ISBN: 979-8-218-78482-9

Cover photo by Laci Dinkle

Book and Cover Design: Erica Clapp

Author Photo: Erica Clapp

Printed in The United States of America

First Edition

www.bryanjoneswriter.com

Also by Bryan Jones

The Farming Game

Mark Twain Made Me Do It and Other Plains Adventures

North of the Platte, South of the Niobrara:
A Little Further into the Nebraska Sand Hills

ADVENTURES IN THE TEACHING TRADE

by
Bryan L. Jones

A memoir

Hermitage Publishing
New York - London - Uranus

THIS BOOK IS FOR
TOM KAUFMAN

Tom was 33 the August I met him. Sweating profusely in a white wash and wear shirt and narrow black tie, welcoming teachers to the sweltering Bladen High School gym for the first faculty meeting of the fall. His Mephistopheles smile made me uneasy. Tom, the new school principal, the sweat hog with the evil grin and military flat top, would be my immediate superior. My future in the school teaching business already looking challenging. This was before I knew a Tom Kaufman from third base and learned his alarming smile had nothing to do with evil intent but merely a genetic hand-me-down from his Jewish/German/Cherokee ancestors. Tom Kaufman smiled because his heart told him to.

During his time in Bladen, Tom frequently used his creative genius to solve the insoluble, from dealing with a grumpy, work-resistant school janitor with lifetime tenure to single-handedly blowing up the school merger with the hated Blue Hill district, a merger everyone assumed to be inevitable. When incompetent school superintendents wore out their welcomes, Tom pulled community levers and gently greased the skids. When a student had a falling out with a teacher, Tom's low-key diplomacy usually put things right. If he found himself saddled with a cocksure, hardheaded greenhorn teacher, who badly needed a mentor, a teacher like me, Tom supplied just enough wisdom and tactful advice to steer the bullheaded jackass away from career suicide. After I threw away the textbooks and began conducting classes without reference to official curriculum, Tom applauded. When I discarded conventional grading and some students and parents objected, Tom supported me. When my senior government class delved into the Civil Rights movement, controversial in 1968, watched films of Martin Luther King Jr. delivering historic speeches, dissected the Kerner Report, which plumbed the causes for the widespread urban riots of 1967, assigned term papers on Fredrick Douglass and Harriet Tubman, all of which irritated the Bladen school superintendent and a couple of school board members, Tom patted me on the back and said: "sic 'em, boy." Tom became so enthusiastic about my classes he occasionally sat in and joined the discussion. Most importantly, he taught me to relax, trust the students, trust my instincts and have fun. For Tom Kaufman, humor was the most essential tool in any successful teacher's skill set.

A hometown hero, Tom held the record for most points scored in a Bladen high school basketball game, played football for the University of Nebraska, achieved the rank of captain during his brief stint in the US Army. Before becoming Bladen principal, Tom ran through several careers, including casualty insurance adjusting and a truncated year of high school teaching/coaching. He was summarily fired from his first teaching/coaching job after yanking the school board president's lazy son from a football game and, on the sidelines, in front of God and the home crowd, loudly calling him out as a "gutless son of a bitch." During his next job selling life insurance, Tom came to believe fervently in the product and invested heavily. He always maintained the best thing he could do for his family was to die young so his kids would be fixed for life. Assisted by a daily diet of five packs of Winstons, mammoth helpings of greasy truck stop food, an occasional fifth of Jack Daniels, and a family history of heart trouble, he achieved his goal, dying of a massive coronary alone in the upstairs bedroom of his modest two-story farmhouse. He was just 3 months shy of his 52nd birthday.

INTRODUCTION

My teaching career came as a surprise, not only to me but to anyone who knew me. I was finishing up a graduate degree in history, opening acceptance letters from prestigious doctoral programs, enjoying the considerable culinary delights of New Orleans. Two days later, I was on a plane to interview for teaching jobs at tiny rural Nebraska high schools. I was to learn the interview invitations and one eventual offer of employment had more to do with the desperate shortage of teachers than my wildly unsuitable qualifications for the job. Despite a complete lack of training or pedagogical talent and possession of an overabundance of egotistical certainty, my teaching career did not crater the first week. Why it didn't had something to do with my irreplaceability. If you've ever achieved irreplaceability, you'll recognize the arrogance that immediately infuses the irreplaceable. Ten feet tall and bulletproof.

My students, demonstrating remarkable tolerance and good humor, gradually eroded the unearned height and the proof against bullets. I will always be grateful.

When I began my unplanned teaching career in the late 1960s, rural schools and parents generally agreed students should know how to read and do math, be able to write a coherent sentence, have exposure to a few science classes, and acquire an understanding of the nation's history and government. They also agreed students upon graduation should be desirable employees or functional college students or dutiful members of the military and be prepared for the obligations of citizenship. Parents and teachers generally cooperated in furthering a student's education. An occasional teacher might turn out to be an incurable bonehead or much worse, but most parents trusted teachers with their children until they proved unworthy.

In the late 1960s, large urban school districts, where top-down Prussian model bureaucracies had been running the show for decades, were not as welcoming to parental involvement. Public school districts in Detroit, Chicago, Los Angeles, and New Orleans, among others, had largely given up on educating students and had little interest in parents reminding them of their shortcomings. School systems in New York, Boston, and San Francisco maintained some semblance of their intended purpose, including high-reputation magnet schools for the brightest students. Parents might not get far trying to influence San Francisco's public schools, but as long as the district strove to educate their charges, parents had less reason to complain. Urban teachers might be subject to firm boundaries on how they should teach and what they should teach. Rebels suffered consequences. But at least in certain large urban school districts, beneficial learning took place.

Employment in a rural school district lacking an authoritarian bureaucracy left my colleagues and me free to shape curriculum, use effective, proven teaching methods, or try something eccentric and unproven. Conformity not enforced, nor encouraged. Every teacher awarded absolute discretion over the assigned classroom. As long as our teaching did not violate community values and our students learned something considered useful, we could expect parental support. If some nitwit from the State Department of Education recommended a new, improved stupid way of doing things, we could ignore the nitwit with impunity. I could not have lucked into a school setting more suitable to my meager talents and lifelong resistance to authority.

Much of this narrative takes place on the High Plains, encompassing the western portion of the American Great Plains before the region screeches to an awkward halt at the foot of the Rocky Mountains. Widely considered flyover country, this is the area explorer Stephen H. Long labeled the Great American Desert. Major Long and his early 19th-century contemporaries regarded the vast expanse as so hostile to farming or any worthwhile enterprise they fully expected a map of the region drawn far in the future, say in the early 21st century, to be as blank and empty of civilization or points of interest as any of Major Long's vacuous maps.

Readers unacquainted with the nuances of High Plains rural society might be surprised at the complexities of daily living. Money, for instance, is harder to accumulate where the uncertainties of mercurial weather, rampaging insects and bipolar agricultural markets can bankrupt overnight. The routine perils of earning a livelihood, a devastating hail storm or a deadly farm machinery accident, frequently add drama to daily existence. Navigating social connections where everyone not only knows everyone else, almost in a Biblical sense, but also everyone's relatives twice removed, plus relevant ancestors, can be far more complex than casual observers suppose. The typical small-town array of characters—the eccentrics, the pharmaceutically challenged, the ancient, the dim of wit, the incurably brilliant—is mostly tolerated and often embraced, giving lie to the expectation of rampant bigotry and bland uniformity.

High Plains schools, like schools in many geographies, often reflect the aspirations and values of their constituents. Successful teaching, especially for an outsider, can depend on how quickly the uneven terrain of local history and family connections can be absorbed and understood. On the other hand, legions of rookie teachers have successfully collected paychecks on their way to brighter lights without exercising the least curiosity about their rural surroundings. My teaching journey, which led from Chicago to New Orleans to small schools in Nebraska and Kansas, depended as much for success on what I learned about the communities I served as on my prior education. Any additional tool in the kit, like a basic understanding of village genealogy, made my job easier.

This is not intended as a how-to book. It might be better described as a what-not-to-do book. I yield to not too many in having a special knack for making self-inflicted mistakes. If you think you have a stronger case, look me up and we can compare disasters. And bring your wallet. On the other hand, a pilgrim on the teaching trail may find some of my more unfortunate experiences instructional. It's possible. Wouldn't rule it out.

National and international events occurring far from the communities where I taught frequently intruded. The Vietnam War, draft protests, the Civil Rights movement, the Great Russian Grain Robbery, Watergate, the roaring inflation of the 1970s and early 1980s, Paul "Cue Ball" Volcker's reckless destruction of the American economy, nation-building wars in Iraq and Afghanistan, efforts to impeach two presidents, 9/11, and the repercussions following the massacre at Columbine High School all affected my students to some degree.

You will also be witness to the periodic imposition of top-down, mandated edu nostrums, like No Child Left Behind, and the toxic effects on the schools and students who were and continue to be victimized. You will also observe principals who performed the thankless tasks of keeping their schools on the rails while helping a hard-headed, sometimes renegade teacher avoid sudden unemployment. For most readers, encounters with the cream of the crop of doofy administrators, moronic educrats, entertaining students, teaching colleagues and parents, both odd and awful, and the inner workings of High Plains communities should drag your buggy through to the end.

Welcome aboard.

BOOK ONE

Elsewhere the sky is the roof of the world; but here the earth was the floor of the sky.

— Willa Cather

Webster County, situated in South Central Nebraska, features the Republican River Valley, former home to infinite bison herds and warring Plains Indian tribes. The Republican wanders west to east along the southern border with Kansas. Limited underground water in the valley forces many farmers to depend on supplementary canal water from the Harlan County Reservoir to the west. The Little Blue River, north of the village of Bladen, traverses the county's northern border. Land in the Little Blue drainage is blessed with more than adequate underground water, fueling a more dependable irrigation-based farm economy. As a result, the farmers in the northern reaches of Webster County tend to be more prosperous than those restricted to the lower yields and inevitable droughts inherent in dry land agriculture.

The Dry Divide, a tableland located along the ridge between the Little Blue and Republican River drainages, is so bereft of underground water a modest stock well can be impossible to locate. Not coincidentally, the Divide was the last portion of Webster County to be settled, often by impoverished immigrant Czech homesteaders. The Divide was also the first section of the county to be abandoned. During the hellish heat and drought of the mid-1930s, Czech farmers, weary of hauling water for family and livestock and discouraged by spindly crops and low prices, often moved in the night, abandoning homesteads and mortgages without giving notice. The Bohemian Desert, an area southeast of Bladen composed of roughly 16 square miles, once boasted a rural school with nearly 300 pupils, most of them Czech. By 1968, not a single school-age child resided within the district.

During years with adequate moisture, the level, fertile tableland along the Divide produces abundant crops. This productivity accounts for the continuing survival of Divide farm families, who, if well-capitalized, can weather a drought year or two. Residents enjoy the bonus of a limitless horizon, perhaps not as infinite as Montana horizons or the astonishing skyline of the Nebraska Sand Hills, but impressive to anyone from east of the Missouri River. During the dry fall harvest months, stainless blue skies stretch the landscape, making it a larger country. Hot, gusty winds of mid-summer subside, creating a palpable sense of peace, despite the dust and noise of frantic farmers and their harvesting machines. In times of extended drought, residents hope the stark white thunderheads boiling up in the west hold more than the all-too-frequent empty promises. They can also track approaching ominous funnel clouds and observe monster blizzards approaching from the southwest or descending from the Dakotas. Weather, which largely determines the year's fortunes, is not only a subject of intense interest and the primary subject of conversation but the most popular spectator sport.

I like to instruct people. It is noble to teach oneself. It is still nobler to teach others and less trouble.
—Mark Twain

Rural school boards traditionally hire teachers who grew up in the community or are related to someone in the community or, lacking superior first-hand information, are known to someone in the community. This may appear an intensely parochial practice, but to a member of a rural school board, it makes perfect sense. Avoiding the extreme difficulties inherent in replacing a teacher mid-year is and should be a top priority. After all, replacement teachers aren't a surplus commodity in sparsely populated rural communities. Any teacher, no matter how superficially attractive, coming from an urban background is immediately suspect. Will a new teacher stick it out if they have not experienced the isolation of rural living? Can they tolerate the lack of fast-food restaurants and shopping options? Will the paucity of people their age cause them to bolt mid-term? Will they carry the unwanted baggage of suspect political views? What hidden personal flaws prevented a larger, wealthier school district from hiring them? Remember that hot-shot football coach from Omaha with the cheerful wife and cute baby girl who got the cheerleader pregnant? Huge mess. We had to testify in front of the Professional Practices Committee to have his license revoked. Nowadays, he'd probably be in prison. Should have been in prison. Took forever to talk Charlie out of retirement to coach one more season. Or how about the librarian from Lincoln we had to hire because she was the only applicant? The one who wore too much makeup and kept a fifth of gin in her desk drawer and fell in the girls' restroom and couldn't get up? We knew she was bad news on sight, but had no choice. Good references are not enough. Resumes lie. College professors lie. Practice teaching supervisors lie. Too often, positive references can be works of creative fiction. Schools have always fired teachers and superintendents and eased the exit by providing glowing recommendations. When was the last time we had a job applicant with lousy references? If we don't already know them or know someone who knows them, we get a little nervous.

Larger school districts typically delegate hiring to the administrators, who sift through applications and conduct interviews. Once they select their top candidate, the administration presents the contract to the board for approval, a yes or no vote. If a hire turns out badly, the administration absorbs whatever public criticism results. A board member of a small rural district has no such buffer. Everyone assumes the board is ultimately responsible for assembling the staff. Mistakes in hiring can take years to overcome. Such mistakes are duly noted and blame assigned. The rural school board, with its deep commitment to the school and community, has every reason to make the best possible personnel decisions. Hiring decisions are deemed too important to be left up to some numbskull itinerant administrator, all too often clueless about both the candidate and the community.

My wife and I flew to Nebraska from New Orleans for the only job interviews we'd been able to secure. We sought two positions, one teaching social studies, the other teaching music. Campbell and Bladen, small schools in south-central Nebraska, ten miles apart, the only ones in the state advertising both positions. My clever mother discovered that a small school teaching position in Nebraska was, in 1968, worth a draft deferment. The doctoral program at the University of Virginia under the supervision of eminent Reconstruction scholar Willie Lee Rose was not. Nor was the graduate history program at Simon Fraser University in British Columbia deferment worthy. The two rural Nebraska schools represented the last chance for a deferment.

During our casual interview at the kitchen table with the Campbell school board president and his wife, we learned the social studies vacancy had been filled the morning before we arrived. As opposed to science or math or music or foreign language instructors, social studies teachers apparently as plentiful as sunflowers. The one hired by the Campbell school board possessed coaching credentials, always a valuable asset to a small school offering multiple sports. My coaching credentials did not exist. Gerald and Carol Bartels were sort of sorry they'd been so precipitous. Clearly, we had much to offer, especially my wife's qualifications to teach not only K-12 music but Spanish. The state education department currently handing out demerits to schools that did not offer at least one foreign language. Hiring a music/Spanish teacher, as rare a commodity as an albino Angus steer, would have solved a couple of thorny staffing problems. Alas, their hands were tied. If things didn't work out with the recent social studies hire with coaching credentials, the Bartels said they'd sure be interested in us. Campbell teacher salaries, we learned, were not based on a formal salary schedule. This meant individual teachers negotiated wages with the school board every year, a practice which gave the school board wide latitude in handing out large raises to teachers they liked and giving skimpy raises or no raises to teachers they didn't like. Gerald was certain, should the opportunity present itself, the Campbell school board would offer us several thousands more in salary than any other rural school in the state.

Bladen? You're interviewing at Bladen? Bladen, the despised rival of the Campbell High School Cardinals? Bladen, the school that always hired crooked referees for their home games? Bladen, home to the smug Methodists who thought they could simply snuff the Campbell school out of existence in recent, one-sided merger negotiations? Gerald and the Campbell board shot down that crazy idea, hadn't they? The Bartels said Bladenites were stiff-necked, penny-pinching Bible thumpers who didn't know how to have fun. Wouldn't know fun if it walked up and bit them in the ass. Carol and her slightly boozy husband Gerald appeared to know a little something about fun. I felt more than a little wistful the Campbell social studies position had been filled.

After striking out with the Campbell school, the more formal interview with the entire Bladen school board the next evening took on added urgency. If Bladen didn't offer contracts, what was plan C? Head for the University of Virginia and hope the draft board didn't notice? Take the generous doctoral fellowship offer from Simon Fraser University in British Columbia and risk permanent exile? Nothing appealing about either option.

How to present ourselves in the most school board-pleasing manner? We, of course, had no real idea of what a rural Nebraska school board viewed as an ideal job candidate. A wild guess, based on nothing but pure ignorance, was to appear as deadly serious, deeply conservative, but inoffensive job seekers who might be sufficiently formidable to keep a tight rein on fractious students. Not the last time we were to misjudge the Bladen school board.

We sat at a lunch table in the school gym, which even in July, long after school had been dismissed for the summer, smelled faintly of ripe jock straps. With the slick outgoing superintendent serving as facilitator, five polite farmer/stockmen (3 World War II veterans and 2 Korean War veterans) and a kindly-looking retired school teacher asked a few pertinent questions and gave the answers sober consideration. Any judgments based on my shaggy hair and longish sideburns or my wife's hippie appearance remained unknowable behind stony faces. We hailed from New Orleans, a large city. We'd also spent a couple of years living in Chicago, a larger city with an even worse reputation for corruption and systemic evil. Long sideburns or the appearance of extreme hippiness represented red flags, but strictly minor red flags compared to the extensive urban backgrounds.

When the lame-duck superintendent invited us to his office to allow the board to deliberate, I had no clue what the members were thinking. I was to learn the hard way a couple of board members were superior poker players. Superintendent Jim Ossian, bound for a doctoral program at the University of Michigan, hinted the decision would be in our favor. Despite advertising the positions in large circulation newspapers and posting the jobs with the state's teacher factories, candidates had been sparse. The handful who showed up for interviews were bottom-of-the-barrel has-beens with checkered pasts or bottom-of-the-barrel rookies with unpromising futures. We carried unfortunate urban baggage and the appearance of whackadoodle politics and questionable morals (which are exactly the same thing if you think about it). However, fall term was fast approaching and Bladen still needed a K-12 music teacher, a band teacher, a foreign language teacher and a social studies teacher. Failure to fill the vacancies with qualified teachers meant double or even triple secret probation from the State Department of Education, risking both accreditation and state funding. Add it all up, and Ossian had adequate grounds to believe the decision would be favorable. What we didn't know and what Ossian didn't know was the board had obtained private intelligence suggesting we might be less dangerous than we appeared. I had blood relatives living and farming in the county, not one of whom, as far as anyone in Bladen could determine, had served time in the state penitentiary or failed to pay real estate taxes. In addition, my smart school teacher mother was working in harness with the Bladen school board president's wife improving

Methodist Sunday School instruction in the area. The traditional rule for hiring only those candidates who were either from the community or related to someone in the community or known by a member of the community had been met—barely.

While we waited, Ossian painted a slightly different version of the Bladen community from the one supplied by the Campbellites. True, Bladen people didn't drink as much as Campbell French Canadians and Russian-Germans (who did?), although they drank plenty, or danced as often as Campbell people, although they regularly attended community dances in Campbell. Nor did Bladenites borrow as much money as Campbellites to buy foolish things. Campbell farmers often lived beyond their means, using borrowed money to buy new pickups every year and making expensive farm equipment purchases to impress the neighbors. Bladenites held a dim view of ostentatious behavior, which they viewed as unseemly bragging. Modesty trumped flash every time. Living below your means made it difficult for others to guess your true net worth. Living below your means presented less temptation for a vengeful God to remind you, as he sometimes did, of your true worth by visiting your crops with hail or drought or rapacious insects. Not surprisingly, the Bladen practice of driving ten-year-old, high-mileage pickups was *de rigueur*, at least into the late 1960s before Earl Butz's Russian graindealapalooza made area farmers feel semi-rich practically overnight. $7 a bushel wheat will do that.

Ossian did not neglect the uneasy relationship between Bladen and Blue Hill, a much larger town to the east. Bladenites viewed Blue Hill with deep suspicion, believing it inhabited by snooty, undereducated, hard-headed Krauts scheming to absorb the Bladen school district and its impressive property tax base, thereby lowering Blue Hill's self-inflicted, ruinous mill levy. In turn, the Blue Hill Krauts viewed Bladenites as stubborn rubes, unwilling to acknowledge Blue Hill's superior claim on Bladen's tax base and student body, an attitude comparable to Adolph Hitler's controversial views on the Sudetenland before World War II.

Ossian also mentioned an old conspiracy theory coloring Bladen's opinion of the territory-hungry neighbor to the east. Old-timers well remembered Roosevelt's bank holiday during the Depression, when all banks were closed temporarily while the Feds assessed their financial conditions. The same old-timers remembered the Bladen Exchange Bank as solvent at the time, despite the desperate economic conditions, due to prudent, farsighted ownership. "It was the damned McBride family who ruined everything." According to the story, the McBride family, loyal Democrats and conniving owners of the Blue Hill bank, sent word to FDR to keep the Bladen bank closed, ignoring its superb finances. Corrupt Democrat FDR did just that. All subsequent, well-funded efforts to open a bank in Bladen rebuffed by the banking authorities, state and federal, under the evil influence of those damned McBrides. Seeking to wipe the village of Bladen off the map, the Blue Hill bank refused to loan money to Bladen businesses, making new commercial ventures near impossible. Anyone attempting to borrow money from the McBrides to buy a Bladen house experienced humiliating ridicule. Wasn't any wonder Bladen was short on active businesses, and real estate values were negligible. Even in the late 1960s, inhabitable houses could be purchased for twenty-five hundred dollars. Damned McBrides. Damned Blue Hill Krauts. Ossian said any mention of Blue Hill tended to change the tone of any Bladen conversation.

Then there was Red Cloud, the county seat down on the Republican River. Ossian said Red Cloud's attention was largely focused on absorbing the smaller Guide Rock school district to the east. Red Cloud's attitude toward Bladen might have been slightly snooty, but not territorially aggressive. The Bladen area, after all, housed several important historic relics of Pulitzer Prize-winning novelist Willa Cather's early life and Red Cloud depended on Willa Cather worship for much of its *raison d'etre*. The sole, chronic irritation Bladen represented to the Red Cloudians was firm possession of the county fair. The village of Bladen, from 1906 forward, hosted the Webster County Fair. Why not the larger county seat of Red Cloud? Because the early county fairs featured harness racing, which attracted gamblers and floozies, just the sort of sinners the town of Red Cloud had no desire to host. The puritanical Bladen Methodists stepped up, grabbed the county fair franchise and never let loose. That, in a nutshell, Ossian said, tells you all you need to know about the differences between Red Cloud and Bladen.

Ossian grew up in a small Iowa community and rode enough bucking bulls in his youth to prove he could do it. When we met him, he was ambitious and eager to advance his administrative career, but understood rural life and was a keen observer of the Bladen community. Ossian retained his close ties after he left. "Bladen," he said years later, "touched us in a way no other community or school ever did." The more typical strutting, dissembling, exploitive, penny-ante embezzler then occupying many rural superintendencies had little genuine interest in the community temporarily employing him or her. Ossian made himself comfortable in Bladen and, we learned later, had been an overactive social animal. No local gathering, large or small, was complete without Jim Ossian's presence. He came to know the community better than some natives.

Ossian assured us most of our students would work hard, and if they didn't, their parents would insist. With few exceptions, Bladen kids were smart because their parents were smart and valued education. Ossian thought the community, unlike hated Blue Hill to the east or Campbell to the west, was awash with smart genes, even a handful of philosopher genes. Locals placed the highest value on education, encouraged their children to further their schooling after high school. In Bladen, smart, educated people automatically held a more elevated social standing than the merely wealthy. One of the board members debating our futures downstairs held a master's degree in ag economics and supplied the community with an abundance of philosophical thought free of charge. We would find Bladen students literate and well-prepared by their elementary teachers.

Nothing Ossian told us that night later proved inaccurate. What he purposely left out? An honest appraisal of the newly hired replacement superintendent due to take charge of the school on the first of August. In retrospect, Ossian had every reason to keep mum. The only hint of the trouble to come was a vague reference to the new guy being "kind of stuck on religion." No kidding.

Summoned back to the board meeting, we faced the now familiar stoic faces. However, after announcing the favorable decision and determining we would indeed sign the offered contracts, a couple of board members managed weak smiles. Perhaps the board had been as anxious as we were. Don Lewis, the lanky, most formidable-looking board member, hem hawed a bit before raising the troubling question of what would happen if our teaching certificates did not appear in time for the start of school, clearly not a question anyone else wanted raised. The general response when it came, amounted to "Why don't we drive off that bridge if and when we come to it?"

Ossian escorted us out through the gym doors, shook our hands, wished us a safe trip back to Louisiana. He provided the phone number of a landlord with a cheap house to rent and directions to the home of the social studies/football coach I was replacing, a guy Ossian suggested might supply useful intelligence to an incoming teacher.

Nobody who ever met him would describe Paul Heller as a small man or as a grumpy man. Paul Heller could, had he chosen, made a long, profitable career of impersonating Santa Claus. The sweaty, ruddy-faced man mountain interrupted his sorting and packing to welcome us and describe the school and community in such rosy terms, I wondered why he and his wife decided to leave. I don't remember why he left, probably to take a higher-salaried job, but he was given a warm homecoming a few years later when he returned to Bladen as superintendent. Heller predicted we'd find the Bladen community as fun-loving as he had. Take that Campbell school board.

Maybe we'd made the right decision. Our trip back to New Orleans and our sorting and packing duties imbued with the shared assurance our new jobs and living situation would be both interesting and satisfactory. If we'd had a lick of sense, we'd have added challenging to the list.

Novelist Willa Cather spent a brief time during her childhood living on the Divide and later made frequent return visits to relatives. Cather continues to be a presence, not only on the Divide but especially in the county seat of Red Cloud, where she is heavily memorialized. The popular Cather Tour takes Cather fans, domestic, international and intergalactic, to places featured in Cather's works. The annual Cather conference in Red Cloud attracts international Cather scholars and has drawn celebrities as diverse as talk show host Dick Cavett, former First Lady Laura Bush and author Maya Angelou.

Cather's presence extends to the village of Bladen, where Elizabeth Boyd, the daughter of Anna Pavelka, the fictionalized heroine of Cather's *My*

Antonia, ran the cafe for many years and patiently answered ignorant questions from Cather fans when she had better things to do. Anna's granddaughter Antoinette Turner, a Bladen community fixture for eons. George Cather, Willa's wealthy cousin, owned the lumber yard and hardware store for decades, although he hardly needed the money.

Cather-related legends abound. Before he was buried at a crossroads southwest of Bladen, Francis Sadilek, Anna Pavelka's father, had been left hanging in the barn where he committed suicide. Fifteen-year-old Con Wilson, son of Virginia immigrants, and his best buddy were delegated to take down the body and prepare it for burial. Once they saw the distorted, purple features of the hanged corpse, now in advanced rigor mortis, the enterprising boys cut it down, leaned it up against the wall near the door and arranged the arms in a threatening position. And left. Anyone entering the barn enjoyed a rude surprise. Mr. Sadilek, once properly laid out, was refused Christian burial by the local Catholic priest and buried at a country crossroads, where wagons and buggies rolled over his grave. The body was later moved to the Red Cloud Cemetery. On the way to my south pasture, I always drove through the crossroads and never failed to remember Mr. Sadilek, Con Wilson and the stiff-necked priest.

The honeymoon home built for G. P. Cather and his bride, Myrtle Bartlett Cather (full disclosure, Myrtle Bartlett Cather was my second cousin twice removed), sits on a corner lot a block north of the Bladen post office. Willa Cather modeled the hero of her Pulitzer Prize-winning novel *One of Ours* on her cousin, G. P. Cather. 2nd Lieutenant Grosvenor Phillips Cather was killed in action near Cantigny, France, on May 28, 1918. Cather was posthumously awarded the Distinguished Service Cross for exposing himself to enemy machine gun fire while directing his troops to successfully repulse a German attack. Local wags suggested Cather committed a form of suicide rather than return to Nebraska and his harpy bride. Cather's funeral attracted a respectful throng, which overflowed the Bladen Opera House and lined the route to the cemetery.

After G. P.'s burial, Myrtle Cather did not stay long in the honeymoon house, which she deemed too large and scary, and moved to a more modest dwelling a few blocks away. She lived out her 42 years of widowhood as a recluse, seldom attending church, despite her parents' deep piety. Rather than buy groceries or fetch the mail, she hired local girls to do her shopping and mail collection. She also hired local schoolgirls to sleep in her house. They were to enter at 9 p.m., lock the door, go directly to a spare bedroom to spend the night. They were to leave upon awakening in the morning. At no time was there to be contact between Myrtle and the sleepers. Myrtle always left a quarter on the bureau, not bad wages in those humble days when farmers paying hired men a dollar a day were considered extravagant. Myrtle might have died semi-anonymously, but she died rich. The Bladen Methodists, in particular, kept Myrtle's memory alive by remembering the generous, surprise endowments she left the church in her will, which funded additions to the current structure. Why Myrtle left a small fortune to a church she rarely attended remains a community head scratcher.

In the wee hours, following his first school board meeting as the new superintendent, Mr. Dwight telephoned me in New Orleans, taking advantage of free access to the school's office phone (long-distance calls cost money in 1968). Busy as I was, cramming for graduate comprehensives in a steamy, moldy, cockroach heaven of a New Orleans apartment, I welcomed the distraction.

Dwight had much to share. Football practices not going well. Had he told me he was the new head football coach? No? "I played high school football in Pennsylvania. Big Polock kids would run right over you. Joe Marconi (former NFL Pro Bowler for the Los Angeles Rams and Chicago Bears) wasn't a Polack, some kind of foreigner, I think, but he knocked me unconscious once. You had to be tough to play. These Bladen kids just don't get it." Then the problems with the Ditto machine bleeding blue ink all over his football play sheets, problems with the school janitor, guilty of ignoring Dwight's suggestions, problems with his rented Bladen house, complaints so foreign to this hot shot history grad student's ears, he might as well have been speaking igpay atinlay. But mindful this blatherskite was my new boss, you can bet I was giving him my fullest. And eventually, he ran out of complaints.

"What exactly is your background?"

So pleased he asked. Some European history, heavy on World War I.

medieval and Renaissance, a smattering of geography, both economic and political. Solid in American History, with an emphasis on pre- and post-Civil War, ditto Jacksonian History, thanks to Dr. Joe Tregle, one of the most distinguished Andrew Jackson scholars in the country. Throw in coursework in 20th Century, colonial, and American Revolutionary history, studying political science under General Douglas MacArthur's chief advisor on the post-war Japanese constitution, and you'd be in for a long day finding anyone better prepared to teach high school social studies. Dead silence on the other end.

"What I was wondering about was, ah-hem, your family background."

Family background, oh that. "The Jones clan runs 40% Welsh with some English chromosomes floating around. Probably other stuff mixed in there, but we consider ourselves Welsh." Crickets.

"The board was, ah-hem, wondering since you're from the South and carry a common Negro surname and the photograph on your transcript photocopy was a little, ah-hem, dark, if perhaps, ah-hem, you might count some former slaves in your family tree."

The school board saw my lily-white face during the interview a few weeks ago. Dwight's posing his ignorant question as coming from the board was bullshit. I could have gone all huffy snit. Perhaps reminded him of which century we were living in. Instead, this hot-shot, lily-white history grad student attempted diplomacy.

"No, sir, I think the board has its wires crossed." No black guy here, just a broke mostly Welsh kid with $5 in his checking account, 5,000 history books and a beater Ford Falcon with hardly any brakes and a nonfunctional heater.

Dwight wasn't quite done.

"The board has, ah-hem, some concerns whether your teaching certificate is quite in order."

I had a signed contract in hand, but Dwight was troubled by my lack of traditional teaching credentials. Presently attending summer administrator school in Lincoln, Dwight had never heard of a Provisional Teaching Certificate. I explained a person holding a bona fide bachelor's degree could obtain a provisional certificate from the Nebraska State Department of Education by signing up for education classes at an approved college or university and commence teaching public school classes with the full approval of the Nebraska Department of Education.

The sound of nothing.

After some little time. "Uh, I uh don't think, I uh have uh ever heard of ah anything like that."

"Ask around when you get back to administrator's school in Lincoln. Let me know what you find out."

"My family will pray for you."

And they probably did. Dwight's inclusive family prayers extended over an ambitious landscape. No family members, friends, neighbors or qualified members of the United Nations could feel left out. I know this because he recorded family prayers on the school's only tape recorder and did not erase the tapes.

My first exposure to the fleshier version of Mr. Dwight took place in the fetid school gymnasium at the obligatory August faculty meeting before the start of school. With fall football practice underway, the sweat-stained aromas wafting from the boys' locker room added a certain piquancy to the proceedings. New principal Tom Kaufman, seated at a table near the door, handed out rudimentary mimeographed school calendars and policy sheets. My genial fellow teachers murmured to each other and aimed curious glances at the handful of newbies sitting in the newbie section of the bleachers. I was curious about everyone.

Dwight marched to the podium, sporting an enormous, perfectly round head, an exact replica of a Vidalia onion, adorned with prominent ears and a prematurely gray buzz cut. The rear vents of his too-tight sports jacket thrust out above his ample posterior like wing flaps on an airliner, suggesting a purchase made some thirty pounds ago. He grinned. Boy, could Onion Head grin—the taxidermied grin of a lobotomized rabbit. He bounced on his toes like he had a June bug up his ass, exuding both athleticism and bounteous goodwill. I recall next to nothing about his remarks, except he introduced himself as being a little more famous than we probably suspected. His claim to immortality, he said, was being knocked unconscious while attempting to tackle Joe Marconi during a Pennsylvania high school football game. The same Joe Marconi, he reminded us, who enjoyed a Pro Bowl career with the Los Angeles Rams and the Chicago Bears by successfully knocking professional football players unconscious. Heady stuff. He also bragged about his graduation from Bob Jones University, which, if designed to impress, failed. Kearney State College, Doane College, the University of Nebraska or any other Nebraska college or university might have drawn a nod or two. Bob Jones University? What's that? We had to look it up. College founders Bob Jones and notorious Nebraska gasbag William Jennings Bryan united in their opposition to the theory of evolution and against nearly 100% of human activity most of us would find pleasurable. In the fall of 1968, as Dwight introduced himself to the Bladen faculty, Bob Jones University did not admit blacks, nor would it admit unmarried black students for years afterward.

And there were rules:

Male and female students cannot be alone in a classroom, rehearsal studio or other room.

On and off campus, there is to be no physical contact between unmarried men and women. (Side hugs are permitted for photographs.)

Women must wear a neckline that is no lower than four fingers' width below the collarbone.

Students must close the blinds to their dorms when night falls.

Students should watch out for "Scatological realism – pertaining to excretory functions" in media.

I'm abbreviating here in the interest of time. The full list of college rules

21

we later consulted comprised an entire spiral-bound handbook. And some of our colleagues, sad to say, had to look up "scatological." At least one of my new colleagues, specifically the mousy newbie English teacher, concluded any college throwing the term scatological around like they meant it must be a pretty upscale institution.

Onion Head apologized for not introducing the teachers to each other. Joe Marconi's knee to the onion evidently precluded remembering names. We took turns standing and reciting random biographical details. Aside from the vacuous superintendent and the mousey rookie English teacher, my new colleagues appeared competent enough. Maybe, just maybe, my fellow teachers would turn out to be interesting as well.

A sunnier disposition might inhabit an occasional orange, but among noninstitutionalized humans who have crossed my path, Onion Head's equanimity remains unmatched. None of his screw-ups, of which there were gobs, disturbed his stubborn tranquility. If a stranger stuck around for a few minutes of casual conversation, they invariably concluded Joe Marconi's knee had vaporized whatever rudimentary clues to the universe Dwight might have inherited. However, just because a person is sporting a largish onion for a noggin and is dumber than dirt doesn't mean they can't make a rare intelligent decision.

One of Onion Head's first memorable acts as superintendent took place during the opening week of classes. After taking inventory of new sports equipment ordered by former coach Paul Heller, Onion Head concluded the orders to be excessive. The impressive pile he assembled of new playground balls, footballs, basketballs, volleyballs, shoulder pads and football helmets should have equipped the school for the next ten years. Onion Head might be excused for his ignorance of the chronic mysterious disappearance of the school's sports equipment. He didn't realize the pile of new stuff stacked in the entry to the gym represented a rough approximation of what would go missing during a normal school year. He called Hogan's Sporting Goods in Hastings, asked for a salesman to stop by for a large order. When the salesman showed up, Onion Head ordered a single tether ball. "By the way, that pile of equipment you passed on your way in? You can take that back to Hastings and credit our account."

Bold move. Give him points for initiative. Might not make him popular with the folks at Hogan's, but the sight of the paunchy, sweating salesman trying to stuff all the equipment into his modest four-door sedan created some merriment in faculty circles. Score one for Onion Head.

The same week, Dwight began earning his reputation for colossal dimwittedness. Shop/math/physics instructor Ken Berns placed an order for lumber, including assorted sizes of Philippine mahogany. Onion Head approved the lumber order with one exception. He suggested the shop students could make do with "good old American mahogany." Which they might have done, Berns insisted, since they were as patriotic a set of shop students as breathed, had such a thing as American mahogany existed.

Grumbling from the football team. The players took one look at Onion Head's runny-inked, nonsensical football plays and decided to run the plays they'd practiced under their former coach. Onion Head, they said, did not notice the difference. Onion Head, blithely driving a busload of football players into the path of an oncoming semi, also had them off their feed.

The initial evidence Onion Head might not be above petty thievery arrived when it became known he'd driven the school's drivers' training car to the Black Hills for a Labor Day family vacation, charging the gas and other expenses to the school. The school board stuck its collective head under the bed and decided to let that one slide.

The well-maintained Bladen school, built in 1924, was already long of tooth in 1968 but remained in pristine condition. Local historians claimed after a bond issue to replace the existing, deteriorating brick structure went down to defeat multiple times, the new school building boosters took the extraordinary measure of committing arson. A crowd gathered to cheer the daring rescue of a tin basketball trophy and watch the great conflagration. Although some in the crowd detected the smell of kerosene, "no evidence of foul play was ever uncovered." The replacement building was state-of-the-art. Sturdy double brick and steel-reinforced concrete, the Bladen school could easily ignore any run-of-the-mill tornado.

A later bond issue, in the early 1960s, proved more popular, resulting in a new addition, featuring a gymnasium, locker rooms, stage, kitchen, administrative offices and modern restrooms. During subsequent school merger talks with neighboring districts, Bladen always fared well with professional merger consultants, who determined superior facilities made Bladen the logical site for the merged districts. Campbell school patrons whispered the fix was in and rejected any proposal siting the combined high school in Bladen. Campbell school boards much preferred not to spend money on facilities and planned to eventually dissolve the district and allow students to disperse to neighboring districts. Exactly what eventually happened.

The Bladen school, built to last, cleverly designed to promote cross ventilation. Impossibly high ceilings, unimaginable after the minimum security prison school architecture fad took hold in the 1950s, and tall windows situated on opposite sides of the building meant even during the sweltering afternoons of mid-August and early May, a cooling breeze flowed through the classrooms. Except for the classroom I was assigned. At an unknown time in the misty past, temporary wooden panels partitioned off the southwest corner of the library, creating my diminutive classroom. During sunny weather, an expanse of glass on the south wall with but a single tiny hinged window turned the room into a broiler. In those halcyon days, any male teacher hoping to remain in good standing in the teaching profession considered wearing a coat and tie every day, all day, to be mandatory. The massive sweat stains in the armpits of my sports jackets and blazers proof positive of this rookie's devotion to the rules of engagement.

Speaking of the library, it contained more shelves than books. Only a handful of moldy textbooks and a ratty set of Collier's encyclopedias, no history or political science collections, no geography monographs. A virtually bookless library presented this fledgling teacher with a serious impediment to the emerging scheme of assigning student research projects.

In 1968, male Bladen teachers wore coats and ties. Period. Arriving fresh from graduate school and its modest clothing requirements, I badly needed reinforcements. And since I was officially broke until the first payday six weeks hence, the wardrobe additions needed to be either free of charge or dirt cheap.

Fortunately, dirt cheap was just around the corner. As a condition of my temporary teaching certificate, I enrolled in a couple of early-August short-session summer school classes at Kearney State College, an hour's commute to the northwest. The history professor who served as my academic advisor (unpublished, stagnant, doing me a favor by breathing the same air) wore a professionally reassuring, if somewhat frayed, coat and tie. He also wore white socks. Which meant he was marked down as a dodo bird before our conversation began. He scowled at my transcript and determined none of the universities represented—Nebraska Wesleyan, University of Illinois, Roosevelt University, University of New Orleans— held an academic candle to Kearney State College. Therefore… and therefore…, he could not accept any of my 120 hours of undergraduate and graduate history credits as proof I knew anything about history. What I lacked and badly needed were enough credits in education courses to qualify for full-blown licensure, but white sock-wearing dodo bird was forcing me to take at least one history class. And once he made up his mind, wouldn't budge. I'm almost over it.

I wish I could say I accepted defeat with good grace and made the most of the cruel joke of a history class. Instead, I pouted. Pouted long and pouted hard. Sat in the back row scowling my ass off as one ignorant, tedious lecture after the other pounded me into near insensibility. One afternoon, an annoying, too-friendly classmate interrupted my pout with breathless news of the boffo sidewalk sale infecting downtown Kearney, Nebraska, that very summer afternoon.

I arrived in Kearney's business district accompanied by an anorexic wallet. Twenty bucks later, I was a dad-gummed fashion plate. Burnt orange extra wide, double knit bell-bottom slacks, the identical slacks in avocado green, a matching wide lapel houndstooth sports jacket in burnt orange and avocado green, a brass-buttoned blue blazer with lapels from here to eternity, a half dozen extravagantly colored ties approximately ten times as wide as the lone preppy string tie hanging in the home closet, a selection of dress shirts in astonishing colors, each one with pointy collars descending perilously near the navel. My first and last seersucker blazer, striped in blue and highway yellow, paired with black bell-bottomed double-knit slacks. And boots. Two pairs. Mod, high-heeled ankle boots with distinctive mod side zippers. Cool enough to make an insufferable Beatle envious.

It never occurred to ask why the local merchants were practically giving away mass quantities of high fashion. I needed teaching clothes and had little money. My prayers had been answered. Only later, when I observed what passed for regulation male teacher attire in neighboring jurisdictions, did the cruel dawning arise my new threads might have been fashionable at one time, perhaps three or four years in the rear-view mirror. My students and faculty colleagues had much to snicker about.

Lyle Kile did not wear burnt orange double-knit bell-bottoms. Lyle Kile wore bib overalls. No Dickies, no Big Smith, no Oshkosh B'Gosh. Lyle Kile insisted on Key bibbies, always spotless, starched, legs ironed with knife-edge creases, courtesy of his faithful wife, Faye. No neurosurgeon ever went to work wearing a more immaculate outfit. No neurosurgeon ever left work at the end of the day with cleaner clothes, despite Lyle serving as the official Bladen school custodian. Because Lyle's overalls appeared immune to the normal splashings and stainings accompanying typical custodial duties, he took on a similar air of indestructibility. True, he spent a good deal of his working day in the furnace room playing solitaire. His superiors, including Onion Head and Faye, might give him a to-do list. But Lyle's personal to-do list always prioritized furnace room solitaire. Faye, although not yet officially employed by the school, spent eight to ten hours a day cleaning the school into submission. Lyle occasionally mopped up puke in the elementary classrooms during flu season. Elementary teachers, unlike moron school superintendents, could ask Lyle to do things and he would sometimes do them. Veteran elementary teachers tend to have both presence and authority. And here I'm thinking of Irma Ione Gurney, whose width nearly equaled her height and had more authority in her stub of a little finger than Dwight could muster in his entire onion-shaped head. And give him credit, Lyle could also be found providing minimal guidance to a volunteer crew of high school boys in the dog days of summer when they resurfaced the basketball floor.

Not that he ever participated in the actual resurfacing. Rumors circulated he occasionally mowed the football field, although those sightings proved difficult to confirm. Anytime the football field grew rank and unsightly, the football coach or another teacher usually drew the short straw. Frustrated superintendents might have directed Lyle to mow and chalk the field, but he did not always choose to do so. More than once, the school bus bearing the visiting team arrived in the parking lot to find a harried Bladen coach or teacher frantically mowing and chalking the field for the evening's football game.

Lyle might not have mowed the football field as often as he was supposed to, but according to rumor, he bitterly resented the football coach lining out used automobile tires so the boys could run agility drills. Tires, he said, are impossible to mow around, although how Lyle knew this had not been verified, at least not by Lyle. Things were coming to a dangerous impasse when the football coach, who happened to be my predecessor, Paul Heller, shared with his players his high school prank of climbing the school flagpole, hoisting tires via the flag rope and dropping the tires down the flagpole, like a game of giant quoits. Drop the most tires down the school flagpole and you won something, probably a six-pack. No dummies, the Bladen football team grasped the concept immediately. The next morning, when Lyle went out to raise the flag, he found ten well-used tires stacked up around the bottom of the flagpole. He marched into Supt. Adee's (Jim Ossian's predecessor) office and announced there would be no flag raisings until the offending tires were removed. Adee ordered Lyle to remove the tires and raise the flag—immediately. Which he declined to do. The situation festered. Adee insisting the tires be removed. Lyle insisting removing tires from a flagpole wasn't in his job description. Although he finally relented after the school had gone flagless for two entire school days. He sawed the tires in half with a hacksaw. If you've never sawed through a steel-belted tire with a hacksaw, give it a whirl, tell me how it went. By afternoon football practice the following day, every used tire in the vicinity of the football field had been magically removed to a town dump in the next county.

Lyle Kile might have been ornery, but you couldn't fault his sense of humor or declare him completely devoid of initiative. After all, loading and hauling over thirty used tires can raise a sweat. When he observed boisterous students sliding down the school's wooden banisters, he fetched a pocket knife from his overalls pocket and set to work carving notches from top to bottom. The next few banister slides resulted in painful splinters and scrotal impairment. Mission accomplished.

Had we rookies been less concerned with our navels, we might have speculated on how the Lyle we knew had become the Lyle we knew. The most likely explanation, that Lyle had been born with a peculiar view of the world, would have been a popular choice. But perhaps life had dealt him a bad hand? Bladen natives, had they chosen, could have filled in a few blanks. Failed farmer, failed locker plant operator who had lost a son. Business reversals can leave marks. Losing a son can leave a mark. Nah. Even if they'd known or cared about Lyle's backstory, a majority of the new teachers would have chosen the eccentric at-birth explanation.

After Lyle's locker plant went under due to the proliferation of home deep freezes, the community concluded Lyle had run out of options and grew concerned his wife Faye's financial future was at risk. The school board offered Lyle (and later Faye) a steady job. The community's adoration of Faye balanced the feather-ruffling Lyle conducted for most of his adult life. The school board fully expected Lyle would be a dependable pain in the ass. However, they figured correctly Faye would keep the school spotless whether Lyle turned a wheel or not. It was up to the teachers and administrators to ignore Lyle's foibles and let Faye pick up the pieces.

Lyle's placid demeanor proved as bulletproof as his overalls. Stubbornly cheerful to the unobservant, even when repeatedly mopping mud from the hallways after recess on rainy days. However, if you had direct access to his fertile brain, you would have witnessed the hatching of vengeful plots against the multitude who had offended him. As shop/math/physics teacher extraordinaire Ken Berns often said, "If you can help it, don't ever get on Lyle's bad side. Of course, all of his sides are bad."

On the farm, the weather was the great fact, and men's affairs went on underneath it, as the streams creep under the ice.

—Willa Cather

Bladen's morning coffee drinkers could choose between Elizabeth Boyd's cafe and the grain elevator office. Farmers, both active and retired, gravitated to the elevator for current market news and free, if corrosive, coffee. Elizabeth served better coffee, definitely not free, to semi and actively retired women, visiting Cather acolytes, and a handful of non-farming men, including the occasional passing crop insurance adjuster. Gossip ran deep in both locations. Cafe gossip concentrated on social matters, who might be doing whom, projected nuptials, projected break-ups, the scoop on the new Methodist minister, the odd duck the school board hired to teach social studies and his hippie music teacher wife.

Weather dominated the 100% male grain elevator coffee crowd. And speaking of the weather, don't be showing up unequipped with the latest forecast. And don't expect the latest forecast to do more than get your foot in the door. You also had to know your weather history. Sleet storm on the way? Someone would remember the sleet storm preceding the first blizzard of the godawful 1948-49 winter. REA poles snapped like toothpicks. Power out for days. Hail in the forecast? Remember that storm ten years ago? Pounded Carl's corn field 'til it looked like he'd been out there with a tandem disc. Drouthy? The year I was born, 1935, my folks couldn't use what little milk the cows gave because the only grass that grew in that heat and drought was pepper grass. The milk tasted just like pepper. Even the hogs turned up their noses.

High-level public policy discussions also took place in the grain elevator office, where men, laboring under the illusion they were in charge of things, shared weighty opinions, opinions which sometimes included views of the crazy jackass presently teaching high school social studies. Novice teachers, fulfilling their responsibilities with varying success, made novice mistakes, secure in complete ignorance their work was subject to daily community criticism. When we finally opened our eyes, the blinding speed at which news traveled around Bladen came as a shock to those of us raised in larger communities. Indeed, news did not need to be formally shared. Long-time village residents knew the particulars of events, sometimes before they happened. Once the village took your measure, no secret was safe. Within hours of his job interview, everyone was fully aware Superintendent Dwight didn't know his ass from a sperm whale. Mr. Warren might have bridled under Onion Head's classroom intrusions and worried he might lose his job, but the coffee crowds approved of his dedicated classroom efforts and his extraordinary patience when coaching less-than-talented athletes. The fact Warren held the high school state Class D record in the mile run also did not hurt his community standing. I should probably have been interested in how my abilities were being judged, but was too cocksure to worry about public opinion. Years after the fact, I learned certain members of the elevator crowd were not my biggest fans, concerned I was teaching too much left-wing nonsense. Because school board members of the elevator crowd patiently explained the necessity of keeping both my wife and her oddball husband employed to satisfy those pencil pushers at the Department of Education, no angry mobs formed. But there were those who would have brought the tar and others who would have brought the feathers had they received a lick of encouragement.

When not parsing teaching performances or lack thereof, or discussing the chances of moisture or drought or general crop prospects, the elevator crowd expended considerable brain power handicapping future Bladen athletic teams.

That Stutzman kid in 4th grade should grow up to be something. His mom's brother was 6'2" and ran track, pretty good rebounder.

And the Larsen boy, isn't he a 4th-grader too? His uncle on his dad's side was a helluva blocker. Wasn't big, but stout. He'd get down there in the dirt and root 'em out.

What about the Kramer kid? He looks like he might be an athlete.

Nah, none of his people amounted to anything. Too chickenshit to hit anyone. But, now that I think about it, he might make a basketball player. His mom could jump before she had kids and started eating enough for the whole damned family.

30

Anything coming in the 3rd grade?

Not much. Well, maybe the Kraus kid will be good enough to play as a sophomore. He's already an animal. Everyone else in his class is slow and lazy. Slim pickin's. Now 2nd grade, that's a different story. You've got a half dozen kids with strong genes. Larricks, Boyds, Gertens, that Conway kid. He's still going to country school, but he'll play when he gets in here to high school. He might even play college ball. Rangy and smart. His mom was a school teacher, you know.

What about the Berns boy in 5th grade? He's tall for his age.

The trouble with the Berns family is they're too damned smart to get their uniforms dirty. And too slow. That's their grandpa's genes running true.

But wasn't the Berns kid's grandma on his mother's side a Vonderfecht?

Yeah, so what?

I always heard the Vonderfechts had some secret Indian blood.

News to me.

That Berns kid looks a little that way. No ass to speak of, long skinny legs, feet way bigger than the rest of 'em, maybe a little too much nose. He might have more speed than we're giving him credit. You know how it was with the Stoughtons. A smidgen of something back there. Maybe Oklahoma Choctaw? Cherokee? All those Kaufman boys were hellacious athletes. Half Stoughton every one of 'em. The Berns kid? They say he's already doing freshman algebra just for kicks. Brains and speed aren't a bad combination.

Brains and speed. Nods all around.

Barb, the Bladen school secretary, had no peer when it came to dispensing entertaining complaints. And she had ample reason to be irritated. Her desk sat just outside the superintendent's office, fully exposed to whatever racket Onion Head happened to generate. And since Joe Marconi's knee had likely dislodged a portion of Dwight's hearing ability, almost everything he said or did proceeded at high volume. The first development of the school year putting Barb off her feed? Onion Head's loud, repetitive playing and replaying of his tape-recorded family prayer sessions.

Sometimes the prayer sessions lasted for well over an hour.

Dwight: "Let us pray for all of those who are hungry."

Mumble, mumble.

Dwight: "Let us pray for those living outside the light of Jesus Christ."

Mumble, mumble.

Dwight: "Petey, is there anything you'd thank Jesus for?"

Petey seldom had a ready answer, but when he eventually responded, spoke with a high-pitched nasal whine.

Petey: "I just don't know, Father. Do I have to? I can't decide. I can never decide."

Dwight: "What about your food, Petey? Aren't you to give thanks for the wonderful supper we had tonight?"

Petey: "But I don't like lima beans. You said we weren't going to have any more lima beans and then we did. Beans, schmeens."

Dwight: "What about the meatloaf, Petey? Didn't Mommy cook it just right? Petey?"

Petey: "Okaaay! Thank you for the meatloaf."

It went on like that for twenty minutes before Dwight turned his attention to his youngest son Sammy.

Dwight: "Sammy, is there something you'd like Jesus to do?"

Petey: "Would Jesus please bring me a Shetland pony?"

Barb: "If I have to listen to whiny little Sammy pray for a Shetland pony one more time that damn tape recorder is going in the furnace."
Big talk, no follow-through.

Some observers might suggest more rigorous teacher training would have helped me avoid rookie mistakes. My pedagogical preparation up to that moment consisted of one dreadful two-credit education survey course at Nebraska Wesleyan University. If the college hoped to weed out prospective school teachers with at least half a brain, that particular introductory education class could not have been better designed or taught by a more suitable professor. I may have dozed off a few times. Miss Clark's repetitive homilies—"I just know you all will be wonderful, wonderful teachers of children"—represent the only classroom memory I retain.

Serious to a fault about my teaching duties (which did not preclude self-inflicted gunshot wounds to the feet). Could I return to those first days in the classroom, I would do things differently. Bladen students, I eventually realized, represented an ideal set of pupils, both literate and hardworking. Jim Ossian had not oversold them. My stern, authoritarian attitude, even if it had any utility, proved wildly inappropriate for the task at hand. Had I been less obtuse, less concerned with establishing rigid order, it might have dawned I had secured the perfect teaching job for a raw beginner. Bright, willing students, engaged parents. Neither disobedience nor sloth threatened classroom order. Having no understanding of my pupils, I assumed rebellion lurked just below the surface, poised to erupt at the first sign of weakness. My initial unforced error? The misguided attempt to establish classroom discipline by instilling abject, quivering fear in my students. With no desire to be any student's best friend, I scowled as ferocious a scowl as I could conjure, staring down any punk foolish enough to challenge my *authorité*. My demeanor stiff and remote, no particle of personal information passed between pupil and teacher. They were, after all, lowly students, completely unsuited to know anything about me. Armed with my personal information, who knows what mischief they'd commit? I'd once been a nogoodnik high school punk myself and witnessed weak-spleened, loose-lipped teachers lose control for the rest of the year during the first five minutes of the first class. You had to nip rebellion right smack in the bud. Once the animal spirits were loose, no hope for restoring authority. No namby-pamby, touchy-feely getting-to-know-you exercises in my classroom. The ten-foot wall I erected between student and teacher might as well have been topped by concertina wire. A more self-inflated martinet you never met in your life.

Herman Larsen, my revered high school band/boys' glee director, played a small but important role in shaping my views on student discipline. Herm, as everyone called him behind his back, a ferociously happy guy. Always smiling, always quick to praise even the most execrable musical performance, which, in the case of the boys' glee, was all of them. According to Geneva rumor, Herm enjoyed his WWII in a Ranger battalion parachuting behind German lines, murdering sleeping Krauts with razor-sharp KA-BAR knives. The facts were a tad different. Herm served in World War II, all right, but in the South Pacific. His precise role is lost to history, but it involved secret black ops and may well have involved knifing Japanese soldiers in their sleep. No matter, every potentially disruptive boy in Herm's classes minded his manners. Who knew what boyish folderol would trip Herm's placid temper into a combat-inspired psychotic rage? There was, after all, the conical, head-shaped depression in the unfinished plasterboard about eight feet above the floor behind Herm's director's podium, mute evidence of the one time Herm went nuts. Nobody remembered the name of the unfortunate boys' glee member who supplied the head, but collective memory was dead certain the poor sap sassed Herm. Herm snapped, plucked the offender out of his chair by the throat, hoisted him above his head and slammed him into the wall. Whenever I thought about a career in teaching, Herm's absolute, fear-based control of his classes seemed like a reasonable goal. Maybe I could sneak into the school at night and impress a handy head-shaped object into the wall. What worked for Herm just might work for me.

Only the deeply disturbed, self-flagellating student doesn't hope for the best results from a new instructor. Who among us has wandered into a classroom wishing the teacher turned out to be a slobbering half-wit or a short-tempered crank? Self-interest alone creates student optimism, the desire for even-tempered, low-drama instruction. With luck, the instruction will contain useful information. With better luck, grades will be assigned in a wildly generous, humane manner. If the student is extremely fortunate, the new teacher will have a sense of humor and the class will be almost enjoyable. My optimistic, habitually well-behaved Bladen students were puzzled by my scowling, dictatorial approach. They sat, eyes wide, wondering why this madman had been inflicted on them. No one giggled out loud, but they had grounds. Over the next days and months, as they gently nudged my understanding a tad closer to reality, I relaxed, as did they. Not until 20 years later, after several epiphanies, did I come across persuasive research showing likable teachers to be far more effective than harsh disciplinarians.

My second, more serious, unforced error began by quizzing students on material they'd supposedly learned the prior year. Shouldn't senior government students who'd taken American History their junior year be expected to know a little basic American History? The name of our first president? Who was running things during the Civil War? At least, that was my delusional expectation. Of course, nobody would own up to knowing a damn thing. Declaration of Independence? Blank stares. First colonies in the New World? Shrugs. Main combatants in the First World War? Eyes downcast, more shrugs. How about the last election just four years ago? Who was running? Who won? Nothing. I was exposing ignorance and it made my students uncomfortable and not a little resentful. That's when I stepped in it. What in blazes were you studying last year instead of American History? Turned out they were studying American History under Coach Paul Heller, one of the most likable teachers in their experience. I had unintentionally insulted a guy, who, although he'd moved on, remained immensely popular in the community and counted as close friends many of my fellow teachers and members of the school board. I later realized, after a summer break from the classroom, the average student retains an infinitesimal portion of the previous year's instruction, ranging from two to ten percent. This is why elementary teachers, who frequently know what they're doing, spend class time in the fall reviewing the previous year's subject matter. If my Bladen students didn't retain much American History, it wasn't necessarily the result of inadequate effort from their former teacher. Fortunately, my error in judgment did not turn out to be fatal, but did not improve my reputation and was a mistake I tried never to repeat.

Many states require prospective teachers to serve under a mentor before granting licensure. This system allows the fledgling to work within an established curriculum and observe how an experienced teacher goes about their business. Rookie teachers, once ensconced in their permanent classrooms, may choose to follow the mentor's practices or go in a different direction. Experience varies with the school and the mentor, but most teachers probably rate the practice teaching component of their training as helpful. Those who have unfortunate experiences frequently switch to other professions.

Having never practice taught, my first day as a classroom teacher was my first day as a classroom teacher. How to best impart my infinite knowledge of almost everything to the students? Not to worry, I'd been subjected to plenty of teaching and plenty of teachers. Some relied on the sturdy worksheet, handed out, collected, corrected and handed back. A few made half-hearted attempts at class discussion, usually overly reliant on the discussion-killing rhetorical question. "What would you say was the most divisive issue leading up to the Civil War?" Nobody, not even the habitual suck-ups, would offer a guess. The teacher not only knows the correct answer but is impatient to share. Keep your mouth shut and get out of the way. My high school American History instructor kept us entertained by reading from the textbook in a deadly monotone for the entire hour, putting half the class to sleep and causing the other half to contemplate either suicide or homicide. Of the roughly 20 high school teachers in my past, the one who stands out was the biology teacher with a compulsion to dissect. Frogs, mice, fetal pigs, the little guy couldn't resist slicing and dicing, showing us how to cut things open to figure out what made the unfortunate dead things tick. His riveting *pièce de résistance* was crude lobotomy surgery on a live albino rat while one lucky student carefully monitored the patient's oxygen and anesthesia mixture. Not a dry eye in the house when the pale, red-eyed rodent expired on the operating table, but nobody complained about having to sit through a boring biology class.

My college instructors typically conducted undramatic readings of an hour's worth of moldy lecture notes. One elderly literature professor's notes were so yellowed and fragile he had them permanently embalmed in plastic. Our job was to take notes, memorize the notes, regurgitate the notes come exam time. A few professors spiced up their lectures with occasional anecdotes or made spontaneous remarks. Once in a blue moon, a college professor turned out to be both wise and entertaining.

If I hoped to be a once-in-a-blue-moon teacher, worksheets or faux class discussions or deadly dull, embalmed lecture notes were not going to cut it.

Early in my first year in Bladen, the school board budgeted several thousand dollars to our lethargic librarian along with the mandate to bulk up the library collections, collections the educrats at the State Department of Meaningless Jargon ruled woefully deficient, a ruling accompanied by threats of probation and loss of state school aid. At the time, no one had a firm understanding of how librarian Lucille occupied her school day. Her unexcelled ability to stay seated at her library desk, nibbling on snacks, sleeping, knitting, reading and avoiding strenuous movement went unchallenged by any serious competitors, even Lyle Kile. She approached her job with lackadaisical good humor, peering at the world from under a mop of dishwater blonde hair and over the frames of her bobby soxer white plastic eyeglass frames. Careless about her appearance, her teeth were often sprinkled with odd bits of scarlet lipstick. Careless about her attire, she remained stubbornly oblivious to the food and coffee stains decorating her saggy bosom.

Unsubstantiated rumors circulated of morbid diabetes and an addiction to strong drink, rumors of a husband twiddling his thumbs in the state penitentiary. Since Lucille didn't mix or match with faculty colleagues or share confidences with anyone in the community, the rumors remained rumors. In exchange for her paycheck, Lucille took full responsibility for sitting at her desk reading, knitting, sleeping or eating. At times, activities merged. Thousands of unrequested dollars for new books not only overwhelmed Lucille's synapses but outraged her sense of fair play. "Why would they expect me to know how to spend that much money? I've never purchased that many books in my entire life!"

I volunteered to help. Like a starving punk kid set loose on a dozen glazed doughnuts. *Dictionary of American Biography*, the *Dictionary of American Geography*, histories of the Roman Empire, standard biographies of Washington, John Marshall, Harriet Tubman, Lincoln, Denmark Vesey, the Adams family, the Roosevelts, both the good one and the bad one, Eisenhower, any book I could find by British historian A. J. P. Taylor, any Vietnam book by Dr. Tom Dooley, *Narrative of the Life of Frederick Douglass*, diplomatic histories, US constitutional histories, Plains Indian works by George Bird Grinnell, *Red Cloud's Folk* by George Hyde, Civil War histories, Indian war histories, *The Autobiography of Benjamin Franklin*, *Crazy Horse* by Mari Sandoz, medieval histories, ancient histories, Bernard Fall's *Street Without Joy: Indochina at War, 1946-54*, Winston Churchill's multi-volume *History of the Second World War*, maps of everywhere. The fun I had creating a respectable library was almost criminal. As the library grew and prospered, so did the scope of the student research projects.

Once the library was something for the community to brag about, I drove the students like rented mules to research topics in American History, American Government, World History and World Geography. They took their assigned questions to the library, explored, opened books, opened more books, studied maps, reported their findings. In addition to evaluating the results, my main responsibility was coming up with a stream of new research projects, large and small. Some projects might occupy a class period, others several days.

When students compiled and summarized their findings, all duly sourced and footnoted, of course, I supplied the next project. Why is Frederick Douglass famous? What is Liberia's largest export and why does Liberia produce the product? What were the early Greeks up to in Egypt? Why did Alexander Hamilton become embittered toward his long-time mentor, George Washington? Why did Nebraska adopt a Unicameral legislature? Why was that a good idea? Why was that a terrible idea? Which communist nation supplies the majority of arms to the North Vietnamese? Why? Who was Harriet Tubman and why is she famous? I might not be a once-in-a-blue-moon teacher, but I could ask questions like nobody's business. Sometimes the questions couldn't be answered with the materials in our library. This was, after all, long before Google reared its ugly head. In the case of failure, assuming the search had been thorough, a student could earn credit just for digging. I assigned a sliding point scale to each project based on the level of difficulty. The student who accumulated the most total points earned the highest grade and the rest of the students were scaled down from there, often disrupting the status quo. Students habitually earning top grades challenged by those farther down in the academic caste system. Students who had spent their school careers cemented in top-dog positions became unsettled. The recently elevated, encouraged by the open, democratic competition, redoubled their efforts. The library had never seen so much action, sometimes forcing Lucille to abandon her post for the more peaceful teacher's lounge.

A bright, curmudgeonly student accustomed to coasting in the straight-A lane for years balked at the competition. Gene, a hard worker with many after-school irons in the fire, resisted devoting too much of his limited time to a single class. As his grade plummeted and those of his less gifted peers rose, his grumpiness reached the breaking point. His last nerve exhausted, he decided to organize a student strike. Oblivious to my bones, I remained unaware of his sedition and piled on even more challenging research assignments. After receiving some early enthusiasm, Gene's efforts to mobilize the straight-A suck-ups languished. Teacher pleasers aren't often the first movers in an open rebellion. Fortunately for me, Ken Berns, the whip-smart and widely respected shop/physics/math teacher, talked Gene down from the tree. Principal Tom Kaufman may have also conducted quiet diplomacy on my behalf, averting the first student strike in Bladen school history.

The next day, an unrepentant and still irritated Gene requested a complicated research assignment worth more than enough points to put him back on top. Which it did. His position at or near the top of the academic ladder never again seriously threatened. The student assault on Lucille's library continued unabated.

By coincidence, the novel idea of sending students into the library to conduct research, instead of spending their time glued to a desk taking, memorizing and regurgitating embalmed lecture notes, was, at that very moment, gaining popularity. Educrats and education professors had been making war on memorization ever since John Dewey was a lad. Memorizing facts, I'd be the first to admit, can be difficult. Members of the education establishment, who traditionally originate in the shallow end of the intelligence pool, had been working like beavers for a good share of the 20th century squelching the memorization of facts. They deemed facts to be undemocratic for two reasons. Firstly, their personal experience with acquiring facts had been disheartening. Watching smarter, more studious classmates leave them in the academic dust hurt their feelings, lowered their self-esteem. Secondly, facts tended to contradict their frequently recycled, invariably dunderheaded edufads (always clothed in indecipherable edujargon), regularly promoted as the last and best fix for what ailed education. Once supremely hard of thought educrats with dangerously low levels of self-esteem grasped the control levers of the edu-industrial complex, they sought to destroy as much of the fact-based universe as possible. There's a reason economists refer to what educrats do for a living as null interventionism—activity which produces only negative results. Social studies and English proved easy pickings. Math and science frustrated their best efforts until the next century. Defactualizing math and science met with success only after educrats created widespread suspicion in education circles facts were indeed tools of the oppressor class.

The Inquiry Method of teaching social studies, spawned by the New Social Studies movement of the 1960s, was but one manifestation of the permanent war on facts. The premise—a student went into the library to research a topic and draw independent conclusions (widely jargoned as "critical thinking skills")—didn't appear at first glance to be a bad idea, not at all dissimilar to what was happening in Bladen social studies classes. However, educrats can never be entirely comfortable with students wandering around libraries without intense supervision. Assigning a topic and allowing pupils to follow their noses represented a dangerous and unpredictable practice. Who could even guess where their noses would take them? What mischief would newly whetted critical thinking skills produce? The Harvard Social Studies Project went all in on the Inquiry Method and addressed burgeoning educrat concerns by providing materials. Materials? You're probably scratching your head. With an entire library at their disposal, why would students need materials? Glad you asked. By supplying an expensive, prefabricated, fully sanitized set of approved reference materials, along with the prefabricated line of inquiry and a prefabricated set of desired conclusions, any messy and possibly controversial research findings would be avoided. The edu-industrial complex promptly jumped on board, and before you could say get ye to the library, there was no need for a student to pass within a hundred yards of a library. Ads for prepackaged Inquiry Method materials from edu-industrial complex publishers overflowed my mailbox, many of them bearing Onion Head's ignorant scribbles in the margins. State educrats hosted workshops for social studies teachers and pitched the advantages of prepackaged inquiry. Edu-industrial complex sales agents selling pre-packaged materials set up booths in the lobbies, awarded door prizes.

Foisting a set of costly teaching materials on schools across the country also solved another pesky problem. Many educrats, at some point in their lives, have taught school, with results typically ranging from indifferent to miserable, and view all teachers through the lens of their own constricted capabilities. Few educrats possess the talent to supervise a class of curious students free-ranging in a library. Even coming up with original research topics would be a stumper. Knowing where to look? Forget about it. How to evaluate the results? Clueless. As with most edufads, the Inquiry Method advocates did not believe teachers could execute the program without top-down micromanagement of every student's every classroom moment. Had the Inquiry Method been promulgated decades later, after the dawning of Diversity, Equity and Inclusion (DEI) and a hundred similar, heavily jargoned propagandas, you can be sure class materials would have contained as little nonfictional history as possible. A 21st-century instructor might introduce a vague subject with a brief video or musical number promoting simple political slogans, none having relevance to nonfictional history. After brief exposure to a few catchy slogans, students would be free to imbue themselves with their own intelligence—perhaps hone their critical thinking skills by finger painting their inner emotions or choreographing an expressive dance routine. The Inquiry Method, now in disrepute for its ingrained racist, meritocratic leanings (grades, after all, were supposed to be assigned), was not the first, nor certainly, the last national effort to diminish teachers' freedom to employ their talents and instincts in guiding their students' academic efforts. Nor have the subsequent years of dismal student academic performance been a surprise to anyone paying attention.

A few months later, the school board appropriated additional library funds, and Lucille found herself stuck with a new round of unspent riches. She tried out her pity party on several colleagues without finding a pigeon before she returned to the novice social studies teacher.

Within two weeks, every social studies student had a personal subscription to a weekly news magazine. This, you may remember, was before 24/7 cable news and long before social media became ubiquitous. Networks broadcast news once every weekday at 5:30 CDT in the evening, usually before my charges had finished football, basketball, volleyball or track practice. Had they an interest in current events, which they didn't, their exposure would have been limited. Each Monday, I assigned magazine articles, national and international news, sports, entertainment, whatever seemed the most newsworthy. Each Friday, classes participated in an oral team test on the assigned articles. I directed questions to individual team members. If a team member failed to answer correctly, the other team had the opportunity. If they failed, it became a toss-up question and anyone from either team could answer and earn points. I kept a running tally of points scored. At the end of the class period, the team with the most points earned the highest grade. A team's grade depended on every team member studying the articles. Those students who blew off the assigned reading found themselves heckled and abused by those who took a more sober approach to assignments and grades. The weekly news quiz soon became a deadly serious competition. And often boisterous, irritating the teachers assigned to supervise study halls separated from my classroom by those thin, temporary room dividers.

Boisterous news quizzes were the reason Onion Head, while stealing a *Sports Illustrated* from the library, first became aware of the funny business in the Bladen High School social studies classes. His grinning, Vidalia-shaped head appeared in the doorway. He said it sounded like we were having fun, waved and disappeared. Not long after, notes began appearing in my mailbox questioning the appropriateness of teaching current events in a class supposedly focused on the US Constitution or the location of the equator or the rise and fall of the Roman Empire. Dwight was especially enthused about the United States Constitution, as well he should have been. I, too, held the United States Constitution in high regard and hoped to guide my students, albeit using somewhat unconventional approaches, to a sound grounding in constitutional matters. Undeterred by the lack of response, Onion Head continued communicating his concerns via mailbox notes.

"The major aim of social studies curricula should be to promote good citizenship and to preserve the American way of life."

Dwight also opened teachers' personal letters and scribbled his maunderings around the margins. A letter addressed to me from a graduate school friend pursuing a Ph.D. in history at the University of Wisconsin drew this Onion Head response: "Is your friend aware Madison, Wisconsin, is full of communist hippies trying to overthrow the government of the United States?"

Small sample size, but the handful of Madison communist hippies I'd met were more interested in smoking dope and dropping acid than in overthrowing the government. That was well before Madison's communist hippies became more ambitious. And, of course, Onion Head's intelligence sources could have been far superior to mine.

With Mr. Warren, the rookie biology teacher, Superintendent Dwight occasionally took over teaching his classes. In one instance, while Warren was fetching dissecting supplies from the storeroom at the rear of the classroom, Onion Head marched into class and, without introduction, demanded, "Do you believe you descended from a ball of snot washed up on the seashore?" The students, currently thinking less demanding thoughts, gave the snot question solemn consideration but came up empty. If you think there's an easy answer to the snot question, why don't you try it on for size and see how you pan out? Onion Head, noting the lack of response, launched into a stem-winding rant against Darwin's theory of evolution. His opposition likely based on his understanding of the Bible and his Bob Jones University education. Mr. Warren wandered out of the storeroom, found his boss, the superintendent of schools, haranguing his students on the subjects of snot and evolution, and departed for the teacher's lounge, thereby navigating a tricky situation about as well as it could be navigated. Warren was, of course, irritated but also puzzled. He spent little class time on evolution. The biology textbook barely mentioned the subject. From that day forward, Warren's mailbox received a generous percentage of Onion Head's notes, along with religious tracts railing against Charles Darwin and his unscientific ideas. "He usually scribbles his notes while he's standing beside me and reaches over to place them in my mailbox. He could hand it to me or simply tell me what's on his mind, but he likes his notes."

Onion Head only invaded my classroom when he suspected anything civil rights-related might be under discussion. He entered without knocking, leaned against the back wall, never said a word. Summaries of his occasional classroom observations came in the form of mailbox notes, warning me about the infiltration of the Civil Rights Movement by the godless Russian Communist Party. J. Edgar Hoover said so. When he wasn't scribbling notes to Mr. Warren or me, he occasionally installed a handwritten four-page letter in my mailbox. And, bless his heart, he tried his best to be diplomatic. The recurring theme? My approach to teaching social studies was a bit too rational and balanced. He much preferred the cheerleader social studies teacher, one who waved the flag and the Bible and promoted American heroes.

"I believe intellectual freedom on one hand, and intellectual responsibility on the other, represent the difference between anarchy and the truth. I believe the Judeo-Christian ethic is the vary (sic) origin of democracy, beginning when Cain slew Able (sic) and Cain being punished because he was infringing on Able's (sic) right to life, liberty and the pursuit of happiness."

Our local educational service unit in Hastings maintained an extensive film library, which teachers could access for free. Some commie Russian agent must have stocked up on CBS News documentaries on Martin Luther King Jr. and the Civil Rights Movement. The senior government class, basking in the sauna-like heat of the minuscule classroom, just settled in to watch a documentary on the March on Washington featuring King's "I Have a Dream" speech at the Lincoln Memorial, Onion Head looking on from the back wall. He'd been alerted by the label on the film canister when it arrived. The ancient school film projector suffered from chronic sprocket issues, occasionally causing a film to jump a frame or two before settling down. Dwight, clearly annoyed by the loose sprockets, moseyed up to the projector, peered intently into the projector's innards, stuck a thick finger into the offending sprockets, causing them to jump out of the projector and scatter across the floor. The film, lacking guidance, rolled out of the projector in great, ever-expanding loops. Dumbfounded, Onion Head watched the disaster unfolding before fleeing, leaving the door wide open and yards of film rolling onto the floor in his wake.

Sharp-eyed readers may have observed, no badge-heavy federal or state educrat or school district curriculum czar imposed the Inquiry Method on the Bladen social studies department, as happened in larger, more stratified locales. Had the Inquiry Method and attendant teaching materials been spawned 50 years later, things might have gone differently. Like every Bladen teacher in 1968, I conducted my classes according to my muses, mostly free of imposed rules or dictates. Onion Head's clumsy efforts at interference might have been annoying, but had zero influence on the work of the Bladen social studies department. Decades in the future, those in government schools favoring conformity and top-down, politicized edufads were firmly in charge.

While I was bumbling my way through the inaugural school days in a fetid classroom, my hippie wife faced her personal teaching challenges with a much higher degree of success. The woman who moved with me to Bladen was a talented musician, adept in foreign languages and highly intelligent. Like me, she had no previous experience teaching children of any age. Once in Bladen, she had responsibility for the elementary music classes, including instrumental music lessons, the junior and senior high bands, pep band, senior high vocal music, and Spanish classes, introductory and eventually advanced. She planned and directed practices for every public music performance, be it a Christmas pageant or a spring all-school concert. She was also tasked with preparing almost every high school student whose name was not Albert to perform at a district music contest. Although she was ill-prepared for her responsibilities, either by training or inclination, she persevered. Young children, in particular, unsettled her. Their existence served as a living, breathing criticism of her decision not to have any. Few knew of that decision, but having made it, she was always uncomfortable around younger students and resentful of those women who appeared to balance children and productive lives without raising a sweat. Faced with daily exposure to entire classes of fidgety, mucus-dripping elementary students, she held her nose and tried to ignore her inner demons.

Tasked with controlling squirrelly elementary kids and entire high school bands and choruses, this woman, who was never entirely sure who she was or what her next incarnation should be, consistently kept her charges on task. She had few strongly held views, but allowing people to explore and express their distinctive selves to the fullest was one of them. Big on whimsical, short on structure. Going in, all signs pointed to permanent classroom chaos. If I had ever figured out how she maintained orderly classes, I could have learned a thing or two about discipline.

The most complimentary thing you could say about the earnest, hard-working musicians she inherited was they were earnest and hardworking. Over the years, her students earned admirable ratings at music contests, and Bladenites professed themselves entertained by her music programs. Although you know as well as I do, anyone who claims to enjoy a school music program is either deluded or lying through their teeth. Along the way, she encouraged at least one student to pursue a career teaching and translating Spanish. Not a bad record for someone who was, in her head, always on her way to becoming someone else entirely.

We moved into our $50-a-month rental house with typical moving-in-to-a-new-place optimism. Weathered, yellow asbestos siding, shingles at the end of their useful lives, a couple of tiny bedrooms, bath, small kitchen, living room, a slovenly back porch. The house lacked a formal foundation, intent on sinking into the prairie beneath. Floors tipped in random directions. One side six inches lower than the other. The uneven floors focused your attention when you were walking around in the dark. Untended fruit trees grew in the small orchard next to an ambitious garden plot. A barn and corral occupied the back of the property, prompting visions of soon-to-be-acquired saddle horses.

By the modest financial standards of the community, these two formerly penniless graduate students were well off. Courtesy of the Bladen salary schedule (thank you, Jim Ossian), which richly rewarded not only years of service but our recently acquired piles of graduate hours, our combined salaries shaded that of the highest-paid employee in the school district—Superintendent Onion Head. We arrived with no savings but had no debt, no student loans. After deducting the $50 a month rent check, only the winter propane bill, which could exceed $200, made a dent in our bank account. Phone and electricity bills were negligible. Television arrived free via roof antenna. Gasoline averaged 34 cents a gallon. Two weeks' worth of groceries cost $25 and the sacks overwhelmed the car's back seat. After paying expenses, our combined $1000 a month take-home pay (worth $7,684 in inflation-adjusted dollars) remained largely unscathed. Even after we acquired a shiny red $2775 Pontiac Tempest with a high-interest installment loan, we had to shop like drunken monkeys twice a month to keep the bank account from exploding out of control. Two twenty-somethings raised from birth in genteel poverty had no experience handling such riches, something duly noted by the community coffee drinkers. Only after a couple of years of profligate spending did mindless consumption run its course and attention turn to real estate investments.

1968, the year I began my teaching career, witnessed turmoil and conflict on a scale seldom seen before or since. The Vietnam War had grown divisive. Lyndon Johnson, the Great Legislator, lost his mojo. Martin Luther King Jr's assassination resulted in widespread rioting and loss of life. Bobby Kennedy's assassination led directly to the raging battles between Marxist protesters and Mayor Daley's police during the Democrat National Convention in Chicago. Throw in the North Korean seizure of the Pueblo, the Prague Spring, the Tet Offensive, and the entire fractious world had become unusually fractious.

My students focused less on national and international events than on more personal affairs. The boys concentrated on their navels, sometimes sports, and on how to acquire more beer. Farm boys proved resistant to the typical male teen romance with automobiles. After all, they'd been driving since before they could see over the steering wheel. Any rare girl-related thought, invariably hormone-generated and unrealistic, was usually brief and too prurient to include here. Girls, a hundred years more mature than their male classmates, expended their energies putting the best face forward in the predatory hunt for permanent mates. Consternation resulted if a boy had not been roped and branded by the end of 7th-grade, although the boys in question were often unaware they'd made a lifetime commitment. Navels and beer thoughts clouded their vision.

The adult community's attention also rested on matters closer to home—weather, commodity prices, the fortunes of the University of Nebraska

47

football team, weather and anything to do with Bladen High School sports. The community, while not unmindful of the titanic events unfolding on the world stage, had a firm grasp of traditional priorities, which served as effective insulation against the toxic energies running rampant elsewhere. Looking back, it's hard to fault the community's worldview. At the end of the day, local sports, weather and Cornhusker football had more influence on their current and future lives than any transitory drama unfolding in Washington D.C., Hanoi or Birmingham, Alabama.

I plead guilty to harboring warm sympathy for the goals of the early civil rights struggle and many of the participants. Although I was not being paid to convert my students into civil rights activists, I did assume my responsibilities as a social studies instructor included increasing understanding of what was happening outside Webster County, including knowledge of the most transformational social movement of my lifetime. While the senior government class concentrated on the government of the United States and the evolution of the same, I plead guilty to exposing my senior government classes to out-sized helpings of Martin Luther King Jr., nonviolent persuasion, Ralph Abernathy and the Southern Christian Leadership Conference. Most of the exposure came, not through lecture, but through free educational service unit films and a few strategically timed personal stories. No didactic instructor told the students what lessons they were supposed to take away from a film or a story. Their only responsibility to pay attention and, to make sure they were paying attention, answering a few nitpicky pop quiz questions afterward. I have never believed the purpose of teaching was to direct my students to a specific ideology. Those students in the habit of forming opinions were free to form opinions based on what they watched or the stories they heard or the firm beliefs they held before taking the class. Playing devil's advocate to my own point of view, for instance, making the case for the state's rights side of the civil rights argument, boosted my confidence the students were exposed to a balanced perspective. Not the case, of course. It didn't take a psychic to know where I stood.

Although I guarded my personal history from the students, I shared a few, carefully selected stories from the summer of 1964 spent in Atlanta in a Methodist-sponsored work-study program. During the day, participants worked—carpentry, pouring concrete, loading trucks, office work, whatever we could find. Evenings, the secretary of the local AFL-CIO or the head of the local Teamsters Union spoke to the group about labor issues. The man in charge of the Atlanta US Steel plant and the manager of the local General Motors plant supplied different points of view. After observing steel and cars being made, I decided the soft life of a university history professor would be much preferable to the constant noise and physical danger and repetitive toil of factory life. In my opinion, whatever those workers were being paid was woefully insufficient, which was probably the conclusion the program organizers hoped for.

Our program leader, a college chaplain from Michigan, encouraged us to follow our noses around Atlanta and find interesting things to do. I found my way to Ebenezer Baptist Church, home pulpit of Martin Luther King Jr. King and Ralph Abernathy were making regular appearances in the national news with their civil rights efforts. Why not check them out? King had reached the most influential period of his life, fresh off his triumphant "I Have a Dream" speech at the Lincoln Memorial. The Ebenezer church building, old and in mediocre repair, reflected higher priorities than brick and mortar. King's father, Martin Luther King Sr., handled the formal aspects of the church services at Ebenezer, drawing our attention to what he considered paltry contributions to the collection plate. The Ebenezer congregation proved older and less vibrant than the congregations I worshipped beside at Rev. Ralph Abernathy's West Hunter Street Baptist Church or the congregations of other Atlanta ministers who toiled anonymously in the movement beside King and Abernathy. Even the music at Ebenezer was perfunctory and dispirited, a far cry from the visceral, joyful noises made by the choir and congregation at Abernathy's church. Ebenezer Baptist Church impressed as a showcase for Martin Luther King Jr.'s preaching when he wasn't occupied elsewhere. The nuts and bolts of ministering to a congregation, visits to the sick and homebound, providing succor to those in need, counseling and support to the grieving did not appear to be priorities for the ministers of the Ebenezer Baptist Church, evidenced by the detached demeanor of the congregants. However, if the parishioners showed up primarily to hear MLK Jr. preach, they were not disappointed. Unlike most preachers in my considerable experience, King spoke from the inside of his entire being. The pipe organ eloquence rose in peaks and valleys from deep in his diaphragm. Completely extemporaneous. Not a note, not a scrap of paper on the pulpit.

And unlike many preachers, King directed his remarks not so much to the people in the pews but at the ceiling and the world beyond. His tightly reasoned arguments assumed familiarity with both Western and Eastern philosophies and more than passing knowledge of the entire span of human history. This was a style of preaching I had witnessed from old school Southern Methodist preachers, based as much on reason and the classic philosophers as on the theology of a particular sect. King's remarks extracted a smattering of amens from the back pews, but they punctuated King's dramatic cadences more often than the sermon's contents. After all, King's sermons primarily appealed to reason, not raw emotion. By the end of the service, I was congratulating myself on witnessing transcendent eloquence delivered in a building largely empty of the human interactions we associate with communal worship.

"Mr. Jones, (from the beginning, for their own reasons, students addressed me as Mr. Jones), did you have a chance to meet Rev. King afterward?"

Yes, indeed. I made a beeline for the church basement, where a small crowd gathered around an ancient coffee percolator. King briefly held court. A limp handshake and some mumbled pleasantries. King looked half asleep, still occupying a mystical state where he retreated when preaching. I was disappointed, but understanding. You can't preach a sermon that brilliant and remain unaffected. King's wife, Coretta Scott King, rescued her husband from the questions I was about to ask. I admit to being a little starry-eyed as this elegant, self-possessed woman steered me to another part of the room and asked enough perceptive questions to keep my focus on myself. Clever and gracious at the same time.

"Did you ever do anything about civil rights when you were in Atlanta, Mr. Jones? Like demonstrating at a segregated restaurant?"

Good question, and one I should have answered honestly. But my lone stab at active engagement in the civil rights struggle, joining a group of northern liberal friends, including one angry black kid, at a small segregated family restaurant on the outskirts of Atlanta, took not much courage and the results were deeply embarrassing. If Gary Robinson, a militant SNCC activist from "up north," hadn't shamed us into joining him, not one of us would have mustered the gumption. Once we were seated, a smiling waitress handed out menus and filled our glasses with sweet tea. We'd just started on the menu, which offered food to die for, when the burly cook (did I mention he was burly? Also seriously over six feet tall? And seriously angry?) waving a meat cleaver emerged from the kitchen and ordered us to leave, which we did—with unseemly haste. Cleaver Guy 1, Earnest Integrationists 0. Our mostly empty gesture concluded in an embarrassing whimper. I found myself ashamed of interrupting the Sunday dinners of a half dozen wholesome-looking Georgia families—Sunday dinners composed of what appeared to be authentic and delicious Southern cuisine—pan-fried chicken, mashed potatoes and cream gravy, hot baking powder biscuits, fried okra, pecan pie for dessert. Whatever our smug, sanctimonious intentions, the only accomplishment? Irritating folks who had no idea they were on the wrong side of history. No reason for my students to know what a gutless twit they had for a teacher.

Instead, I talked about Gary Robinson, who, like many members of the Student Nonviolent Coordinating Committee, was impatient to force change and employed confrontational tactics that sometimes made older civil rights organizations like the NAACP and the Urban League uncomfortable. Robinson, cocky and fearless, promised us something "big" was going down. He wouldn't say exactly what was going down but said we'd be seeing him in the newspapers any day now. The day after President Johnson signed the Civil Rights Act of 1964 into law, Robinson and two colleagues, escorted by Justice Department officials, including the relentless conscience of the DOJ, John Doar, (who later served as lead counsel to the House Impeachment Committee, which voted to impeach Richard Nixon), attempted to enter Lester Maddox's Atlanta Pickrick Restaurant. Maddox, the most vocal segregationist in Georgia, promptly closed his restaurant, jumped on a bicycle and rode crazy circles around the parking lot. At that point, Gary Robinson disappeared from sight and never shared his version of his brief appearance on the national stage. I wish he had. Robinson could tell a story. Maddox, who later became governor of Georgia due to a bizarre set of circumstances, appointed more blacks to government positions than did all previous Georgia governors combined and integrated the Georgia State Patrol. Go figure.

My students also heard about a memorable automobile trip from Atlanta to the rugged hills of northwestern Georgia. This was the summer of the Mississippi Burning disappearance of civil rights workers Chaney, Goodman and Schwerner. If I hadn't been aware of the risks of active participation in the civil rights movement, I sure as hell was after news of the disappearance and massive search hit the newspapers. The slightly dicey incident in northwest Georgia that followed did not embellish my credentials as a big-time civil rights guy. My role strictly passive, and my survival due not to any bravery on my part, but to the lead foot of the northern fat-assed liberal driving the car. Although not the hero of this story, far from it, I didn't mind sharing it with students to illustrate the risks actual civil rights workers assumed.

Four earnest university students from above the Mason-Dixon line and one worldly Angolan motoring around NW Georgia in a 1955 Pontiac with a V8 engine and Michigan license plates.

Ismael Martins, Angolan civil war refugee, currently serving as the only male secretary in Martin Luther King Jr.'s Southern Christian Conference Atlanta headquarters. Izzy, as he preferred, fluent in multiple languages, as refined and elegant as the rest of us were not. His father, a high functionary in the colonial Angolan government, sent his brightest son to Portugal for his early education, where he acquired refined Continental manners, a taste for dapper clothing and an umbrella. Once the Angolans rebelled against their European colonizers, Izzy's father joined the rebellion, was arrested and incarcerated in a Portuguese concentration camp. Izzy joined the insurgents in the bush, participating in the usual guerrilla pastimes, blowing up stuff, ambushing enemy patrols, figuring out where his next meal was coming from. He was the first person in my experience who had deliberately killed a fellow human being. He said killing Portuguese soldiers didn't bother him in the least, an impassive admission which made the rest of our party a little nervous.

Although he never shared the details of his escape from Angola or how he came to be studying economics at Lycoming College in Pennsylvania or how he landed a job with Martin Luther King Jr., he was happy in his work. According to Izzy, his duties were undemanding and the female secretaries uniformly attractive and easily persuaded to accept his attentions. Life was good, right up to the day he was walking to work, formally dressed and twirling his umbrella. A pickup pulled up beside him and a large fellow with a double-barreled shotgun ordered him to "get on your knees, Sambo." (except he didn't say Sambo). No stranger to guns, Izzy complied, but afterwards never carried himself with the same confident, urbane attitude. Some air had gone out of him.

Keith from St. Paul had a gift for languages and was already fluent in five. He could play almost any tune by ear on the piano and attracted an appreciative party crowd if a piano were in the neighborhood. He later served in the Peace Corps in Thailand, returned to serve with the CIA for thirty years. When in our company, he spoke infrequently and mostly minded his own business. He was also a complete, 100% physical coward, although his job that summer involved loading and unloading trucks, no job for weaklings.

Big Man on Campus from Carleton College played college football and attempted to keep the rest of us in order. You may remember Carleton, which 60 years ago was regarded as one of the top liberal arts colleges in the country. Carleton located in Northfield, Minnesota, where Jesse James and Cole Younger were victimized by the formerly peaceful townspeople during a botched bank robbery. Joseph Lee Heywood, Carleton College's treasurer and a cashier at the local bank, shot and killed for refusing to open the safe. As our group's self-designated responsible party, BMOC could never fully relax and enjoy himself with the rest of us. He was smart, disciplined, honest to a fault, later became a pillar of his community and enjoyed a long and distinguished legal career.

Mike from Duluth. Crazy when sober, out of control violent when drunk. Mike not so secretly wanted to physically attack anyone he identified as a segregationist. On this trip, he got his wish, sort of. He later married the sister of the Grand Titanic Kleagle Cyclops Muckety-Muck Poobah of the Birmingham, Alabama, Klu Klux Klan. Over the succeeding years, Mike took involuntary vacations in mental institutions in Kansas and Georgia before his unreconstructed segregationist wife divorced him and he permanently sank from sight. I'd give an even nickel to know what happened to him.

Tom from Michigan, a rounder guy. A wider guy. Five feet two inches and 250 pounds of devout religiosity, Tom spent his evenings on the bottom bunk of our shared Emory University dorm room wearing shorty pajamas, basking like a beached whale as the large electric circulating fan blew gusts of humid Atlanta air over his roundness. So round he could not see his toes while lying on his back, or, come to think, while standing upright. He balanced religious novels against his stomach and read his nights away. *The Robe, The Big Fisherman, Shoes of the Fisherman, The Big Fisherman Catches a Large Carp* all rested at one time or another atop his generous tummy. While he read, classical music played on his transistor radio. He kept time to the music with his toes, which were mostly invisible to him, but not to me. Tom served as our designated food scout. If the KFC restaurant at the local chain motel offered an all-you-can-eat Sunday brunch, he informed the crew, and we all showed up to make mincemeat out of KFC's bottom line. Every Wednesday evening, the local Howard Johnson offered all-you-can-eat fish. Tom sat in his designated booth in the designated section of his favorite server. The rest of us occupied the adjoining booths. He ordered all-you-can-eat fish and we ordered sweet iced tea. Tom's designated server kept the entire crew, freeloaders included, supplied with all the fish and fries and hush puppies and coleslaw we could eat. Like many rounder people, Tom was a dainty eater, kept his fingers licked and took judicious small bites, which he chewed until they were thoroughly masticated. After everyone but Tom was groaning and bloated, we slipped the waitress the $10 we collected between us, doubling her day's wages. She was happy and we were miserable. Tom, the most devout Christian in the joint, believed all was fair in food and war. If Howard Johnson were cheated in the process, it bothered him not at all. Did I mention Tom owned the only available automobile? A red and white 1955 Pontiac two-door equipped with a large V8 engine, overdrive and a metal sun visor?

Late July, Atlanta's sub-tropical heat index cranked up to heat stroke. Our seminar leader arranged a weekend outing in the cooler Blue Ridge country of Northwestern Georgia. By then, most of us had been living in unairconditioned dorms for too long, spending our fetid days and nights loading and unloading freight trucks, earning Teamsters Union negotiated wages (thank you, Jimmy Hoffa, wherever you are). A couple of days goofing off out of the heat struck us as timely. Our seminar leader, who often surprised us with his resourcefulness, miraculously pulled together enough food and drink for a picnic, an actual ski boat equipped with water skis. Our destination? The recently dammed Coosawattee River, which eventually played a prominent role in *Deliverance*, James Dickey's popular novel, and the movie starring Burt Reynolds, a squealing Ned Beatty and a squinty-eyed banjo player.

Following the enjoyable picnic/ski boat outing, five of us, including Izzy, loaded into Tom from Michigan's Pontiac and headed back to Atlanta. Unfortunately, Tom from Michigan hadn't filled his gas tank recently. He drove for 30 miles on a narrow blacktop through the red dirt scrub pine without finding a crossroad, never mind a gas station. Nobody in the car relished the idea of being stranded along the side of the road in squinty-eyed banjo-player country. The vanished Chaney, Goodman and Schwerner lurked in our heads. Palpable relief became palpable when a tiny one-pump, ramshackle gas station appeared in the distance.

Tom from Michigan pulled up to the pump and waited for someone to pump gas. This in the days before self-service. Custom dictated parking at the appropriate pump and someone eventually appearing to pump your gas, maybe wash your windows, check your oil or even check the air in your tires. A humpbacked, skeletal middle-aged guy wearing a wife-beater shirt, cigarette dangling from the side of his mouth, moseyed out to the unairconditioned Pontiac from Michigan, walked around the car, noting the out-of-state plates. After giving the car and its occupants the fish eye, wife-beater moseyed back to his shack and slammed the rickety door.

Mike from Duluth, riding shotgun, kicked open the passenger door and stomped towards the shack. Mike's explosive temper had earned him several assault and battery convictions, one incident getting him kicked clean out of Hamlin University. Loose cannon didn't adequately describe him. One of us needed to be in that shack before Mike landed all of us in serious trouble, maybe locked up in a redneck jail by a redneck sheriff. Twang a twang twang twang. One of us turned out to be me.

Purple-faced Mike from Duluth had wife-beater by the throat, pinned against the wall, demanding he pump our gas. Wife-beater wasn't having any. "I ain't pumping gas for no Sambo." (except he didn't say Sambo)

Miracles do happen. Mike was still processing wife-beater's firm position and resisting my flimsy efforts to control him when our fair-haired BMOC stepped inside, wasted no time getting behind Mike and installing a choke hold. All 115 scrawny pounds of me hit Mike at the knees, creating an inelegant dog pile on the floor. We somehow dragged Mike out the door towards the car. Tom from Michigan, Izzy and Keith from St. Paul, who never said much, stuck religiously to their roles as UN Peace observers. If Mike hadn't run out of fight, we could never have managed. He was stout even when he wasn't enraged.

Time paused while we struggled to load Mike into the car. Mike finally allowed himself to be pushed into the back seat when an ancient stake bed truck drove in, a stake bed truck loaded to the gills with bony white guys in overalls and beat-up straw hats, a couple carrying pitchforks. Wife-beater must have made a phone call. The hat brigade stared expressionless. Silent. As the truck slowed to a stop beside us, Tom didn't pause to check for intentions. The Pontiac from Michigan, which had never broken the speed limit in anger, spun red dirt and clods all the way to the blacktop, where Tom promptly buried the speedometer for the next 20 miles. With the exception of Mike, who was spouting nonsense about going back to settle up with the wife-beater, the rest of us were grateful for the Pontiac's oversized V8 engine and Tom's willingness to break the traffic laws of the state of Georgia.

No way of knowing Tom's thoughts, because Tom stopped talking to us, or, in fact, to anyone, but the episode might have prompted his decision to become a Trappist monk. BMOC went to law school. Mike married the Klan sympathizer and lost the last of his marbles. Keith from St. Paul, who never had much to say, went off to Thailand and became the most fluent non-native Thai speaker in the United States of America.

Izzy disappeared from our lives. He never attended another seminar session. Who could blame him? His time in Atlanta, featuring rednecks with shotguns and rednecks with pitchforks, had been an uneven experience. Izzy later resurfaced in Germany for postgraduate study in economics at the University of Mannheim, then earned a degree in economic development from Oxford University. Until Portugal granted Angolans independence, Izzy bounced between various United Nations bureaucracies in Geneva. Once Angolans were in charge of their affairs, Izzy served in several high-level government positions, including finance minister and trade minister. Since 2001, Ismael Martins has served as Angola's permanent representative to the United Nations.

"What do you think those guys on the truck would have done if they had caught you, Mr. Jones?"

"Nothing good. We probably wouldn't be having this conversation."

By now you might think my students were constantly hammered with civil rights talk, and I wouldn't blame you. But the usual topics that come up in history, government and geography occupied most of our attention. However, more than enough civil rights stories to upset some people in the community, although I was oblivious to the discontent. A handful of farmers, including several in the grain elevator crowd and a couple of school board members, got their backs up. Superintendent Onion Head, of course, perpetually suspicious and annoying. Notes piled up in my mailbox, sometimes a half dozen a day.

"If Americanism needs definition, then somebody is thinking the wrong history. Intellectuals who only see gray in semantics and not black and white, will someday suffer under the black or give in to the black."

Onion Head might have been irritating, and might eventually decide to get rid of me, but he posed no immediate threat to my employment or any other employee's. His credibility dissipated as the school year progressed. Teachers told Onion Head stories. Students told Onion Head stories. The school kitchen staff told Onion Head stories. He became a regular source of community amusement. The school board might not have been among my biggest fans, but choosing between a renegade social studies teacher with a hippie wife currently keeping the state educrats mollified by teaching both Spanish and music and a bumbling blockhead of a superintendent was not particularly difficult.

In the not-too-distant past, the public's fickle attention focused on unacknowledged racism and white privilege. This prompted a brief re-visitation of the 1968 version of Bladen, Nebraska. Whether Bladen's racial attitudes circa 1968 were more or less civilized than any other High Plains village is impossible to determine. In the absence (mostly) of a resident black population or interaction with same, casual conversation provided the majority of the evidence. And race seldom came up. Weather and sports dominated. Most considered discussions of race to be bad form, as were political or religious conversations. The cruelest racist remarks usually came from veterans who'd served beside segregated black units in Korea. Infrequent racist comments, masquerading as humor, uttered while in a state of drunkenness. No doubt if the community hadn't concluded I was a wild-eyed liberal on racial matters and censored their speech accordingly, I would have been privy to more frequent irritating remarks.

At the time, fanatical devotion to Husker football was gradually converting a good share of the populace to a superficial brand of color blindness. Any coach, star player or student trainer, black or white or Inuit, had first call on the community's unqualified adoration. Case in point. When the news leaked the black star of the current Husker team, an All-American and eventual Heisman Trophy winner, held up a Lincoln gas station, had been convicted of felony armed robbery, and yet continued to play Husker football, Bladen's attitude? "So what?"

For decades, Bladen housed a single black resident, Wylma Fletcher, a classically trained singer from Chicago. Fletcher, when she wasn't touring, made her home for nearly 40 years with a local Methodist minister. Rev. Gertrude McCallum occupied a pulpit, not in Bladen, but in Cowles, a tiny village a few miles to the southeast. The pitiful salary would not have paid her gasoline bill, let alone paid for her tires or wear and tear on her car. She also served as Fletcher's manager and personal driver. Gertrude booked appearances at churches around the state, making the odd couple a modest living from the free will offerings following the performances. On a Sunday afternoon in the early 1950s, Wylma Fletcher performed at my father's church in Neligh, Nebraska. Dad must have done his part to advertise the show because the pews were packed with ruddy-faced farmers and their families. Wylma Fletcher did not disappoint. In addition to being the most beautiful human being I'd ever seen, Wylma's operatic voice was like nothing I'd ever heard. Head over heels in love. Unlikely as it might seem, my instantaneous love for Wylma Fletcher exceeded even my deep and abiding affection for Mrs. TomJack, my raven-haired, alabaster-skinned second-grade teacher. And I often camped outside Mrs. TomJack's front door, hoping to catch a glimpse of her. And once or twice, after she spotted me lurking, she invited me inside for a warm cookie, which did nothing to discourage her stalker.

Gertrude McCallum was a product of the Plainview community south of Bladen, bordering the Bohemian Desert, where she attended the Plainview Methodist Church. Resident philosopher Don Lewis, who was married to one, often referred to those who grew up in the Plainview community as Plainview Puritans. Plainview Puritans carried a reputation for harboring overly severe attitudes towards harmless sins like card playing, drinking, casual cussing and dancing, in addition to the more serious sins of lying, stealing and fornication.

According to local legend, John McCallum, Gertrude's wealthy father, insisted on consummating the wedding with his bride Della at the first opportunity. Della had grown up in the Plainview community, sheltered from the harsher realities of life. John, five years Della's senior, treated the world as his oyster while becoming wildly successful as a farmer and businessman. After the ceremony, John drove Della home in a stylish buggy drawn by a handsome, matched team and wasted no time getting down to business. The shock and awe proved too much for Della and she soon filed for divorce, a tad too late to prevent the pregnancy which eventuated in Gertrude.

The local legend suffered from slight exaggeration. Della did indeed divorce John, but did not pull the trigger until months had passed. However, Della shared with young Gertrude her deep mistrust of men and their uncontrolled animal instincts. Della never came within a hundred miles of remarrying. John, on the other hand, soon married a woman 16 years his junior and fathered additional children. Even so, he did not neglect his first child, helping Gertrude pursue her ambition to become a minister and providing for her in his will.

Gertrude and Wylma lived quietly in the most impressive Victorian house in town. Gertrude fetched the mail and the groceries. A black man from Chicago occasionally visited, but whether he was Wylma's relative or a suitor remains an open question. Wylma sightings were infrequent. The last time I saw Wylma Fletcher in the flesh was during her performance in the Neligh Methodist Church. She accompanied Gertrude to church services in Cowles, but never in Bladen. Early in her residency, the first time Wylma worshiped at the Bladen church, there'd been trouble. One vocal, bleeding asshole of a crapbag announced to one and all she would never again grace the church with her presence if Wylma Fletcher were in the building. Bladen being Bladen, the word got back to Wylma. The harridan's attitude did not reflect the general feelings of the community. The most racially insensitive Korean war veteran would not have raised an eyebrow if he found himself in a pew with Wylma Fletcher. When people talked about Wylma, it was with affection. But Wylma assumed the bleeding asshole's views represented the community's. And like Myrtle Bartlett, became a virtual recluse.

A rat in a maze is free to go anywhere as long as it stays inside the maze.

—Margaret Atwood-*The Handmaid's Tale*

"I've spent my whole life trying not to be a trained rat." Whenever Tom Kaufman was into his fourth pack of his daily allotment of Winstons and halfway through a fifth of Jack Daniels (always Black Label), his dim view of urban living bubbled to the surface. The first time he appeared at our door, well into fall football season, he offered a fifth of Jack Daniels (Black Label) as a hostess gift and smiled his disconcerting part-Cherokee smile. Searching for the bottom of a bottle of decent bourbon at our hand-me-down kitchen table, invariably on a school night, Tom's conversation turned to the poor bastards living in large cities. "They wake up, drink bad coffee, crawl out to their cars while it's still dark, get on the freeway maze with all the other trained rats, bump and curse the other trained rats as they chase the cheese to their job. Or they pack themselves like sardines on the subway or a commuter train to make their way to the cheese. At the end of the day, they crawl back in their cars or commuter trains, bump and curse the other trained rats chasing the cheese through the maze back to their cookie-cutter houses with cookie-cutter lawns. By the time they get home, it's already dark, their wives and kids are home, pissed off and worn out from scurrying around their mazes all goddamned day.

"Even worse, after they run their mazes for a few years, they no longer think like individual rats; they become incapable of independent rat thought. If the TV news says there's a crisis, like the seasonal flu, and instructs them to be afraid, all the rats immediately panic. If a TV ad tells them they should run out and buy something, they run out and buy the same thing. You've spent time in a city, Jones. Haven't you seen the rats lined up outside a restaurant or a movie? Sometimes a rat will come along, see the line, and go stand at the end, just because the other rats are standing in line. The rat doesn't need to know why there's a line. There's a line; he has to go stand in it."

"True, I have witnessed this behavior."

"Jones, you're my friend. Right?"

"Yes, sir."

"No real friend would let another friend become a trained rat, would they? Promise me you won't let me become a trained rat."

"Do not worry, Thomas. I will do my level best."

And I meant every word, but had no clue how to prevent trained rat- ness. It seemed to me then and seems to me now, trained ratness can- not be prevented by intervention, no matter how expert. You are either born with trained rat genes or you're born some variety of anti-social misanthrope, who should live in a sparsely populated rural area with- out mazes. At opportune times, I shared my brilliant, Jack Daniels-in- formed trained rat insights with Tom. He did not disagree, but insisted, every time the bottle reached a certain level, on solemn pledges of future rescue. I concluded Tom had been tempted, perhaps more than once, by the offer of a high-salaried job in rat maze territory. Perhaps his will to resist the next temptation was in question. After all, he had an unstable wife and four young children to support, future college educations and weddings to fund. His principal's wages, boosted by a small stipend for assisting Onion Head coach football, exceeded the average teacher's salary, but not by much.

Kitchen table conversations with Tom covered many subjects, most of them Bladen-related. Of particular value were his lectures on extended Bladen families. Knowledge of the intertwined family trees informed my new desire to become an integral part of the community. With each passing day, Bladen became more appealing. I wanted to fit in. Be accepted. Bladen, previously considered a strictly temporary, hick domicile, might become a permanent home. Tom's genealogy lessons also proved essential in my daily teaching. If Scott held a permanent grudge against Kevin, it might have nothing to do with recent school politics, like which kid was starting on the basketball team, but have everything to do with Kevin's grandfather screwing Scott's grandfather out of the 80 acres he was supposed to inherit from their mutual ancestor. Once held, the grudge would never go away, which meant, at least in my classroom, Scott and Kevin's assigned seats were never within ten feet of each other.

Bladen families kept genealogy charts in their heads. No blood relatives intermarried, although there were occasional emergency interventions when cousins several times removed threatened to become more than pals. A high school of 60 souls, give or take, offered limited romantic options certified not to be some kind of relative. This might account, at least in part, for the early, deadly serious pursuit of scarce, genetically qualified permanent mates by the girls.

Newcomers to a small rural community have a choice between waiting to be invited to social events or creating social events. Not long after receiving our first fat paychecks, we began hosting casual parties, inviting teaching colleagues and school board members and the few members of the community we knew. As the year progressed and our circle of acquaintances grew, so did the parties and our liquor bills. The socializing proved to be a capital idea. New friendships blossomed. The community came to accept the oddball social studies teacher and the hippie music/Spanish instructor as less threatening than they first appeared. Free food and booze can do that. Not all school board members were regulars, but the ones who came stayed late, often until breakfast was served. Breakfast regulars became life-long friends. Return invitations multiplied.

With the Vietnam War temporarily boosting prices for livestock and grain, the local farm economy, which had become moribund after the Korean War, showed signs of renewed prosperity. Farm families allowed themselves the forbidden luxury of guarded optimism, enough optimism to host an occasional social gathering. Said gatherings usually featured an open bar and staggering amounts of venison summer sausage, which settled science has determined to be the primary cause of both terminal flatulence and attendant wobal glarming. Jim and Ginny Kral's warm kitchen on the Dry Divide became to us almost a second home. Plentiful food and spirits paired with Ginny's astonishing knowledge of breaking community news and Jim's avuncular presence made for memorable late evenings, evenings which invariably led to wee hour mornings and then to communal breakfasts as ax-murdered, rosy-fingered dawns broke on the eastern horizon. No one would have blamed Jim and Ginny for bailing much earlier, shooing lingering guests out the door before the rooster's crow. But they took pride in being the last ones standing. And they were always the last ones standing.

Ginny had no peer in the storytelling department. Every community tale she told contained an abundance of forbidden deliciousness. She could perfectly mimic the speech of anyone who lived within twenty-five miles. Pacing? Perfect. All in good humor and without being the least bit mean, she could puncture the pompous, twit her husband's failings, twit her failings, and have the boozy assemblage holding their collective sides.

A Korean War vet who contracted malaria guarding North Korean prisoners, Jim served as president of the school board and other area boards. The community instinctively trusted level-headed Jim Kral to listen to their concerns and make sound decisions. Jim was never more in his element than when hosting a large social gathering or skipping fieldwork for an impromptu trip to the horse races at Fonner Park in Grand Island. Ginny, who shared Jim's social instincts, grew up a Blue Hill Lutheran, which, in Jim's eyes, permanently tainted her claims of steadfast allegiance to Bladen causes.

Jim's suspicions concerning Ginny's true loyalties proved well-founded after a gregarious single woman moved to Blue Hill and promptly infected two dozen devout Lutheran town fathers with gonorrhea. The local medical clinic subsequently conducted a land office business treating businessmen and their wives. Some wives arriving at the clinic under the impression they'd been summoned because their husbands had contracted a particularly virulent flu bug. After the *Omaha World-Herald* published a state health department report listing Blue Hill as having the highest per capita venereal disease rate in the state, the laughter in Bladen could be heard as far away as Blue Hill… and Campbell…and Red Cloud. During the early morning hours of the next social gathering, Jim proposed Blue Hill's accomplishment deserved recognition—an addition to the "Welcome to Blue Hill" sign. "Welcome to Blue Hill, VD Capital of Nebraska" discussed, voted upon, and passed almost unanimously. Although there was no shortage of volunteer graphic artists, Ginny put the kibosh on the project by threatening to call the sheriff and rat out every prospective artist.

Jim and Ginny's open-handed generosity, never crimped by drought or low commodity prices, gave the impression they were made of money. Although they owned a medium-sized farm and a quality Angus herd, they were not exactly printing money. Rather, their philosophy was the opposite of the miserly. Why don't we have a good time with our friends and neighbors and figure out the money part later?

Resident philosopher Don Lewis and his wife Geneva hosted smaller gatherings in the house built for war hero G. P. Cather and his eccentric, harpy bride Myrtle. Lewis parties coalesced around the kitchen table, usually ending well before midnight and made up in quality for what they might have lacked in quantity. The Lewis household read books, gobs of them, hardly any of them light reading. Don possessed the next best thing to a photographic memory and if you disputed him about any shared reading material you'd have your ass handed to you on a platter. The Lewis children's considerable brains had not been degraded by exposure to television before they entered junior high, and then only after considerable parental debate. Neither child showed ill effects from the deprivation.

After graduate school, Don worked as a field rep for American Crystal Sugar in the Platte Valley. And Geneva taught school. They commuted on weekends to farm until they saved enough to move to Bladen and farm full-time. Although not a tightwad, Don had to watch the pennies while the farm enterprise got off the ground. For several years, his farm equipment was second-hand and undersized compared to his neighbors', not that he minded. Like Jim Kral, Don was a Korean War veteran, serving at Camp Hale near Leadville, Colorado, training raw recruits for winter warfare. Like Jim, he served on the school board, where, unlike Jim, he closely questioned the living crap out of any administrator selling typical administrator bullshit. Unlike Jim, Don intensely followed current events, local, state, national and international. If intergalactic news had been in circulation, he would have formed cogent opinions about those developments as well.

Table discussion might turn to the current urban riots, resulting in loss of life and widespread property damage, or the anti-war demonstrations shutting down universities across the country. A party guest might propose using the National Guard to reestablish order since the police had been ineffective. Don began his soliloquies with much harrumphing and corn cob pipe pounding.

"Remember the riot at the state penitentiary? 1955? I was in graduate school at the time and earning money as a guard. About half the place was on fire. Pissed-off prisoners running all over. The idiot governor sent in the National Guard. Most of those guardsmen were scared shitless. Never had training in riot control. Good kids, most of them, but when you're scared to death in a situation that's out of control and you're holding a loaded rifle, bad things can happen. Making those kids relax, move their fingers off the triggers wasn't easy. Took some time and a lot of conversation. Now insert untrained kid guardsmen in the middle of an urban riot. Riots are messy, no defined battle lines, punks throwing bricks and Molotov cocktails, maybe taking a few potshots at you. How well do you think that is going to turn out? Take those same untrained guardsmen and send them to control a draft riot at a university. Maybe the rich draft dodgers have occupied a building or two. Maybe they've taken a dean hostage. These punks despise soldiers. They've got bad mouths. They spit. The national guardsman has a loaded rifle and no clue how to proceed. Got bad written all over it."

Not infrequently, Don discussed the latest chemical weapons in his take-no-prisoners war against crop pests—insect, vegetable or pathogen. Don hated bugs, root worms, corn borer, various aphids, cutworms, spider mites, ear worms, any munching critter that might adversely affect his yields. Don also hated weeds, but not as much. He could control weeds with diligent pre-plant cultivation and pre-emergent herbicides, and in a worst-case scenario, actual row crop cultivation. It was insects that kept him up at night, visions of marching legions of ravenous corn borers making sausage of his formerly healthy corn stalks, root worms slicing and dicing the tender corn roots. In an era before Bt technology, which produced plants that paralyzed the larvae of crop destroyers, Don had access to a limited number of chemical tools, none of which ever provided a 100% kill rate. Consequently, Don developed warm friendships with area spray plane pilots, those uninsurable nutballs who eat life-threatening situations for breakfast. During one memorable kitchen table discussion of the evil town to the east, an itinerant spray pilot offered, if someone paid the chemical bill, to distribute Agent Orange over the entire town of Blue Hill. There was no shortage of generous offers, but the plan mysteriously went missing before it could be executed. Whenever the pesticide of choice fell down on the job, Don called in the spray planes, tanks often loaded with the nerve gas parathion. Take that you corn borer bastards.

"If it weren't for that goddamned Nixon, we wouldn't have the goddamned EPA canceling every chemical that works worth a shit. He created the damn thing, didn't he? Anyone hold a gun to his head? Hell no. You just wait, once the EPA finds out parathion works like a charm, they'll be banning it. Look what happened to DDT. You had millions of little kids in third-world countries surviving malaria who would have died without DDT. A couple of sissy eagles lay defective eggs, they ban DDT and the kids start dying again. Rachel Carson has killed more people than Hitler and Stalin put together."

I have never had a clear understanding of pipe smoking rituals, although rituals appear essential to the sport. Don kept four pipes in various pockets. As soon as one was loaded, packed, ignited and a few puffs extracted, it was tucked away in the designated pocket to await the next tour of duty. Without interrupting his train of thought, Don extracted the next pipe in the assigned order, pounded out the partially burned tobacco in the general direction of an ashtray, reamed out the accumulated carbon with his pocket knife, loaded, packed, repeated. A near tragedy occurred at a fall football game when, engrossed in the proceedings, he stuck a smoldering pipe in his coat pocket and set himself on fire. He survived, but the coat was a total loss.

At the kitchen table, Don's long legs and suitable placement of same created chronic difficulties. After extensive trial and error, he usually settled back in his chair, one leg crossed over the other, puffing contentedly on his corn cob pipe until it was time to rotate pipes, at which point the leg arranging process recycled. Anything related to domestic duties defeated him. An empty iced tea glass resulted in, "Tea, wife."

Geneva, always cheerful when answering the call, but often stymied by Don's long legs blocking her path to the refrigerator. Much grumbling if Don had to re-situate himself to create an opening. You might be wondering why Don didn't open the refrigerator door, two feet away, grab the tea pitcher and refill his glass, but that would misunderstand the rules of the Lewis household. Food preparation, food serving, cleaning, ironing, laundry, bed making, anything classified as household duties resided securely in Geneva's bailiwick. Any intrusions by domestically challenged husbands unwelcome and actively discouraged. Sure, Don could have grabbed a pitcher and poured his tea, but rules were rules.

According to community wisdom, the average IQ of any social gathering rose by 20 points if Don and Geneva were in attendance. The nincompoops running the world in 1968 could easily have put paid to their nincompoopiness had they listened to the wit and wisdom circulating with the pipe smoke under Don and Geneva's 14-foot kitchen ceiling. But they were, after all, nincompoops.

Sharp-tongued and tightly curled, 75-year-old Nettie Boom, head school cook, guarded lunchroom pennies as if they were hundred-dollar bills. Each year, the school board increased her budget, hoping she would offer a more varied and appealing menu. Every spring, Nettie proudly handed over a check representing significant unspent funds. Nettie's lunch menu, which relied heavily on USDA surplus commodities, frequently featured gourmet treats like spaghetti with peanut butter and sauerkraut gravy. Nettie encouraged students to eat everything on their plates by standing watch over the exit garbage can. Students hoping to sneak unconsumed spaghetti with peanut butter and sauerkraut gravy into the garbage had to contend with one irate cook. Once Nettie's crusty eye fixed on a student, nothing to do but return to the table and clean the plate.

One serving of spaghetti with peanut butter and sauerkraut gravy terminated my interest in Nettie's offerings. Lunch at home or eaten at my desk sufficed for the rest of my Bladen teaching tenure. There was a penalty, of course. Nettie did not approve of those who chose not to eat her food. Every time I passed by the lunch room, which was seldom, Nettie fixed me with a hostile glare until I left the vicinity. Teachers she liked, the gourmands who smacked their lips and asked for seconds, could sample her fresh cinnamon rolls. My understanding from the chosen was the cinnamon rolls were delicious.

She may have been well into her 70s, but nothing wrong with Nettie's spidey senses. She disliked Superintendent Dwight from the first sighting. Ever vigilant in tracking her food inventory, Nettie noticed in mid-September her cache of hamburger in the two school chest freezers diminishing at an unusually high rate. No dummy and naturally cynical, she suspected theft and had a suspect in mind. Nettie began locking the freezers when she left the building and waited for developments. Developments not long in coming. On a promising autumn Monday morning, replete with frosty air and tinted leaves, Nettie entered her kitchen to discover the handles of both freezers ripped off, leaving the freezer lids sprung wide open, soggy food defrosting inside. Twenty packages of hamburger, by Nettie's count, gone missing since the previous Friday. She wasted no time in calling the county sheriff in Red Cloud, who showed up only three hours later with a spiffy new fingerprint kit.

Did I mention Onion Head was preternaturally strong? Especially for a shorter, dumber guy? Bladen football linemen, once they'd been hammered by Coach Onion Head during blocking instruction, avoided further instruction. Onion Head stumbled into the crime scene investigation by accident. He'd seen the sheriff's vehicle in the school parking lot and, gregarious fellow that he was, rushed downstairs to chat up the sheriff of Webster County, perhaps share a Joe Marconi story. Confronted with the broken handles and lids of two chest freezers covered in fresh, accusing fingerprint powder, Onion Head immediately took responsibility. He'd been relaxing at home with his Bible studies the night before, glanced across the football field to see lights flicker a few times at the school. Worried the lunchroom freezers might have been deprived of power and valuable food might be spoiling, Dwight rushed over to check things out. He had no idea the freezers were locked. They'd never been locked previously. When he tried to open the lids and couldn't budge either one, he had to use more force. He said he must not have known his own strength. The person who locked the freezers should have informed the office. That person, Dwight said, staring right at Nettie Boom, was to blame for the mix-up. Nettie stared right back.

The Webster County sheriff had been elected to multiple terms in office, not so much for his crime-fighting skills, which were minimal, but because of his keen political instincts. Nothing to see here. He packed up his new crime scene kit and departed for Red Cloud. Let the Bladen school board members sort it out. Which they did at the next board meeting, directing Nettie Boom to keep the new chest freezers locked at night and Supt. Dwight to call Lyle Kile if he suspected a power outage. Although he was allowed to keep the stolen hamburger, Onion Head's feelings were bruised. He did, however, keep his mitts off the lunchroom freezers for the rest of the year.

Onion Head maintained a low profile for almost a month, concentrating on the spiritual redemption of Albert. No one argued Albert couldn't use a little spiritual redemption. A recent graduate of the Boys' Training School in Kearney, Albert enrolled in Bladen High School several weeks after the fall term began. At that point in his life, Albert was good-natured, but functionally illiterate, and had so many bees up his ass it was near impossible for him to sit still. He was also the best natural high school athlete I ever saw. Albert, had he ever earned a high school diploma, would have been offered college scholarships in multiple sports. 6'3", 190 pounds, fast, gifted with remarkable hand-eye coordination and superhuman strength, Albert could throw a football, catch a football, block and tackle better than any boy in the conference. Had he been academically eligible, which he never was, he would have been the shooting star of the football, basketball and track teams. They're still looking for the baseball he hit with his first swing.

For Albert, sitting quietly in a classroom proved an impossibility. If reprimanded, he'd apologize, promise to do better. Two minutes later, he'd be flicking the ear of the unfortunate classmate seated ahead of him. Within a week, he'd been permanently kicked out of every class. I like to think if I'd known then what I know now about teaching limited-ability kids, I could have worked with Albert on simple skill-building assignments he was capable of completing and given him a chance to be successful. Asking him to research a topic in the library was beyond ridiculous for a high-energy man-child who couldn't read or write. Expulsion from every class left Albert with days filled with study halls. As luck would have it, two of those study halls were supervised by Mr. Jones. Albert tried to behave, "reading" every picture magazine in the joint until the covers dissolved. But should an underclassman take a seat within range, Albert was obliged to send multiple spitballs his way. An inveterate tripper, Albert loved to sneak a foot into the aisle at the last moment, face-planting pimply freshmen boys—although always deeply sorry afterward. The day Albert left my study halls permanently, Twyla, who either lost her bearings or intended to tease Albert, wandered too close to his desk. Grinning like a delirious raccoon, Albert grabbed her bra strap and pulled it back the absolute maximum distance before releasing it. The resounding snap awakened everyone in the study hall. Outraged, Twyla yelped once and gave the side of Albert's smirking head a healthy swat.

"Albert, you need to go home now. Go straight home. Do not dawdle along the way. Do not pass go, do not collect $200."

"You're kicking me out of school, Mr. Jones?"

"Yes, sir. If your mother has any questions after you get home, have her call the school."

Albert went, but mopey. He enjoyed being in school, hanging around other kids, snapping random brassiere straps. It was the schooling part of school he found troublesome.

Principal Kaufman appeared in the doorway ten minutes later. "Albert's mother just called. Did you kick Albert out of school?"

"Yes, I did."

"Can you do that?"

"I have no idea."

"I think we're supposed to go through certain channels and procedures before we kick someone out of school."

"This way seemed simpler and quicker."

"You might be right."

Tom pursed his lips, turned the problem over in his massive brain, turned it over twice more, went off to chat with Onion Head. By the next day, Onion Head, bless his heart, had assumed complete responsibility for not only Albert's education but his eternal soul.

With Albert permanently incarcerated in the superintendent's office, except for lunch and frequent trips to the restroom, Onion Head had to figure out what to do with him. First-grade reading books proved too challenging, and Dwight lacked the skills to teach reading. Arithmetic stumped both Albert and Onion Head. Onion Head grabbed older magazines from the library and left Albert alone for long stretches to study the pictures. Albert eventually tired of magazine photos, which he'd already reviewed countless times, and he became a distraction to Albert's default supervisor, the school secretary.

Onion Head then shifted his focus to saving Albert's endangered soul. He loaded the tape machine with the "Petey, what are you thankful for this evening?" Onion Head also provided Albert with a few lessons in prayer giving. "Albert, can you think of anything you're thankful for?" Often as not, Albert, brow deeply furrowed, failed to come up with an answer. Onion Head, despite initial optimism, gave up on prayer instruction. Albert continued to devote his divided attention to the tapes as they repeated and repeated. Then he became antsy, and an antsy Albert was headed for trouble. When bored, Albert enjoyed gripping the arm of the 1924 model student desk and, pushing up with his feet, long jumping himself and the desk as far as possible. The resulting banging and scraping was considerable. Barb, the school secretary in the next room, began taking two-hour coffee/smoke breaks in the teacher's lounge.

Onion Head did not reveal the source of his next inspiration, a series of vintage recordings of an ancient ex-nun describing the Satanic rituals she'd been subjected to in a French nunnery. Her reedy, querulous voice, complete with a Midwestern American accent, filled Dwight's office and the secretary's office beyond.

"In the dead of winter, they took us outside and made us take off all our clothes and beat us with cruel, knobbed clubs and made us roll in the cold, cold snow."

"They made the novices eat mud pudding for every meal."

"Whenever a nun had a baby, they killed the baby with huge swords and made us drink the blood."

Sometimes after a particularly gruesome tale, Onion Head paused the tape to ask Albert, "Aren't those Catholics awful?"

Albert always nodded his head off. The tape resumed.

"If we were virgins, they poked out our hymens with a long, sharp spear made of oak. I screamed, but they stuck a rag in my mouth and told me to be quiet or else."

If Albert's soul had budged an inch toward salvation or if he had firm opinions about what he was hearing, he kept those things to himself. Barb, the school secretary, who after a couple of days, could do a passable imitation of the nun's squeaky voice, did not keep her opinions to herself. "If I have to hear about baby-killing hymen punchers one more time, I'm going to throw that damned tape machine in the furnace." We'd heard that empty threat before, but wouldn't have blamed her if she'd done much worse.

One afternoon, Albert, alone in Dwight's office, dutifully listening to the whiny nun, the next day he was gone, permanently expelled. No reason given, although word on the street theorized Dwight's precious nun tapes had been vandalized. Barb professed shock and ignorance. Speculation centered on the value of the tapes. Maybe Dwight had borrowed them from Bob Jones University's library and was on the hook for their safe return? Days passed, and no other suspects emerged. We eventually lost Albert altogether, endangered soul and all. He later served a stint in the state penitentiary, which made him mean. A few years later, he met violent death on a frosty Sand Hills road trying to outrun the State Patrol in a stolen car. By then, Onion Head and his querulous nun tapes long gone and unmourned.

Rookie Bladen teachers looked forward to their first fall teacher's convention. Most veteran staff members accepted the two-day break from students as an excuse to shop or work cattle or goof off. The novice teachers, curious and possessing a vague sense of professional obligation, attended at their first opportunity. Few ever repeated the exercise.

Of the sessions I attended that fall, only a handful made lasting impressions. The first was a presentation on health insurance by John Lynch, long-time executive director of the Nebraska State Education Association. The NSEA had been around since before Methuselah was a long yearling. However, its power in the late 1960s was limited to larger school districts, primarily in the Lincoln-Omaha area. The organization's eventual dominance of both the state's public schools and state politics far in the future. Two more decades passed before the NSEA could block any state legislation they opposed By then, the NSEA's political contributions dwarfed the combined political contributions of the state's commercial and agricultural interests.

Meanwhile, the union identified sympathetic local teachers to recruit for leadership roles. The union offered salary negotiation workshops, which provided essential bargaining skills. Teachers with the "right attitude" could expect additional training in union procedures and philosophy. Vague offers of high-paying employment at union headquarters and the chance to earn gold stars from professional colleagues kept local union enthusiasts eager to recruit new members. And also helped local union members overlook the union's bizarre positions on political and social issues, which were usually far left of the state's mainstream politics. Three decades passed before administrators and school boards began avoiding dismissing even grossly incompetent teachers because they feared the inevitable appeal hearings where NSEA teacher reps routinely exposed the schools' incompetencies—improper to nonexistent teacher evaluations, failure to provide adequate time to correct identified deficiencies. Failure to document teacher incompetencies fatally damaged administration cases so frequently the administrator profession should have resigned *en masse*. In finally coming to the defense of most NSEA members from arbitrary dismissal, be they from Omaha or Thedford, the NSEA provided a vital service to its members. Before the NSEA's ascendancy, it was a rare teacher who didn't have first or second-hand knowledge of a fellow teacher fired for no good reason.

John Lynch's chore for the hour was convincing teachers in the room of the unbelievable bargain represented by the Blue Cross-Blue Shield health insurance package he'd personally negotiated. No health insurance available in Nebraska featured the generous benefits he'd negotiated. No insurance premiums were cheaper. And I, for one, believed him. The NSEA trumpeted the cheap insurance offered teachers by Blue Cross-Blue Shield at every opportunity. Our school mailboxes overflowed with BC/BS advertisements. Why would they lie?

One possibility—taking public credit for cheaper health insurance would keep existing members in the fold and attract new dues-paying members.

You know how it is. When someone's high-pressure selling becomes annoying, it can kick you in the suspicious bone. After returning home, I called my local insurance broker, asked about rates on Blue Cross-Blue Shield health insurance for a benefit package identical to the one John Lynch bragged about. My local insurance broker apologized for the rate he could offer, which seemed high to him. The premium identical to what the school and I were jointly paying for my Blue Cross-Blue Shield health insurance. Any civilian walking in off the street would pay the same rate.

Why, you might be asking, would John Lynch negotiate insurance coverage and rates on behalf of the largest union in the state and end up with the same premiums any random mope might pay? Albert could have negotiated a better deal. I never found out. No NSEA representative ever answered the question, although they faunched and squirmed. Sometimes, making a prevaricator squirm is its own reward. But we sure can speculate, can't we? By sheer coincidence, John Lynch, in addition to serving as the executive director of the NSEA, also served on the board of directors of Blue Cross-Blue Shield Nebraska. His long tenure on the BC/BS board meant he was compensated accordingly. This was years before Blue Cross-Blue Shield Nebraska occupied an opulent $98 million state headquarters in Omaha. But even in more Spartan times, as a board member of long-standing, he could take advantage of the all-expense-paid company board meetings held not in boring Omaha, but in swell places where tourists liked to congregate. Whether Lynch ever attended meetings in Las Vegas or Miami is unknown (no attendance records are available), but he had more than adequate opportunities.

Ignoring the prominent Horace Mann insurance kiosk in the convention lobby proved difficult. Testosterony, crew-cutted young men accosted teachers with free Horace Mann ballpoint pens and Horace Mann shopping bags. You'll no doubt remember Horace Mann as the influential 19th-century American educator who did more than anyone to impose the Prussian, highly bureaucratized top-down industrial education model on American public education. The same Horace Mann who decreed parents should have no say in their children's education. Horace Mann property insurance? Check. Life insurance? Check. Automobile insurance? Check. Retirement annuities? Have we got a deal for you. Comparing the special car insurance rates "offered only to educators" with my current rates led to disappointment. By changing my coverage to Horace Mann, I would be raising my premiums by almost 5%.

Over the succeeding years, Horace Mann representatives waved the flag at every teacher's convention and many teacher in-service trainings. The details of the incestuous relationship between the NSEA and Horace Mann remain clouded, but one back clearly was and is rubbing against the other's. Then and now, administrators granted Horace Mann reps special access to their teachers. Pressure applied for teachers to buy high commission, high annual expense, low performing retirement annuities exclusively from Horace Mann. Teachers choosing to invest 403B retirement contributions with financial institutions other than Horace Mann were too frequently informed Horace Mann was the only "legal" choice. Another memorable session during that first teacher's convention, also hosted by the NSEA. NSEA teacher representatives described to the assemblage as one of the many services NSEA members enjoyed. Of those services, the promise to defend any NSEA member against unjustified termination of particular interest to some of us. 1968 was not far removed from a time when single female teachers could be dismissed for getting married. In the 1930s, my smart mother taught at several rural schools under contracts with those termination clauses. Teachers who disagreed with their administrators, no matter if they did so in a professional manner, could find themselves on the street. Teachers who didn't bow and scrape in the presence of the more self-inflated administrators could find themselves looking for a job. Those sorts of firings happened infrequently, but the threat remained in some school districts in the late 1960s. If the NSEA could protect my job from the likes of Superintendent Onion Head, I was all ears.

If an NSEA member in good standing were terminated, the NSEA teacher reps promised they would meet with the school board, explain teacher employment law as it then existed, use persuasion to reach the best outcome. Failing that, the NSEA had crackerjack attorneys on retainer who could easily best any school board in court. If you want to keep your job, you can keep your job. Thinking of the unpredictable Onion Head, this was welcome news.

Three middle-aged veteran teachers had questions. Hailing from Holbrook in South Central Nebraska, known as the City of Beautiful Elms before the American elms arching majestically over the highway through town expired of Dutch elm disease. All three teachers had taught in Holbrook for ten years or more. All three well settled into the community, married, had children, members of local churches. None of them, to their knowledge, had ever been the subject of complaints. Still in shock after their contracts had not been renewed without explanation. A more sorrowful trio of teachers never graced a teacher's convention. The most senior of the union teacher reps asked them to stay afterwards, excused the rest of us. I decided to stick around.

The rumor circulating in Holbrook blamed the termination on the recently adopted salary schedule. Said salary schedule negotiated with guidance from the NSEA, which, after factoring their years of experience and graduate credits, made the trio too expensive, at least according to the school board.

"How can they fire us when we haven't done anything wrong?" The union teacher rep, overflowing with empathetic drivel, expressed his deepest sympathies. Outrages like this could not and would not be tolerated. If the NSEA ignored this incident, other penny-pinching rural school boards would be encouraged to do the same. The Holbrook board deserved to be sued until they begged for mercy.

"Will you represent us? Take to school board to court? Get our jobs back?"

Unfortunately, as much as the rep wanted to fight this battle, NSEA's resources were limited. Not enough unionized teachers outside of Lincoln and Omaha. Currently, annual dues could only support so much teacher advocacy, and, for now, those efforts had to be focused on teachers in Lincoln and Omaha who paid the majority of union dues. He hoped this would soon change. If enough outstate teachers saw the light and became members, the union would be in a better position to help rural teachers.

"But we belong to the NSEA, have been members for years."

"That's good, that's very good, excellent in fact, but you have to understand how limited we are. Be patient, we're gaining outstate members every year, we'll get there eventually."

After the initial, troubling introduction to the Nebraska State Education Association, I found it difficult to justify giving them hundreds of dollars in annual dues. Something which became ever more difficult when it became apparent the NSEA had outsized influence on the State Department of Education. In fact, the two entities were joined at the hip, favoring policies that often gored my goat. Like the educrats in Lincoln, the NSEA pushed to close small schools and merge them with larger districts. Both organizations argued, without producing a lick of proof, small schools did a poor job of educating kids. No coincidence—teachers from small districts were less likely to become dues-paying members of the teachers union. State educrats and the union also argued per-pupil costs at smaller schools were too high, which meant larger, more cost-effective districts were being asked to subsidize less efficient districts. This claim ignored the disproportionate percentage of state aid given to the largest school districts and the paltry amount received by small rural districts. Local property taxes have always provided the bulk of funding for Nebraska's rural school districts. A big chunk of sales and income taxes small school patrons send to Lincoln ends up supporting the "more efficient" larger schools. Educrats and the union also ignore the substantial income from leasing state school lands, in recent years roughly 60 million dollars annually. Most of the state's school land is located in western Nebraska. Lease money comes from farmers and ranchers who also fund local schools under ruinous property tax assessments. Lease payments flow to the Board of Educational Lands and Funds, which in turn forks over the millions to the State Department of Education in Lincoln where it is distributed primarily to Lincoln and Omaha schools. The NSEA, due to the enormous power it wields in the Nebraska Unicameral and its ability to shape state aid formulas and tax policy, bears the largest responsibility for denying adequate state aid to rural school districts and the confiscatory property tax burden borne by outstate rural residents. Having a vested interest in the Bladen school district assembling the maximum pile of money to pay its teachers, I came to resent the NSEA's dedication to undermining the Bladen district's financial well-being and, by implication, mine as well.

Why does the state's most powerful union oppose tax relief for Nebraska's farmers and ranchers? Perhaps the socialist-leaning NSEA takes pleasure in seeing greedy capitalist farmers and ranchers penalized with heavy property tax burdens. And, if you think about it, why shouldn't farmers and ranchers and other rural residents who often vote in opposition to wise NSEA guidance be taxed out of existence? Until the day when the NSEA's Politburo successfully orchestrates the consolidation of farmers and ranchers on agricultural collectives, sending the recalcitrants in chains to remote Gulags, the NSEA will continue to bear unbearable financial burdens. Just consider the difficulties and expense the NSEA encountered in securing legalized marijuana in Nebraska. Or the high cost of NSEA lobbying to keep disadvantaged minority children trapped in dysfunctional Omaha Public Schools. Or the expensive fight to keep biological males in women's sports and restrooms. Anything the NSEA can do to eliminate farmers and ranchers makes its job easier.

The difference between intelligence and stupidity is intelligence has its limits.

—Ancient Adage

Stupid edufads appear with the regularity and consistency of monkey bowel movements. Departments of Education, state and federal, teachers unions, and teacher factories promote stupid edufads with all the enthusiasm brain-dead institutions can muster. Employees of these worthy institutions, particularly if headquartered in capital cities, have never abandoned the premise they were placed on earth to exemplify to the unwashed what sophisticated cultural attainments and lofty social status can do for you. Educrats' greatest collective fear? That, despite their best efforts to create a country populated by ignorant voters, public school students will somehow acquire useful knowledge and persuade their legislators to defund institutions spending billions in public funds on the flatulation of jargony gibberish. That Departments of Education, teachers unions, and teacher factories remain in charge of public education is an unfunny cosmic joke which has yet to be rectified.

All edufads, if religiously adopted, assume a Prussian, bureaucratic, dictatorial education policy. As with the infamous Inquiry Method of teaching history, edufads assume any new miracle teaching methodology will be imposed on schools and classroom teachers by state and federal bureaucracies. After all, why would the average, unenlightened classroom teacher ever adopt a superior methodology without pressure from above?

The NSEA never saw an edufad it didn't embrace or didn't lobby educrats to adopt. Over time, the incestuous NSEA/educrat partnership has severely restricted the freedom classroom teachers once enjoyed to design and implement the best instruction for their classrooms. Any rural teacher worth their salt practicing their profession 70 or 80 years ago wouldn't have put up with this micro meddling for a New York minute. Although teachers of that era were not unfamiliar with attempts at similar micromanaging. My smart mother, who knew a thing or two about running her classroom as she saw fit, provided excellent advice:

"Don't argue with them, whether it's your principal or the county superintendent or a state education department employee giving a workshop. Just smile and nod your head, even promise to do things their way if you have to. Once you're back in the classroom, do whatever you intended to do. Only the vocal rebels attract attention. It's a rare administrator who knows what's going on in an individual classroom. Keep your head down, teach the way you want to teach."

Which is what I tried to do my entire career. Usually, the advice worked, but in later years, after fellow teachers became the self-appointed enforcers of each new stupid edufad, previously accepted, but now disfavored teaching methods became more difficult to practice.

By 1968, the conduct of the Vietnam War, lack of popular support, resistance to the draft, marches and campus protests became unavoidable hot-button issues. Except in Bladen, a community that went to bed early and slept soundly, where the weightier concerns of sports and weather took precedence. Although the War occasionally came up for discussion in senior government class, I had little interest in making it the topic *du jour*. My conflicted attitude toward the war had not a little influence on the relative lack of attention. While still in high school, I'd concluded if the United States became militarily involved in Vietnam, the results were going to be disappointing. I was also well aware of Russian support for their North Vietnamese proxies. And since anything the communist Soviet Union supported was, by definition, evil, I felt morally obligated to back the US effort in Vietnam. Except, except, except the effort was so poorly executed. Perhaps American involvement was doomed before it started, a view that grows in popularity as memories of actual events fade. In 1968, the images on my two-channel black and white TV lacked the kind of clarity you can achieve by looking in a rearview mirror. What had become clear, at least to me, was those in charge of the war effort were unworthy of our trust or the trust of the soldiers who were paying the ultimate price. This long before the CIA's notorious Phoenix program of targeted assassinations became public knowledge. The national leadership, from reckless cold warrior JFK to pathological liar LBJ and his coterie of smug former JFK advisors to the CIA to some of the top generals situated on well-defended bases in Vietnam, was so obviously incompetent, so many American soldiers and South Vietnamese dying for no purpose, it became difficult to wave the flag and root for the home team. The country would have been much better served in future conflicts if an example had been made of a random assortment of high-ranking incompetents (there would have been legions to choose from) by court-martialing them and sentencing them to significant terms of military imprisonment.

Exposure to Pulitzer Prize-winning *New York Times* reporter Harrison Salisbury also impacted my views, although not in the way he might have intended. Salisbury recently returned from a visit to North Vietnam with shocking descriptions of the American bombing campaign, descriptions which portrayed the bombing as ineffective and serving to strengthen North Vietnam's resolve. Salisbury's interview subjects included the happy citizens of the barbarous North Vietnamese regime. Said interviews could never, of course, include questions about the brutal subjugation the North Vietnamese communists inflicted on their citizens following partition in 1954. (After partition, 900,000 North Vietnamese voted with their feet by fleeing to the South.) Although under near-constant threat from the skies, the happy North Vietnamese not only kept their equanimity, according to Salisbury, but were in perfect agreement with their North Vietnamese oppressors, who bore principal responsibility for their suffering.

Salisbury's lecture tour gained him fame and fortune, but his primary purpose was to generate public pressure on the Johnson administration to negotiate with Ho Chi Minh. He bragged about the resourceful North Vietnamese building makeshift pontoon replacement bridges within hours after American bombs had destroyed the originals and deploying bicycle brigades to transport Soviet and Chinese weaponry to the communist forces in the south. He made the case the North Vietnamese could not be defeated with the bombing campaign on which Johnson and his military advisors had staked so much political capital. The obvious answer, according to Salisbury, was for the Johnson administration to open peace negotiations.

My question to Salisbury, posed during a Q & A after his lecture in Chicago: if the North Vietnamese are barely inconvenienced by the bombing campaign and appear well on the way to defeating their enemy, why in blazes would they negotiate?

Afterward, the custodians peeled quite a few bits of Salisbury off the ceiling. He did not suffer to answer the question but attacked the questioner as an LBJ surrogate sent to disrupt his presentation with irrelevant questions. Salisbury's haughty, straw man prevarications didn't do much for his credibility, but it took no leap of faith to credit his descriptions of effective, primitive solutions defeating the best efforts of a highly industrialized enemy. LBJ hadn't the stomach to risk widening the war by punishing North Vietnam's military suppliers. A clear-eyed look at the systemically corrupt, Viet Cong-infiltrated South Vietnamese war effort, which had few successes to show for billions in American arms and thousands of American and South Vietnamese lives, also did not inspire confidence. Spend billions more, see more Americans and South Vietnamese die, bomb the communists to kingdom come, and wouldn't the scrawny little guys wearing tire sandals involuntarily toting guns and ammunition down the Ho Chi Minh Trail continue to do what they did so well?

Once the inevitable became inevitable, at least to me, I didn't want the responsibility of stoking my students' patriotism and inadvertently inspiring them to join a lost cause. In most cases, I'd match my loyalty to country against anyone's, but on this issue, I took a powder. While avoiding outsized attention to the war, the senior government class did take an interest in the unconscionable mistreatment of our returning Vietnam veterans. Nobody in the room had any sympathy for the privileged college kids protesting the war, burning fake draft cards, throwing blood on returning soldiers. My students' views matched exactly the attitude of the Bladen community. The grain elevator crowd was no more interested in promoting an optimistic view of the Vietnam War than I was.

The only person in town demanding fervent support for the war effort was Supt. Onion Head, devoting many a mailbox note to the subject and more than once trying to stir up war fever at school assemblies. Onion Head's overt patriotism caused him, just before the start of a basketball game, to run on the floor yelling for the band to stop playing the national anthem. The band's usual rendition of "The Star Spangled Banner" was earnest enough but lacked pitch and sufficient polish. After Onion Head's interruption, the grinding, discordant descent into silence particularly awful. Onion Head had neglected his self-assigned duty of turning on the spotlight illuminating the flag on the gym wall. Once the oversight was remedied, he ordered the anthem to resume and turned out the overhead lights. The brightly lit American flag the only visible object in the room. Striking image, but the darkened gym presented a problem for band members who relied on their sheet music.

"Lights!" Screamed an irritated hippie band director. And the lights grudgingly came on. The band fired up the national anthem, in bits and pieces, a few squeaky instruments at a time. Not the band's best performance, but under the circumstances…

Quick, name one of your high school social studies textbooks that jolted you awake and made an indelible, favorable impression. I'll wait. For the first half of the 20th century, history and civics textbooks earned the reputation of being crushingly boring, if utilitarian subject guides. By 1968, history and government textbooks, chosen for adoption by committees of fact-averse educrats and politically motivated union members, were often factually flawed ideological propaganda directed at students and teachers with fourth-grade reading abilities. Which is why I chucked them at the first opportunity.

Fortunately, the high school storeroom contained dusty riches. A former English instructor (rumored to have been a Blue Hill fifth columnist) left behind an assortment of novels. *The Grapes of Wrath, The Good Earth, Anna Karenina, The Scarlet Letter, Moby Dick, Madame Bovary, A Tale of Two Cities, All Quiet on the Western Front, Red Badge of Courage, Brave New World, 1984,* Elie Wiesel's *Night.* He also left behind *Catcher in the Rye,* but the rookie English teacher appropriated *Catcher* before I could figure out how to justify the assignment to an American History class.

Following the study of China, it's theoretically possible but highly unlikely Bladen's World Geography students remembered assorted facts concerning the nation's important physical features, form of government and primary exports. After reading *The Good Earth* as a supplementary text, it's possible a handful, especially the girls in the class, remembered Wang Lung the farmer and his despicable treatment of his loyal wife. A few of them might still be spitting nails. Along the way, students might have stored impressions of Chinese peasant life before Mao's genocidal communism. World History students read *The Long Walk*, courtesy of the school textbook budget. The Polish storyteller took his readers on a perilous escape from a Soviet slave labor camp in Siberia through Mongolia, the Gobi Desert, and over the Himalayas to safety in British-ruled India. Some students couldn't resist reading ahead to find out what happened. Not the reaction you typically see with an educrat-approved textbook.

World History students read *A Tale of Two Cities* in conjunction with studying the French Revolution, and got along with Dickens tolerably well. Assigning *Anna Karenina* for its tenuous connection to the Russian Revolution a leap too far. I believed assigning an extra-thick Russian novel engorged with twenty bazillion family trees would build character. *Anna* mostly built resentment and outright rebellion. A couple of girls might have soldiered to the end, but only because it was a chick book. *All Quiet on the Western Front* by Erich Maria Remarque, perhaps the most powerful war novel ever, seasoned our study of World War I.

While studying the frontier, American History students read *Old Jules*, the warts-and-all biography of Mari Sandoz's Nebraska homesteader father. Jules Sandoz's harsh treatment of his wives did not win him popularity awards from the female students. American History students also read *The Grapes of Wrath* while studying the Great Depression. I thought it a logical assignment at the time, and the story worked as intended to illustrate the desperate conditions of the Dust Bowl. I had no idea the book had been widely banned, and had I known, I would have been puzzled. This was, after all, 1968, long before the next century's rampaging book censors consigned hundreds of formerly well-regarded authors, like Dr. Seuss, Harper Lee, Mark Twain, J. K Rowling, Laura Ingalls Wilder and Margaret Mitchell to the burn pile. The country had not yet grown accustomed to having its reading material judged and censored by unelected left-wing nut speech police.

American Government students took time away from intense constitutional studies to read *1984* and *Brave New World* and invent visionary Utopian worlds of their own. Student utopias often bore a marked resemblance to the world they presently inhabited, except for a much younger legal drinking age.

Library research remained the central activity of the high school social studies classes. Students competed in weekly current events contests. I sometimes supplemented their reading with Dittoed copies of appropriate articles. Every morning, teachers lined up at the A B Dick Spirit Duplicator, better known as the "Ditto Machine." The "spirit" involved was mostly alcohol. Barb, the school secretary, claimed she could get high just sitting at her desk watching teachers churn out blue-inked worksheets and quizzes. The school did not yet own a photocopy machine, which meant each article had to be transcribed on double-ply-inked duplicator sheets on a typewriter, a process so laborious it kept teachers (mostly) out of the bars.

Whether toiling in the library or studying the latest Ditto handout, I expected students to have a command of the appropriate timelines and maps. After repeated testing, most of them could do a passable job identifying all the countries and capitals on a blank map of Europe or Africa or Asia or South America. If an American History student couldn't place the Mexican-American War on a continuum, he might as well transfer to algebra. A World History student needed to know not only what was up with that whole crusade thing, but be able to date and describe each one. I might have been a peach-fuzzed 23-year-old, but old school about creating a framework of dates and places to improve a student's understanding and sense of process.

Fall football season winding down. The team, no means terrible, but leaderless under the direction of Coach Onion Head. Dwight's assistant coach Tom Kaufman explained during a regular weeknight visit, "Onion Head's play calling is so stupid they've started calling their own. Good thing we have a smart quarterback. Sometimes they make up plays in the huddle. 'You run here, you block that guy, you block that other guy, hike on four.' The offense is better and the kids are having more fun. Dwight's so dumb he can't tell which play came from where. You'd think he'd have remembered a little something from playing high school football. Pennsylvania high school football is a big deal, produces hundreds of college prospects every year. Either he wasn't paying attention or Joe Marconi's knee clabbered his brains."

That first October in Bladen saw a geometric increase in two rookie teachers' discretionary spending as the impact of our outsized salaries took full effect. Guns, registered dogs, a sporty new car. And horses. Which meant saddles, bridles, vet bills, hay and oats. Horses, unlike cattle, eat pretty much 24/7. If you desire an infinite black hole into which to throw your money, a horse is an excellent choice. The first horse, a high-strung American saddle-bred mare, purchased at an area farm auction, turned out to be smooth riding but clinically insane. The first owner spoiled her by beating her around the head, something she remembered every time someone tried to bridle her. She'd take the bit, fuss when you put the bridle over her ears, pretend to behave. Once your attention moved to the blanket and saddle portion of the operation, she took careful aim, swung her head against yours, the shank of the metal bit smacking full bore into your skull. Tripper earned her name with her strategic falls, cunningly plotted and executed, intended to inflict maximum physical harm on the rider. She succeeded more times than she failed. My uncle Milton Tupper loaned a second horse, Lady, a comely 3-year-old bay mare which might, if she were well rested, have beaten a Galapagos tortoise in a foot race.

Since owning a horse bestowed, at least to my imprecise understanding, the official designation of cowboy, money needed to be spent on proper cowboy attire. And not just any attire. For instance, you didn't want to be caught dead in Lee jeans, worn primarily by those wide-beamed, flat-assed pseudo cowboys, the kind of clueless tourons who show up at Cheyenne Frontier Days. Levi jeans possessed a respectable working cowboy past but had recently been appropriated by movie stars and slumming stock brokers. This left the proletarian Wrangler jean, cut so generously, even expanding middle age could insert itself. Almost every area farmer, working or retired, wore Wranglers. With few exceptions, like Lyle Kile and the at-home version of Ken Berns, bib overalls were a thing of the past. Then came the boots, not Tony Llama, an excellent choice for formal occasions, but not for slogging around a shitty corral. Justin made fine dress boots, but their waterproof work boot bestowed both practicality and the imprint of good sense on the purchaser. Sturdy Hyer boots served almost as well. Not many cowboy hat wearers in the Bladen community. Free seed corn and farm chemical baseball caps dominated. The notable exception, resident philosopher Don Lewis, wore a suitably sweat-stained, beat-up Rowdy Yates model cowboy hat of indeterminate manufacture. But then, he always had distinctive style, a style he believed could only be maintained by wearing correct habadashery and periodically enriched with judicious dollops of harmless sin. Stetsons, considered mandatory in some jurisdictions, earned no compliments in Bladen. Too pretentious. That left practical cowboy straws in summer and modestly priced Resistol felt hats in the cooler months. Not that a school teacher wearing any brand of cowboy hat wasn't considered pretentious. $350 later you couldn't have decked out a pretending not to be pretentious pair of pretentious school teachers any better.

If you really want to hear about it, the first thing you'll probably want to know is where I was born, and what my lousy childhood was like, and how my parents were occupied and all before they had me, and all that David Copperfield kind of crap, but I don't feel like going into it, if you want to know the truth.

—Holden Caulfield—*The Catcher in the Rye*

The first-year English instructor, a fellow greenhorn, matriculated from Grace Bible Institute in Omaha. Grace Bible shared some theological and student conduct philosophies with Bob Jones University, specifically, Bible-centered instruction and strict prohibitions against male-female panky hanky. Some have described Miss Murphy as plump mousey. However, an alert observer would not call Miss Murphy a sourish, fundamentalist prude. She laughed nervously at whatever anyone else found humorous, shunned disagreement as too disagreeable. A glass-half-full brand of painfully shy optimist, her students did not find her oppressive. On the contrary, her classes featured spirited paper airplane warfare. If she became accidentally aware of flying objects and accidentally detected the source, she might, but only if seriously provoked, timidly request the miscreants write "I will not throw paper airplanes" ten times on the chalkboard. Given her macaroni backbone and eagerness to please her youngers, it was beyond cruel for Superintendent Onion Head to saddle her with coaching volleyball, a sport with which she had only nodding acquaintance. He also tasked her with the sponsorship of both the freshman and sophomore classes, supervision of the chronically fractious pep club and the production of both the junior and senior class plays, extra duties which landed on her plate because she was new and easily browbeaten. Her play productions made up in chaotic hilarity for what they lacked in polish. Holding play practices, not on the school stage, as was customary, but in her home, led to harmless pranks, like shutting off her alarm clock and generous deposits of lead BBs in her bathtub.

Since she avoided her colleagues during the school day and inviting a graduate of Grace Bible Institute to a booze-filled social gathering didn't occur to anyone, Miss Murphy's private life remained obscure. The class play participants knew her much better than her teaching colleagues. For instance, they knew she had an actual boyfriend. Perhaps a Marine. Knew when they were betrothed. After the boyfriend abruptly left her in the lurch and she flushed the engagement ring down the toilet, they knew about that, too. And they knew when she burned his letters in the trash barrel behind her house (all but a special few). Miss Murphy found herself torn between deep humiliation and self-reproach. She never wanted to hear from the jerk Marine for the rest of eternity, but couldn't help staring at the mute black telephone, hoping for a reuniting ring. Mostly, she tortured herself by speculating on what she could have done differently. If only...? Would he have abandoned her? After a month of deep mourning, Miss Murphy straightened her knickers and turned to tutoring a troubled youth in her home — late at night. A step over a line which should never, ever be crossed.

When I wasn't paying attention, Miss Murphy filched the entire stock of *Catcher in the Rye* paperbacks from the high school storage room. Not that I had any current application for the much-banned 1940s classic coming-of-age novel, but never say never. She asked the junior class how long they estimated it would take them to read it. After due deliberation, they decided if they applied themselves to the maximum, most of them could finish in three months, a challenging regimen of three pages a day. Miss Murphy signed off and to provide motivation, made the final exam over *Catcher in the Rye* the semester final, worth half the semester grade.

The night before the final exam Miss Murphy got busy reading *Catcher* for the first time. She had to create a test by the next day. Hard to know what she expected, but Holden Caulfield shocked her to the quick. Come the next morning, a red-faced Miss Murphy called off the final exam and spent twenty minutes apologizing for assigning a book that was clearly the work of the Devil.

Once a school year begins, usually in fits and starts, the year gradually assumes a final destination, a certain momentum and a future passage of seasons. At some point, summer freedom for teachers and students becomes the goal line. After a few weeks of autumn football and volleyball, especially if the scores tell sobering tales, eyes turn toward the coming basketball season. Hope reappears. Well before the first basketball game, traditionally after Thanksgiving vacation, the grain elevator crowd will have handicapped every basketball game on the schedule and prove to be prescient. After all, they knew the gene pool, not only Bladen's, but the genetic determinants swimming in competing small towns. For example, the Campbell game could be chalked up in the win column before the first practice. Every few years, usually during a rare solar/lunar/ Jupiter/Uranus eclipse, Campbell fielded a competitive football team. Husky Russian-German lads paired with a few quicker French boys sometimes made Bladen-Campbell football games interesting. Campbell basketball seldom proved competitive. Bladen owned a richer tradition. District tournament winners frequented the 1930s and two teams made it all the way to the state tournament in Lincoln. The elevator genetics professors never tired of reliving Tom Kaufman's near single-handed dispatch of hated Blue Hill at the Webster County tournament. Also, fresh memories of Ermine Krewson's gravity-defying flights above the rim. No Bladen Bulldog ever jumped higher or hung in the air longer than Ermine Krewson. And nobody who didn't have his head inserted completely up his ass had forgotten the athletic 1966 district champions, which not only set several school scoring records but contributed willing hands when it came time to drop automobile tires over the flagpole.

Basketball, a sport played by only five players, which, if they were talented and well-coached, could sometimes compete with teams from larger schools. The dreams of the elevator genealogists rested on the periodic assemblage of four or five respectable basketball players on a single team. Predictions for the 1968 team modestly favorable. A dependable outside shooter, a quick defensive guard and a set of scrappy, if undersized, rebounders will win some ball games. Mr. Warren, the rookie coach, represented an unknown. The guy was as athletic as they came. Tall, rangy, could run forever. Still held the state record in the mile run, didn't he? Chances were good he played basketball in high school, but scouting reports were none. Given the choice, would you rather have an athletic guy who played the game or some dinkphod who'd never dribbled a basketball in his life? Mr. Warren would probably do.

No surprise, the first game of the season attracted an above-average crowd. And the game progressed according to biological script, with the home team more than holding its own. The pep club and cheerleaders, employing cheers and routines learned under a previous sponsor, clearly welcomed performing in a more confined space with far superior acoustics to a cold, wind-blown football field.

Give me a B!

B!

Give me a U!

U!

Give me an L!

L!

Give me an L!

L!

Give me a D!

D!

Give me an O!

O!

Give me a G!

G!

Give me an S!

S!

What's it spell?

BULLDOGS!

What's it spell?

BULLDOGS!

What's it spell?

BULLDOGS!

YEEEEAAAAAH TEAM!

The spirited cheerleading on this night packed the added oomph of the formerly absent black and orange pom poms. During a warm fall practice on the schoolhouse lawn, they'd been left where they landed when the cheerleaders took a water break. When they returned, the pom poms had vamoosed. Lyle Kile, the first person they approached, confessed ignorance. Following Thanksgiving vacation, the prodigal pom poms magically reappeared in the visiting locker room shower. This, after extended pleadings from the rookie pep club sponsor and a patient Tom Kaufman directed at one Lyle Kile. But one example of Lyle relentlessly practicing his strict philosophy—everything has its proper place, be it used automobile tires or cheerleader pom poms.

Pom poms represented an infinitesimal fraction of the items gone missing during a typical school year. The average lifespan of a playground kickball ranged from days to hours. Any basketball, football or volleyball left lying around by a careless student or coach disappeared. Unguarded student property, including shoulder pads, shoes, coats, textbooks and entire gym bags, joined the playground kick balls in whatever mysterious hidy hole they might be residing. Since petty theft was virtually unknown in the school or in the community, likely suspects didn't exist. Theories enjoyed brief currency and expired without gaining favor. I developed a pet hypothesis after an entire set of next-day quizzes disappeared from my desktop overnight. The only person with opportunity was Lyle Kile. Motive? A gentle reminder to keep my desktop operating room sterile. Following the disappearance of a half dozen pickled frogs from the biology room, Mr. Warren proposed a stealthy late-night reconnaissance of Lyle Kile's downstairs utility closet. Lyle kept the closet, the only unexplored territory in the entire building, locked up tighter than Dick's hat band. Why? We assumed it held mops and brooms and harsh cleaning chemicals. But perhaps, just perhaps, a half dozen embalmed frogs might be hiding in there. Besides, the locked door suggested other items worth suspicioning. Approaching midnight. Lighting provided by a single restricted-beam flashlight. The many-talented Mr. Warren picked the lock without breaking a sweat. His small-town boyhood had not been completely wasted on grueling trips around his high school's cinder track.

The door creaked open, a tad too creakily for comfort, the penciled flashlight beam explored the extensive closet interior, the floor-to-ceiling shelving, rows upon rows of pristine kickballs, footballs, basketballs, shoulder pads, gym bags, shelves stuffed with winter coats, sneakers, mittens. What about the missing frogs? The burglars first had to scramble over the clunky floor polisher, assorted mop pails and an assemblage of five-gallon chemical buckets blocking the closet entrance. The hidden riches, for the most part neatly shelved, stretched forever. In the far corner, back behind the kick balls and gym bags, on a shelf five feet above the floor, Mr. Warren unearthed not only the wayward frogs but a dusty gallon jar of embalmed clams. Nestled close to the clams, which appeared to be in prime condition, Mr. Warren discovered a large beaker containing what appeared to be chunks and bits of floating starfish debris. Chances were excellent the starfish were older than the burglars. Although he debated leaving the frogs where he found them, Mr. Warren had use for the frogs—and the clams. Abandoning the fragmented starfish, he hauled the frogs and the clams back to the biology lab storage closet, now featuring a sturdy new padlock.

Although the early-season basketball crowd, both home and visiting, maintained its enthusiasm throughout the first half, people began commenting on the dimly lit gym. The action on the court could be followed, but it was like squinting through smoked glass. During a timeout, the visiting coach approached Coach Warren, pointing to the numerous burned-out bulbs in the overhead lights. Coach Warren, in turn, sent a student manager to inform Superintendent Onion Head, currently munching his way through the pep club candy stand's shrinking offerings. After the buzzer ended the first half, a good share of the men in the stands, including a working majority of the school board, migrated to the lobby, where they puffed feverishly on cigarettes and at least one pipe, befouling the entire area with clouds of blueish gray smoke. The lobby crowd would provide reliable eyewitnesses to Lyle Kile's entrance and quick exit.

Lyle, a devoted fan of the wildly popular *Gomer Pyle: USMC* TV show, made it his business to never miss an episode. Tornadoes nor floods nor thermonuclear war not withstanding. He arrived at the gym clad in scrupulously clean Key overalls, a scrupulously clean matching Key denim jacket and a scrupulously clean denim engineer's cap. Did I mention his visible annoyance to be called away from Gomer Pyle? Once he discovered Onion Head had dislodged him from his favorite recliner and TV show to change out the non-functioning gym lightbulbs, he graduated from annoyance to stubborn outrage.

"I'm not climbing any ladders. Haven't climbed a ladder in years and I'm not about to start now."

"I guess you will climb a ladder and change those light bulbs."

"You'd be wrong, mister. I'm not doing it."

Onion Head, already infamous for questionable decision-making, decided to go hard. "If you expect to have a job on Monday morning, you'll change those lights right now."

Lyle turned on a dime and stomped out through the lobby doors, delivering a parting shot over his shoulder at Onion Head and the entire lobby of interested smokers, "I'll be here long after you're gone, buddy."

That Lyle's prediction came up roses was no surprise to the lobby crowd. In fact, you'd have found no takers on the other side of the bet. Lyle had nothing to fear from a competent superintendent, never mind a blithering MO-ron.

After Lyle called his bluff, Superintendent Dwight's blithe spirits showed little decline. Cheerful to a fault, he continued to open teachers' personal mail and scribble deranged notes on the envelopes. Sometimes, if the mail supply proved insufficient, he answered personal mail before the designated recipient had seen it. A practice that often confused the original correspondent, who most likely had no idea who an Onion Head might be or why he was writing to them about communism or citing inappropriate passages from the Bible. Should the incoming mail lack political or social content, he tackled junk mail, often contenting himself with random, scribbled Bible verses. His visits to my classes dwindled. He couldn't understand the concept of library research, and crackerjack student performances during current events quizzes might have made him feel inadequate. If he stumbled into a discussion of the ups and downs of the Spanish-American War, his eyeballs glazed and he discovered more important business elsewhere. He continued to tape and replay his family prayers, but once little Petey began whining, secretary Barb took off for an emergency cigarette in the teacher's lounge. Nobody knew what tasks Onion Head might have been doing, but if he did anything, everyone believed it was with the familiar lobotomized rabbit grin on his face.

How to pinpoint the tipping point that persuaded the board not to renew Onion Head's contract? The much-publicized lunchroom hamburger pilferage of the previous fall not forgotten. Continuing sharp complaints from Nettie Boom about most anything Dwight-related. Complaints from faculty didn't count for much unless they came from teachers who were also Bladen natives. As the year wore on, complaints from the natives grew more insistent. Meanwhile, compulsory reports to the educrats in Lincoln remained uncompiled and unsent. Onion Head bolloxed the school's finances. He paid bills twice or not at all. The school district's true bank balance anyone's guess. The board would have suspected a more clever superintendent of embezzlement, but clever and Onion Head didn't occupy the same planet. Board secretary Don Lewis, who knew his way around both dollars and cents, tried mentoring him for a time, but Dwight's concrete, onion-shaped skull proved impervious. Lewis reluctantly took over the bookkeeping and, with the school secretary's help, managed to get through the school year in close proximity to the black. Since managing the school's finances and keeping the educrats in Lincoln happy were included in Onion Head's job description, his abject failure at those tasks could not be ignored.

Then there were Onion Head's school bus-driving misadventures. Not one to pass up free meat or any addition to his paycheck, Onion Head volunteered for a regular school bus route and any available extracurricular bus driving assignments. He could manage picking up a handful of school children on sparsely traveled rural roads unless the roads were drifted with snow or muddy. If mud or snow were in the forecast, parents along Dwight's bus route made sure to park a tractor of sufficient horsepower, loaded with a heavy log chain, near a likely trouble spot. Kids needed to get to school no matter how erratic the bus driver. A few near collisions on highways when hauling students to distant activities went down in the ledger, but the board hesitated. Until…until… Onion Head drove a bus to district music contest at a school fifty miles to the north. Since nearly 100% of Bladen High School and junior high students participated in at least one music activity, they filled the district's two largest school buses. Onion Head pulled rank and took point on the trip home. Just south of Hastings, he decided the car in front was not traveling fast enough. He abruptly pulled out to pass without signaling or checking his side mirror, oblivious to the car in the process of passing him. While the passengers in both buses looked on, the passing car took the ditch, continued until it hit a culvert, flew for a spell, and landed on a driveway, wheels splayed, hood popped open, engine smoking. Sad end to what had been a sporty car. Onion Head never saw a thing. The cherry on top for Onion Head's final performance as a bus driver.

Had he accepted the loss of bus driving privileges with a smidgen of grace he might have saved his job. The school board, mindful of the difficulties of replacing staff, mindful of the last sorry group of flawed superintendent candidates they'd sifted through to arrive at Onion Head, had no stomach for a termination. But Onion Head refused to admit the latest incident ever happened. If something maybe, might possibly have gone amiss, it wasn't anything to get excited over. This despite the testimony of a school board member who witnessed the whole deal from the trailing bus. Whether Onion Head were aware or not, he had settled his hash. Contract extension talks remained on hold. He showed up in the office for the rest of the school year out of habit, but he was done. Glee abounded when the news reached the Bladen faculty. Little did we know Onion Head was not the sorriest school superintendent on the menu. Something more sinister than doofy Dwight was headed our way.

Summer brought three months of relative freedom for Bladen students and most of the faculty. The rookie teachers from New Orleans were not among the free, having obligated ourselves to rack up the required education hours for actual teaching certificates sooner rather than later. Consequently, we took nothing but education classes during pre-session, regular session and post-session summer school at Kearney State Teachers College. Had to be done and no easy alternative, but so many education courses packed together caused permanent psychological damage. Like being forced to drink a five-gallon bucket of castor oil, the first taste might not be a deal breaker, but there are still five more gallons to go. Torture victims frequently block out the memories. Indescribable pain shocks them into a form of amnesia. Summer school education classes may not have involved yanked fingernails or sparking electrodes applied to the testicles, but the effects were similar. Only vague memories of that traumatizing experience survive. What I do recall is each so-called professor was more stupid than the previous one. The best of the worst could remember perhaps two percent of what they'd been taught. The entire two percent composed of pure oatmeal. No surprise, since the IQs of education majors exceed only those of social justice majors. Because low-ability professors could hardly burden low-ability students with challenging assignments, the professors divided the class into small groups so we could discuss educational topics of the day, imbue ourselves with our own intelligence and report to the class. Grades? Each of us received an A. As was and has been the case for decades, education majors traditionally sport the highest GPAs of any college department.

A discussion in an educational psychology class led to the predetermined conclusion ability tracking students was bad because some students might feel slighted. A conclusion that predated by decades the anti-meritocracy edufads of the next century. Two turtleneck/gold chain-wearing profs besotted with their coolness co-taught the class. They might have had Malt-O-Meal for brains, but they could out-emote anyone, anytime, any place. The primary goal? To foment ad hoc group therapy sessions which often began with a question. Did any of you experience a teacher praising another pupil for outstanding achievement? How did that make you feel? Less valued? Depressed? Unfortunate college students prodded into serving up repressed memories of classroom marginalization could expect an overdose of syrupy sympathy and the unwelcome introduction of two cloying pests into their lives. Once the turtlenecks unearthed a self-identified abused student, they honed in on the poor wretch, extracting additional outrages and blubbering over the confessions. The rice paddies of Vietnam never looked so inviting.

As I gritted my teeth and plodded my way through summer school, little on the national scene intruded. The war in Vietnam dragged on, the daily body counts a regular highlight on the nightly news. Protests against the war multiplied and became more strident. Business as usual. Although had it been general knowledge Nebraska boy Lt. Bob Kerrey had directed a messy CIA-ordered massacre of 13 men, women and kids in the Vietnamese village of Thanh Phong, we might have read about it in the *Omaha World-Herald*. Or not. Ted Kennedy managed to escape serious penalties after Chappaquiddick. The spelling of Chappaquiddick and Mary Jo Kopechne eventually became regular questions during the Friday news quiz contests. My students might not have known every amendment to the United States Constitution by heart, but they sure as hell could spell Chappaquiddick and Mary Jo Kopechne. Neil Armstrong walked on the moon. His moon walk would have been more impressive to Bladenites if he could also throw a football and been enrolled at Nebraska U, where Bob Devaney's teams had been scuffling the past two seasons. Woodstock happened, I'll take their word for it. The event barely made a ripple in my world, although I later purchased the album and played it until the grooves gave up.

While enduring my education classes and the long commute to Kearney, I lost track of current Bladen school developments. Over the summer, Miss Murphy departed for parts unknown, for reasons unknown. I wish I had been more curious. Her replacement, Mr. Warren's vivacious wife, hired to teach English classes and French. Most of Miss Murphy's extracurricular assignments parceled out to the existing staff, Librarian Lucille burdened with an extra large helping. A new superintendent had been hired almost before Onion Head's protruding ass disappeared over the eastern horizon. A hiring that struck some of us as odd. Bladen's lowly status as a small school located in a tiny rural village meant plausible superintendent candidates, if they applied, did so after they'd exhausted superior possibilities. If this new guy had agreed to a contract so early in the hiring season, he must, by definition, be desperate.

In 1969, rural superintendent candidates relied on job postings and tips from their friends when seeking the best opportunities. If they chose to apply for a job, they competed with all the other candidates looking for a new situation. This before the present system of hiring superintendents came into being. If a Bladen school board, should one still exist, were in the market for a new superintendent, employing a headhunting firm would be the first order of business. The firm might be connected to the state association of school boards or might be an entity put together by a couple of enterprising educational administration profs at Kearney State. For a fee which would far exceed Superintendent Onion Head's annual salary, the headhunters would take over the selection duties.

Why, you might ask, don't rural school boards conduct their own due diligence on superintendent candidates and save themselves both money and potential grief? The Nebraska Association of School Boards conducts training workshops for school board members and actively discourages school board members from becoming private detectives, which could give malicious small-town gossip, based on fact or fancy, too much weight. A bunch of amateurs poking around in a candidate's past has bad written all over it. Much better to leave due diligence to the professional consulting firms. Fellow school administrators know a great deal about each other, but sharing inside information with a prospective employer violates the unwritten rules. Even if amateur sleuths focused on public records, little information is available. Past performance, unless a superintendent is convicted of a criminal offense or been sanctioned by the state board of education, hidden from the public. His or her current school board provides a glowing recommendation just to get the miscreant out the door. In recent years, the former employer, wary of legal trouble, may provide no information beyond the dates of employment. The privately owned, for-profit Nebraska Association of School Boards advises local boards to hire headhunters (the Nebraska Association of School Board's in-house headhunters would be happy to serve you) to navigate these tricky waters and most follow the advice.

Freed at last from a summer's incarceration in education classes and eager to share my frustrations with my Bladen colleagues, I looked forward to the day teachers reported for the fall term. We crowded on bleachers in the pungent gym. A favored few who patronized the school lunchroom munching on Nettie Boom's rumored to be excellent cinnamon rolls. I had little opportunity to unload a truckload of snarky summer school observations before our brand-new superintendent marched to the podium. Bigger guy stuffed into a cheap suit two sizes too small. Eyes two sizes too small stuffed in a bulging face. Crew cut. Face so red he resembled an engorged tick. Not a glib smiler. Our new sup was more into glaring, daring us to challenge his authority. Whatever deficiencies the staff harbored, and we knew there were no shortage, Richard Brommer promised to unearth and punish every one. "You may think I'm not paying attention, but you better believe I will monitor everything happening in this school. You screw up, I'll notice. Anyone who doesn't get the message will be fired on the spot." And off he marched.

So much for an uplifting message to get the new school year started on a positive note. So much for our fragile self-esteem. We don't know this fat jackass from a cow chip and he's threatening to fire us? What the hell? After the peppy talk and abrupt departure, I followed Brommer to his upstairs office. He was surprised to see me. I introduced myself, welcomed him to the community. Asked if he was happy with his new position so far, a question which proved a stumper. Happy and Richard Brommer were not on speaking terms.

Might as well get down to it.

"When you mentioned firing teachers, were you talking to me?"

"Not at all. From what I'm hearing, I'm sure you're going to be one of my top teachers. I was addressing some of those losers. You can probably guess who."

"I have no idea which of us you were addressing."

"Nothing to worry about. Just keep your nose clean and you'll have a successful school year."

There you have it. Richard Brommer, blowhard bully. No more substance than a defunct gym light bulb. He could beller 'til the cows came home, nobody need pay a particle of attention. Call his bluff, he'd fold. Meanwhile, my Nebuchadnezzar oven of a classroom was calling.

When Tom next came to the house, he got a kick out of my foray into Brommer's office. "He's a bully all right. Stand up straight and he'll back down. Have you met his wife? She's a piece of work. Little bitty thing. I'd be more worried about crossing her than crossing him. She's a mean one. There was trouble at his last school and she was in the middle of it."

Why had Brommer been hired so early in the hiring season? Wasn't his availability a red flag? Tom's version, sourced from his postmistress mother: The Bladen school board found itself stuck with only one applicant. Said applicant came with impeccable credentials, glowing recommendations. If he appeared a bit of a bully, what of it? If they didn't hire him, it wasn't like dozens of suitable candidates were beating down the door. According to the grapevine, the board already regretted the hire, but it was too late to reverse course. With luck, Brommer would be sending enough correct paperwork to the state educrats to keep them happy. With luck, he wouldn't be stealing gobs of district money. Meanwhile, batten down the hatches and hope we can ride out the storm.

While I was enduring the most mindless, jargony oatmeal the Kearney State College education faculty could inflict, Tom Kaufman spent his summer relaxing with other students taking graduate administrative classes at the University of Nebraska. Gossip from the insular world of Nebraska school administrators flowed freely. Who was leaving which superintendency and why? Who were the up-and-comers? Which schools had rogue school boards? Which schools had shaky finances? When I complained about my mind-numbing education classes at Kearney State, Tom smirked. "I took one 12-hour seminar. The only requirement was to read a book of my choosing and hand in a one-page report at the end of the summer. Class attendance was optional. Everyone got an A. Sorry about your summer, Jones."

Late August scorched its way into dusty September. Tractors pulling wheat drills left graceful etchings in the brown soil. Combines churned through desiccated milo fields. September eventually yielded to October and corn harvest. Bundled-up fans huddled along the sidelines watching frosty football games. The Bulldog football team won a couple of games they were supposed to lose. The mediocre volleyball team flew below the community's radar. Lyle Kile sized up Brommer and found him inconsequential. Brommer sized up Lyle and decided to leave him alone. Lyle played solitaire in the furnace room, Faye cleaned the school and Brommer holed up in his office for hours, usually accompanied by his diminutive wife. What the heck did they do in there? No evidence of friskiness. Whenever they emerged, they emerged scowling. Eventually, aided by Secretary Barb's keen powers of observation, we learned the paranoid Brommers spent their days searching under the couch cushions for plots against their regime, searches yielding scant results. So desperate were the Brommers for insurrection rumors, they created their own. Perhaps Mrs. Brommer shared the women's restroom and the teacher didn't greet her with sufficient enthusiasm. Better keep an eye on that teacher. Isn't the business instructor taking administrative courses at Kearney State? Won't be long before he wants this job. After all, he parties with school board members. He'll be making up stories trying to get me fired. Lying bastard.

If the Brommers hadn't been obsessed with uncovering and stamping out real or imagined subversion, plotting a coup would have never occurred to any staff member. Lyle had his life arranged just the way he drew it up. Most teachers, occupied with class work and personal lives, largely ignored the noxious fumes emanating from the superintendent's lair. Ken Berns could smile at any threats to his position. If he weren't already an icon in the Bladen community, his sharp tongue and combative personality made him the least likely target of a blowhard administrator. Nettie Boom could recognize a wrong number when she met one, but except for scalding Brommer's fat ass behind his back, tended to her own knitting.

By rights, Brommer should have made an example of Doreen Sanders, an old-fashioned schoolmarm who ran her 7th and 8th-grade classes with humor and military precision. Doreen spoke her mind, no clutch involved, and voiced her dislike of the new sup at every opportunity. Brommer had to be aware, but gave Doreen a pass in favor of a more flaccid personality. Lucille, the slovenly librarian, the first to feel Brommer's wrath. A more unlikely plot originator could not be imagined. Lucille's crime? Chatting up the postmistress and complaining about the hot temperatures in the school library. Somehow, Brommer got wind of the conversation and immediately called a faculty meeting in the basement Home Economics classroom, the coolest room in the building. Once again, the engorged tick marched in, red-faced and scowling. Without preliminaries, he pounded a meaty fist on the podium and announced, "All of you are gonna to be fired. If you're wondering why, loose lips sink ships." And marched out.

Doreen Sanders was outraged. "Who died and made him king? What a jerk!" Ken Berns laughed. Soon everyone was giggling, some more nervously than others. I, on the other hand, was irritated. I confronted scowling Brommer in his office. Brommer's diminutive spouse scowling at me from her perch behind his desk.

"When you were talking about firing people down there, were you talking about me?"

"Not at all, I was just warning some of the losers to stop spreading lies around town. You're in no trouble."

I should have taken my winnings and left. But as a founding member of the young and stupid club, I couldn't let it go. "Just a friendly suggestion, Mr. Brommer. Next time you have a problem with a teacher, talk to them, please don't involve the rest of us."

Dick Brommer would not forget.

Despite the paranoid superintendent and his paranoid wife, my second year of teaching proved more rewarding than the first. Relaxing and interacting with students as fellow human beings largely to blame. Students adapted to the changed atmosphere. Freshman Scott asked if I'd like to go along on a coon hunt. I was delighted by the invitation, which led to a long rainy night trudging around the soggy Blue River bottoms trying to locate coon dogs gone missing in action. They appeared two days later at a farmstead ten miles south of town.

Lori, a recent arrival from Guam, charmed the class with her exotic experiences as a military brat, roaming the island with her older brothers free as feral cats. Her father's recent death brought her widowed mother and her children to Bladen where relatives eased the transition. Still grieving and confronted with an alien society, Lori spent most of her time scuffling to adjust.

Then there was Mary, self-assured majordomo of the sophomore class. Following minimal urging from her friends, Mary explained her dating brain trust. Mary had to deal with multiple suitors, which made her a bit of an oddball. Most Bladen high school girls formed permanent, monogamous relationships at the earliest opportunity, usually prior to high school. Dating multiple suitors just not done. Mary broke convention by not only entertaining invitations from local boys, but from boys in surrounding towns. So many boys made overtures, she used a Ouija board to sort good prospects from the not so good. Presented with a difficult choice, Mary engaged her dear, dead grandmother via Ouija board. "She's never been wrong, not once. If she gives her approval, the boy always turns out to be a good person. The ones she gives the thumbs down, even if they seem okay, always have issues. You hear things, even from other towns. If someone has a loose screw, word eventually gets around." Mary offered the use of her board to other girls, but her grandmother refused to communicate. Mary blamed the breakdown on her classmates' skepticism. "If you don't think it works, it won't work."

In spite of the more casual atmosphere, students worked their tails off, as did I. Keeping my students fully occupied required considerable planning. As their library skills improved, assignments took less time to complete. The faster they worked, the more they produced. Their annual production, over 50,000 pieces of paper, absorbed a considerable chunk of my after-school time, time I might have spent riding newly acquired criminally insane horses. Not that I found the workload burdensome. After all, minds were being sharpened by research, students acquiring a depth of knowledge largely absent from the vacuous textbooks—written by dimwits and approved by politicized committees—gathering dust in the storage closet down the hall.

Pheasant hunting season opened for business. Corn harvest concluded. Semis lined up at the local elevator to haul the new crop to feedlots in Kansas. The incessant bawling of newly weaned neighborhood calves interrupted sleep. Football morphed seamlessly into basketball.

Brommer did not repeat his Home Ec. Room tirade. Instead of threatening teachers, he became invisible. When not holed up in his office, he and his wife traveled to distant professional conferences. Wandering Bladenites reported sighting the glowering Brommers shopping in exotic places like Lincoln and Grand Island. With Tom Kaufman nominally in charge, the school saw little drama.

If you don't count the day before Christmas vacation.

Afternoon high school classes cancelled, elementary classrooms hosting holiday festivities. The entire high school, students and faculty, gathered in the library/study hall for the annual Christmas party. The Brommers blew town the previous week, relieving the faculty of the awkwardness of inviting them and watching the scowling couple piss all over the party atmosphere. Ken Berns challenged the multitude to simultaneous chess games, and, as usual, handily defeated all comers. Most party goers engaged in desultory board games with one eye glued to the prominent Regulator pendulum clock high on the library wall marking the glacial minutes until two weeks of freedom. Meanwhile, a few generous teachers distributed red and green popcorn balls and snickerdoodle cookies. Nothing quite like a homemade snickerdoodle cookie to pass the time.

Like Jacob Marley's ghost, unannounced and uninvited, a grim-faced Lyle Kile appeared in the doorway. He slammed the study hall doors shut, held out for inspection what appeared to be the assorted ashes of partially burned playing cards. "Nobody leaves until the guy who burned my cards admits what he did."

Quiet descended on the festivities. Silence so absolute we could have heard a newborn mouse fart.

We later learned Lyle returned to his cozy furnace room from a leisurely sojourn in the boys' bathroom to discover his solitaire deck had gone missing. After a frustrating search, he opened the furnace door and rescued the sorry remains, a blackened spade, a barely there pair of charred hearts. Party attendees tempted to laugh studied Lyle's face and didn't.

So we sat and sat and sat some more. Nobody confessed. We looked at one another, shrugged our innocence. The Regulator clock teased us with much ticking and gonging. That no one made a break for it was testimony all of us, teachers and students, knew Lyle was not someone you crossed. Not if you valued your most prized possessions. So we sat and sat and sat some more. How long I couldn't say. Seemed like hours. The snickerdoodle supply didn't last.

If it weren't for Faye Kile, we might still be unhappy detainees, staring at the clock, hoping for a SWAT team rescue. Did I mention Faye was usually soft spoken? She jerked open the French doors. "What do you think you're doing, Lyle Kile? The buses have been waiting for the last 20 minutes."

Lyle admitted he was holding hostages until the guilty party owned up to burning his solitaire deck.

"I threw your cards in the furnace, you dummy. I got tired of you wasting time down there not lifting a finger to clean this school. I've had it. Had it up to here," pointing to her throat.

Lyle hung his head and left. We were too stunned to snicker.

Shortly after classes resumed in early January, a dreaded letter from my draft board arrived. Mr. Warren received a similar missive. Both draft boards noticed we were no longer claiming student deferments. Were there pressing reasons we should not be subject to the draft? Although we never discussed it, the threat of being drafted had been hanging over our heads. My smart mother thought a small school teaching job to be better protection from the draft than graduate school. But what if she were wrong? My sweet teaching job in Bladen, where I could teach what and how I wanted to teach, where the students worked their fingers to the bones and the parents supported the teachers, might be history. Instead, I was facing a rushed trip through brutal basic training at Ft. Leonard Wood and a front row ticket to a losing war.

Mr. Warren asked Brommer to write a letter to his draft board explaining the problems small schools were having attracting qualified teachers. He agreed. I didn't ask Brommer to write any letters, but did float the idea of his accompanying me to a hearing with the board. "No problem, Jones, just tell me when."

My draft board set a hearing date two weeks in the future. As the day approached, something told me, Brommer being Brommer, to hedge my bets. Should Brommer be a no show, Tom Kaufman and Bladen school board members Don Lewis and Jim Kral reluctantly agreed to accompany me and plead my case. Sure enough, two hours before we were supposed to leave, school secretary Barb stopped by my room to inform me Brommer wasn't going. Brommer didn't bother with lame excuses. A wild guess? This was payback for my confronting him over his random threats to fire teachers.

On my way out the schoolhouse door, Mr. Warren stopped me, said he'd heard from his draft board. Brommer had written a letter all right. Told the board Mr. Warren "lacked maturity" and "the army would do him good." Lucky for him, Warren's board decided to ignore the letter and grant a one-year's deferment to a hometown athletic hero.

Bless their hearts, Tom, Don and Jim showed up, although in skittish condition, chatting nervously about everything but tonight's draft board hearing. Don might have set a world record for pipes smoked during a one hour car ride. Jim and Tom chain smoked cigarettes. Jim asked if Geneva, Nebraska, had a bar "worth a shit."

I can only speculate what the draft board, made of up of older, deadly serious local farmers, thought of the Bladen crew's appearance and presentations. Some of them might have remembered my forgettable, but gutsy football career as a 112-pound wide receiver/defensive back for the Geneva Wildcats and held a favorable opinion. Some might have remembered the same forgettable football career differently or not at all.

Tom's brief remarks made the earnest, but improbable case exhibit A, the shaggy-haired guy sporting long side burns and an avocado and burnt orange checked sport coat, was irreplaceable. Jim Kral con-structed a more elaborate brief, citing the paucity of candidates for teaching positions and the unwillingness of most of those to teach in a small rural school. When it was his turn, Don Lewis began by as-suring the board "all of us are veterans who proudly served our coun-try." Which might have helped the cause, but flashed an unfavorable light on the only nonveteran in the room, namely the guy wearing the bizarre sports jacket. Then he went clean off the deep end, including a bit of yelling for emphasis. "Bladen has one lousy gas station! There's a cafe, but it's only open a few hours a few days a week! Rental housing is almost nonexistent! Damn little of that has indoor plumbing! Why in bloody hell would a single teacher take a job in Bladen? Just try finding an unmarried woman who isn't ugly! You can count the eligible bachelors on two fingers and they're even uglier and much dumber! Do you think I'm kidding?"

These were mostly true statements, except for the indoor plumbing part, but ignored Bladen's bustling tavern, the functional grocery store, the elevator, the county fair and rodeo, the post office and the most reliable mechanic shop in the entire area. By the time Don finished trashing his home town, a town he would, in other circumstances, have defended with his last breath, the demeanor of the draft board had gone from deadly serious to bemused.

After murmured consultation, the draft board president announced I'd be informed of the decision in a few days. Some twinkling going on behind his bifocals. I allowed myself a bit of optimism.

Blanke's Tavern on Geneva's town square only served beer and not the hard liquor Jim Kral preferred, but met with the Bladen delegation's approval. The town characters in attendance, mostly full-blooded Bohemians whose legendary beer consumption was a matter of public record, impressed even fellow Czech and legendary imbiber Jim Kral. We celebrated until closing time, Don's oration recounted and savored. As the local patrons left, most took a case of beer to go. Just enough for a night cap with a couple of cans left over for a tomato beer breakfast in the morning.

The letter from the Geneva draft board provided a one-year reprieve. I needed to reapply for a deferment every year, an application they dutifully approved in subsequent years until I aged out of the draft. Tom and Jim and especially Don Lewis had made the case. They never once reminded me of the huge debt I owed them.

A nasty version of Type A flu hit the community in early February. No canceled basketball games, but the boys and girls played like zombies and inferior opponents handed them humiliating defeats. Every teacher, with the exception of the annoyingly healthy Ken Berns, taught with red noses and low-grade fevers. A substitute teacher might be rounded up for a teacher with a new baby or a long-term illness. In the case of strictly minor infirmities like the Type A flu, teachers bucked up and did their jobs.

Since he seldom left the furnace room, even when healthy, only Faye knew Lyle was under the weather. A fearsome headache and a raw throat up to his ears finally forced Lyle to do something he'd never done, leave school early. Although he went straight to bed, chest slathered with Vick's VapoRub, the epizootic was not deterred. By midnight, the only thing on Lyle's mind was his pounding head and a sore throat from Hell. Lyle made some wretched, quacking calls for help, but Faye, in the guest bedroom, exhausted from nursing a crabby patient, proved unresponsive.

From somewhere deep in Lyle's fevered brain, he summoned the inspiration of a warm salt water gargle. He assembled box of Morton Iodized Salt and a glass of warm tap water, stirred up an opaque slurry and commenced gargling like his life depended on it. Well into his third round of salt water, head thrown back and eyes tight shut, Lyle opened his eyes to see—only inky blackness. He fumbled around, found the light switch. No light. At that point, he did what any rational person in his situation would have done, he panicked. Stumbled out of the bathroom yelling for Faye. "Help, I'm blind, I'm blind, I'm blind." During his flight down the hall from the bathroom he became disoriented and veered into the living room where he encountered Faye's grandmother's china hutch. Most of the contents did not survive.

Faye, who arrived on the scene in groggy condition with flashlight in hand, took her sweet time getting her head around what all the noise was about.

"You think you've gone blind? How did this happen? You were gargling in the bathroom and your eyes suddenly quit working? Can you see this flashlight? You can? Good. Get over here by the window, Lyle. Look outside. Can you see the streetlight out front? No? That's because the power went out, you dummy."

February drifted into March. The flu bug, which affected so many, disappeared and passed from memory. District basketball tournaments took center stage, and optimism ruled. The grain elevator wise men determined most of the talent on the boys' team to be too young, maybe a year away, but with luck, the boys had a remote chance of defeating an unimpressive district field and securing a trip to the state tournament. Wouldn't that be something?

Lousy free-throw shooting and a pair of referees who were clearly bought and paid for ended the Bulldog season and jump-started speculation about next season. Faculty spirits revived with the bombshell news the unloved Brommer had resigned. Arrogant to the end, he presented the school board with a list of teachers he demanded be fired. Only a handful of elementary teachers, judged innocent of treasonous plots, escaped the list. The board demurred. Brommer threatened to resign if the board didn't change its mind. A polite summary of the board's response: "See ya."

At that point, even the most timid teachers lost their fear of the Brommer regime, a regime which disappeared from sight. He was a no show at school for the rest of the school year. Tom said Brommer and Co. were on the road, applying for superintendencies at larger, better paying schools. Word from the school administrator grapevine suggested he was the top candidate for two positions representing significant promotions and sizable raises in salary.

Have I mentioned Tom Kaufman's formidable persuasive powers? That semester, Tom browbeat me into teaching an independent study psychology class. In their pursuit of closing every small school in the state, the Lincoln educrats had, once again, upped the requirements for accreditation. Bladen was obligated to offer more hours of instruction or go on probation. The educrats said they weren't kidding around this time. We had only so many students (about 60) and only so many high school teachers (9), not a qualified teacher of psychology among them. My background in the subject could not be described as extensive. A semester of undergraduate Psych 101 and a six week joke of an educational psychology course the previous summer. Tom promised me textbooks and a set of gifted, eager psychology students. Stronger people than I hadn't been able to say no to Tom Kaufman.

To qualify as an official course, at least two students needed to enroll. After considerable bush beating, Tom produced two earnest senior boys, willing enough, but lacking an overriding interest in any particular academic subject, never mind psychology. Tom provided the elderly textbook they browsed for potential research projects. Descriptions of the work of Ivan Pavlov and B. F. Skinner decided them to experiment on rats. With the help of shop/math/physics instructor Ken Berns, the boys built a maze. The proposed experiment designed to measure the IQs of white rats before and after they'd been exposed to a goodly amount of maze running. I requisitioned a few red-eyed albino rats. The students' scientific methodology might have been a little fuzzy, but that didn't stop them from sending albino rats repeatedly through the maze and engage in a little pari mutual side wagering. They used the school furnace room to house their livestock and conduct their research. Lyle soon began to resent the smell of rodents and loud interruptions of his meditative solitaire games. Words were exchanged. Aggrieved members of the class rigged up a bucket of water on the furnace room door, which worked as flawlessly as any bucket of water on top of a furnace room door ever has. Lyle went home to change clothes. The next morning, when the eager psychology researchers trooped down to the furnace room to resume their experiments, they discovered 100% of their experimental subjects in various stages of rigor mortis. The uneaten remains of D-Con rodenticide told the tale.

Far from being discouraged, the boys expressed relief to be rid of the rats, as the maze running had become tedious and devising methodology to measure rat IQ proved more difficult than supposed. They decided on the spot to engage in different, rodent independent lines of psychological inquiry for the few weeks left in the school year. Tom's psychology textbook might have been dated, but didn't lack for research models. After a few minutes study, they pronounced Sigmund Freud "too weird and probably a pervert." Alfred Adler and Carl Jung struck them as boring. However, a few illustrated pages explaining Hermann Rorschach's visual psychological testing grabbed their imaginations. A sympathetic elementary teacher supplied construction paper, tempura paint and a dusty, squatty bottle of genuine India ink. Creative juices bubbling, they went to work. Over the next couple of days they produced enough Rorschach tests to submit a good chunk of the human race to psychological examination. Sometimes they stuck with tradition, creating ink blots by the dozens. They eventually extended their scope, using bright shades of tempura to construct images of horses, windmills and, in the case of Rob, who fully intended to farm for the rest of his born days, an impressionistic rendition of a John Deere tractor.

As you may recall, Rorschach theorized a subject's reaction to various images could provide keen insights into the unconscious mind. My students lacked the baseline research reporting the reactions of hundreds of subjects to their artwork and matching said reactions to particular psychological profiles. Circumstances and time constraints prevented proper test validation. The students winged it and hoped for the best. Each "test" carried clear instructions on the back explaining which responses meant what. Anyone foolish enough to see a stick horse in the image of a stick horse, like Kurt in the sophomore class, was determined to be a potential ax murderer. If a subject, for instance classmate Shirley, identified a globby inky blot as a globby inky blot, as in "that looks like a globby inky blot," said test subject would be identified as a manic-depressive, probably someone with Blue Hill origins. Randy's guess the images fashioned from tempura paint were the fuzzy shape of a John Deere tractor, produced the alarming diagnosis—"this subject is crazier than a mouse in a cream can."

Hermann Rorschach no doubt churning in his grave at warp speed, but the boys had enormous fun, which after the abrupt termination of their rat experiments, was the whole point. As the psychology class wrapped up its business and headed out the door for greener summer pastures, the suspicion gained circulation Hermann Rorschach was full of shit, a conclusion which drew no counter argument from their instructor.

Bladen High School teachers traditionally rotated class sponsorship duties. Freshman and sophomore class sponsorships included little more than supervising a single organizational meeting for the election of class officers. Junior class sponsors had the most on their plates. The junior class had to raise a couple of thousand bucks to produce the junior-senior prom. Choosing the prom's theme consumed multiple, often rancorous class meetings. "Love is Blue" might compete with "Pieces of April" or "The Impossible Dream."

Each theme garnered fanatical proponents. Once settled on a theme and a band, came the weighty decisions on the banquet menu, which typically involved meetings with the junior mothers, some of whom held conflicting menu visions. Whatever menu items survived the cut would be prepared in Nettie Boom's kitchen. Not every class sponsor capable of the diplomacy involved in gaining Nettie's permission and cooperation. Sponsoring the junior class appealed to some teachers who viewed it as a precondition for sponsoring the senior class and the attendant all-expenses-paid sponsorship of the annual senior sneak day trip. If tasked with sponsoring a class, I would have chosen the freshman class, as there were no activities, no fund raising, no refereeing of disputes over prom themes, no supervising frisky seniors up to God knows what when unleashed on the Ozarks or on downtown Omaha.

My first year in Bladen, I was assigned sponsorship of the junior class, I did not see the job as a stepping stone to bigger and better sponsorships, but as the time-consuming drudgery it was. Multiple bake sales, car washes and pop bottle round ups earned money, but at a glacial pace. Fortunately, someone remembered a school carnival a few years back which netted a significant profit. We'd sell tickets for a dime apiece, tickets collected at each booth. Proposals encompassed various games of chance including roulette, hide the peanut, balloon darts, guess the card and a bean bag toss with the hole in the center of the target too small for bean bag admission. Although some loser soreheads complained, the juniors made bank with the bean bag toss. Carnival profits put the prom fund over the top.

The prom itself arrived and expired with mixed results. The banquet menu offered rubbery poultry hidden under Velveeta escalloped potatoes. Mothers cooked, popular freshman and sophomores served, the junior class spokesperson welcomed seniors and faculty, the senior class spokesperson responded with awkward thanks.

By popular demand, Tom Kaufman served as keynote speaker. Most of his remarks are lost. His opening statement is not.

"I'm grateful for the opportunity to speak to the junior and senior classes. I'm also grateful for the opportunity to speak to the esteemed members of the Bladen High School faculty. Mostly, I'm grateful for the opportunity to stand up and straighten out my underwear."

The ancient hearse tasked with transporting the band, The Undertakers, broke down on the trip from Geneva. The students long departed for pasture beer parties before the band finally appeared. The Undertakers performed covers for the then-popular band Blood, Sweat and Tears, music no human at any time or place has ever considered dance-friendly. But some of us tried.

The next fall, after Brommer and Company took control, the senior class sponsorship passed to me. I was tempted to decline the honor, but was trying to pull my weight, or at least appear to. Not easy for a social studies teacher not coaching a major sport. If I wanted to keep my employers happy, I had to make myself useful outside the classroom.

For as long as anyone could remember, Bladen senior classes raised the bulk of the senior sneak trip funding by selling magazine subscriptions, common practice in rural schools across the state. A smarmy retired coach/grifter making the rounds of small schools showed up in early September. He promised thousands in profits, offering the most productive sales people cheesy prizes like Styrofoam beer coolers. No surprise, the prizes never appeared, nor did most of the magazine subscriptions. The subscribers, primarily friends and family of the seniors, never saw their *Sports Illustrateds, Cosmopolitans, Wee Wisdoms* or *Good Housekeepings*. The seniors were lucky the grifter's company paid them their commissions. Other schools were not so lucky. The next fall, when the grifter showed up at Bladen High School he was unceremoniously mailed back from whence he came.

Magazine sales nearly met the required sneak trip budget. The seniors figured a soup supper would put them over the top. Last home football game. A coterie of senior mothers spent the afternoon in Nettie Boom's kitchen preparing chili and chicken noodle soup and consigning the soups to several large electric roasters to simmer until half time of the football game. Other parents brought in assorted fruit and cream pies. Pie sale revenue usually shaded soup sale revenue by a substantial margin.

Near half-time, senior mothers left the game to make final preparations for the post-game soup supper. Upon entering Nettie Boom's kitchen, they discovered the electric roasters and the entire soup supply missing. After a failed search of the school, including the locker rooms, I was summoned from the football field. Faye Kile answered the phone. When I stated my business, she handed the phone to Lyle. Lyle had no knowledge of the missing soup. Nope. Hadn't seen any soup, missing or otherwise.

"If the mothers don't find the soup, there are going to be a lot of hungry people after the game. The seniors were counting on this fundraiser for their sneak trip. Is there any place in the school you can think of, maybe a place most people wouldn't consider, where the senior mothers might look?"

Lyle pondered the question at some length. Pressing him would only get his stubborn up. I heard Faye chirping in the background. After more ponder, he finally gave it up. "If someone were to open the doors under the gym stage and pull out one of the trolleys loaded with folding chairs, they might find something or they might not. I have no idea."

Taking the senior class to Lake of the Ozarks or Omaha, popular sneak trip destinations in the past, held little appeal for me. The casual suggestion of sneaking off for Denver and Colorado Springs, virtually uncharted territory, gained instant popularity. With the help of Bladen alum/travel agent Colleen Borwege, the senior brain trust lined up the bus, hotels and a visit to the Cheyenne Mountain Zoo in Colorado Springs. What should the seniors explore while in Denver? The well-regarded Museum of Nature and Science? The Colorado State Capitol building? What about a visit to Lakeside Amusement Park where the kids could eat cotton candy and ride a roller coaster until they puked? Nope. Instead, I made a few phone calls and succeeded in unsettling the Denver public school bureaucracy.

"You're seeking permission for a senior class from a rural school in Nebraska to visit a Denver high school with a high percentage of minority students? That's, ahem, a bit unusual. Let me connect you with someone who might be a position to address your situation." Four DPS educrats later, the Bladen senior class was scheduled to visit Manual High School, one of the oldest schools in Denver, one with a primarily black student body. The fourth educrat bragged up Manual as the jewel of the Denver Public School system. Manual High, recent recipient of millions in federal dollars, had installed in-house cosmetology and secretarial schools, state-of-the-art metalworking and woodworking shops. Manual, the only school in the country to operate a full service gas station. Metal shop students built a functional full-sized airplane and were only weeks away from a test flight. The Bladen seniors would be visiting a school with so much innovating going on it would set their rube heads on spin cycle.

In the wee hours, we departed Bladen in a comfortable tour bus, plenty roomy for 11 seniors and a couple of sleep-deprived sponsors. Anyone who has sponsored a bus trip involving hormone-supercharged high school kids would appreciate our good luck. Not a single romantically inclined couple in the bunch. Discouraging panky hanky on the darkened bus a breeze. Cruising through the predawn dusk in a silent, hermetically sealed tour bus, we headed for Colorado, an exotic place few of the passengers had ever visited. The Kent State Ohio National Guard shootings earlier in the week, which persuaded so many Americans the Vietnam War was a lousy idea, did not enter into it.

We hit the first obstacle outside Manual High School when the students refused to leave the bus. While I was inside finalizing arrangements with the principal, Manual students strolling past asked if the students huddled inside the bus wanted to "see blood." You tell the students no big deal, right? Trash talk is trash talk. You shame them into getting off the bus and scuttling into a mammoth school building where some mean-looking, smack-talking students might be lurking.

Once inside, the wispy principal, who had lost his energy at birth, served as tour director. He showed off the empty 100 chair cosmetology shop, the empty state of the art metalworking and woodworking shops. The equipment appeared new and expensive and unused. The building spotless. But where were the students? One over there, three over there, but the zillion square-footed vocational program areas had everything except students.

The Bladen rookie math teacher/coach took half the seniors to visit an honors senior math class. The other half accompanied me to an honors senior English class. As we navigated the halls, we encountered dozens of students hanging in stairways engaged in not much of anything beyond listening to massive boom boxes. None of them, thank goodness, asked if we wanted to see blood.

"Who are you? Why are you here? Where did you come from?" A slight, carrot-topped, pimply faced student rushed up, pumped my hand like a jack handle. While I explained our presence, he teared up. "It's so good to see white faces. I'm the only one, the only one. Do you know what that's like? Every day, the only white kid. I gotta get outta here, somehow I've got to get outta of here." And off he rushed to his next class while the Bladen seniors chewed and digested what they'd just witnessed.

The honors English instructor, a stylish, middle-aged white woman, provided a warm welcome and introduced us to her class of fifteen senior students. Most of the male students deep in sleepy repose. A couple of girls flirted openly with the Bladen senior boys. When the teacher asked for a show of hands by those who remembered to bring their textbooks, the two flirts raised their hands and waved their textbooks as proof. This achievement earned the girls bonus points towards higher grades.

The teacher then asked a purely housekeeping question, "How many of you read the assignment? Nobody? Nobody? Retha?"

Retha mumbled a bit before allowing she'd read "some of it," but found it boring. Which left the teacher with complete responsibility for the rest of the class period. She soldiered on, smiling and animated, providing keen insights into the background and obscure meanings contained in Poe's *Tell Tale Heart.* The two wakeful class members paid attention and were suitably impressed. "That story say all that?"

My students were also impressed. This was red meat, even if it were secondhand. Not something they'd experienced all that often in their own English classes.

Meanwhile, in honors senior math, the teacher also handed out bonus points to the quartet of suck ups who remembered their textbooks. According to the rookie Bladen math teacher/coach, the instruction was devoted exclusively to addition, as in 12 plus 8 equals 20. The teacher wrote problems on the board and asked the same four students to solve them while the rest of the class rested their eyes. The Bladen seniors had suffered through the rigors of Algebra, Geometry and Advanced Algebra, with some introductory work in Calculus. What they witnessed unfolding in a senior honors math class at a fancy dancy big city high school left an impression. As the Bladen kids were leaving the classroom, the senior honors math teacher confided to the Bladen sponsor his hope he would have enough students who could master arithmetic next year and might be able to tackle a little basic algebra.

Following our visits to the math and English classrooms, the principal invited us to his spartan office to wrap up the visit and answer any questions. His bargain basement suit pants might have been a bit shorter than you'd like to see, short enough to reveal a pair of slightly yellowed white athletic socks and a pair of translucent, hairless shanks. Clearly a lifer administrator, who last experienced anything surprising or interesting at least 30 years ago, he remained stubbornly unflappable. You couldn't disturb his equanimity with a well-timed grenade. Asked a potentially embarrassing question, he'd use his index finger to nudge his black framed eyeglasses back up the bridge of his nose and answer the question.

Why are so many students lounging in the halls and stairways? Shouldn't they be in class?

"Many of our upper-class students have completed their course requirements for the semester and are waiting to visit with their friends who are still attending classes."

What percentage of the Manual student body attends school on a given day?

"It varies, of course, depending on weather and illness. Our official enrollment runs about 850 students. If thirty percent of our students are in attendance we consider it a good day. Many of our students come from broken homes and may have responsibility for younger siblings. We try to be understanding."

We've visited the impressive metalworking and woodworking shops, the cosmetology school, heard about the airplane and the student operated gas station. Do you have an estimate on how many of your graduates are employed in any of those fields?

"Good question. Let's see, the programs have been fully operational for about four years. And you have to understand, we don't always know what our graduates are doing after they leave us. Let me think. Four, I'm almost certain I know of four."

Four with jobs in those specialized fields?

"I was referencing graduates with jobs of any kind, although there's no guarantee those former students are still employed at those jobs. The community we serve is often subject to changing circumstances."

Would you be able to estimate the total amount of federal funding Manual has received over the past four years?

"Sure. Vocational grant funding is spread out over a multi year period. You might have heard we have received some outlandish amounts. Actually, on a yearly basis, the grant only supplies roughly 1.7 million dollars per annum."

6.8 million over four years?

"That sounds about right."

So if we do the math, 6.8 million dollars divided by four employed graduates would represent an expenditure of 1.7 million dollars per job?

(Chuckles) "That probably sounds like a great deal of money, but you have to understand the full contextual picture. Our students leave here with skills they'll use for the rest of their working lives. They might employ those skills next week or ten years from now. There's no expiration date on those skills or the life skills we also teach. It's virtually impossible to put a dollar value on the Manual High School experience."

Life skills?

"You know. What you teach your students to do. How to fill out a job application. How to dress for a job interview. How to prepare for a job interview. How to fill out applications for food stamps and dependent children assistance. The usual."

Blank stares all around.

On our way to Colorado Springs, the bus detoured to the Colorado State Penitentiary at Canon City. Three-story red sandstone 19th-century cell blocks baking in blinding sunshine. No wind. No inmates visible. According to our stout guide, who imparted information in a robotic monotone, Alferd Packer, Colorado's most famous Democrat-eating cannibal, spent his spare time building intricate doll houses in one of those cells over there. Angel-faced Antone Wood, incarcerated at the tender age of 11 for murder and robbery, also spent time in one of those cells. Because of his age, Antone had been paroled early, despite an unsuccessful prison break, and graduated to a responsible position in the Salvation Army. While he recited these examples of crime and punishment, our guide trained a stern fish eye on a couple of fidgety senior boys, letting them know he'd taken their measure and seen certain incarceration in their criminal futures.

When the Bermuda shorts-clad senior girls trailed our guide into the prison yard, an animal roar like nothing you'd likely hear in church arose from the cell blocks and continued unabated until the girls disappeared into an administration building. I assumed the girls were terrified. Hell, I was shaken. The girls handled the enthusiastic attention with outward aplomb and a few smiles, like they had been subjected to appreciative male animal howling their entire born lives. So much for assumptions. The afternoon visit to the Cheyenne Mountain Zoo in Colorado Springs proved a popular choice. For most seniors, a zoo was a novel experience. Watching enormous gray-backed gorillas delicately dissect and nibble on bananas and oranges hypnotized the crap out of them. We had to return to the monkey house to retrieve some laggards for the next excursion. After the bus hauled us up to the Garden of the Gods and the kids dutifully sweated their way around the colorful rock formations for an hour, we hit the hotel and ate dinner at a local restaurant. The girls chose to walk around downtown Colorado Springs trolling for animal catcalls until bedtime. The rookie math teacher/coach volunteered to chaperon the senior boys if he could find a suitable movie playing in the area.

The next morning at breakfast, when the boys let it slip they'd visited an X-rated movie house and were plenty impressed with what they'd seen, I was as dumbfounded as a person could be dumbfounded. My co-sponsor, presumably a responsible adult, had chaperoned an excursion to a porn movie palace. He was young and didn't know much, but still inexcusable. The best-case scenario involved a lifetime ban from sponsoring future senior sneak trips. Not the worst outcome I could imagine. But more dire things could happen, like losing our jobs. The boys' parents might not complain, boys being boys, but the girls' parents included some Plainview Puritans who took their morality seriously. With Brommer's eagerness to fire people for no reason, what if he had a reason? Should I plead ignorance? Rat out my fellow sponsor? He was just a kid himself with less than optimal good sense. Did he even realize what he'd done or understand the possible consequences? To come clean or let it ride? I stewed the entire bus ride home. In the end, I let it ride. And nothing happened. It was like the porn movie episode never occurred. Whatever views the senior parents held on the matter, they kept tucked away. You could bet they didn't forget, but whether or not they added a black mark to my resume remains impossible to know.

I expected Brommer to rub my nose in the X-rated movie embarrassment, as he had every right to do. That he didn't, was convincing evidence he and his diminutive wife had moved on, mentally and spiritually, to greener pastures.

High school graduation in early May. A sophomore girl pounded her way through "Pomp and Circumstance" on a tinny piano. The salutatorian and valedictorian thanked parents and teachers for helping them beat out nine other seniors for top academic honors. Both painted a rosy future for those who dared to dream and were willing to work their asses off. A glowering Brommer wordlessly handed out diplomas and boogied immediately afterward, never again to grace the streets of Bladen. No one longed for his return.

Summer meant an unwelcome renewal of daily trips to Kearney and a soul-crushing procession of education classes. One positive development, my time on the road to and from Kearney had been shortened by a spiffy new Volkswagen Squareback, the only one in the village. The VW offered a higher than strictly legal top speed and decent gas mileage, a marked advantage over my former ride, even though gas was selling for a modest 36 cents a gallon. Classes devoted to curriculum and social studies teaching methodology blurred their way toward August. Audio Visual Aids class provided a bit of comic relief. The instructor, one Tom Sawyer, reminded us every day he wasn't actually the Mark Twain character. While explaining the intricacies of the film strip projector or helping us prepare transparencies for the overhead projector, Mr. Sawyer rolled the end of his tongue into a perfect taco-shaped U before each burst of instruction. Counting those epic tongue rolls and rooting for a new daily record helped pass the time.

Infrequent visits with Tom Kaufman that summer kept me in the loop on school developments. The new superintendent, Tom reported, seemed smart enough, if a tad rough around the edges. Navy vet with the tattoos to prove it. An English major who liked to quote poetry couldn't be all bad, could he? Tom, always fiddle-footed, was exploring a career change. Buying a franchise business was at the top of his list. Fried chicken. Didn't everyone like a good piece of fried chicken? He'd done enough research to know profit margins on fried chicken could make up for an inexperienced restaurant owner's mistakes. Now he was focused on the right location. Hastings? Grand Island? Either one would be a gold mine.

Bob Heckathorn proved far more skilled at avoiding controversy than his immediate predecessors. He soon formed a fast friendship with shop/math/physics instructor Ken Berns. The pair came to dominate teacher's lounge discussions with testosteroney guys being guys talk, which, along with the choking clouds of cigarette smoke generated by our new sup, thinned out regular lounge attendance.

For unstated reasons, I was excused from sponsoring the senior class, as was the rookie math teacher. I could look forward to another junior class fundraising marathon, a welcome relief from cosponsors escorting senior boys to porn movies.

Any jackass can drive a car on a paved road. If you can handle a car in mud up to the hubcaps, you're a pretty good driver.

—Tom Kaufman

As long as I served under Tom Kaufman at Bladen, he taught the drivers' training classes. Tom believed students should learn to drive on less-than-ideal road surfaces. If there were a muddy dirt road anywhere in the vicinity, Tom had his student drivers take a crack at it. Tom argued a successful trip through deep, tire-burying mud created the kind of confident and highly skilled drivers you couldn't duplicate by having them drive on wussy black-topped highways. Consequently, the drivers' ed car often returned to the school parking lot covered with goo, the mud coating the windshield relieved only by the paths of the windshield wipers. Superintendents, including Heckathorn, who borrowed the drivers' ed car for trips to meetings and emergency shopping, were resentful. Showing up at a meeting of their peers in a mud mobile, even if it were this year's model, created embarrassment. They could have driven their own cars, of course, but a free ride is a free ride, gas included.

The social studies classes not exactly on autopilot, but the students, except for the incoming freshmen, knew how to dig into the library and argue research-based positions. There is no greater waste of time than providing an attentive audience to ignorant opinion. Come back when you know something. The weekly news team tests on Fridays raised the profile of the classes and kept the competitive juices flowing.

Meanwhile, I'd been spending spare time in Red Cloud with my maternal grandparents. Bryan and Edith Tupper told compelling stories of their homesteading experiences in Wyoming during and after World War I. Grandpa tried his best to educate me in the business aspects of agriculture. Told of cutting a fat hog in the ass on a recent sale of yearling steers or coming up short on a set of dry sows in the middle of the Depression when sows sold for less than two cents a pound. Talked about the price of land and how to determine a fair price. His purpose was not to convert me from teaching to farming. In his opinion, I was living on Easy Street with a safe gummit job with benefits and a fat state-sponsored retirement plan. Grandpa didn't suffer fools, whether they were gummit employees or more important members of society like ranchers and farmers. He had a low opinion of gummit employees, myself included, because he thought they were a shiftless tribe who typically "didn't know too much." Male school teachers ranked barely above the life insurance salesmen, bankers, preachers, and IRS agents at the bottom of the community septic tank. Anyone associated with the Federal Reserve system lacked enough brains or common sense to be ranked. Grandpa was only trying to help me learn things he assumed correctly I didn't know, so I wouldn't be a complete economic ignoramus walking the earth disgracing the Tupper family. Had he considered it, the idea of a guy who could barely drive a tractor giving up a cushy gummit job in exchange for the risky, capital-intensive farming game would have been laughable.

However, Grandpa's informal efforts to supply an ag education yielded unintended results. I began scheming to abandon teaching and get into farming. Who wanted to be a gummit employee, scorned by the productive members of society like my grandfather? Making a living with my brains and hard work appeared more attractive than having my life organized by moron administrators and gummit educrats.

I'd been renting a farmstead on the west edge of town. More room for horses (my grandfather ranked skilled horsemen higher than any community of human beings) and an expanding dog kennel. When the owner, Lawrence Grandstaff, a courtly former Bladen teacher, offered to sell at a reasonable price, I didn't hesitate. The decision to buy proved consequential in several respects. Even though my income over the past few years should have provided a hefty nest egg. I had no nest egg. Plan A, spending paychecks like a deranged gerbil, hadn't included saving money. The Hastings Federal Land Bank gave tentative loan approval, but a neighboring farmer, one of the more unpleasant, greedy, jealous, paranoid jerkwads in the Bladen community, who not only served on the Bladen school board but on the Federal Land Bank board of directors, vetoed the loan. Not that I hold any remaining bitterness. I had no choice but to hit the road with my beggar's cup. Against his better judgment, Grandpa Tupper loaned me $7,000 at 8 percent interest, and my father, who had no savings worth the name, borrowed the other $7,000 against his life insurance policy. By begging loans of $14,000, I'd gained full possession of a milk barn with a leaky roof, a granary with a leaky roof, a chicken house with a leaky roof, a set of disintegrating corrals and 70 acres divided between woodsy Blue River bottom pasture and heavily eroded farm ground. I'd also purchased a well and water system designed in his spare time by Satan himself and a drafty late 19th-century house which cost $500 a month to heat. Although I continued to accumulate summer school education hours and earn a decent paycheck teaching school, my energies increasingly focused on building the farm into a self-supporting enterprise. Working for jealous, paranoid jerkwads who could veto the previously approved loans of possible competitors was not my idea of satisfactory employment.

With the new focus on farming and livestock, one thing led to another. The kennel expanded from Norwegian Elkhounds to Old English Sheepdogs and Great Pyrenees. A couple of high-kicking dairy cows added milk, cream, and cheese to the farm's direct sales offerings. I purchased a well-preserved barn with a decent roof and a hay mow at public auction and had it moved to the property. It served as a budding profit center, housing bottle calves until they were weaned and a warm place to lamb out a set of young ewes.

At the end of spring semester, Tom resigned his principalship and moved to Grand Island to operate a junk mail delivery franchise, which prospered for about five minutes before he took over management of a Kentucky Fried Chicken restaurant. Losing regular contact with Tom meant losing track of current community opinion and the invaluable gossip he gleaned from his postmistress mother. More importantly, I was no longer able to follow the school board's increasingly unpredictable moods. I completely missed the news a couple of board members resented my acquisition of a modest acreage with a decaying set of buildings. If school teachers were paid so well they could afford to compete with hard-working farmers for land, they were being paid too much. As a result, over the next three years, years which saw inflation spike, the board granted no raises in base salary.

The spring semester when Superintendent Heckathorn was sailing through his second year at the helm, he encountered minor turbulence. The issue didn't amount to much. Word reached Heckathorn some patrons disapproved of his habit of leaning over the railing outside his office chain-smoking cigarettes while students traveled back and forth from the gym. The critics felt he was setting a bad example for the students. Crude and not a little insensitive, for sure, but many adults in the community exposed students to smoking. Half the households in the community contained at least one smoker. Although his job was never in danger, Heckathorn spooked. Who knew a tough, lavishly tattooed, foul-mouthed, poetry-quoting Navy veteran would scare so easily? He grabbed a superintendency in his home territory in Northeastern Nebraska and skedaddled.

Alarmed by the rapid turnover in superintendents, three sups of varying competency in four years, the board chose to go with the devil they knew and promoted the current principal, who had loyally served the district for several years as teacher, coach, and bus driver. Although the decision to elevate a former teacher to head administrator came with questions, like whether former colleagues would accept his authority, the appointment didn't cause faculty grumbling. Despite a boyish face and a lower lip which protruded under stress, the guy was a whiz at bookkeeping and could decipher state educrat rules written in obscure edu jargon better than most. He also brought welcome grant-writing skills to the job. A knee-jerk people pleaser, Mr. Reimers had few if any enemies. If alcohol got the better of him, as it sometimes did when he attended area dances, he was in good company with some of the faculty and certain school board members. If he sometimes made married women uncomfortable with his persistent attentions, he received a pass because his romantic efforts were so clumsy and his groveling apologies after being rebuffed so abject.

That school year also closed out my long pursuit of genuine busthead, aged in the keg, official Nebraska teaching credentials. Although I'd been teaching for five years, the state Department of Education insisted on nine weeks of successful practice teaching. The only school willing to accept me was a junior high in Superior, Nebraska, some 60 miles away. I remembered Superior from my high school days, when the Ed Weir Relays in Superior were a highlight of spring track season. Ed Weir, All-American Husker football player and legendary Nebraska University track coach, watched from the stands and visited with old friends. Weir had the distinction of being instrumental in the defeats of a Red Grange-led Fighting Illini team and a Notre Dame team featuring the Four Horsemen, coached by Knute Rockne. I kept an eye on Weir as I labored around the cinder track on the anchor leg of the two-mile relay. If I were to embarrass myself by yielding the fourth-place standing I inherited along with the baton, I didn't want Ed Weir to be watching when it happened.

Superior's salad days as a wealthy railroad trade center were a distant memory, memories kept on life support by a well-preserved business district and an abundance of stately Victorian houses in a certain part of town. A meager tax base relative to the size of the student body meant the Superior public schools had been chronically underfunded for years. The claptrap ruin of a junior high building built 50 years previously, appeared nearing collapse, one imperceptible earthquake from catastrophic disintegration with attendant mass slaughter of hundreds of both innocents and guilties. The local cement plant (now an EPA Superfund site), Superior's largest employer, attracted unskilled workers from the surrounding area. Children of cement plant workers seldom aspired to attend college or join a profession. Many had been shortchanged by their elementary educations.

After teaching in Bladen, enjoying the unusual good fortune of a smart, ambitious student body and well-maintained facilities, Superior provided a different reality. The junior high staff, most of them lifers, were a mixed bag. The elegantly coiffed and clothed 8th-grade English teacher quoted poetry and effortlessly managed her classroom. She shared her lunch in the teachers' break room with Barney Crook, the ignoramus local cop, who worshiped her so slavishly he made the staff uncomfortable. Two burly male math instructors taught their subjects with chalk in one hand and brass-bound meter sticks in the other. Any student who irritated a math teacher could expect a meter stick across the shoulders or upside the head. The ever-present meter stick might not have been accepted best teaching practice at the time, but the Superior math teachers had no trouble keeping order. Had I been willing to buy and employ a brass-bound meter stick, the sadistic math teachers might not have directed so many sneers in my general direction. My standard coat and tie put them off their feed when I walked in the door. They favored the knit golf shirt with an animal on the pocket and regarded those who donned coats and ties as snooty, probably gay, pond scum.

126

Don't even get them started on a coat and tie-wearing, effete sissy who refused to employ a brass-bound meter stick.

My practice teaching assignment included 6th and 8th-grade social studies classes. The 6th-graders studied Nebraska history with Miss Viola E. Mayhew, one of the more effective, low-key teachers I ever observed. She never raised her voice. In her late 60s, she seemed much older, her lumpy figure packed into gingham which might have first seen the light of day in the early 1930s. She seldom lectured, but scuttled around the classroom helping individual students with their chosen class projects. Like most experienced teachers, Miss Mayhew had her own way of doing things and, in her case, they worked. My services had not been requested and were, in any case, unwelcome. I might have taught school for a few years in some faraway hick town, but she wasn't about to trust me not to mess up her class. She came to tolerate my presence, but only as an observer who could keep his mouth shut and didn't interrupt the proceedings.

Dave Watters, principal 8th-grade social studies teacher, served as my primary supervisor. Bigger guy, not above paddling a recalcitrant student criminal, but unlike the math Nazis, did not enjoy the exercise. Given his size and air of authority, the wooden paddle usually rested on top of the office file cabinet accumulating dust. Watters proved to be an ideal supervising teacher. Unlike Miss Mayhew, he wanted me teaching his classes to free up time for his expanding administrative responsibilities. He watched a few minutes of my first class and disappeared for the duration. He assumed a guy who'd taught for five years might be able to do the job, a job comprised of handing out, collecting, and correcting worksheets. Given the opportunity and more adequate resources, I might have employed less constricted teaching approaches. Watters, a devout Christian, was one of those rare humans whose behavior matched the theology. He cared deeply about his students, knew them and their families, and did what he could with small acts of kindness and concern to offset the dysfunction many experienced at home. His classes operated on autopilot. The students entered, sat in their assigned seats, accepted their daily worksheets, worked quietly until they finished.

My job also on autopilot. The only interruption came three days in when, with no warning, a ruddy stick of a girl threw a spastic fit as

I greeted the class. She stayed seated, her body twitching violently, flailing her arms over and around her head while kicking in random directions and screaming. "Blaaaaah, blaaaaah, blaaaaah, Screeeeeeeeech, Screeeeeeeeeeeeeeeeeeeech!"

I assumed she objected to my opening remarks. Although the grins on her fellow students' faces indicated they had seen this movie previously, no one volunteered to translate. Give her credit, she could scream at a higher pitch for considerably longer than most people. When she showed no sign of fatigue, I thought about calling in an exorcist. The decision taken from me when the girl sitting next to her mentioned Mr. Watters and the paddle he kept on his file cabinet, whereupon the spasms and screams ceased. Over the succeeding weeks, I anticipated a fresh spasm/screaming outbreak at any moment. However, the girl proved to be a psycho in lamb's clothing for the rest of the semester, which didn't keep her from giving me the stink eye early and often.

I also supervised a study hall immediately after lunch. One hundred-twenty ancient armchair desks crammed together in a sweltering, claustrophobic, converted bus barn. Students entered sweaty and stoked from roaming untethered during the noon hour. My task, creating quiet, studious conditions, made near impossible by choosing to go unarmed. I could nag, correct, threaten after-school incarceration until my blood pressure exploded, but the students smirked and ignored. Without a meter stick backing up Mr. Wussy Student Teacher, nobody took my threats seriously. They regarded me as fresh meat provided by their zookeepers for both sustenance and entertainment. Unwilling to admit failure by appealing to Mr. Watters for support, I gradually upped the level of verbal violence, and the students grudgingly acknowledged my authority. After a rough couple of weeks, we finally came to an understanding. If I stuck my nose against the end of a student's nose and screamed myself hoarse, the action was accepted as the rough equivalent of being whacked with a meter stick. As long as I was prepared to scream in a student's face, I was never again required to raise my voice to maintain order. A huge relief to my blood pressure and my study hall charges, who evolved into a collection of perspiring copacetics.

In addition to the harsh disciplinary practices at Superior Junior High, I had to adjust to lower ability levels. The majority of my Bladen students were smarter than average, not a few much smarter than average. At Superior Junior High, the average kid was, well, average. And there were a handful with IQs in the low 70s. Mr. Watters advised I stick to the dependable worksheet. After taking stock of my students, I had to agree with him. Turning my Superior students loose in the woefully stocked library would have yielded paltry results even if the library had been better equipped. Worksheets it was. Some of my students, whose literacy only extended to writing their names, could not write their names on the designated line. For some, the effort involved in writing their names consumed most of the class period. My mentor advised to give them extra credit if they wrote their names anywhere on the paper. He had no illusions the lower-ability kids would stay in school after their sixteenth birthdays and believed promoting them until they aged out of the school system to be best policy. "Who are we," he said more than once, "to postpone their productive careers earning good money at the cement plant?"

During the last week of school, Dr. Mike Shada, my genial supervisor from Kearney State, appeared while I was handing out worksheets. He observed the class for almost five minutes before beckoning me to follow him into the hallway. "Both Mr. Watters and Miss Mayhew tell me you know what you're doing. That's all I require. Congratulations."

I will own up to celebrating after arriving back home. Although I wouldn't have chosen to teach again at Superior Junior High, the experience taught me to respect the teachers who toiled in the trenches, cared about their charges, made the best of teaching with limited resources without resorting to brass-bound meter sticks.

Life in Bladen changed that summer. With Tom in Grand Island and generally unavailable, I was unaware the purchase of the small acreage west of Bladen had bent some school board noses out of joint and left me ignorant of the stronger reaction to the subsequent purchase of a rough 240-acre dry land farm south of Bladen and half interest in 160 acres of good grass in the Republican Valley, purchases which burned some board members' bacon beyond recognition. Paying for the land purchases necessitated the addition of what was supposed to be an income-producing cattle herd, acquired on easy credit from the Blue Hill bank. In the space of less than two years, I owned more heavily mortgaged land and cattle than a couple of jealous school board members.

According to the pencils I pushed every evening, by borrowing more money, purchasing more land and cattle, I could expect my farm income to far exceed what I was earning in the classroom. The school board, for reasons best known to them, had not given the teachers a raise for the past three years. Perhaps the advent of teachers competing with honest farmers for land made salary raises a low priority. Teacher-initiated negotiations proved unproductive. Following the only, somewhat heated negotiating session, one board member accused the new business teacher, our lead negotiator, of learning his communist ideology during his growing-up years in Blue Hill. The failed negotiators met with their fellow teachers and explained the impasse. Doreen Sanders, the most vocal proponent of higher salaries, cough talked "that's acoughbunchacoughbullcoughshit."

The next step was notifying the state department of the stalemate and requesting a fact-finding. Fact-finding would compare Bladen teacher salaries to those of a sample of similar-sized schools. The negotiators had done their research on comparable schools and were confident fact-finding would result in a significant raise in pay. However, even the teachers, like Doreen Sanders, who had complained the loudest about their low pay, refused to authorize the request for fact-finding. They guessed the board would make a better offer the next year if the teachers kept quiet and didn't do anything crazy, like requesting fact-finding.

If my plans included teaching in Bladen for the next 30 years, the board's parsimony might have been more discouraging. However, I was too intent on getting rich in the farming game to lose much sleep. In a year, two at most, income from the expanding cattle herd would dwarf the school paycheck. And I'd be acquiring more land and more cattle, all with borrowed money. A blind squirrel could play that game.

Classes resumed in the fall. Teachers showed up for work. Lyle Kile showed up for solitaire. A senior class, which contained more intelligence and ambition than should have been strictly legal, replaced the previous senior class which possessed even more brains and ambition. The contrast with the recent experience at Superior Junior High couldn't have been more stark. My students, except for the freshman geography class, could dig into a library better than certain of my fellow graduate history students back in New Orleans. The school year began full of promise, even if that promise didn't include a raise in salary.

Belinda created the first minor bump in the road. A senior girl who disdained the library or anything else resembling work. What she lacked in scholarly ambition, she more than compensated with cleverness. The previous spring, her plot to prod Mr. Warren into an angry overreaction worked to perfection. She waited until Mr. Warren entered the study hall, made sure she and her boyfriend, a kid Mr. Warren had clashed with previously, were engaged in a heavy-duty display of public affection. One thing led to another, the another being some physicality directed at the boyfriend. With the Nebraska State Education Association MIA and confronted that evening by a panicked administrator, Mr. and Mrs. Warren handed in their resignations and left the area. Belinda did not disclose why she held a grudge towards Mr. Warren. She didn't necessarily need a good reason to dislike someone, but passed her grudges around like stray confetti. After Mr. Warren went down the road, Belinda moved on to her next project, putting the run on the social studies teacher, a guy who'd assigned her a desk beside a boy she'd briefly been involved with romantically but now loathed. Belinda's general resentment of school work wasn't a patch on her loathing of the weekly team news quizzes in senior government class. If she didn't read her assigned news magazine pages, which she never did, her teammates suffered the consequences. Not all of them took defeat in stride. More than one rude boy began to refer to her as Be-Dope.

Through the community grapevine, Belinda knew one school board member, the father of another senior girl, didn't approve of studying current events in government class. He thought the Constitution and the three branches of government to be the only proper subjects taught in government class. He'd passed on his concerns to Mr. Reimers, the new superintendent, who passed them on to me. I nodded and ignored the concerns. A frustrated Belinda finally bullied her female classmates into backing her play to get rid of the detested news magazine assignments and the weekly team quizzes. With the other girls hiding red-faced in their clothes, Belinda, grinning with the confidence of someone holding a straight flush, announced the senior girls would no longer participate in the weekly news quizzes. Instead, they wanted to concentrate on the study of government and only government. Period. The end.

Fine by me.

I handed each of them a weighty government textbook and mailed them into the study hall next door along with a longish reading assignment. Their male classmates catcalled "Yooooou girls are really stooooopid."

With the girls' schedules rearranged by the obliging guidance counselor, my former planning period became Senior Government II. The US Constitution? They didn't learn it quite by heart, but they probably had nightmares rooted in the US Constitution and/or the Federalist Papers. Any semi-educated government teacher could spend years on each branch of government. We didn't have years, but it probably seemed like years. If a student failed to recite the history and the implicit and implied powers of the judicial branch, she had many additional opportunities to do so. While the girls wallowed in punishing boredom, the Senior Government students continued to compete fiercely on Fridays and pursued their research projects the rest of the week. I never had more fun teaching school.

Another shoe dropped. Superintendent Reimers, without the courtesy of a heads-up, canceled the individual student subscriptions to the news magazine. When pressed, his excuse was a lurid cover story a few weeks previously, which I'd excised from the magazines before handing them out. Both of us knew the real reason. That left no choice but to create multiple copies of each assigned news story (thank you, brand new office photocopier). A little more work for me, but the news quizzes lived to fight another Friday.

The final shoe drop/bump in the road emerged one promising spring morning in the teacher's lounge during a private chat with Mr. Reimers. Although obsequious and apologetic, I wasn't convinced he was all that disappointed the school board had unilaterally changed the salary schedule by eliminating merit raises in extra duty pay they'd previously awarded the music/ Spanish teacher/hippie spouse. The merit raises had appeared unsolicited after remarkable increases in the size of the band, the creation of a large and spirited pep band and superior ratings aplenty for Bladen's large contingent of musicians at district music contests. I'm afraid I may have taken the news with poor grace. Mr. Reimers never again risked being alone with me in a small room with but one exit.

Already irritated with the school board for their parsimony and meddling ways, the cut of merit pay broke it. No way we could work for this low-rent outfit another year. Grandfather Tupper thought us crazy to reject so much money earned with so little effort. Easy for him to say. He had enough pride to have never gone to work for such a low-rent gummit outfit. We handed in our resignations to a puzzled school board president. He pronounced himself mystified as to why any recent action of the school board would result in losing two teachers. And, given the mental opacity of the board president, he might have been telling the truth. As we were leaving his house, he asked if we would reconsider if the current superintendent were let go.

Since the school board president mentioned "letting the sup go," chances were "letting the sup go" was going to happen. This was news.

Most members of the Bladen community were aware of the superintendent's suspicious financial shenanigans. As sponsor of the junior class, I had again been tasked with fundraising for the junior-senior prom. This year's fundraising relied heavily on snack sales at basketball games. When the juniors learned of the insulting low-profit margins on candy purchased from the regional wholesaler, they opted instead to sell homemade cookies, brownies, Rice Krispie Treats and small cups of Kool-Aid. Margins went from 5% to 95% and the junior snack stand began minting hundreds in profits every time out. After the first night of a two-day tournament, Superintendent Reimers came by to collect the change bag for safekeeping in the office safe. Had we counted it? Not yet. The juniors, including the kids of a couple of school board members, had, of course, counted it twice. The official receipt total, revealed to class representatives the next morning, fell short by a couple of hundred bucks from the student count. Everyone kept mum. They knew exactly what they were about.

The next night after the last game, Reimers again asked if the cash had been counted. Again, no one would admit to doing so. The next morning the take came up $150 short. Trap sprung. Released from their resolve to keep quiet, the juniors complained, boy did they. All fingers pointed in the same direction—the squishy beer belly of the current superintendent. When he heard the rumblings, Reimers posted a stern admonition in the morning school bulletin warning students who'd allegedly accused the school secretary of theft, something which had crossed precisely no one's mind. His muddying of the waters worked as well as you'd expect.

In addition to aggrieved juniors and their parents, rumors had been circulating for months about peccadilloes gone too far, angry husbands appearing at board meetings promising public scandal unless certain dismissals took place. Book-ended with the public exposure of petty theft and skirt-chasing gone wrong, the Reimers' goose had become fork-ready.

Reimers' impending demise had no influence on our exit plans. He'd lost my vote when he canceled the news magazine subscriptions and stole from the kids. Whatever extramarital mess he'd gotten himself into was none of my business. If past were prologue, he'd be given a glowing recommendation so he could work his magic in another Nebraska school. His Bladen replacement would likely be a deeply flawed someone. School board members who thought land-buying teachers should be punished would remain. Our course was set.

Looking back, the decision to resign might have been a mistake. Opting out of the classroom to devote full time to the nascent livestock operation a case of dreadful timing. The cattle market promptly tanked. The region was hit with the worst heat and drought since the 1930s. I ended up selling old bag o'bones cows for less than 25 percent of what I'd paid. Land prices declined. A couple of steady paychecks would have slowed the flow of red ink.

My grandfather's prescient warnings fully realized. Sometimes the best outcome of a financial beating is a change of course. The cow-calf operation absorbed gobs of high-interest borrowed capital and returns did not cover expenses. Once that epiphany hit me amidship, I should have ditched the cow-calf business and concentrated on enterprises with higher profit margins—like hogs and short-term grass cattle. I jumped into the hog business and began buying and backgrounding feeder cattle, both dependably profitable, but I couldn't quit cow-calf entirely. A sad addiction suffered by many in the cattle business. Hogs, grass cattle, bottle calves, a small sheep flock and direct milk sales kept the boat afloat for a few more years. But the cow-calf operation remained in the welfare line.

In August of 1979, when Federal Reserve Chairman Paul "Cue Ball" Volcker, Jimmy Carter's appointee, began jacking up interest rates, eventually reaching 23.5% at my friendly local bank, my "get rich in a jiffy" heavily leveraged farming operation went on life support. Land prices, which had risen to record levels, eventually collapsed under the weight of Volcker's usurious interest rates. My net worth dropped from healthy to below zero. For millions of farmers and small business people who went belly up during Volcker's heavy-handed reign of terror, borrowed money, which provided a tailwind to so many entrepreneurial enterprises during the 1970s, became a fatal curse. Bankrupt farmers and businessmen committed suicide so often suicide hotlines were invented. A bankrupt farmer assaulted my banker at the local country club, leaving him with two black eyes and a missing tooth. Banker Bob crawled back on his bar stool and expressed relief he hadn't been shot, like that unfortunate banker in Iowa.

The publication of *The Farming Game* in 1982 briefly revived hopes for survival. The first book originally published by the University of Nebraska Press to be reviewed by the *New York Times, The Farming Game* brought minor fame in the form of appearances on national TV and a lucrative series of speaking engagements as far away as Boston. Significant sales resulted in encouraging royalty checks. The auction of the paperback rights, another first for the Press, added more thousands to the bottom line. But a 23.5% interest rate eats money like a starving tapeworm. The first royalty check barely paid six months' interest on the bank loans. I spent weeks writing a bad novel I hoped would net a huge advance and bail out the farm. Maybe if I'd written a novel which didn't stink. Despite the earnest efforts of three different literary agents, rejection notices piled up—almost as fast as the interest bills.

Retired school board member Don Lewis invited me to join his brand-new real estate business. I took the courses and passed the test. Selling slow-moving Bladen real estate was a slow-moving train to fortune. Lenders, notably the Blue Hill Bank, the Federal Land Bank, and the Farmers Home Administration, refused to extend loans on Bladen real estate, limiting purchases to cash or contract sales, depressing prices. We ran a few classified ads in the Los Angeles Times for $2500 Bladen houses, the grocery store, and the local saloon. Although we did a brisk business for a few months, none of the purchasers stuck around. A couple of them set fire to their newly acquired real estate for the insurance money. Consequently, our efforts to market Bladen real estate to strangers from California were not universally applauded by the community. In any case, paltry real estate prices meant modest real estate commissions, split in half. Twenty-three and a half percent interest scoffs at modest. Twenty-three and a half percent interest only respects the immodest, the kind of profits common in the dope business, the kind of profits rumored to be available running a house of ill repute.

Once you're dead broke by several magnitudes, even a thick-skulled pilgrim might recognize the need to do something differently. The decision to return to teaching didn't prove difficult. Like Mark Twain's cat, who, having sat on a hot stove, would never sit on any stove, whether hot or cold, I was cured of pursuing risky entrepreneurial ventures. No barbecue joints, no Amway distributorships, no chinchilla farms. Teaching promised steady, if modest earnings, and I had the hard-earned credentials to qualify. Almost.

It took a full year of additional classwork at Kearney State College to earn an English teaching endorsement. As much as I enjoyed teaching social studies, coaches dominated the field and schools often reserved social studies positions for coaches, either current or prospective. In contrast, language arts positions were less frequently reserved for members of the coaching profession. Unlike in 1968, when I last sought a teaching job, no shortage of teachers currently existed, except for math, science, foreign language and music. In 1985, English teachers weren't as scarce as math teachers, but they were less plentiful than social studies teachers. If a year studying with the Kearney State English department would improve my marginal employment chances, I was game.

The Kearney State English Department could not have been more different from the Education Department across the lawn. Approachable, student-friendly, staffed with professors who were teachers and nurturers first. I arrived during a golden age, the department churning out talented, motivated English teachers by the busload. The nationwide takeover of college English departments by nihilistic, Marxist, perpetually angry deconstructionists had not yet breached the walls of Kearney State College. As a result, the now disdained standards of collegiality, open inquiry, and civilized debate prevailed. Poet Don Welch infected the entire department with his wry sense of humor and genial nature. Staff linguist Dwight Adams, versatile Vernon Plambeck and preeminent Mari Sandoz scholar Helen Stauffer, comported themselves in similar fashion. The only indoctrination practiced by the Kearney English faculty involved infecting students with a love of good literature. The only brainwashing in evidence the gentle prodding to produce the best writing a student was capable of producing. The bizarre notion of an English faculty member haranguing students with personal political views would have been viewed as the equivalent of farting in chapel. After enduring a dreary series of inane classes conducted under the auspices of the education faculty, the Kearney State English department renewed my faith in the human race.

During decades of interdepartmental turf wars, the Kearney State education department repeatedly tried to snatch English teaching methods courses from the English department. Let your imagination run wild just long enough to contemplate a course in the teaching of poetry overseen by an ignorant philistine from the constipated bowels of the Kearney State education department. I'll give you a moment. Harry Hoffman, dapper English department chair, who did not purchase his sartorial elegance from the J. C. Penny sale rack, made the instruction of English teaching methods to prospective teachers something of an obsession. Hoffman wrote academic papers on the subject and was well-prepared to fight a turf war with mental midgets. Every time the Education department made aggressive noises, the English department responded with total warfare, political debts foreclosed, the English department's most effective and persistent lobbyists unleashed on whatever hapless administrator happened to be serving as chancellor. The educationistas had far more students and therefore higher standing than the English department, but, lucky for me, the methods courses, at least for the time being, remained under the English department's jurisdiction.

A Teaching Secondary School Reading methods course under Dwight "Dewey" Adams eradicated many of my former teaching theories, replaced with a new whole language approach. *Hooked on Books* by Daniel Fader served as the class bible. Dewey's mantra? If you want kids to read better, have them read more. Student reading speeds will increase, along with their vocabularies and comprehension. If you want kids to write better, have them write more and have their peers review and critique and give the students an opportunity to revise. In the early days of that particular version of the Whole Language movement, Dewey's theories encountered push back, especially from my classmates who'd spent time teaching reading to 1st-graders. They insisted phonics should have a role. Dewey would have none of it. "If a kid reads more, he'll read better. Phonics study gets between a student and the text." In Dewey's defense, his course promoted teaching methods for older students, not beginning readers. Dewey's absolutism was the kind of nonsense the whole language advocates passed down as holy writ. Like with other fads *du jour,* once they've been appropriated by the educrats, a distorted, heavily jargoned, narrow version of whole language was eventually adapted. If Dewey realized he was a running dog for the educrats he would have turned in his doctoral hoodie and fled to the wilds of Montana. He'd picked a fight to prod his students into thinking and reacting, making his classes more entertaining for Dewey.

Talk about setting a room full of hair on fire. Nothing more enjoyable than a college class with professor and students pounding on one another. I knew enough about teaching reading from my smart mother to suspect Dewey's whole language theories might not be much help to beginning readers, something he probably knew. Didn't make his classroom brawls any less enjoyable for a spectator. The ever-acerbic Dewey Adams, when given the choice, picked the path of most resistance. If he could irritate someone, the worst outcome would be he captured the irritated's attention. After the strum and drang settled to simmer and outrage and gave way to fresh questions, he'd accomplished at least one partial conversion. I believed Dewey's radical theories would work with older students, who presumably could already read at some level of proficiency. Worth a try. Plans for next year's classes began churning.

To make myself even more marketable while sailing through my English classes, I picked up a coaching endorsement by taking courses in first aid, strength training, sports psychology, and coaching methods for track and football. The legendary Kearney College track coach taught the track coaching class. Heavily reliant on the rhetorical question, he might begin the first class with "What do we know about the hurdle?" Good question. Stumped the class. The answer, obvious as all get out if you think about it: some hurdles are taller than others.

"What do we know about athletes who run the 400-meter dash?" One experienced track coach answered correctly. 400-meter dash runners should be sprinters first. Speed is primary. Endurance will eventually appear.

My classmates were high school coaches earning graduate credits to move up the salary schedule. They knew their business and class discussions increased my paltry coaching knowledge from none to almost some. A school perusing my college transcript might note the athletic department coursework, assume I was the cat's meow in the coaching world, and not do any further checking. That was the hope. In any case, I was feeling better résuméd for pursuit of my next teaching job, if only I could locate one.

BOOK TWO

Teaching, like writing, has helped me develop and clarify my own thoughts. Charlie calls this phenomenon the orangutan effect. If you sit down with an orangutan and carefully explain to it one of your cherished ideas, you may leave behind a puzzled primate, but will yourself exit thinking more clearly.

—Warren Buffett

What do we know about Robert Day? In your face, rabid atheist? Left-wing nut job? Funny to the bone? Kansas City button-down preppy transported to the flat plains of west-central Kansas? While teaching freshman English at Ft. Hays State and dating a school teacher from tiny Gorham to the east, he spent time on a ranch south of Hays, soaking up cattle culture and the complex nuances of rural family life. And wrote himself a helluva first novel—*The Last Cattle Drive*, set on the same flat, dry Kansas plains featured in Peter Bogdanovich's classic film *Paper Moon*.

The book earned a Book of the Month Club selection and Robert Day a high-dollar tenured teaching position on the East Coast. His new class load, one class every other semester, allowed him adequate time to write and indulge his fascination with the south of France where he and his wife rented cheap farmhouses and sampled local vineyards. Day optioned the novel several times to movie producers, but aside from swelling Day's bank account, the options resulted in no movie. However, *The Last Cattle Drive* became the most-read, most-quoted novel of the year in Bladen, Nebraska. Don Lewis, in particular, saw himself in Spangler, the hard-nosed, hard-drinking rancher who decided to drive his cattle to Kansas City instead of paying truckers ruinous freight rates and who beat fourteen kinds of shit out of Hollywood types who interfered with the drive. Nobody from Bladen had visited Gorham, Kansas, which figured prominently in the book, but it sounded like Bladen's kind of place, populated by our kind of rugged individuals. Did I mention *The Last Cattle Drive* was a work of fiction?

The Gorham school district was absorbed in 1967 by the larger Russell School District to the east (thanks to the collectivist educrats in Topeka). The community managed to keep the local high school attendance center open until 1984, when the Russell District finally pushed for a full merger. Gorham residents resisted. Early and often. Rather than force a set of hard-headed, stubborn German Catholics into an unpopular marriage, the Russell district sold the Gorham school facilities, lock, stock, and football field to a private consortium of parents and oil wealth for one dollar. Each year, the community raised $40,000 with sand volleyball tournaments, slo-pitch softball tournaments, car washes and bake sales. A shrewd local businessman, rumored to have built his initial stake in the oil bidness by bootlegging during Prohibition, wrote an annual $450,000 check for the remaining operating expenses.

While we were searching for jobs late in the hiring season, the independent and private Gorham Junior-Senior High Institute watched a couple of teachers leave after school dismissed for the year. Once we learned of suitable openings in Gorham, home of *The Last Cattle Drive,* our eventual destination became destiny. Gorham took one look at my wife's music credentials (Gorham preferred its existing German classes to Spanish) and offered us contracts without bothering with interviews. My duties included 9th-grade English, 7th and 8th-grade

English and reading classes and coaching junior high volleyball and girls' basketball at the whopping salary of $17,242 per annum, a significant raise over the last salary I'd earned in 1974. Ignoring the fine print dedicating $1500 from my annual pay to cover estimated health insurance costs, insurance I was free to purchase at my own expense, I expected to run comfortable budgetary surpluses every month.

Following the fire sale of our beef and dairy cattle, horses, farm equipment and miscellaneous personal effects, my parents sweetheart loaned me enough to get out of the country, pay a few bills and make deposits on utilities and Gorham rental housing. However, the half million dollars remaining on our bank loans, accruing interest charges at the annual rate of 23.5% every damned day (Thank you, Cue Ball), cast shade on the new enterprise. As did the impending dissolution of my marriage. Sis and brother-in-law helped load two pickups and stock trailers for the 130-mile trip south to Gorham. A troubling omen in the form of the violent cloudburst as we crossed the Kansas state line soaked the contents of both trailers. My prized autographed copy of *Old Jules* by Mari Sandoz pounded into a glob of soggy papier-mâché. Despite the waterlogged household goods, looming domestic disentanglements and massive indebtedness, the move represented a fresh start of sorts. In Gorham. Home of *The Last Cattle Drive*. Home to ornery ranchers who drank Green Gables Scotch whiskey directly from the bottle. Home to sturdy souls who'd just as soon punch an arrogant Hollywood director through a jukebox as look at him. Cautious optimism stuck its ugly snout from under the scattering, empty rain clouds.

By moving from Bladen, Nebraska, to Gorham, Kansas, I traded life on one dry divide for life on another. Gorham, like Bladen, composed of roughly 300 souls, sat on a dry divide, this one between the Smoky Hill and Saline River Basins. Annual moisture in Bladen averages 27 inches per annum. Gorham 26 inches. Primary crops on both divides in 1986? Milo and wheat. The dry divide south of Bladen lacks underground water. The dry divide surrounding Gorham has no abundance of underground water, but what exists often tastes of salty rotten eggs and, given time, will remove the chrome from every plumbing fixture in your house. And also from your gizzard.

My rented house, built a few years previously, already sported disfigured plumbing fixtures. The modern 3-bedroom ranch with a fenced yard came with a monthly rent of $350 a month. Seven times, if you've been paying attention, to the monthly rent for my first house in Bladen. The oil man writing the checks keeping the Gorham school afloat built spec homes in his spare time. This one hadn't sold before the oil price crash and he offered it up to any incoming teacher in need of housing. That would be me. Had there been someone to share the rent and utilities of the most luxurious house I'd occupied up to that time, the cost wouldn't have been burdensome. However, after storing most of her personal possessions in the basement, my soon-to-be ex packed a suitcase and left for Hays, where the lights were brighter, leaving 99% of her stuff behind.

By moving from Bladen to Gorham, I entered a less formal version of the Federal Witness Protection Program. I didn't require a new identity or a new passport because Gorhamites knew next to nothing about me. I arrived as a blank slate, as much a cipher as any luckless, relocated foot soldier who'd offended the Brooklyn mob. Gorhamites could fill in blanks if and when pertinent information arrived. But only if they were curious. For my part, I knew so little about my new community I might as well have relocated to an isolated mountain village in Peru. I promptly set about acquiring knowledge of my Gorham surroundings. Whether the townspeople had a lick of interest in my past or present remains unknown. They were not, on average, in the habit of asking nosy personal questions.

I never tried to explain to anyone, teacher or student or neighbor, why my wife and I had taken teaching jobs in Gorham when we were on the cusp of a dissolution. Maybe I couldn't come up with an explanation that didn't sound lame. The plainest fact? We took the first jobs offered because we were broke, figuring things would eventually reach a logical conclusion. But the situation made for awkward moments with questions unasked and unasked questions unanswered. It also made for awkward personal finances. Paying full rent and utilities for more house than a single teacher required exhausted my monthly paycheck. Taking sole responsibility for repaying half a million bucks in farm debt might have been a generous gesture, but I was in no position to be generous. My confident projection of regular surplus funds from my teaching paycheck proved a fantasy. I have no idea what my fellow faculty members thought of my domestic situation. If they had opinions, they had the good manners to keep them private. My students took their time sizing things up. Once sightings of Gorham music teachers hanging out in Hays bars began circulating, opinion shifted to modest sympathy for me. Unwarranted sympathy, to be sure.

Germans from Pennsylvania initially settled Gorham. Pennsylvania Germans, as well as Norwegians, Czechs, and English, comprised the first Bladen settlers. Although descendants of many ethnic groups inhabited the Gorham area, staunch Catholic Germans were over-represented. The imposing Catholic Church the only religious edifice of any consequence. The Methodist Church served the same dominant role in Bladen society. Both communities enjoyed vast horizons and spectacular storm clouds, although Bladen's sunrises and sunsets provided superior technicolor. Both communities regarded past, present, and future weather as prime conversation topics. Gorham enjoyed more frequent tornadoes. Every Gorham student had personal experience with at least one. When the sirens sounded, Gorham residents toted lawn chairs out to their yards to ensure clear views of what might be approaching. Most times, beer coolers were involved. During one particularly stormy Sunday afternoon from my backyard lawn chair, I spotted sinuous funnel clouds hanging in the westerly, southerly, easterly and northerly directions. A full-time job keeping track of current weather developments.

The similarities between Bladen and Gorham had mostly to do with size, climate and small-town mores. The differences included religion, the frequency of tornadoes, and the oil industry. Since the 1920s, the area surrounding Gorham rewarded oil exploration and the oil services industry. The extraction of large quantities of oil created not only millions of dollars in new wealth but massive amounts of salty brine, which eventually led to less than pristine groundwater. The Fairport field north of Gorham produced 1,847,785 barrels of oil in 1926. By the time I arrived in 1986, production had fallen to just north of 614,000 barrels. A boy graduating from high school expected to find ready employment in the oil business and make enough to not only buy a new pickup, but support a family should one come along. The immediate rewards of going to work after high school diminished interest in post-high school education. The majority of my Bladen students planned a future with college or trade school as a career building block. For Gorham students, high school represented an unwelcome delay, time wasted confined to a desk before assuming an outdoor job with lucrative wages. The two graduating senior girls in the Class of 1987 (comprised of four girls) who attended Ft. Hays State in nearby Hays represented the first college attendees in recent memory. The plunge in oil prices, from $23.29 to $9.85 a barrel (Thank you, Cue Ball Volcker) and attendant retrenchment in local oil service firms over the preceding 18 months might have been a factor in their decision. By the summer of 1986, one experienced operator complained he was losing two dollars on every barrel he pumped, forcing him to shut down low-producing wells and lay off well service and office workers.

Although Bladen landowners typically possessed comfortable wealth, Bladen's personal income fell short of the oil-plumped average Gorham income. Egalitarian Gorham culture did not encourage ostentation any more than Bladen's but a quick drive around town revealed an assortment of speed boats and newer pickup trucks parked in the driveways of modest ranch-style houses. Although Bladen residents valued hard work, they valued education more highly. The ethic of hard work permeated the Gorham community. The concept of sloth as a personal choice would have been considered ridiculous had it ever been publicly voiced. If we're breathing, we're working. So is everyone. It's what we do.

Religion stood out as the least common denominator between Gorham and Bladen. All religious sects have their quirks. Some, like the Methodists, abandoned their revivalist, fundamentalist roots eons ago. By 1986, any well-indoctrinated Methodist would have been hard-pressed to name a mortal sin. What would be the point? If you start focusing on sin, pretty soon you're thinking up punishments, or rather, you're intuiting what kind of punishment a vengeful supreme being will hand out. Opposition to punishment eventually became so dominant, Methodists began forgiving everyone, even hardened, violent criminals who hadn't made a formal request. Locate a mass murderer minding his own business, bring him to public attention, and the Methodists will knock each other down in the rush to not only forgive him, but give him money and fruit baskets. They will forgive him absolutely, without the lingering suspicion he might revert to untoward behaviors. They will do so in a manner suggesting it is they, rather than the criminal, who bears ultimate responsibility for his misguided ways.

Full confession. I grew up in a Methodist home. Since committing venial and mortal sin was my stock in trade, I appreciated the forgiving atmosphere. However, a nagging question persisted in my partially formed brain, persists to this day in my aged brain. Is it possible a sin punished in the present might be a sin avoided in the future?

Bladen Methodists produced well-mannered, self-confident children, not regularly threatened by the wrath of an irritated supreme being. If they suffered any life-altering harm from the lack of supreme judgmental oversight, I have no way of knowing.

As with most religious sects, some Bladen Methodists attended church services regularly. Some only on Christmas and Easter. Some never. Most younger kids in town attended Vacation Bible School for a week or two each summer. It's impossible to determine if any of this casual religious exposure made a lasting impression. Most Bladenites agreed every Bladenite, except for a few objectionables they could name if you really wanted to know, was a decent sort of person. Not that tongues didn't wag when sins became public. It would be a dull town indeed that didn't take note of the real juicies. But to call down divine wrath on the miscreants? Just not done. After all, most of us are decent people.

More importantly, talking about personal religious matters wasn't a thing. Bad manners. None of your business or anyone else's. As with personal political views, you were expected to keep your opinions to yourself. Settling down in front of a cup of barely brown coffee at the Bladen Cafe and sharing your weighty opinions about those dumbass bastards in Washington D.C., unless you were philosopher Don Lewis, would label you a rude, eccentric crank who might best be avoided. If you wanted to earn the reputation of a deranged blatherskite, get busy sharing your beliefs or lack of belief in this or that religious precept. Current or past preachers could be bashed or lauded, mostly bashed. But don't get into what you've done lately to get right with the Lord. Nobody...wants...to...hear...about...it.

Like Bladenites, Gorhamites did not routinely call on higher authorities to retribute on others. Nor did they consider religion or politics proper subjects of polite conversation. However, many Gorhamites, raised from birth on the milk of the Holy Roman Catholic Church, had an active preoccupation with their personal sins. Repeated terroristic threats from above delivered during multi-year catechism classes will do that. Habitual trips to confession will do that. Like Bladenites, Gorham adults attended church according to their internal compasses. But it was rare for people to miss the big ones, the Easters, the Advent season services, the Ash Wednesdays, the Maundy Thursdays. As in Bladen, if you lived in the Gorham community, the working assumption was you were a decent person, even if you never darkened the door of St. Mary's Catholic Church. The local priest might have held a different opinion.

What became evident as the year progressed was the tiny sliver of self-doubt internalized in most Gorham kids. They'd learned to identify their shortcomings. Some rejected the concept entirely and carried on as if they were white as snow. Their companions crudely branded those with a casual attitude towards their own shortcomings as "He thinks his shit don't stink."

A few students had grown obsessive, worrying over religious laws broken, even unintentionally, and the certain punishment to follow. This created a stressful resting state. 8th-grader Emily, despite attending confession as a personal hobby, fretted constantly over her mostly imaginary transgressions, etching permanent worry lines on her forehead. My most competitive 7th-grader, on the other hand, raised in the same faith as Emily, suffered from her peculiar demons, but they were personal, grounded in her family's dysfunction, not in any sect's religious teachings. She spent less of her head space on personal shortcomings than on how to properly kick the ass of the last person who'd offended her.

Two communities. One mostly Methodist. One mostly Roman Catholic. United in stern opposition to public discussion of religious matters. To a casual observer, both villages might have been inhabited by practicing atheists. However, only Gorham proved to be inhabited by riotous sinners capable of earning the school double secret probation and the threat of an athletic death sentence.

Gorham students, well prepared by their elementary teachers, out-worked any students in my entire teaching experience. Goodness knows, I drove them hard, a matter of personal survival. I had charge of the squirrelly 7th-graders for both reading and English, each hour-long classes. Ditto the 8th-graders, more mature, but not folks you wanted to leave to their own devices for two hours a day. Supervising the 9th-grade English class, as serious and well-behaved as you could hope, scarcely raised a sweat.

On the toasty first school day in August, students filed into my over-heated classroom, wide-eyed with smiling expectations. Shouldn't they be fearful and a little shy of a strange new teacher from somewhere far away? Stubbornly cheerful, Gorham students did not view a new teacher as a potential threat, but as someone who might assign them new and interesting tasks. When do we start? No getting-to-know-you exercises for these kids. Five minutes in, they were deep in their reading or writing assignments, competing to finish early, even if the hurried results lacked perfection. This is not to say occasional grump-iness might not infect a student. Not every kid owned an idyllic home life. Kids have been known to show meanness to one another. But Gor-ham teasing didn't often descend into dehumanizing personal insults. Most students had known each other from their first venture inside St. Mary's Catholic Church. They regarded fellow students with the vague fondness of people so familiar they'd forgiven one another long ago for the small, annoying peculiarities humans inflict on others.

The Gorham Oiler High School English program's mission statement (mission statements the freshly hatched brain fart of the educrats in To-peka) dictated that by the time a student graduated from high school, he or she would have read a wide sampling of what were considered lit-erary classics. Twain, Thoreau, Austen, Dickens, Tolstoy, Steinbeck, Al-cott, Stevenson, H. G. Wells and other major authors listed on the offi-cial menu. The current principal and my new boss, Mr. Beeman, largely responsible for adopting the ambitious literature goals. By loading the curriculum with classic literature, Beeman overruled the long-time senior high English instructor, who viewed time spent reading as time subtracted from the more important study of grammar. The resulting pissing match lasted for as long as Beeman served as principal. The fall

I arrived, Beeman bullied the high school English teacher into mandating senior students read at least one book prior to graduation. Seniors could be heard in the hallways bitching about the unreasonable requirement which they predicted would absorb 100% of their free time until graduation day. My English Department cohort, who religiously wore short-sleeved knit shirts with little animals embroidered on the pockets, took the new reading requirement with ill grace. He believed the study of English was the study of grammar. Period. No reading. No writing. Grammar. His students could complete grammar worksheets in their sleep. As could mine. They'd had grammar pounded into their skulls from the first day they'd darkened a schoolhouse door. Although friendly in a superficial sense, my new English colleague took umbrage at my habitual coat and tie, which he assumed I intended as an insult directed at his casual attire. What is it about guys with little animals embroidered on their golf shirt pockets?

Unaware of the discord between my English colleague and Mr. Beeman, I employed Dewey Adams' "reading more is better" philosophy. With a twist. Beginning with my Gorham reading classes, every new book introduction for the next 20 years included a warning: "As you get into this book you're going to find quite a bit of sex and violence. If it's too much, we can find you a different book to read. But please think twice before telling your parents. We don't want this book to be banned, do we?"

Thus were *Anne of Green Gables, Call of the Wild, Tom Sawyer, Great Expectations, Where the Red Fern Grows,* and other examples of prurient literature introduced to my reading classes. You want students to open a book with anticipation good things will happen. Of course, it didn't take long for students to understand I was funning them, but in the hearts of not a few 7th-grade boys rested the lingering hope this next book would actually contain generous helpings of sex and violence.

Beeman provided the books I requested and, given his ongoing feud with my colleague English teacher, did so with a certain amount of relish. During the 1986-1987 school year, each of my charges read at least 45 books, a feat which did nothing to endear me to the animal on the pocket guy down the hall. The sight of 9th-grade boys and girls spending portions of their lunch hours entranced by *Anne of Green Gables* pushed him over the edge. He told his students, who told their parents, I was not teaching what they were supposed to be learning. Wasting time on reading and writing assignments instead of studying grammar represented impending disaster. Given enough time in my classroom, none of the 7th, 8th or 9th-graders would be able to pass his classes.

The backstabbing campaign came to my attention when a forthright 9th-grade girl, granddaughter of the gentleman writing the large checks to keep the school open (and my landlord), raised her hand.

"Mr. Jones? Some people are worried we aren't studying enough grammar. Some people think we'll fall behind where we're supposed to be and it will be hard for us to catch up."

Student journals and writing assignments disappeared, replaced by grammar textbooks and grammar worksheets. Two unrelenting weeks of grammar instruction proved to the students and their parents the students' grammar chops were not eroding. Perfect worksheets every time. Nothing had been lost. The exercise also reminded students how crushingly boring grammar study can be. English classes returned to daily writing assignments, completed assignments submitted to peers for editing. Anyone committing grammar or usage sins could expect correction. And there was no shortage of grammar or usage sins. Perfection achieved on grammar worksheets had no predictive value for writing assignments. Students sprinkled "We was" "They're cat" "We won't loose the game" freely throughout their writing. It was as if they'd never been exposed to English grammar or usage lessons, never completed a grammar worksheet, let alone obtained perfect scores.

Mr. Animal on the Pocket continued sniping for the rest of the year, but his wad was shot. The students came to prize writing over grammar worksheets and eventually converted their parents. Reading books, an assignment first regarded as another welcome task, became, for many students, almost enjoyable. Early journal assignments might require 25 words on why an annoying sister or brother might not be their favorite person—a safe assignment in a Catholic community where brothers and sisters were in surplus condition. Later in the year, once in the groove, they might turn out 300 words during a class period on their worst nightmare. Not a shabby output for kids who had never been required to compose more than a sample business letter in 6th grade. Like many writing teachers, I discovered negative writing prompts stimulated more creative responses than treacly suggestions. What do you consider your best quality? Gag.

7th-grade journal entry. Prompt: Describe the meanest thing you've ever done.

"The meanest thing I've ever done was I kicked my brother in the balls really, really hard. My punishment was to be grounded for one week and I had to hug my brother and kiss him on the cheek. My parents forgought after 1 day that I was grounded. I was not sorry at all, because my brother makes me madd all the time. He deserved it more than anyone I know. He still makes me madd, but not to much anymore and whenever he does I just kick him in the balls."

Gorham, like Bladen, sported an unofficial genealogical society, which predicted athletic success or failure based on family bloodlines. Bladen's genetic soothsayers met for coffee at the grain elevator. Gorham's met at the local beer joint, where they were sometimes joined after practice by the football players and their coaches. It was said no football player or coach had to buy his first beer, but after that, he was on his own dime. The year I moved to Gorham had long been predicted to be a banner year for Oiler athletics. The girls' sports teams on a roll, coached by a pleasant tyrant they idolized. Boys sports had been in the doldrums, last year's football team going winless and not by just a little bit. But last year's team also featured a rugged sophomore running back who'd been anointed with area all-state status. A couple of beefy linemen and a scrappy, hard-nosed toothpick of a wide receiver of Irish descent added to the general sense the football worm was about to turn.

Those in the optimist camp pointed not only to the area all-state running back and enough bigger kids to open the holes, but a much weaker schedule. A half dozen opponents expected to have down years. One team, the homecoming opponent, might not be able to muster 8 players. Even if they did, half the team would be puny freshmen. Pessimists hung their hats on a long record of failure and two nincompoop coaches. Head coach Ray, well-versed in demanding conditioning drills, had a limited concept of offensive football—or defensive football. He installed four running plays featuring the area all-stater, plays he called in every circumstance. If the opposition stacked all 8 players near the line of scrimmage, he did not change strategy. Throwing a forward pass? Too risky. No matter how often the players begged him to call a pass play, he refused. Even if they had a point, players had no right to an opinion. Had he been head coach, easygoing Assistant Coach Tubby would have called a few passing plays. But he lacked the gumption to challenge the head coach. Coach Ray believed implicitly in his own authority. His long-term career ambitions did not involve coaching high school football and basketball. He regularly applied for a job with the Kansas State Highway Patrol. Passing the screening tests proved a stubborn obstacle. He believed the next time would be the charm. He'd be locked and loaded, full Sam Brown belt and uniform, cruising the state highways busting anyone who drove 2 miles over the speed limit.

To prepare for his future law enforcement career, he regularly searched my room. Coach Ray, who wore athletic T-shirts to his day job as a social studies teacher, did not appear to be scandalized by my coat and tie. But there was funny business going on in that Jones guy's classroom. Laughter. Loud bursts of laughter. You can't have laughter in school. School is serious business. Besides, laughter is disrespectful. He was also disturbed by students lounging around reading books, a feeling reinforced by whispered conversations with my English colleague. Coach Ray's success at motivating his social studies students, despite his hard-assed approach, was minimal. If my students were reading books, it must be due to some nefarious juju business. He didn't have a clue what the motivator might be, but he knew if he searched my room enough times, he'd find out. Coach Ray could have searched my room in the wee hours every night for months and not come close. The cumulative point grading system, tried and true, which provided every student with a chance at the top, worked as well in Gorham as it had in Bladen. More importantly, the compulsive Gorham work ethic drove students to meet or exceed the previous day's accomplishments. Find a book in the library you might find interesting. When you're ready, sit down with Mr. Jones and talk about the book. Not many, actually nobody, tried to bluff their way through a second time. Depending on the book and the relative challenge it represented to the specific reader, point totals might grow as uncontrolled as the Russian thistles on summer fallow wheat ground outside town.

Anyone who has taught junior high kids knows the junior high mind, wired in strange and wonderful ways, can tolerate considerable silliness. Upon finding a desiccated lizard on a hike around brackish Wilson Reservoir a few miles to the northeast, I incorporated the mummified lizard into our Friday classroom pep rallies. Every upcoming opponent was designated as the Lizards. As in, the Tipton Lizards, the Natoma Lizards, the Lucas-Luray Lizards, et al. A single cheer comprised the entirety of each pep rally.

Give me an L!

L!

Give me an I!

I!

Give me a Z!

Z!

Give me an A!

A!

Give me an R!

R!

Give me a D!

D!

What's it spell?

Lizard!

What's it spell?

Lizard!!

What's it spell?

Lizard!!!

Followed by thumbs down gestures, jeers and loud stomping of junior high feet. You give kids a chance to yell and stomp their feet during school, and they're bound to take advantage.

Our classroom cheer culturally appropriated a Plains Indian tradition. It's always a dependable motivator when confronted with a superior foe to taunt and degrade them until they appear weaker than advertised. Although the lizard never shared its innermost feelings about the rallies, the taciturn lizard, from his or her perch on my desk, absorbed the taking of his or her name in vain with remarkable equanimity. Cool customer him or her. Not so cool were Coach Ray and Mr. Animal on His Pocket, who complained to Mr. Beeman about the disruptive noise. All for naught. Mr. Beeman had distinct counterculture tendencies, as any observant person would have concluded from the unsightly hair growing down over his collar and all over his face. Beeman's motives for having my back had mostly to do with the ongoing conflict over the English curriculum and Coach Ray's pitiful performance as a coach and teacher. Had Coach Ray won a few more football games, his complaints might have gained traction. Another factor in my favor was law and order Coach Ray's ill-disguised contempt for the "hippie" principal, who didn't discipline students with enough severity and whose wife had chosen to leave Gorham and live separately from her lawfully wedded husband in godforsaken Kansas City. If that didn't make the case against Beeman, there was the whole diet thing. Beeman shunned beef and bacon in favor of skinned chicken breasts. The fact Beeman's father died young of heart trouble and his 40-something brother had already suffered a heart attack didn't mean it was okay to eat like a danged limp-wristed hippie. Although his blithe, slightly-distracted demeanor led people to assume he wasn't all there, Beeman often demonstrated his keen awareness of school politics, so wired in he was nearly impossible to surprise. Just try telling him some newsy tidbit he didn't already know. His discipline practices might have been wussier than Coach Ray's, but the lack of repeat offenders spoke well of their effectiveness. Beeman had a genius for persuading the student criminal to take personal ownership for preventing further offenses. He believed his focus as principal should be on hiring talented teachers, discovering what teachers needed to be successful, doing his level best to provide— then staying the hell out of the way. In my view, the perfect philosophy for any principal anywhere. Beeman supported most of the staff. Those few who disappointed him, even though he was never unpleasant or badge-heavy, discovered he paid scant attention to anything they felt like sharing, for instance, requests he do something about something.

Mr. Beeman might have resembled a hippie and sometimes exhibited suspect hippie attitudes, but when it came to academics he was cold steel. Early in the fall term, when the first down slips came out, he instituted a mandatory after-school study hall for any slacker who'd received one. Varsity athletes included. The after-school study hall sentence lasted until the student raised the offensive grade to at least a C. The mandatory study halls worked so well no student, with one exception, received another down slip for the rest of the year. Kevin, 8th-grade class clown, enjoyed the attention he received as the only screw up still standing and ramped up his efforts to earn down slips in every class, including PE. He almost drove me crazy when it was my turn to supervise. Would—not—shut—up. What was I going to do? Sentence him to more after-school study time?

The junior high volleyball team took my rookie coaching efforts in stride. Lucky for me, their coach the previous season had not been Coach Stephens, the beloved current high school volleyball coach, a talented teacher/coach who enjoyed success at every school that employed him, coaching winning teams in each sport he was assigned. His business classes at small rural high schools always won the statewide annual stock-picking contest, which matched them against teams from larger, richer suburban schools. My predecessor as junior high volleyball coach left no strong impression on her charges. My junior high team assumed my emphasis on fundamental drills had some basis in standard volleyball coaching practice. The drills, digging, passing, serving, absorbed our allotted daily practice time. The favorite drill, by far, involved bumping a volleyball into the basketball hoop from the free throw line. Drills also closely resembled work, and the girls, true Gorhamites, were all about work. If I failed to make them run lines before and after practice, they were sufficiently occupied with drills not to grumble too much.

They even accepted the notion of relaxation and visualization as part of the pregame ritual. Doyle Fyfe, a coaching genius at Kearney State College, taught a class in sports psychology. Instead of rah rah pregame speeches, he advocated assembling the team in a darkened locker room just prior to the game, having them lie on the floor, close their eyes and allow their breathing to become regular. Once they'd relaxed, they were to visualize performing a particular skill, like bumping the ball over the net or digging a hard spike. A basketball player might visualize repeating perfect free-throw shooting form. A quarterback might visualize making a difficult sideline throw. Once the volleyball team grasped the purpose of the technique, they took to relaxation and visualization as if they'd done it all their lives. Impossible to say how much Doyle Fyfe's theory contributed to their relative success, but the team came out of the locker room preternaturally calm, without the nervous pregame jitters young athletes typically experience.

The team boasted three 6th-graders standing less than five feet tall. The 8th-grader at five feet two inches and two 7th-graders at five feet four inches towered over the rest. Did I mention the 6th-graders not only lacked height but were uniformly puny? The challenge of serving a volleyball over the net defeated them more often than not. Naturally, they all wanted to serve overhand, which raised the level of difficulty by several progressions. Not wanting to squelch their ambitions, I set the bar at 20 consecutive successful overhand serves in practice before they could serve overhand in a game. Not one player made the cut, although the two 7th-graders came perilously close a couple of times.

Rudimentary. An accurate summary of the team's volleyball skills. The Gorham Junior High team did not run plays, did not set to certain players in certain situations, did not make strategic substitutions to counteract an opponent's best players. We were equipped with a single substitute and her name was Melanie. Blocking drills? Impossible. Only a couple of kids could sometimes reach the top of the net. Our practices concentrated on digging and passing.

It's a rare volleyball player who doesn't aspire to elevate high above the floor, delivering thunderous, gym-rattling spikes. Adulation awaits those who can regularly spike a volleyball with attendant violence and soul-satisfying noise. Our team devoted wee bits of practice time to setting and spiking. The 8th-grade setter did her job to perfection, but so eager were her spike-happy teammates to murder the ball with all the frustrated force they possessed, the attempts either flew into or under the net. During the entire season, the Gorham Junior High team failed to record a single successful spike. However, they bump, bump, bumped the ball over the net with enough regularity to force opponents into mistakes. Enough mistakes to win a handful of games, even though they were usually matched against teams populated with taller, more experienced 8th-graders. As they exceeded expectations, their own and everyone else's, their confidence grew, and some of the less puny members adopted a certain swagger. Then they played Paradise.

We rode the school bus to Paradise, a picturesque settlement of 35 souls 20 miles north of Gorham. Ensconced in the meandering Paradise Creek Valley, the village claims an impressive WPA-era water tower built of local limestone as its singular claim to fame. We traveled north through flat, treeless farm ground, showing the sere stalks of harvested milo and the greening parallel tracks of newly planted winter wheat. When we passed some of the highest-producing oil wells in Russell County, the legendary Fairport Field, I may have been the only one on the bus to take note. To my charges, oil wells were too common to notice. Instead, much to the bus driver's displeasure, their attention focused on the raucousings coming out of their boom boxes. I was about to request a general drop in the noise level when the bus pulled off on the shoulder. The driver, a retired oil field roughneck who drove school buses as an unpaid volunteer, suggested the girls turn off their boomboxes for the duration "or this bus is headed back to Gorham. Now." Worked for him.

As we neared Paradise, we passed through patches of rougher grassland, where Gorham farmers sometimes pastured their cattle during summer grazing season, the same area devastated by the massive

169,000-acre Four County grass fire in 2021. Driven by 100+ mph winds, the rapidly moving flames burned houses and barns, killed people and hundreds of cattle and horses. Local history buffs claim Paradise owes its name to a 19th-century grass fire that burned up the countryside, but spared the town. The 2021 fire did not completely spare the town.

Tiny Paradise didn't impress the Gorham volleyballers, who had little reason to feel superior. While Gorham had more people and a few more businesses, it wasn't exactly the shopping mall in the nearby metropolis of Hays. But when the Paradise team, made up entirely of 8th-graders, strolled onto the gym floor, the Gorham girls had the same question I did. How in blazes did the dinky community of Paradise produce so many 8th-graders, all of them relative giants? Some almost 5' 10"? And athletic. No wonder they were leading the conference. They might have taken Gorham lightly, especially after they watched our diminutive squad take warm-ups, struggle with serving, blasting practice spikes under and into the net. But when the match began, Gorham's disciplined bump, bump, bumping prevailed in the first set. Halfway through the second set, with Gorham leading and Paradise in disarray, I decided to substitute Melanie, the shortest 6th-grader who had yet to see action. The Gorham school rule for junior high sports stipulated everyone played. Winning was deemed less important than providing every student with game experience. Melanie, a 4' 8" 6th-grader, would not win any popularity contests with her teammates. I never knew why. She had limited athleticism, but so did the other 6th-graders. Nonetheless, the two 7th-grade players chose Melanie to despise. True, she often appeared lost in her own reality, thinking hard on matters far removed from volleyball. Sometimes she allowed balls to drop at her feet without noticing. But she wanted to play, badly enough to emit silent, deadly farts designed to force me to send her into the fray. I can't say I wasn't sorely tempted to do exactly that more than once.

Once Melanie checked into the game, Gorham's disciplined play disintegrated. Paradise rediscovered its groove. Timeouts and attempts to restore calm had no effect. The team, except for Melanie, was furious with me. "Why did you put HER in? We had them beat." This from the most competitive 7th-grader. Retrieving Melanie and returning her

159

to the sidelines to stink up the bench did nothing to put things right. Gorham lost the final two sets and neither of them was close.

I would not choose to relive the bus ride home. Melanie sat alone behind the driver, absently disappearing the contents of her personal cooler—sandwiches, potato chips, icy cold Coca-Colas. The rest of the team huddled together in the rear, aiming death glares at the back of my head. Although we played a few more matches, our season was effectively over. Mr. Jones made the unpardonable error of losing a game against a superior opponent by inserting the hated Melanie at exactly the wrong time. They would never trust me again.

Coaching meant tedious hours riding school buses to faraway places. Some bus rides, like to Paradise, took less than an hour. Bazine, Lincoln and McCracken involved more distance and more bus time, allowing the bus driver opportunities to feed himself. The bus driver might not have been paid a handsome salary, but he knew every fast food joint on every bus route. Given the choice, he stopped at those offering free food to bus drivers. As many servings as he could eat. I suspected he might have occasionally taken a longer route to stop at a place offering bus drivers free meals. During basketball season, the boys and girls junior high teams traveled on the same bus. The girls brought along substantial lunches. The boys brought full-sized coolers. I'd never seen a group of human beings consume so much food. They ate constantly on the way to games and all the way home. If the bus stopped at a fast-food joint, they ate some more. You might suspect some obesity going on, but the Gorham kids were fit. Not scarecrows exactly, but despite their awe-inspiring calorie intake, they were athletic. In this, they resembled their parents. Gorham people ate generous portions at every meal and in between. You might encounter an occasional morbidly obese person shuffling around a grocery store in Hays, but not in Gorham.

The Gorham cafe served lunch. Typically, a bieroc dinner (hamburger and sauerkraut filled bread rolls), composed of two bierocs weighing a half pound each, a massive helping of German potato salad and a drink would run you a little over two dollars and fifty cents. I couldn't begin to finish, but most Gorhamites, none the worse for wear, not only polished off the massive lunches but stayed tuned for a dessert or two. They had not inherited the same genes I had. Like the ones that add five pounds if you pass within three and a half miles of an Oreo.

A private house party early in the fall semester. Maybe a wedding anniversary? Everyone except for the new teacher drank beer. Gorhamites much preferred beer to any other liquid. The food table, stacked with a wide assortment of cheesy hors d'oeuvres and meaty snack items, featured a mountain of raw hamburger as the centerpiece. The custom, I learned, was to load up a soda cracker with raw hamburger, some folks added salt and or pepper, some didn't, and munch. I overcame initial squeamishness enough to eat a couple of loaded crackers, congratulating myself for unbounded courage. Not bad. The balance of the bloody pile, surrounded elbow to elbow by the male attendees, disappeared in less than an hour, along with the rest of the food. Beer, in prodigious quantities, flowed all evening. The atmosphere of well-fed, beery bonhomie couldn't have been more welcoming.

Homecoming. By virtue of my 8th-grade class sponsorship, I supervised the construction of the class's homecoming float. Poor Emily, the only 8th-grader to show up for duty, had to shoulder 98% of the job. The other 2% shouldered by her pouting younger brother and the lucky sponsor. Emily, nothing if not ingenious, cobbled together a ramshackle trailer, chicken wire, and enough colored tissue paper to create a patriotic papier-mâché-headed effigy clad in shoulder pads and a Gorham Oiler jersey. The effigy closely resembled the Kansas folk art on display in at the Garden of Eden and the Grassroots Art Center in Lucas, just a few miles up the road.

S. P. Dinsmoor, an eccentric Civil War vet, who, due to a computer error, received two pension checks, created the Garden of Eden from home-brewed concrete mixed furtively in the black of night using local limestone and his own urine. The pension checks, added to his dead wife's fortune and the ten-cent admission he charged visitors, kept him well supplied with cement. The Garden of Eden, populated by concrete representations of biblical all-stars Adam and Eve, Cain and Abel, Satan, a human-tempting serpent and other dignitaries (several of whom bore strong resemblance to Emily's homecoming effigy) ranks among the top ten folk art attractions in these United States of America. Dinsmoor, a concrete enthusiast, lies moldering in a limestone mausoleum inside a concrete casket with a clear glass window revealing Dinsmoor's shrunken, desiccated face sprouting a healthy crop of black mold.

The nearby Lucas Grassroots Art Center has plenty of its own charm, elaborate sculptures fashioned from 1970s aluminum can pull-tabs and displays of artworks created from dryer lint or well-chawed chewing gum or barbed wire or ancient grapefruit rinds, not a few sculptures doppelgangers for the strange effigy riding front and center on Emily's homecoming float. Whether Emily fancied herself a folk artist or not, her creative talent would later impress Gorham parade watchers.

The homecoming parade, past the school and on to the downtown, launched on time. Mid-October sun. A few casual thunderheads hanging far off in the west. No wind to pester brightly colored tissue paper stuck haphazardly in chicken wire. I stood with Coach Stephens near my two 7th-grade volleyball players watching the marching band and the other hastily assembled floating entities pass by. The paraders outnumbered the parade watchers by approximately two to one. We watchers did our best to make a joyful noise. A convertible, top down, loaded with a diverse group of celebrating Gorhamites, rolled past. The most competitive 7th-grade volleyball player's mother, when she tried to stand up in the back seat to wave, tumbled out over the trunk and landed splat in front of us. Too drunk to stand, her companions gathered her up and deposited her back in the car before the parade could continue. Seeing your mother make a public spectacle of herself not high on a list of what most adolescent girls wish to witness. Under her helmet of tight blonde curls, the girl's face and neck turned scarlet. She bit her lip. Neither Coach Tom nor I could think of anything to say, at least nothing which didn't seem lame, nothing which wouldn't make her feel worse. And then she was gone. Home, probably. Who could blame her? And what facile homily would you have recited? Pay no attention to what everyone in town will be chattering about for the next week? You have no responsibility for your mother's behavior? This, too, will pass?

Drunken antics during the homecoming parade a prescient omen of the drunken disaster to unfold that evening. Several years previously, the local saloon soothsayers guaranteed a Gorham victory at this particular homecoming game. The opponent, as predicted, was winless, and had been winless two of the three previous seasons. Gorham, also winless, had an area all-state football player and several sturdy juniors almost as talented. Gorham's losses had not been as lopsided as usual. A couple of games had actually been close for a quarter or two. Homecoming Friday's enthusiastic classroom pep rally rocked the rafters with jeers and insults aimed at the evening's hapless lizard foe. Anticipating a rare football victory, Gorham fans, including school board members, backed pickup trucks to the sidelines early, pickup beds featuring lawn chairs, an occasional keg and coolers packed with ice and beer.

The party began an hour before opening kickoff, which, by the way, the visitors returned for a touchdown. The male members of the Gorham crowd, including school board members, followed the usual practice of abandoning their pickups to follow the action up and down the sidelines, beers in hand, aiming well-chosen criticisms at the referees and Coach Ray. The supposedly hapless lizard visitors not only refused to fold, but stuffed Gorham's predictable running plays, found holes in Gorham's predictable defensive formations, forcing rinse repeats of punts and lizard touchdowns. By mid-second quarter, the designated patsy opponent led 41-0. The Gorham pickup crowd turned from ebullient to surly. Sensing defeat and an ugly aftermath, I headed for home.

Bolts of jagged lightning grounded themselves in the milo fields to the west. According to reliable sources, with the second quarter due to expire, two Gorham players initiated a shouting match with Coach Ray over his unimaginative playcalling. Shouting escalated to shoving. Assistant coach Tubby came to Coach Ray's defense. Punches thrown, although whether any landed is doubtful. The skies opened up. Not just a little bit. Sheets of driving, frog-strangling rain turned the football field into a lake. The field lights flickered.

By leaving early, I missed the referees tossing the football upwards into the downpour, calling the game at halftime. News of the decision, based on the lop-sided score, inclement weather and the mini-riot on the Gorham sideline, took minutes to circulate through the Gorham crowd, long enough for the referees to gain a head start toward the school's semi-official referee locker room—tiny by any standard, but with a formidable deadbolt, which locked the sturdy steel door from the inside.

Once the tipsy crowd became aware the refs had called the game, the situation went completely haywire. Deep-throated cries of "Those crooked sonsabitches!" "They can't get away with this!" "Where'd they go?" The enraged mob began slogging through the underwater football field in the general direction of the school and the semi-official referee locker room. They arrived outside the referees' cozy refuge in an outraged, inebriated, thoroughly sodden state. When the refs refused to abandon their sanctuary, one recent graduate proposed borrowing a cutting torch from the school shop. Following earnest discussion, he was overruled. The steel door, even if it currently sheltered the worst kind of crooked referees, belonged to the community. Damaging community property, maintained by so many bake sales and car washes, proved unthinkable. The mob meandered back to pickups and beer coolers. Only the frightened refs remained, too scared to open the door to see if their tormentors were gone. They were still holed up at two the next morning when members of the Kansas Highway Patrol arrived.

Unfortunately, neither the state patrol's courageous action nor the general sheepishness on display around town the next morning ended the matter. Prodded by hysterical complaints from the relatively unscathed referees, the governing board of the Kansas State High School Activities Association held an emergency meeting the very next week. Mr. Beeman, just returned from visiting his wife in Kansas City, summoned for questioning. As were a couple of school board members, who, unlike Mr. Beeman, had attended the game.

The ruling, when it came, could have been more severe. Most Gorhamites, once they sobered up, agreed. But it wasn't nothing. Five years of strict probation, including a death penalty for all Gorham Junior-Senior High Institute sports if the fans ever repeated their disgraceful, drunken behavior. Pickup trucks loaded with beer and lawn chairs backed up to the sideline? Banned forever. School board members roaming the sidelines beers in hands? Banned forever. Mobs chasing referees and holding them hostage? Don't even think about it.

Football season whimpered into "there's always next year" country. Two more games against superior opponents, one of them the Lucas-Luray squad. The Gorham community, including the coaches and players, expected resounding defeats. Any flicker of optimism now deader than Percy's cow thanks to the KSHAA's draconian edict and the simmering bad blood between coaches and players. The inevitable thumpings delivered by the last two opponents only ensured the player-coach enmity continued into basketball season.

I was too involved with my own personal challenges, professional and financial, to closely monitor Coach Ray's preparations for the upcoming basketball season. His players made no secret of their disdain for him, but every boy the community expected to play basketball turned out to endure Coach Ray's brutal pre-season conditioning drills. For the junior high language arts department, the academic version of the school year to that point couldn't have gone better. Once writing was understood to equal gainful employment, the Gorham work ethic kicked in. My charges wrote reams—every day. Not much of it a threat to the literary firmament, true, but most kids developed a distinctive voice and became comfortable giving and receiving criticism. The reading classes burned through books like life savers. Books they chose in the library for extra credit points, books assigned to everyone from the limited selections in my room's spacious supply closet. Kearney State College prof Dewey Adams preached the virtues of ambitious daily reading assignments, always followed by a short quiz the next day, quizzes graded (by the teacher, never fellow students) and handed back the same day. According to Dewey's theory, instant gratification for those who read and instant consequences for those who didn't led to disciplined reading habits. Gorham students read in class, students read in study halls, students read in the hallways during lunch hour, students carted books home to read after school. Dewey was a genius.

Weekly spelling tests became a ritual. To many of you, this may seem an outdated practice. Insisting on correct spelling has gone the way of ABCDF grading in many education circles. I was less than hopeful assigning spelling words would increase spelling prowess, something which has never been proven. However, I expected time devoted to spelling would have a salubrious effect on student vocabularies. Each Monday, I pronounced and defined twenty words selected from their upcoming assigned reading and included a few previous words that had proven challenging. It was up to them to grab dictionaries and figure out how to spell the words and write a sentence that demonstrated they knew the meaning of each word. Twenty words, twenty sentences. In the process of looking up the correct spelling and meaning for each word in a physical dictionary, students exposed themselves to hundreds of additional words and their definitions. Something which doesn't happen when someone looks up a word on a personal electronic device. Sometimes the resulting sentences demonstrated imprecise understanding.

Ricochet-*I ricochet when alone.*

Infinity-*You add 12 and infinity and the answer would be just a little over infinity.*

To move the process along and make Mondays a little less of a slog, I allowed students to choose a partner and share the work fifty-fifty. Allowing students to choose their partners and allowing those students to choose which words to look up gave them a sense of ownership. A simple concept, but classrooms offering choices are, in my experience, not that common. Jim Fay,* noted classroom guru from Colorado, once explained the importance of offering students choices, particularly those kids who have little control over their crappy lives at home.

"Tell a kid he has to complete twenty problems. If dad beat up mom last night and the kid couldn't do anything to stop it, he might refuse to do any of them. But give him the choice between doing the even-numbered problems and the odd-numbered problems, he might do half the problems because someone finally gave him a tiny bit of control over his life."

Fridays, in addition to hosting lizard-hating pep rallies, featured weekly spelling tests. I promoted spelling tests as hugely important, important

*Fay grew up with a father who believed in harsh, uncompromising discipline. Fay began his teaching career as a strict disciplinarian. Following a physical altercation with a student, Fay experienced a revelation, read widely on child development and teaching methodology. He went on to enjoy a long and successful career as a teacher, administrator, and educator of teachers.

enough to warrant modest cash payments (a shiny twenty-five-cent piece) for 100% scores. To reiterate, promoting spelling tests as vital to the future of the free world was not done with any faith they would make my students better spellers. They would spell, probably dreadfully, with or without spelling tests. The aim was to motivate the student to talk to someone, parent, sibling or friend, into drilling prior to the test. One more chance to cement the meaning of the word into youthful craniums. Come spring and the annual achievement tests, student vocabulary scores reflected substantial progress. Once in a blue moon things work out.

Dunderhead-*I ain't no <u>dunderhead</u>.*

I wish my finances had shown as much improvement as my students' vocabularies. The chief culprit was the decision to keep paying rent and steep utility bills on a larger house than was strictly required after the hippie music teacher moved to Hays. Accumulated stuff. Twenty years of stuff. I could have found a smaller, cheaper place, discarded some of my stuff, stored the rest. But that would leave all the hippie music teacher's stuff, some of it her irreplaceable family heirlooms. I lacked the backbone to make the reasonable request she deal with her stuff. Then there was Luke the Wonder Dog, the loyal Aussie/Border Collie I'd brought along from Bladen. Used to traipsing free and easy around hundreds of acres, he did his best to adapt to semi-citified Gorham life. The rental house featured a large fenced backyard, easing Luke's transition. Even if all the stuff disappeared so I could fit in a smaller, cheaper rental, Luke had earned the elbow room. After all, it wasn't his fault he had to leave the farm because his owner borrowed too much high-interest money and sociopath Paul "Cue Ball" Volcker took charge of the Federal Reserve. The hefty premiums on a bare-bones health insurance policy also became a monthly strain, as did desultory payments on the half-million dollar farm debt. By the time my modest paycheck arrived each month, I was lucky to have five bucks in my checking account. My fault and completely avoidable, but you can understand why I was especially attentive to any rumors of future pay raises.

The God that holds you over the pit of hell, much as one holds a spider or some loathsome insect over the fire, abhors you, and is dreadfully provoked; his wrath towards you burns like fire; he looks upon you as worthy of nothing else, but to be cast into the fire ... you are ten thousand times so abominable in his eyes, as the most hateful and venomous serpent is in ours.

— Jonathan Edwards-(1703-1758)

Coach Ray had his way of conducting basketball practices. I had mine. Coach Ray saw himself as a modern-day Jonathan Edwards, saving youthful sinners by subjecting them to hours of punishing physical conditioning, the kind of unrelenting drills that can cause even the fittest athlete to throw up on his or her basketball shoes. Most successful coaches devote the majority of practice time to fundamentals, preparing for the next opponent's strengths and tendencies, teaching new offensive plays, new defenses, new out-of-bounds plays, then putting the concepts in place by scrimmaging. Some coaches include blocking out and rebounding drills in every practice. Some insist on athletes making X number of free throws before they head to the locker room. Ray's practices left little time for anything except brutal calisthenics and running lines. Gobs of lines.

For those unexposed to the line running drill, a coach usually lines up players in no more than three groups. The gym floor divided horizontally into sections, sometimes by temporary tape, sometimes by setting up line-designating folding chairs on the sidelines. The whistle blows. The first of each player group runs to the first line, touches the floor, runs back to the start, touches the floor, runs back to the next line, usually the free throw line, touches the floor, back to the start, then to the half court line, back to the start, then to the farther free throw line, back to the start, then to the next line, back to the start, then to the far end of the gym at full bore. Sometimes the drill continues until everyone has run ten sets of lines, sometimes twenty, sometimes, with Coach Ray in charge, until his players were three-quarters dead.

While I wasn't philosophically opposed to physical conditioning, fundamental skill drills, learning offenses and defenses, free throw shooting, had a higher priority for our limited practice time. My junior high

168

girls were bitterly disappointed I didn't ask them to run more lines. Coach Stephens made them run lines last year. Coach Stephens knew what he was doing. If I knew anything about basketball, I'd make them run lines until the cows came home. The absence of line running was to fester all season.

There was no reason for the seven, count 'em, junior high team members to have a shred of confidence in their basketball coach. Based on the debacle at the Paradise volleyball game, everyone but Melanie would cheerfully swear out a warrant for my arrest. The entire sum of my basketball experience consisted of a melancholy couple of years sitting on a junior high basketball bench. Truth of the matter? My actual basketball coaching credentials were as nonexistent as my volleyball coaching credentials. As nonexistent as any extra duty pay for this assignment. The girls had many reasons to compare my basketball coaching chops unfavorably to their last year's coach, the beloved Coach Stephens, currently coaching the winning high school girls' basketball squad. Unlike the current Junior High coach, Coach Stephens knew what he was doing. A patient but demanding teacher, Coach Stephens emphasized the toppy conditioning required to play pressure defense. He took the time to convince his players defense wins basketball games when the offense goes badly. When he demanded maximum effort at all times, demanded his girls run lines, they knew, unlike with Coach Ray, it wasn't done out of sadism, but for the shared goal of winning basketball. Coach Stephens might have been soft-spoken, but the younger sibling of a large Catholic family could be as strict about rules as any Jesuit. Missing a practice, for instance, disqualified a player from the next game. Didn't matter why she missed practice. Illness, the funeral of a close relative, say a mother, an earthquake, a heathen communist nuclear strike, no excuse excused. You missed a practice you didn't play. Let your imagination discuss how far Coach Stephens' strict rules would fly in today's squishy feely public schools.

Because he was a teacher first, because he played no favorites, because his players believed in him, they would do anything he asked. Any Gorham Oiler foe knew they would be facing a fanatical defense, a defense that would out-hustle, outlast their opponents. They would also be facing a team that shot free throws with steady accuracy. Lights-out defense and decent free-throw shooting will win basketball games, even against physically superior opponents. In addition to various zone defenses, Coach Stephens' teams played man-to-man defense a good share of the time. He believed man-to-man defense required more energy and focus than zone defense. If a team played zone defense too often, they often lapsed into lazy habits, forgot to be aggressive. But he mixed things up. If an opponent began setting screens, successfully peeling off defenders, scoring easy layups, he'd switch gears and smother them with a tenacious zone defense until they gave it up.

At the first junior high practice, the most competitive 7th-grader announced, "Mr. Jones, we don't want to play man-to-man defense. We like zone defense. So please don't ask us to play man-to-man. And we like to run lines, so have us run lines."

Didn't matter if the beloved Coach Stephens, the coach they still worshipped, required them to play man-to-man defense the prior year. They were dug in. I explained playing man-to-man helped their defensive skills, even if they played zone most of the time, but they weren't having any. Maybe if I hadn't screwed up the Paradise volleyball game they wouldn't have been so adamant. Maybe if I'd announced they'd be running lines by the hour. Maybe. But no, zone defense. Period. The end.

Sometimes you fight wars you know you can't win, but it's not a practice with much utility. The Gorham Junior High girls' basketball team played zone that season. But they played zone like their lives depended on it. They played zone like they'd been practicing man-to-man defense their entire natural lives. Opponents won, but seldom by outlandish scores. The girls forced opponents, no matter how talented, to earn every point.

But what do to about the offense? Emily, the only 8th-grader, stood 5'2" in her Chuck Taylors. Excellent ball handler and defender, not a confident shooter. The two 7th-graders, who represented 90% of the team's offensive ability, barely topped 5'4." That left three 6th-graders. One a weak-limbed, but gutsy scarecrow who lacked the strength to shoot a layup, the other an athletic, fanatical defender. Neither one cleared 4'10". Then…there…was… Melanie, our only substitute, 4'8" inches of gaseous vacuity. I needed an offensive mentor. Yesterday. Although he would have been a valuable resource, Coach Stephens politely declined to become involved. Probably foresaw an approaching train wreck and didn't want to get any on him. No basketball coaches in my Rolodex. Or maybe there was one. Doyle Fyfe at Kearney State College, rumored to be a basketball genius. I needed more than a mere genius. I needed a basketball Einstein.

The following Saturday morning, I was buying Doyle Fyfe breakfast at a downtown Kearney cafe while he diagramed plays on napkins. Rumors about Fyfe's basketball genius turned out to be understated. After listening to a thumbnail description of the team, Fyfe grasped the physical limitations, the reality they'd always be matched against taller, older girls. The plays he designed did not depend on long-range shooting ability or superior height. What became the team's favorite play involved one of the 4'10" forwards setting a moving screen on a taller opponent to free up the baseline for an easy layup. Then, as now, moving screens were illegal. But as Fyfe predicted, referees typically ignored a diminutive player setting a moving screen on a much larger opponent. Only after considerable complaining by opposing coaches did the refs call the foul. The other gift, a gift which kept giving all season, was the out-of-bounds play Fyfe drew up, one he'd employed for years. It proved effective against every opponent. When combined with the press break he supplied, Gorham routinely broke full-court presses, often for wide-open layups. Teams that tried to press didn't choose to continue. There was more—his favorite dribbling and passing drills, loose ball drills, block out drills, denying the ball to the opponent's best shooter drills. A basketball Einstein's compendious knowledge handed out free of charge on a growing pile of napkins. Then a little inside basketball.

"Did you ever notice, Bryan, how most kids aren't comfortable with close physical contact? If you're playing zone. You're going to be playing zone, right?" This delivered with a pitying stare. "Have your girls crowd those without the ball. It's how most people react to close talkers. Someone whispers right in your face, you naturally back away, create more distance. When a kid gets crowded, she's gonna take a step back, then another step back. Before they realize what's happened, they will be pushed a long way from the basket, a long way from their favorite shooting spot, a long way from any chance at an offensive rebound.

Messes up the whole offense to have players stuck clear out on the perimeter. (This before deadly three-point shooters became ubiquitous) Your kids can even move a strong, taller post player from under the basket. Just keep crowding; they don't have to touch them, just stand really close. If they move back, stay close.

"I'm not recommending this, you understand, but once upon a time back in Colorado, I had a kid always suffering with a cold." Fyfe is chuckling. "Snot running constantly. Something bad wrong with him, but he was tough. He usually defended the opposing team's best post player. As you know, (I didn't), post-players typically have a certain way of doing things, embedded habits. They have a couple of favorite shots, and they work on those. Not many of them are comfortable shooting too far from the basket. Every time this snot-nosed kid got to dripping, he'd grab a handful and wipe it on the post guy's arm or jersey. Yuck, right? But it worked. Didn't take long for those post guys to lose their appetite for rebounding or anything else which might take them near my guy. Like I said, not a recommendation, but it sure was fun to watch.

"You know about the belly poke, right? No? You're kidding. No? I forget you've never coached basketball. You always teach your kids to block out after a shot? Right? Let's say there's a gal on the other team with a nice 15-foot shot. She can make that shot blindfolded; she can make that shot in her sleep. Once the ball leaves shooter's hand, have your kid turn to face the basket, stick her butt up against the shooter, blocking the shooter from a rebound. Have her reach back and poke the shooter in the stomach. The shooter, the refs, the crowd, the coaches, everyone in that gym will be watching the basketball headed toward the basket. Nobody will notice if your kid gave the shooter a little poke to the gizzle. Doesn't have to be a hard poke, just firm, right below the breastbone. Not many shooters have the same accuracy after a couple pokes in gizzle. They're flinching. They're shooting farther from the defender, farther from the basket, farther from their favorite spot. They're not thinking about anything except the next poke in the gizzle. And it will work for your shorter players too. Even better, because nobody, especially a ref at a junior high game, pays much attention to a short player."

I'm dead certain I never thanked Doyle Fyfe adequately for saving my bacon. If only he could have seen the Gorham junior high girls set moving screens at every opportunity, break opponent presses at will, take pure delight in gizzle poking.

Incoherent-*When you wake up from a comma you may be* *incoherent.*

Coaching without enough warm bodies to scrimmage proved frustrating. A 3 on 3 scrimmage might be better than no scrimmage, but practicing shorthanded offenses and defenses is a poor substitute for a 5 on 5 scrimmage. Unexpected assistance came from Mr. Hake, the junior high boys basketball coach. Mr. Hake, who doubled as the school's math teacher, came from Tipton, where his family had economic interests, broad and deep. He planned to teach until he returned to Tipton and the family businesses. His starters, all 8th-graders and all gifted athletes, were so good they obliterated his second and third-stringers during scrimmages. Second and third-teamers seldom able to bring the ball past center court or take an uncontested shot. His scrubs couldn't practice offensive plays because his first team proved too disruptive on defense. "What would you think of having your girls scrimmage against my scrubs? That way, your girls could practice at full strength (all six of them) and my kids could run their offensive plays enough times to get comfortable. Now they can't get off the dime. From what I've seen of the girls' team, they should be competitive with the boys."

Halfway through the next practice, Mr. Hake led his 12 scrubs into the gym—with unexpected results. The boys, assuming the girls were easy pickings, played with all the energy of a group of self-admiring Rico Suaves. The girls, on the other hand, played for reals. Five minutes in, the girls had five baskets and the boys had none. The boys, on the short end of the score, had taken a physical beating as well. Scrimmages typically ran on the honor system. If you thought you had been egregiously fouled, you could make the call, shoot the foul shot. In actuality, fouls were seldom called. Nobody wanted to look like a weenie. Imagine how reluctant a boy would be to declare he'd been fouled by a girl. Exactly. And the two 7th-grade girls took full advantage. Grabbing, poking, eventually engaging in full-metal mugging. Even Melanie got in a few licks. Eventually, the boys tired of being victimized and did some body banging of their own, no dirty pool, just hard, aggressive play. From then on, the teams scrimmaged on an equal basis. Both sides wanted to outscore the other, of course, but the contests became deadly serious, with everyone giving maximum effort. The boys always won by a couple of baskets, but in the process, the girls earned respect. During subsequent scrimmages, both teams improved. The boys polished their offense and gained confidence. The girls, playing several times a week against physically superior opponents, learned to adapt and ramp up their own skills. As the season unfolded, the teams cheered and encouraged each other with genuine enthusiasm. Mr. Hake's experiment worked out better than he could have hoped.

The basketball team's final game of the season. Downs, Kansas. 70 miles north of Gorham. Both town and school three times Gorham's size. My experiences with coaches and teachers from competing Kansas schools formed a general impression most of them knew their business and had professional standards. The Downs Junior High coaches were a cut above. They'd taught and lived in Downs for years, knew their athletes and their families. Downs coaches were organized and systematic. I never saw one become visibly angry or yell at their charges. No matter what the sport, Gorham coaches knew when facing a Downs team, their teams better be well-prepared—and lucky.

An early railroad center, the combination of railroad employment and fertile surrounding Solomon River Valley farmland allowed Downs to grow and prosper. It cannot boast of a Garden of Eden, like Lucas, forty miles to the south, or the largest ball of twine in the known universe, like Cawker City, six miles to the east, but on one summer weekend a year, you can enjoy the Kansas Storytelling Festival.

The week before the contest with Downs, a type A flu bug struck Gorham. Not many escaped. The students especially hard hit, including every member of the junior high girls' basketball team except for Melanie. Barely able to stand or put one foot in front of the other, they shambled around school, shambled through practice. I did not hold long or demanding practices. No fast break drills, no running lines. Yet no one, including the most competitive 7th-grader, complained.

The bus ride to Downs saw the girls slumped in their seats, wrapped in multiple layers, only their slitted eyes visible, no boom boxes blaring, everyone still as wool, unless they were coughing up lungs. The silent bus passed through Russell, the largest area town and hometown of Senate Majority Leader Bob Dole, turned left to pass through Osborne on the way to Downs. We did not stop at the Osborne County Courthouse, the Richardson Romanesque edifice at the town's center. Constructed in 1908 for the improbable sum of $54,000. The structure, fashioned of native limestone, blue sandstone and septarian creation (sedentary rock often mistaken for fossilized turtles) with floors of mosaic tile and interior walls of Tennessee marble, provides mute testimony to the optimism and public pride of the founding generation. During construction, John William Wineland, a busybody septuagenarian farmer, wandered into town each day to micromanage the stone masons. The helpful suggestions of the acolyte of Brigham Young/California Gold Rush miner/Indian fighter/Union army veteran so irritated the stone masons they carved a less than flattering version of his face into the south wall of the clock tower. If you find yourself in north central Kansas, block out enough time to contemplate the Osborne County courthouse and John William Wineland's buttinsky face. You might also wander a few miles west to add Victoria's unique WPA limestone water tower to your completed bucket list. And please do not neglect the eccentric splendors of the Garden of Eden nor the world's largest ball of twine in Cawker City. While in Lucas, check out the dryer lint sculptures at the Folk Art Center and pick up the best beef jerky on the planet at Brant's Meat Market. You won't be sorry.

After Downs opened the game by scoring the first 15 points, the Gorham girls sucking air, the Downs coach slowed things down. No fast breaks, patient passing offense, no presses. Not one gray-faced Gorham player whined when I switched them out for Melanie. Melanie stepped up, mostly by contributing a warm, gaseous body. Early in the third quarter, the Downs coach replaced his starters with second-stringers and his second-stringers with third-stringers. By the fourth quarter, Gorham girls had a choice— either rest on the bench or collapse on the court. We played shorthanded, sometimes four players, sometimes three for the rest of the game. Downs chose not to exploit the advantage. After the game, I thanked the coach for his mercy.

"I could see your kids were a little under the weather."

A little under the weather, but game. As awful as they felt, the girls continued to scrap, expending the little energy they had. Although I was not responsible for their heroic effort, they were only doing what they were wired from birth to do; I couldn't have been more proud. And told them so on the way home. Wrapped in layers and mostly comatose, a couple of girls cracked their eyes open until I finished talking. If they had voiced an opinion, they would have pointed out they'd lost the game. Not only lost the game, but been drubbed. Winning the game might be a reason for this loser coach talking pride. However, losing was losing. No way to pin a rose on it. Please shut up.

Cyst-*Last year I had a <u>cyst</u> in between my utarise and my rectum.*

Following basketball season, rumors circulated Mr. Beeman might be flying the coop at the end of the school year, rumors circulating so vigorously they reached my cloistered ears. I looked him up, asked him about his plans. He said he wasn't unhappy with his job or the school. Said running his own show in Gorham was the most fun he'd had in his entire life. His wife, on the other hand, was not returning. He didn't say why. To keep his happy home, he was looking for a job closer to Kansas City. Hadn't found one yet, but was confident. Rumors of the identity of Beeman's impending replacement soon circulated.

Mrs. Roberts served as Gorham's part-time guidance counselor. The wife of the Russell superintendent of schools, she was widely suspected of being a double agent, gathering intelligence for the enemy district everyone assumed still had designs on absorbing Gorham's students. According to the rumor mill, Mrs. Roberts grew up on Army bases, usually as the daughter of the commanding officer, accustomed to enlisted men catering to her every whim, saddling her horse, currying the horse after her frequent rides, feeding and watering her horse, getting their asses kicked if the horse wasn't in the pink. No surprise she came to Gorham equipped with a highly exaggerated sense of personal power. Although she didn't wear jodhpurs or knee-high cavalry boots or cruel spurs or carry a riding crop, she carried the attitude.

Coach Ray became her personal favorite. Thick as thieves, those two. Humid, furtive glances during rare faculty meetings. Coach Ray assumed the role of chief stooge. During the past school year, Mrs. Roberts kept her low opinion of Mr. Beeman undisclosed, at least to most of us. But later, after school shut down for the summer and Mr. Beeman left for his new principal's post in Kansas City, she let it be known his wishy-washy treatment of student criminals and underperforming teachers was beneath contempt. New regime, fresh attitude.

Luke the Wonder Dog enjoying the cool morning air with me on the back step while I sipped a vile cup of coffee brewed with vile Gorham water. Luke's nervous whines a reminder he deserved a long, unfettered run, maybe around the rugged shores of Wilson Reservoir. Luke, who'd been clocked at 35 mph, needed a long, flat-out run every once in a while to keep his sanity. Better get on the road to the lake before the hot part of the day.

The distant ringing of a phone. Mrs. Roberts requesting my presence in her office at my earliest convenience. The very morning she officially assumed the job of Grand Poobah of the Gorham Junior-Senior High Institute from the recently departed Mr. Beeman.

Once she directed me to the chair in front of Mr. Beeman's former desk, she wasted no time on pleasantries. She tilted her head back, the better to peer at me over her aquiline nose. A vaguely Southern drawl laced with whiskey and tobacco. Mr. Beeman ran a loose ship, she said, students out of control, teachers not teaching. Change long overdue. "I understand, Mr. Jones, you took a reading class outside one day this spring without permission and forced them to read on the lawn. Many of your fellow teachers were upset." Who might be upset besides Coach Ray and perhaps my English department colleague, I couldn't imagine.

I pled guilty. With the room thermometer tickling 97 degrees and the kids wilting in their own sweat, I made the executive decision to expose them to shade and weak breeze by parking them against the east wall of the school. They read, when not observing birds or passing cars or the fresh zit on their best buddy's nose, but they read with more attention than if I'd kept them cooped up in that inferno of a classroom.

"Next year we won't be taking students outside of the school building without permission, will we, Mr. Jones?"

I should have told her to piss up a rope or curry a horse or whatever would have been appropriate. However, I'd probably violated a formal, written-down official board policy. My position further weakened by not having an alternative job offer in hand, currently owing a Nebraska bank a cool half million bucks and my checking account balance resting at near zero. I swore I would never in a million, jillion years, pull that stunt again. She aimed a tight victory smile in my direction. But she wasn't quite finished.

"Do you recognize this?"

Sure enough, during one of his periodic classroom searches, Coach Ray unearthed the mummified lizard and delivered the crime clue extraordinaire to his partner in humid perfidy. Completely on me for thinking I could move the lizard from his or her habitual perch on my desk to behind a set of dictionaries in the spacious storage closet. Completely on me for thinking the lizard, which had been the focus of so many spirited pep rallies, would be safe from Coach Ray's intrusions until the fall term. Only a wide-eyed optimist would believe for one second the famous mummified lizard, wildly popular with Gorham students, could escape Coach Ray's determined efforts. Coach Ray was, after all, a permanent candidate for employment with the Kansas State Highway Patrol. For all I knew, he'd borrowed a goldanged bloodhound from local law enforcement. Would have been just like him.

"What, may I ask, is this horrible, disgusting thing! doing in your classroom?"

At that point in the proceedings, the worm turned. As eminent biologists often say, even the lowliest invertebrate, if pushed too far, sometimes discovers a bit of spine. Offering up groveling promises to never again expose my reading students to the dangerous wilderness of the school lawn was one thing. Promising to dispense with the great and powerful desiccated lizard, which had earned an enduring place of honor at the Gorham Junior-Senior High Institute, was a bridge too far.

"I have no idea. Never saw it before."

178

Shaken, but not stirred, she regrouped. "It was found in your room. Surely, you're not going to sit there and tell me you haven't seen it before."

"Fraid so. I would remember. Wrinkled up little devil. Is it a he or she? How do you sex a lizard anyhow? Never sexed a lizard in my life. Wonder how he or she got in my room? How long do you suppose he or she's been there? Maybe you could ask one of the teachers who's taught here longer than I have. Coach Ray might know something; he keeps up with school business pretty well."

"I don't think so."

"I'll ask around, let you know if somebody knows something."

With that final smart-assed remark, I plucked the great and powerful lizard from Mrs. Roberts' desk and boogied from the scene. I should have been more worried about my job. No teachers union to protect me. Unlike the Nebraska teachers union, the Kansas National Education Association had yet to extend its tentacles into small rural Kansas school districts. The Gorham school board did not recognize the KNEA as an employee representative. But when you boiled it down, Roberts couldn't fire me without justifying the decision to the school board. There would be questions, some of them embarrassing. Like, how had the lizard come into her possession? Either she admitted her stooge had searched my room or she made up a big fib about searching my room herself. In either case, the egg would be well distributed over her face. And the inevitable question from the board, should things get that far, "why make a big to-do over a little dried-up lizard? Are you nuts?"

Which she was, of course, in the limited sense of being an entitled, dictatorial, horse-riding, stooge-riding, unrecovered alcoholic creepazoid.

She didn't fire me, not yet (her payback would arrive soon enough). But I could be certain, come next fall, if not sooner, she would inflict her most sadistic cruelties. I'd be crawling on my belly, eating sand out of the road to hang on to my job. Time to get serious about alternative employment.

Teaching jobs proved scarce. I applied for the handful matching my credentials at small schools across Wyoming, Kansas, Colorado and Nebraska. The first to offer an interview? Dewitt Tri-County, a consolidated school southwest of Lincoln, Nebraska, seeking a junior high reading teacher. Some coaching assignments "might be available," eduspeak for any successful candidate better be able to coach multiple sports—well. In the case of DeWitt Tri-County, a school with a long tradition of athletic success, I could expect far more interest in my coaching credentials than in academic qualifications.

The town of DeWitt rang a couple of memory bells. Every farmer I knew had several VISE-GRIP pliers within easy reach. Not much needing fixing couldn't be remedied with a pair of VISE-GRIPS. Pliers invented in DeWitt and manufactured in DeWitt for many years before the company was sold and manufacturing moved to heathen communist Red China, causing 300 local workers to lose their jobs.

I associated DeWitt with high school athletic prowess. I also remembered riding with my dad when he served as Methodist district superintendent, visiting small Methodist churches in Saline County, the county DeWittians call home. I've always enjoyed chatting up old-timers. Old timers well-represented at the carry-in church dinners which typically followed Sunday worship services. Have you by chance tasted a genuine busthead Czech kolache, those heavy-doughed sweet rolls with jam in the centers? If you have, you know why I accompanied my dad to Saline County.

Old timers tend to talk about what they want to talk about. Sometimes, elderly Czechs talked about the times of trouble back in Bohemia after some high and mighty Catholic muckety-mucks burned reformer John Huss at the stake. Subsequently, much bloodshed between the muckety-mucks and loyal Huss supporters. The warfare caused Czech farmers and their families to migrate to America. Substantial numbers settled in southeast Nebraska. A stubborn minority remained bitter against the Catholic Church. The old timers remembered neighbors who sicced the family watchdog on any priest who showed up. Often, any minister, even a Methodist, who appeared at the front door with religion on his mind received a lesson in running back to his car with an angry farm dog hot on his ass.

Some Czechs were good Catholics. Others steered Protestant, mostly Methodist. But many were staunch unbelievers, just like their fathers and mothers and grandparents. After the Papists burned John Huss for no good reason, religion of any flavor held no attraction for many Saline County Czechs.

Going into the interview, I knew three things about DeWitt. The school had a tradition of strong athletic teams, DeWitt was home to the invaluable VISE-GRIP plier and if you were in the general vicinity of DeWitt, you might find yourself getting on the outside of a genuine Czech kolache, possibly baked by a stone atheist.

After scanning my paltry coaching resume (no conference or district championships), my three administrator interviewers, all wearing graying crew cuts and short-sleeved golf shirts with little animals on the pockets, understood my candidacy was dead on arrival. However, they had the good manners to greet me warmly and treat me as if I were the most outstanding applicant they'd ever met. The teaching part of the job, which should have been my sweet spot, consisted of handing out pasteurized, homogenized, strenuously edited "stories," which lacked the faintest suggestion of drama or humor or the human condition. Purchased from a publisher in good standing with the edu-industrial-government complex, the stories made *Fun with Dick and Jane* seem wildly entertaining by comparison. The canned reading program, I was told, had proven highly effective in other schools and eliminated all the guesswork in choosing reading books for the classroom and the school library. By limiting the students to pasteurized reading materials, the school avoided messy complaints from parents about troubling language and/or subject matter.

While we toured the reading classroom, the interviewers explained the nuts and bolts of the teaching assignment. I would be handing out pasteurized stories, directing students to read the stories, then handing out worksheets with questions about the stories. The heavy lifting occurred after I collected and corrected the worksheets and recorded the grades. An untrained monkey could have done it with one paw tied behind his or her back.

I had a few questions.

The reading classroom held a single dictionary. Would it be possible to purchase a few more?

The worksheets provide all the definitions needed.

Was the school opposed to the students reading books of their own choosing for extra credit?

We find there is less controversy if the students stick to the assigned reading materials.

Is spelling part of the official reading curriculum?

No.

At that point, I no longer wanted the job, not that I would ever be offered one. At that point, it was clear to everyone in the room the interview was over. The animal on the pockets administrators did not bother with coaching questions. I thanked my way out the door and into my ancient car for the long drive back to Gorham and the lizard-hating Mrs. Roberts. For old times' sake, I took a brief detour through Bladen to see how my farmstead was faring with the new renter. Junk everywhere. Corrals torn out and replaced with nothing. Shingles missing from outbuildings. The place gave off the distilled aroma of abandonment.

Two weeks later. Gorham experiencing typical mid-June temperatures in the low 100s. The electric bill for the rental house air conditioning would certainly break the monthly record. Meanwhile, teaching jobs disappearing from the board every day. What if I couldn't find a teaching job? Would I return to Gorham for another year? A year that would see Mrs. Roberts using me as her go-to scapegoat? I began, not for the first time, to consider a different occupation. Prison guard? Too depressing. Small town librarian? I'd need to brush up on all that Dewey Decimal business. I was too old for the army. How about a cushy job as some kind of federal bureaucrat? Friends with no specific skills had taken the civil service exam, landed jobs with Alphabet Nation, the SSA, the BIA, the BLM, the USPS, the...hold on there, Chester. The United States Postal Service? Now you're talking. Those folks make bank, fabulous retirement and health insurance, vacation days up the wazoo. I wouldn't necessarily have to work at a sprawling industrial sorting facility in firearms-friendly downtown Chicago. Maybe I could score a job in a cozy rural village, get to know the residents, bake cookies, pass gossip around like a pro. No one would be more pleased than Luke the Wonder Dog, especially if I could find an acreage on the edge of the ideal village where he could roam at will.

Speaking of Luke the Wonder Dog. He has joined me on the back step. The morning air not so much cool as not quite as oppressive as yesterday afternoon. Vile Gorham coffee. The phone. By the way, not just any phone, but a phone attached to the receiver by a stout, coiled cord, said receiver attached to the wall, just as God intended. McCook Junior High in McCook, Nebraska, wondering if I'd be up for an interview for the 7th-grade reading position in the next couple of days.

My parents spent some of their most productive years ministering to the congregation of the McCook Methodist Church. Dad making sure the sheep were fed, particularly the unloved, universally despised sheep. Mom serving as a reading specialist for the McCook Public Schools, a job that suited her to her toes. I did not connect McCook's interview offer with her previous employment by the district, but I should have. As with most schools, McCook administrators felt more comfortable if they knew a job candidate or knew a close relative of the candidate.

BOOK THREE

The man who does not read books has no advantage over the man who can not read them.
                                        —Mark Twain

Situated in Southwest Nebraska in the Republican River Valley, McCook served as the trade and medical center for both Southwest Nebraska and Northwestern Kansas. The divide between the Republican and Platte Valleys a half-hour drive to the north, considerably drier than the divides near Bladen and Gorham. Irrigation water on the divide between the Platte and Republican not abundant, but a five-hundred-foot well and a low-output center pivot irrigation system could raise a crop if you were willing to pay the exorbitant energy bill to pump the water. Farmers, with few dependable helpings of moisture, lived one drouthy period away from disaster. They were a serious lot, taken as a whole. Fun-loving did not come naturally to those one drought or one hail storm away from financial ruin.

A railroad town, McCook experienced resounding boom times in the 1950s and early 60s with the discovery of significant oil west and southeast of McCook. Federal flood control and irrigation projects in the Republican River Basin added additional high-wage employment, resulting in a growth spurt. Enterprising speculators built cracker box Cape Cod-style houses around the edges of town, available to anyone who could beg or borrow $3500. McCook's progressive business owners valued education. When taking their obligatory turns as school board members, they did not pinch pennies; hired crackerjack administrators. Ralph Brooks, a 1950s superintendent hire, went on to a distinguished term as Nebraska governor.

By 1987, McCook's glory days were in the past; visionary community leaders succeeded by parochial lesser lights more interested in protecting the town from change than in expanding opportunities for all. The public schools, however, maintained high standards, hiring talented teachers and administrators even if they weren't born and raised in McCook.

Known as the Banana Belt of Nebraska, the McCook area featured mild, sunny winters and unrelenting dry summers, usually accompanied by monotonous, sing-songy, dust-filled winds gusting in from Kansas and Eastern Colorado. No wonder early settlers ate rat poison. McCook's vast western skyline often held clues to the area's mercurial weather. Thunderheads boiling up by the thousands of feet, innocuous, fleecy cirrus clouds, the occasional ominous wall cloud predictive of high winds and hail. Multiple bolts of gravedigger lightning strikes sometimes lit up the western horizon in the best Gorham homecoming tradition.

The local radio station, affectionately nicknamed "Chicken Little Radio," broadcast breathless weather warnings designed to keep listeners alert to approaching storms. The possibility of a tornado, no matter how slight, became urgent advice to head for the basement, or if you didn't have a basement, to the nearest inside closet, or if you didn't have an inside closet, to the nearest road ditch where you were supposed to lie face down and cover the back of your head with your hands, a maneuver which would also provide protection from Ruskie thermonuclear devices. God help you if "freezing fog," whatever the hell that was, threatened. Never clearly defined, freezing fog ranked right up there with Class Five hurricanes and EF5 tornadoes as threats to human existence. We might not have been able to define freezing fog, but that didn't mean we could ignore the warnings without risking dismemberment or death.

McCook's religious sects covered the usual suspects: Methodists, Episcopalians, three Lutheran flavors, multiple Baptist congregations, Church of God, Assembly of God, Church of Christ, Congregationalists, Evangelicals, Church of Latter Day Saints and a baker's dozen of fundamentalist nondenominational churches. Of all the churches, the Catholic Church had the most adherents and a parochial elementary school. The Graffs, a prominent local banking family, provided oursized support for the church and school. A heathen resident could hardly blame lack of options for maintaining his or her pagan status.

McCook featured the special attraction of my Uncle Willis and Aunt Lucille Jones. Ask the Jones cousins to name their favorite aunt and uncle and Willy and Lucille would be elected by acclamation. More kid-doting humans have never existed. Willy took visiting nieces and nephews fishing on one of the lakes he helped build while working for the Bureau of Reclamation. Lucille mothered us and laughed at our antics. Unlimited fried crappie or unlimited servings of Uncle Willy's famous tacos and slabs of Willy's highly regarded apple pie kept us fat and happy. Once you stayed with Willis and Lucille, you'd be wishing you could visit again forthwith, if not sooner. The idea of teaching in the same town Willy and Lucille called home only whetted my interest.

The red flags came from my mother after she learned of the impending job interview.

"You'll find McCook people to be friendly in a superficial sense. But they don't accept outsiders easily. No matter how long you live in McCook, it's unlikely you'll be treated as an equal. And by the way, McCook people pay special attention to their lawns and the lawns of others. You might want to mow once in a while."

Having witnessed the mixed results of my lawn tending, my smart mother had a right to be concerned.

Strange job interview. Sun blistered parking lot. Luke the Wonder Dog waiting in the hot car, window down, head and tongue hanging out, one blue eye and one brown eye searching the area for his master. I sat for the interview with a single McCook administrator, Mr. Backer, the soon-to-be-retired junior high principal. Sat in a sweltering office inside a sweltering building. Mr. Backer, clad not in a golf shirt with a little animal on the pocket, but in a short-sleeved white shirt and tie, did not appear inconvenienced by the heat. He also did not ask many questions. Just one, to be precise.

"Any questions?"

Fresh off the DeWitt interview, I had a question. Available reading materials?

Mr. Backer led me down the hall to the 7th-grade reading classroom. Books, books, more books. My predecessor (more about her later) clearly knew her business. Class sets of quality fiction and nonfiction books for every interest and reading level. Dictionaries, gobs of dictionaries. Machines designed to build word recognition in struggling readers. My smart mother employed machines like these, which flash words on the screen before a kid can blink, imprinting the subliminal memory. She often said a few weeks on one of these babies could make miraculous improvements to a kid's reading skills.

As you probably remember from bitter personal experience, not everyone welcomes the impromptu, loud, discordant hosanna. Mr. Backer didn't seem like a guy who would appreciate a loud, discordant hosanna. But I sure as hell felt like aiming several in his general direction. The reading classroom contained all the necessities for a sound reading program. If anything were lacking, the evidence of substantial money already spent indicated there was more money where that came from. Sugar plums danced in my head.

Back in his office, Mr. Backer asked if I had further questions. I considered asking about the salary schedule, but refrained for fear he'd consider me too materialistic. He didn't look like a guy opposed to materialism, but looks don't always tell the story. Instead, I asked if he had any questions for me. He didn't. We were done and done.

188

I never saw him again.

I drove back to Gorham convinced I never had a chance. Either that or the decision to hire me, one Mr. Backer didn't necessarily favor, had been made before I showed up. Three weeks later, when McCook hadn't accepted or rejected my candidacy, I assumed I was not going to be moving to McCook.

My Gorham post office box did scant business. I was too new in town to qualify for much junk mail. The letter with the red-lettered return address from Franklin, a Class C school in the Republican Valley, an hour east of McCook, couldn't have been more of a surprise nor more welcome. Franklin Public Schools requesting an interview, bless their hearts. I didn't remember the particulars of the job I'd applied for months earlier, but had a faint recollection of multiple Junior High Language Arts classes and a smorgasbord of extra duty assignments.

Franklin, the county seat of Franklin County, the county where my smart mother grew up and taught school before she married my father. Situated on a narrow section of the Republican Valley, which limited the number of productive, irrigated acres feeding the overall economy. Franklin's business community in 1987 nonetheless retained a full range of shopping and services. Franklin High School produced perennial state champion sand greens golf teams, which almost made up for the historically mediocre basketball and football teams. Tim Kolb, Franklin's most famous genius native son, graduated from Franklin High School. Maybe I'd encounter a few more student geniuses.

The interview, conducted by the high school principal (white shirt and tie) in a frosty air conditioned office, included several questions from him, which I took as a sign of serious interest. In his mid-30s, my interviewer bright and personable. My prospective classroom included dictionaries and a few actual books. Unfortunately, the job, which recently reopened when a previous candidate backed out, should have been, in the interest of transparency, described as multiple jobs. Two Junior High English classes, a 7th-grade reading class, a high school speech class, a high school journalism class, a study hall, Junior High girls basketball, volleyball and track coaching, junior and senior class play sponsorships, competitive one-act play and speech team coaching, supervising production of the school yearbook and school newspaper. This 24/7 job monster would require keeping a cot and a change of clothes in my classroom.

Without other job options, I fully intended to take the position if offered, a position offered the day after I returned to Gorham. A two-thousand-dollar raise over the Gorham salary, full health insurance and enough responsibilities to keep me out of the bars forever. Still contemplating life as a small-town postal clerk, I risked a three-day delay before committing. On the third and final day, a letter arrived in the post office box with a red lettered return address from the McCook Public Schools. Inside a teaching contract for the 1987-1988 school year for the princely wage of $21,500, a four-thousand-dollar raise from my Gorham salary, without considering generous district paid health insurance and retirement contributions. I tried to keep the glee out of my voice when phoning my regrets to the Franklin principal. Less glee after a vengeful Mrs. Roberts charged me $700 for release from the Gorham teaching contract for the 1987-1988 school year. Sometimes smart-assedness has consequences.

The $700 bill for my freedom sent me back to Dad for another "loan." Another addition to the half-million-dollar hole I'd dug. On the bright side, sociopath Paul "Cue Ball" Volcker had been ousted from his position of Federal Reserve Chairman, where he'd committed so many crimes against humanity. In his place, the permanently incoherent Alan Greenspan, who, in a couple of months, would preside over the most precipitous stock market crash since 1929. Thank you, Federal Reserve System.

Designed by architects from the same uninspired schools of architecture responsible for the raft of newer minimum security prisons around the country, McCook Junior High's deliberate lack of cross ventilation assumed the presence of central air conditioning. The assumed air conditioning failed to appear after the construction bond issue had to be downsized to meet voter approval. This created a one-story, blond brick minimum security prison with neither air conditioning nor cross ventilation. My former Bladen social studies classroom boiled the inhabitants during the warmer months of August, September and May. The McCook 7th-grade reading classroom, located along the interior hallway, lacked a single window and, due to a school furnace with a hyperactive thyroid, boiled the inhabitants year-round. A reason, perhaps not a persuasive one, but a reason, why so many of my male colleagues wore knit golf shirts with little animals embroidered on the pockets.

Not Dr. Eugene Rider. Never wore a golf shirt in his entire natural life. Doc, the 7th-grade world history teacher and the occupant of the next-door classroom, never threw anything away. Hence, the yellowed wash and wear white shirts and the frizzled neckties circa 1956, often paired with expensive banker's suits. Doc was also responsible for the leftover, moldy, fossilized food dating back to the 1880s he squirreled in the teacher's lounge fridge.

After his military service during the Korean War, Doc earned his Ph.D. in history at Denver University, his doctoral dissertation written on the corrupt 19th-century Denver police department. In 1987, Doc was likely one of the more overqualified junior high teachers on the planet. Any soldier who has spent time in the trenches teaching young adolescents will tell you possessing default cynicism and firsthand experience with crime cannot be overvalued. Although wary of junior high students if he happened to think about them, Doc did not possess a criminal mind. Intelligent to a fault, Doc looked at things through rosy, 1950s-tinted spectacles. Incapable of lying or deceit himself, he could not credit similar behavior in others, unless they happened to be Democrats.

Speaking of criminal minds, Mr. Berry, Mr. Backer's replacement as Junior High principal, stopped by my classroom while I was unpacking and taking stock. He earned high marks off the bat for wearing a white shirt and tie. He asked questions. Paid close attention to the answers. Paying close attention to answers is the mark of a skilled interrogator. I was to learn when it came to solving junior high crime, Mr. Berry had no peer. He often knew the identity of the criminal while the deed was only in the planning stages.

Stirrup-*I am going to stirrup trouble.*

Still out of sorts from the DeWitt interview, I handed Mr. Berry an earful. Made it clear this reading program would employ dictionaries, actual books, good books. No dumbed-down, soul-crushing, pasteurized, prepackaged, edu-industrial-government complex "stories" in this classroom. Ever. In light of subsequent events, I should have made a much stronger case. As it was, I must have worked myself into a lather, because he took a step back, then another as he eased himself out the door. A lunatic reading teacher, every principal's fondest hope. Perhaps not the best of beginnings, but we ended up friends, two new kids on the block, both of us under scrutiny from the veteran animal on the pockets contingent. Two of which, I later discovered, had applied unsuccessfully for Mr. Backer's position. In a word? Bitter.

I walked into the Gorham Junior-Senior High Institute for the first time, ignorant of the existing tension between my English colleague and Principal Beeman. Not that I would have made different choices had I known. Walking into the McCook Junior High for the first time, I was equally ignorant of the resentment harbored by the two rejected candidates for the principal's job. The two animals on the pockets grumps had taught for many years, were respected by their colleagues and the community. Their opinions carried outsized weight.

In those halcyon days, the teachers' lounge provided safe harbor for the handful of teachers who smoked tobacco, teachers who comprised the primary opposition to the new principal. Twirly smoke signals gathered under the water-stained ceiling tiles, along with muttered outrage at Mr. Berry's latest efforts at creating a pleasant teaching environment. A power of positive thinking homily in the school bulletin might set them off. A note in one of their mailboxes praising them for a mundane accomplishment never failed to raise a sneer. Mr. Berry, always a bulldog, never gave up trying to win them over. Despite mixed results, Mr. Berry periodically handed out forms so the faculty could anonymously evaluate his job performance. Typical response? "He wears nice clothes for someone so unfortunate looking." A more thin-skinned administrator might have reacted with anger and revenge. Mr. Berry had a hide of wang leather. Any teacher with a problem, whether a fan of Mr. Berry or his more ferocious critic, could expect Mr. Berry's full support. Kid giving you grief? Send him down, I'll check his oil. Need someone to cover your last class on Friday? No problem. Want to switch lunchroom duty days with Carl? Sure, you two can work it out.

Veteran teachers who served on the principal search committee the previous spring wisely kept their heads down. No telling who the malcontents would attack next. However, once the committee members sized up Mr. Berry and determined he was likely to not only stick around, but be successful, whisper word circulated the two malcontents had not interviewed well. In fact, neither one showed much interest in the job. Mr. Berry, on the other hand, not only demonstrated keen interest but came with the gold-plated credentials of a rising rock star in Nebraska administrative circles. Wildly successful teaching and administrative experience, laudatory letters of recommendation from an impressive assortment of Nebraska VIPs. The committee's decision to recommend Mr. Berry shouldn't have been close, and it wasn't. Only a certified sorehead could have argued with the result.

Once I took stock of my room and noted the books chosen by my predecessor, I realized I was following a reading teacher who knew what she was doing. I called Lisa in Omaha, where she was teaching middle school 5th-graders. The only conversation we ever had, but I learned how she built the reading program in McCook, why she'd selected this book, why she might not choose that book if she had a do-over. She was already homesick, wishing she were back at McCook Junior High teaching 7th-grade reading—her new assignment with the Omaha Public Schools not a patch on her former job. When the kids went home at 3:35, Lisa spent the next two and a half hours filling out OPS paperwork. Did a student meet personal learning goals for the day? If not, why not? There's a form for that, one per student. Had Lisa stated the purpose of each lesson at the beginning of class? There were forms for that. Had Lisa summarized at the end of each period what she had taught and what had been learned? OPS forms for that. In addition to paperwork covering attendance and student health, OPS provided forms for setting fresh individual student goals for the next day. Once she finished with the students, she could turn her attention to self-grading her own daily performance and filling out forms setting teaching goals for the morrow. A humorless sergeant major employed by the principal's office collected the forms at the end of the day and made sure every required form had been filled out—no blanks allowed. The piles of dead and processed trees forwarded to OPS headquarters, where dozens of highly compensated assistant administrators sorted and filed and forgot.

Far in the future, after Mr. Bennett retired, after the Hoehners left the scene, when my McCook assignment became less pleasurable, I sometimes considered teaching in a larger metropolitan district for higher wages and presumably more professional colleagues. Those thoughts didn't get much traction. Memories of Lisa's unhappy experience kept me in place.

Doc Rider held himself far above petty school politics. He had no interest and no time. Often preoccupied with thoughts, and nobody had deeper thoughts than Doc, he frequently checked out of the present to ponder more important matters. The price of gold (he had a basement littered with the filthy stuff), the current status of his garden empire, which included vacant lots distributed around town. Fifty tomato plants on this one. Cucumber vines and twenty-five tomato plants on that one. Another devoted to jalapeño peppers, key ingredient in his gourmet dill pickle recipe. Doc's sideline businesses included delivering the *Denver Post* and the *Omaha World-Herald*. As he trucked his papers from doorstep to doorstep, he kept an eye out for vacant lots he might farm for at least one summer. Doc also performed services for the elderly, scooping walks, mowing lawns, cleaning gutters. He didn't have the time to spare, but social services paid good money, something Doc prized. During summer vacation, in addition to his paper routes and tending his garden empire, Doc worked as a flagger on area road construction projects. Again, the money was good. Doc invested his accumulated pennies in Krugerrands or stock in Newmont Mining and Barrick Gold or penny Canadian gold mining stocks. Doc subscribed to financial newsletters aimed at gold bugs like himself. He often dithered for weeks between investing in this penny stock or that major gold mining venture. Once he jumped in, whether he lost money or made a fortune, he never spoke about it. It was on to the next investment decision and another stretch of dithering.

Doc's investing philosophy came straight from his father's playbook. A long time family dentist in Wauneta, Nebraska, Frank Rider and his wife Maryan operated the Chateau movie theater as a sideline and stocked their basement with gold bullion. Doc loved talking about his parents' gold stash. Meeting or exceeding their accumulation became Doc's obsession.

Although his father practiced dentistry for over 60 years, Doc, fearful of any medical provider, only consulted one if he were in terrific physical pain. Balky gall bladder? Doc had to be dragged to the emergency room. Deathly afraid of cancer, Doc believed as long as he didn't allow a doctor to perform an exam and he ate a daily handful of almonds, he was safe. His aversion to doctors extended to dentists. He waited until a tooth fell out not to see a dentist.

Each autumn Doc "put up" the bounty of his scattered garden realm. He canned vegetables and pickles into the wee hours, showing up at school unshaven and haggard. On those days, he spent his planning period snoring in the teacher's lounge. His shock of snow white hair, regularly butchered by the cheapest barber in town, in disarray. Missing teeth, front and center, also detracted from his appearance. A casual visitor to McCook Junior High might be excused for thinking Doc had wandered in after a long, dirty ride on a passing freight train.

Autumn also turned Doc's deep thoughts to gambling. Not usually football betting, although a teaching colleague fronting for a local bookie made the rounds collecting wagers every Friday and dropping off any winning bets the next Monday. Doc focused on Keno. Legalized only recently, several of Doc's favorite watering holes featured the ubiquitous back lit Keno boards. He determined to configure a system which would predict the correct numbers, numbers randomly selected by computer. A typical weeknight found Doc in McCook saloons playing Keno until the bartenders booted him out at closing time. He kept every Keno card, crunched the numbers looking for patterns. If Doc visited the school bathroom he carried his most recent collection of Keno cards. If tasked with lunchroom duty, he leaned against the far wall making notations on old Keno cards, so deep in calculations a food riot with multiple fatalities would not have disturbed him. He soon determined each saloon Keno screen had its own set of patterns.

Numbers predicted to pop up at the Coppermill Lounge, for example, might not show up at the Real's Bar. After much trial and error, he settled on the Coppermill Lounge as his primary seat of operations. And his system, continually perfected and fiddled with, began paying off. Lounge denizens noticed he was cashing winning Keno cards. Keno players begged for his predictions. After a couple of beers, Doc would oblige anyone, even a practicing Democrat. Wherever Doc sat, kibitzers and serious players moved their chairs to surround him, serious players including attractive women, some of them blondes. Doc's romantic fantasies ran heavily in the blonde direction. Deep thoughts about Keno took Doc to heights of popularity he'd never experienced.

Doc's popularity with the Keno crowd did not necessarily translate to his students. Junior high kids tend become restive or doze off during droning lectures. Who doesn't? Doc assumed significant class time should be devoted to lectures—Babylonian gardens, Egyptian pyramids, Grecian politics, Roman military matters, the first fifty-seven Crusades. He read through his stash of yellowed, crumbling, dog-eared world civilization lecture notes in a soprano monotone.

Doc loved maps. Crusades? Maps for those. Greece? A map for Greece. Roman conquests? Maps for those. Maps were to be colored as neatly as possible. Maps to be colored without using either red or green crayons. Doc was colorblind. Red or green registered as gray. Coloring maps took up a significant portion of non lecture class time, class time which could not be used for mischief.

Once the patient librarian taught him how to use the overhead projector (not a job for sissies), he sometimes lectured using overhead transparencies of highlights from his lecture notes while the record player on his desk emitted obscure dirges.

By rights, students should have rebelled. Filled the air with spit wads and paper airplanes, engaged in surreptitious, lewd, contagious coughing fits. Didn't happen.

If he somehow became aware of misbehavior, it was something impossible to overlook. Doc then decreed the miscreant write 500 sentences saying "I will not chew gum in class" or 600 sentences saying "I will not pass notes in class." Doc's punishments might have deterred some criminal behavior, but exactly how big of a wuss would you have to be to fear writing a few sentences?

Against all odds, full-scale student eruptions failed to erupt. Doc's earnest Boy Scout persona might have dampened resentment. He also exhibited the polished, old school manners which have become so rare. Good manners occasionally have a quieting effect on potential felons. He kept his distance from students, regarding them as a benign, but probably alien life form. In turn, Doc's students recognized the vast distance separating them from Doc. His world so removed from theirs the idea of misbehavior, which might narrow the distance, didn't often enter in. To my knowledge, Doc never learned a student's name or any identifying personal details. In not prioritizing names, he maintained consistency. The first semester was coming to a close before he asked Mr. Berry the name of "that new teacher" in the neighboring classroom.

Several times a month, Doc promised his classes a future treat, something to excite their imaginations and create a lifelong love of history. "The chariot race," he said, "we're going to watch the chariot race." And they'd look at each other and wonder. Wonder what the hell Doc was talking about. They found out. After dispirited, dirty lumps of winter snow frittered away and Easter season approached, Doc wheeled in the school's ancient film projector and treated his students to the chariot race from the 1959 Ben-Hur movie. Charlton Heston and Stephen Boyd pounding around the arena for fifteen excruciating minutes to raucous cheers and blaring trumpets. The razor sharp blades on Stephen Boyd's chariot wheels threatening Charlton Heston's vulnerable wooden chariot wheels on every turn. Charlton Heston passing up no opportunity to grimace in his inimitable toothsome, lock-jawed manner.

The joyful noise generated by the chariot race easily penetrated the temporary vinyl curtains separating Doc's room from mine. Dutiful 7th-grade reading students trying to get a head start on tomorrow's reading assignment assaulted by periodic trumpet blasts, the constant pounding of horses hooves. Doc, like me, taught six class sections each

day. Six times a day, for what seemed like an eternity, the hooves pounded. Six times a day, trumpets blared and blared again. Six times a day, the
arena crowd roared and roared again. Doc never failed to pronounce the
chariot race film fest as a huge hit with his students. Which might have
been a true fact. Although no student ever nominated, at least in my presence, the Ben-Hur chariot race as a personal favorite.

Necromancy-Some people practice _necromancy_, and others soccer.

We should probably visit about the Class from Hell. The 7th-grade class
entering McCook Junior High in the fall of 1987 carried a reputation of
being difficult. Explaining with precision why they were difficult stumped
their middle school teachers.

"I don't know, they're just different."

"Never taught a class like them. They're wired funny."

"Good luck. You're' going to need it."

"They're pleasant enough. Maybe something in the water when they were
conceived?"

"You get the impression they'd be happy if they never turned a wheel, just
sat around visiting with their friends."

A congenial bunch, give them that. A few more class members than usual
eventually spent time housed in Nebraska's penal system, but criminal
activity wasn't what earned the Class from Hell its reputation. Attitude.
When given an assignment, they looked at the teacher with mild disinter-
est. They were thinking, "What happens if we don't do it? Then what? We
kinda hope you'll get mad, slobber all over yourself. Please threaten us to
punish us. Be fun to watch, wouldn't it? We've survived tougher teachers
than you. And if you inconvenience us too much, we'll tell our parents
you're mean and unreasonable. Our parents will talk to other parents and
some of them will visit with the school and you'll either back off or be
shown the door. The sooner you understand how it works, Mr. 7th-grade
Reading Teacher, the sooner we can get back to doing nothing much."

I'd be the first to admit, teaching Bladen and Gorham students left me unprepared for the Class from Hell. I'd been stupid lucky to have so many bright, hardworking pupils. All too easy for me to attribute their successes to their extraordinary, multi-talented teacher. Every day, the Class from Hell reminded me of my shortcomings. No wonder their middle school teachers wished me good luck. Junior High colleagues complained about them at every opportunity. Except for Doc, who never realized the Class from Hell differed from any of its predecessors.

Most class members, slow to realize the full implications of the cumulative point system, remained on familiar cruise control until first quarter report cards and parent-teacher conferences. Several students, accustomed to receiving straight As, earned lower marks. Not many failing grades, but Cs and Ds. The lines of parents waiting to see me during conferences stretched down one side of the lunch room. Not all parents were upset. The parents of students who took advantage of the point system by earning extra credit and tackling more challenging books, were surprised and pleased. The disappointed parents behaved like their children, composed, confident. No rants. No threats. Just a consistent line of questioning focused on how the point system worked and why I thought it preferable to the regular, conventional grading system they and their kids found much superior. The talking points from each set of parents so similar, a casual observer might have wondered if the parents had been holding meetings over coffee.

The only tenuous moment occurred when an impatient mom on a mission cut in front of an impatient dad who'd been waiting in line for over an hour. The dad a local real estate agent famous for his short fuse. Bloodshed averted. But things were nippy and tucky for a few moments.

When the community talking points fell on a couple of deaf ears, parents tried emotional appeals.

"Sarah has never received less than an A on any report card. This will devastate her."

"How will we explain this grade to him? He's a straight A student. This could really affect his self-image."

I assured one and all their smart, admirable, handsome, congenial children would likely adjust and earn higher grades the next time. Or they wouldn't adjust, and continue to earn crappy grades. Not every set of parents went away happy, but the spectacle of long lines of pissed off parents at my table was never repeated during the next twenty years of parent-teacher conferences. As predicted, students adjusted. I also benefited from the infusion of new teachers every year, some of whom lacked the brains of an oyster and couldn't teach their way out of the proverbial wet Kleenex. Those unfortunates proved magnets for parental scrutiny. I should note not all new teachers lacked ability or ambition. McCook Junior High snared a number of rookies as talented as any I ever taught beside. If only there had been a few more of them.

Speaking of a particular, top heavy, rookie band teacher, quickly nicknamed by the animal on the pockets crowd as "the girl who walks downhill." Like many band instructors, she required students to hand in practice reports on a regular basis. Each report to be certified as accurate and signed by a parent. At fall parent-teacher conferences, the line in front of her lunchroom table stretched around the entire room. She'd handed out zeroes for every missing practice report. Firm, you might say, but justified. Except only a handful of parents had been informed of the requirement. In all the excitement of returning to the classroom, 99% of the band students neglected to carry blank practice reports home or explain their purpose. The band teacher, although young and possessing unusual posture, stuck to her guns. The zeroes stuck. A zero earned in band carried the same weight as a zero earned in math class. GPAs sank. Band students quit in droves. The junior high band program, formerly composed of three concert bands, a jazz band and a marching band, shriveled over time to a single, much diminished concert band.

In addition to Doc's classroom, I shared a temporary vinyl curtain with the 7th-grade English teacher. Approaching retirement age, a bright, funny, grandmotherly woman. The Class from Hell knocked her completely off her bearings. Pencils, pens and miscellaneous objects flew under the curtain into my room. Muffled laughter from beyond the vinyl divide, followed by a grandmotherly voice in full yell. In my shoes, most veteran teachers would ignore such trifling

interruptions and carry on. My classes carried on. No sense inject-
ing myself in the mess next door. Meanwhile, new sets of class rules
appeared periodically on the English teacher's white board.

1. No throwing objects under the curtain.

2. Anyone caught throwing objects under the curtain will spend 10
minutes after school.

3. Anyone caught throwing objects under the curtain a second time
will spend 20 minutes after school.

4. Anyone caught throwing objects in the curtain a third time will
spend 30 minutes after school.

5. Anyone caught laughing after another student throws an object
under the curtain will receive the same punishment as the student who
threw the object.

Other lists of rules covered the usual. Students will be respectful,
followed by an escalating list of punishments. Students will hand in
their homework on time, followed by an escalating list of punishments.
Students will be polite to one another, followed by an escalating list of
punishments. Makes me tired to think about the lists, which had about
as much impact on student behavior as you'd expect. More than one
future prison inmate took each new list of rules as a personal challenge.

The more lists the English teacher posted, the worse her classes behaved and the more she unraveled. Mr. Berry made diplomatic suggestions, but locked into rules and punishments, she couldn't see another
path. And at that stage of the festivities, whether a different approach
would have worked was unlikely. The Class from Hell firmly in the
driver's seat. The bright, funny woman I met the first day of fall classes
had become an angry, distracted version of her former self. Already
qualified for a full pension, come spring she pulled the plug, took the
pension, fled the building. Not the way she hoped to end her career.

I've never been an advocate of formal classroom rules. Why burden a
collegial atmosphere with rules? If you establish a rule, then you have

to think up a suitable consequence. Classroom situations too fluid to conform to rigid rules. What if a kid is having a bad day? Do you want to make it worse by dishing out a predetermined punishment? If a kid went heavy into jerk mode, I might ask him if he was going to make me think up a rule and a nasty punishment for breaking it. And I was warning him ahead of time. If he made me interrupt what I was doing to think up a rule against whatever he was doing, the punishment would be so godawful he couldn't imagine how awful. I can't remember ever being forced to think up a rule, let alone a punishment. The lack of formal rules and suitable punishments also eliminated the need to get to the bottom of every crime. Often the second or third actor is the one detected and punished.

Let's say Jerome is poking Samantha in the back of the head with a ballpoint pen. I might be unaware Samantha has been whispering to Jerome under her breath, telling him he smells funny. Which he probably does. Jerome has been known to trail visual aromas in his wake. But Samantha's whispering represents a vexation. It might not be the first time Samantha picked on Jerome this week. What rule do you formulate and then enforce to cover a complicated, fluid situation?

No formal rule in my classes against poking someone in the back of the head with a ballpoint pen. Which didn't mean the poking was something to be encouraged. The first order of business would be to ask Jerome what he was doing. (Jim Fay 101). Not why are you doing that? Asking the offender the why of a behavior opens up the entire abstract spectrum of physical, geological, climate-related, metaphysical, psychological causation. Chances are, no matter how seriously Jerome considers the question, he won't have a clue why he's poking Samantha in the back of the head. It might be as simple as revenge. He might be feeling grouchy because he missed breakfast. He could be curious in a sciency sort of way about how much ink the skin on the back of Samantha's head will accept. Or more likely, he just feels like doing it. Asking for the why diverts attention to the infinite vagaries of motivation. Much better to ask Jerome what he is doing, help him identify his own behavior.

"Hey, Jerome, what are you doing?" The question sets off a chain of events in Jerome's brain.

"What am I doing? Where was I? Think. Pretty sure I was poking Samantha in the back of the head with my ballpoint pen. That's what I was doing all right. But Mr. Jones probably thinks it was a bad thing."

"Hey, Jerome, do you think you could stop poking Samantha in the back of the head with that ball point pen?" This again directs Jerome's attention to his current behavior. Once he becomes fully cognizant of his behavior, Jerome has to consider the new question, doesn't he? Can he stop poking Samantha with a pen if he chooses to? A question which goes to his fledgling manhood as a stud duck 7th-grade boy. If he can't stop poking Samantha, what will it say about him? He is also being handed a choice, as per Jim Fay 101, giving him some control over the situation. He can decide he indeed has the power to stop poking Samantha's head with a ballpoint pen. Samantha will be happier, his teacher will be happier and he will have demonstrated to one and all he is in charge of his own behavior. Kudos all around. Or he is free to choose door #2, thereby conceding he has no self-discipline and be subject to general ridicule and perhaps even subject to a godawful as yet to be determined punishment. Then there is door #3. Jerome could immediately surrender, take the kudos, wait until the bell rings, catch up with Samantha in the hall as she's being congratulated by her buddies for making Jerome look stupid, give her a sloppy Wet Willie as he passes her.

It was my job to make those difficult choices easier.

By accepting the position in McCook, I avoided lonely nights on a cot in a Franklin classroom. Other aspects of the Franklin assignment might have turned out peachy keen. The principal who interviewed me appeared competent. My Franklin students and colleagues might have been competent. But the job itself would have been a booger. No life outside the school building. The McCook position supplied the stability of a larger school system, a decent wage, adequate funding for reading materials. The job also entailed working under top notch administrators. Previous to my hiring, I'd never met Superintendent Harold Bennett, the man largely responsible for bringing me on board. I knew him only by reputation. My mother, a woman who could read people, held Bennett in high regard.

"Mr. Bennett is a man of integrity. He values good teachers. If your students perform, Mr. Bennett will support you." She was right on all counts.

Bennett bore zero resemblance to bumbling former Bladen Superintendent Dwight. For instance, Bennett knew what he was doing and had the resting demeanor of an exacting professor. An enthusiastic Nebraska State Education Association member, raising teacher wages Bennett's priority #1. He was also keen on offering teachers wide-ranging opportunities to attend workshops and conferences in teachers' subject areas, workshops and conferences of their choosing. Unfortunately, Bennett also ordered up way too many teacher in-services pushing the latest educrat nostrum for what ailed education. I choose to believe had Bennett attended these vacuous, time-wasting workshops himself, he would have inflicted them on his staff less frequently. Except for teacher wages, Bennett was famously careful with the district's money. Bennett's shabby office furniture gave mute testimony to his budget priorities. Bennett believed in hiring the best obtainable teachers (excepting the coaching staff, where he sometimes agreed to hire a successful coach, who might not have been a classroom whiz). He also had our backs. Any parent complaining about a teacher might be given a polite hearing, but the complaint better not be frivolous. Bennett did not suffer fools, nor whiny-pantsed parents. An administrative philosophy any teacher could appreciate.

The fall I arrived, Bennett had four superb administrators in place. Along with Bennett, they composed the brain trust which shaped school policy, put out fires, planned the future. Bennett's administrative team would have been the envy of any school district anywhere. I didn't realize at the time, but Bennett and his team represented a golden age for the McCook Public Schools. Bennett recruited LeRoy Hoehner from a successful superintendency at a smaller school. Hoehner, wired into the upper regions of the Nebraska School Activities Association, served as head principal and liaison to the McCook community. A product of a hardscrabble upbringing (his father died young), Hoehner's athletic prowess at McCook Junior College led to his lifelong partnership with the brainy head cheerleader, a four-year degree, successful high school coaching and eventually a superintendency. Hoehner turned 50 the year I arrived. He remained a force of nature, darkly handsome, tall, athletic. It took no imagination to visualize him clad in helmet and shoulder pads, laying waste to opponents on the gridiron or excelling on the cinder track. Although the almost familial relationship between Bennett and Hoehner was sometimes fraught, their spirited disagreements always mended. Both Hoehner and Warren Everts, the high school principal, formed lasting relationships with students born without silver spoons or much of anything else. Pat Hoehner, the brainy cheerleader and Mr. Hoehner's able partner in every sense, directed the district's gifted programs and special services. Nobody ever ran a better meeting than Pat Hoehner, soliciting opinions, helping participants formulate opinions from random thoughts, forging a consensus, even when none existed. Most importantly, Pat Hoehner's meetings stayed on topic and ended on time. After LeRoy's untimely death, she departed for the University of Nebraska at Kearney's Educational Administration Department, a department she chaired for years, where she turned out a procession of confident, bushy-tailed school administrators. Then there was Mr. Berry, the bright new Junior High principal hire, whose analytical mind worked better than most and who supported his sometimes contrary opinions with quiet tenacity.

Spring semester. Cheerleader tryouts completed and squads selected for the various sports. A disgruntled group of mothers descended on Mr. Hoehner's office. I know this because he kept a second office at the Junior High across the hall from the Junior High principal's office. The same office where teachers filled their coffee cups with wretched coffee (usually diluted with gobs of sugar and carcinogenic faux creamer), and picked up their mail. The mothers' agenda? The wrong side of the tracks girl who'd won a tryout for the wrestling cheer squad needed to be dropped so their daughters wouldn't have to associate with her. Mr. Hoehner heard them out. When he spoke, he didn't leave it at no. He articulated at some length how loathsome he found their behavior. Those of us sipping bad coffee in the office across the hall, ears attuned, had no trouble hearing him. It's been many years, but I don't remember him leaving out any relevant adjectives. The mothers slunk out of the school like the deflated shit weasels they were. A proud day for the McCook Public Schools.

Freewheeling administrative brain trust discussions sometimes left bruises. If you wanted to be heard, you'd better be able to back your opinions with forceful arguments and plenty of evidence. Not a forum where timid snowflakes or weak of thought humans would feel comfortable. Imagine, if you will, a collegial university department, far, far in the distant past, perhaps a history department prior to 1960. Long before enforced herd opinions and strident ideology destroyed academic freedom. Long before tenured professors could be vaporized for opinions that ran counter to the prevailing groupthink. Try visualizing professors socializing with colleagues with differing political views. Imagine professors maintaining friendships with colleagues of opposing opinions who regularly attended faculty parties and engaging them in friendly intellectual donnybrooks. Good luck imagining, but that was Bennett's brain trust in a nutshell. The freedom administrators were granted to argue oppositional views had everything to do with the quality education offered by the McCook Public Schools.

Pat Hoehner's fervid support of the McCook gifted program kept it afloat, even after educrat opinion shifted and gifted programs became viewed as elitist, probably racist and somehow unfair to dumbasses. She saw to it teachers who offered a differentiated curriculum in their advanced classes wanted for nothing. Thanks largely to Pat Hoehner, the value of books in my room soon exceeded $80,000 in 1987 dollars (roughly $227,100 in the current version of chump change). Not all McCook Junior High teachers altered their approach or requirements for advanced classes, viewing the effort as too much work. Incentives did not always trump indolence. Although Pat encouraged and cajoled, motivating a lazy tenured teacher is like pushing on a wet noodle.

A few of the dimmer-bulbed teachers, and I'm pleased to say only a handful, resented bright students, imputing a snobbish attitude. True, students in advanced classes saw their elevated designation as a point of pride. No doubt, some viewed their status as separating them from the hoi polloi. Backyard gardeners know if you plant yellow corn, you get yellow corn. Snobby parents produce snobby children. It's also true students in advanced classes were much smarter than the dim bulb teachers. It was my experience advanced kids enjoyed challenges. Many of them had been bored to madness during their previous years in school. It's possible slothful teachers who failed to challenge their students suffered some push back. After all, advanced classes were advertised as advanced, not the same stuff the kids in regular classes were being offered. Instead of creating a challenging classroom, the resentfuls dug in and chose to hate on their most capable students. Because a union-negotiated salary schedule determined teacher compensation, the resentful sloths were paid the same whether they did their assigned work or not.

McCook Junior High tracked students according to ability, a practice now under fire from those intent on destroying merit-based education. If properly implemented, as it was in McCook, ability tracking allowed teachers to tailor material and approaches to give students their best chance for success. The classifications were not necessarily permanent as they often were in larger, heavily bureaucratized school systems. If assigned to a regular classroom, McCook students could earn their way into an advanced class. Modified (edu jargon for remedial) students could earn their way into a regular classroom, although my modified reading students seldom accepted an offered promotion.

In addition to a flexible class assignment system, making accurate initial student placements based on test scores, grades and teacher recommendations was key. When I arrived on the scene, the middle school reading teachers were schoolmarms in the best sense. They sometimes knew their students' abilities better than the parents did. If they thought a student could do advanced work, the kid could do advanced work. They were never wrong. Not once. They might recommend a kid without toppy reading or IQ test scores because the kid always did whatever it took. I didn't ignore grades or test scores, but I always heavily weighted the middle school teachers' recommendations.

You will never hear me arguing multiple intelligences, some impossible to measure, do not exist. The ace computer hacker or the diesel mechanic who can fix anything may not score highly on conventional IQ tests. The gifts of artists, musicians, tech entrepreneurs or extraordinary athletes might not be subject to accurate measurement. What standardized tests can predict is how well a student will perform in a particular subject area—like reading.

One popular meritocracy-hating theory postulated by vapid educrats and wackadoodle, multi-billion dollar foundations suggests all classrooms should be a Duke's mixture of abilities, undifferentiated by racist constructs like standardized test scores. What happens in practice? Undifferentiated classes sentence gifted students to permanent boredom. No persuasive evidence exists an average kid can magically begin solving complex math problems merely by being assigned to the same classroom with students who can. What is certain is putting a student in position to succeed guarantees better results than placing` a student in position to fail. Any objective person who has studied the precipitous decline of student mastery of reading and math over the past 40 years can measure the damage done by the meritocracy-hating educrats who, when they were students, rarely qualified for an advanced class.

Plagiarism-*I plagiarism to the flag.*

When I recall my time at McCook Junior High, the modified classes spark the warmest memories. To qualify for the class, a student had to be recommended by the middle school reading teacher and score below average on reading and IQ tests. With few exceptions, the modified students arrived in my classroom with an ingrained dislike of school. They had been pushed through the system like so many constipated turds, receiving the poorest grades, become accustomed to teachers chiding them for lack of effort, teachers using them as classroom exhibits for what not to do or what not to be. Many also arrived with the baggage of socio-economic family dysfunction. The girl whose mother pimped her out to transient harvest workers staying at a local motel. The girl whose father was murdered by her best friend's father in a love triangle gone bad. The quiet boy whose mother faithfully attended parent-teacher conferences, but never sober.

The first priority was to create a safe environment. Safe from teachers who despised them, safe, if only for a few hours a week, from ugly stuff at home. Safe from fellow students who could be vicious to those they viewed as social inferiors. As long as they were in my classroom, doing quality work and earning good marks, they didn't have to think about what went on in other classrooms or in the halls or the place they called home.

Not an easy task to change a kid's attitude toward school, especially after 6 or 7 years of frustration and failure. Once more, my savvy mother offered sound advice.

"Most of your modified students will be perfectionists. I know that sounds crazy, but it's true. If they don't do perfect work, which is difficult for them, they'll often throw up their hands and quit. They might not even make an effort on the next assignment. These students too often don't have much support at home. They may be the only responsible person in the household, may be the only stable presence for younger siblings. They are no strangers to chaos. Completing an assignment perfectly makes them feel they have the power to create better outcomes, even for a single class period.

"You need to assign work they can do. Always, and this is vital, give them the questions first. Then have them look for the answers in their assigned reading, which forces them to read, even if they're reluctant readers. Then insist they answer the questions perfectly. As many times as you have to return the assignment for corrections, make them work until it's perfect. Once they've received a 100% on a few assignments, they'll be correcting mistakes on their own. You'll be surprised how eager your students will be to get to your classroom and how much they'll accomplish."

I added a few wrinkles of my own, greeting them warmly as they came in the room like I was happy to see them. Not an act, I was happy to see them, smug enough to think this would be a day a kid's life might be a little brighter. Kids who've been scarred by past school experiences can smell a phony baloney ten miles away. They dearly hate false cheerfulness. They especially hate false praise, the careless "Good job, Traci," when Traci knows she's produced nothing special. Let me do solid work, earn a decent grade and for the love of God, have the good sense to keep your lyin' mouth shut. Please don't spoil my achievement with your cheap praise handed out to deserving and undeserving alike.

I made it a rule never to praise modified students, no matter how well they performed. The class required top performance, perfect work. If they performed, they earned top grades, reward enough. If they fell short, I wasn't shy about pointing out errors, errors they were duty bound to fix. Most of them appreciated being held to a high standard, instead of being awarded barely passing grades for crap work.

Modified kids had a heightened need for acceptance. Not phony, platitudinous praise, but genuine acceptance, which acknowledged their flaws and annoying eccentricities. This is where a teacher who likes kids, no matter how unlikeable, can build bridges. Taking the time to give a casual "How you doin'?" and listening to the answer to the kid who is scuffling, volunteering a kid whose home situation blew up last night to perform a routine classroom duty, like checking attendance. Although it would likely get you thrown in jail in the current environment, I also handed out reassuring pats on the back. Some kids connect best in a physical way. They've learned talk is cheap. A casual hand on the shoulder tells them you accept them and their baggage in a form they can process. If a kid complained of feeling sick, I checked foreheads for excess heat. A hot forehead meant the kid went to the nurse's office. I'm not recommending anyone teaching in the present tense try this. Too many predator teachers, both male and female, under the bridge. Too many of those predators have not been hanged.

Corey came to school late—*every day. Neither his meth head father, last seen in county court for starving six dogs to death, nor his father's meth head girlfriend, nor his meth head sister, nor her meth head boyfriend could roust their druggie asses out of bed in time to haul Corey to school. Corey loitered on the sidewalk outside for several hours after school, hot weather or cold, before a family member remembered to fetch him. He became something of a pet. Doesn't take much with kids like Corey. You ask them how their day is going. Ask if they approve of the day's weather. Ask them if they've ever considered moving to Alaska. Ten minutes later they're still talking. Next thing you know, they're following you around like a runt of the litter pup.*

Corey carried a playlist in his head. Not any music genre you'd recognize. He composed fresh discordant melodies every day, humming them remorselessly while he went about his business. If interrupted, he soon resumed humming, not where he left off like you'd expect, but with a brand new tuneless tune. He had a million of 'em.

Science Teacher Mr. Smock's annual Conservation Day in the park. Groups of 7th-graders attended sessions hosted by wildlife officers and rangeland specialists. They also played softball. I caught for both teams, also called balls (many) and strikes (few). Neither team volunteered to accept Corey as a teammate. He couldn't hit a ball if it were glued to his bat. Didn't run so much as stumble. Couldn't catch a ball. If you threw it in his glove it'd fall out. I arbitrarily assigned Corey to a team, shushed potential bitching with my fiercest glare. Don't you dare even think it. Corey struck out every time, missing the ball by a couple of feet. Someone upstairs was looking out for him, because nobody hit a ball within fifty feet when he was standing in the furthest reaches of right field.

On his way to the waiting bus at the end of the day a humming Corey stopped by, big grin.

"You're a really good catcher, Mr. Jones."

If you've been the only kid in a class without an appropriate nickname, you know how bereft you felt. The nickname, bestowed by the teacher or classmates, often performs the miracle of making a misfit kid feel he's somebody special. The uncoordinated kid who slip slides into an inelegant landing on his way to the pencil sharpener might become known as "Crash." A taller kid might become known as "Tree." A diminutive kid who wears glasses and a studious expression might be called "The Prof." Even if the pipsqueak isn't a deep thinker, he will see the humor and delight in the elevated status. A small brown kid with arms like toothpicks could become Jesse "The Body" after famous wrestler Jesse "The Body" Ventura. By the way, giving a nickname to a 7th-grade girl is just asking for trouble. 7th-grade girls are fragile by definition. "Skeets" or "Kid" might work, but woe to anyone who assigns a girl the sort of nickname a boy would wear with pride. Don't, for example, expect optimum results by nicknaming the girl with a chronic cold "Kleenex Girl."

Inserting my students' names in tests and study materials helped keep them fully engaged. Think about it. You're working your way through a quiz and right there in black and white is a multiple choice question with your name as one possible answer. Not something you're used to seeing in a quiz, is it? Let's say students are slogging their way through *The Outsiders*. Perhaps not great literature, but 7th-grade reading class was designed to improve reading skills, not create sophisticated literary critics. At the time, most kids, even reluctant readers, could identify with the Tulsa hard luckers portrayed in *The Outsiders*. It might be the first book that fully engaged them, the first book they didn't stop reading when they'd finished their daily assignment. During the first weeks of school, it was vital students become accustomed to 30-40 page daily assignments. Much easier to condition them if they liked the book.

The daily quiz over *The Outsiders* material might include questions like these:

Ponyboy Curtis is the kid brother of (a. Two Bit b. Dallas c. Tree d. Darry e. Steve).

We learn (a. Crash b. Johnny c. Cherry d. Bridget e. The Prof) is spying on the Socs for the Greasers.

The greasers fight with the rival Socs led by (a. Jerome and Wilbur b. Bob and Randy c. Donald and Steve d. Sonny and Cher e. Jesse "The Body" and Slim Whitman).

Revamping the daily quizzes each year to include new names and nicknames might have taken extra time, but well worth it if kids chuckled while they were taking a quiz. If you detect laughter during a chapter quiz, your students might anticipate the next one with something other than dread.

As the year unfolded and the students became more accustomed to their reading teacher, I came to value dependable routines, especially for the modified classes. Experiencing unpredictable chaos in their home lives, the students appreciated the rituals of Monday vocabulary/spelling sentences, Tuesday, Wednesday, Thursday reading assignments and quizzes, Friday spelling tests and, if available, a snippet of the movie version of the book they were reading. And, once in a blue moon, Krispy Kreme doughnuts for everyone.

Just to mix things up and create additional challenges, I sometimes required students to begin each vocabulary sentence the same way.

Example: The sticky waffleman…which might lead a sentence like this:

Discreet-*The sticky waffleman* <u>*discreeted*</u> *behind a bush.*

Monogamy-*The sticky waffleman committed* <u>*monagamy.*</u>

Some assignments required geographical place names.

Rwanda-*Then the sticky waffleman went to* <u>*Rwanda*</u> *and got eaten by missionary cannibals.*

A Christmas season prompt.

Euphemism-*"Drat those pesky elves," said Santa. "Oh,* <u>*euphemism!*</u> *They broke Mrs. Claus' lamp."*

Students sometimes had to include the name of a famous person or historical figure in each sentence.

Louis Pasteur-<u>*Louis Pasteur*</u> *ain't gonna be saving Old Yeller's life anytime soon.*

President William Jefferson Clinton-<u>*President William Jefferson Clinton's*</u> *most obvious foibles include pretty young women with big mouths and a ball-breaking wife.*

Savage-*Tom Cruise's woodchuck-like teeth could tear through human flesh like the teeth of a* <u>*savage*</u>*.*

John Wilkes Booth-<u>*John Wilkes Booth*</u> *was a better president than Jimmy Carter.*

Methuselah-<u>*Methuselah*</u> *was what you call an old fart.*

Richard Nixon-<u>*Richard Nixon*</u> *is a dumbass.*

Mozart-<u>*Mozart*</u> *was a famous composer. What's he doing now? Decomposing?*

Speaking of Mozart, his music became a staple of 7th-grade reading classes. Once the students dug into their reading assignment, Mozart,

Bach, Chopin, but mostly Mozart, provided background music. Even before the mass frazzling of kid brains by personal electronic devices, student brains were well frazzled. Video games, blaring televisions, constant telephoning all contributed to chronic attention deficits. Once books were opened and defrazzling music descended on the classroom, concentration improved. By Mozart's second or third day, the music became an ingrained prompt for the brain to turn off competing stimuli. I would have even been more impressed if Mozart hadn't already proved magical in classrooms across the country.

About once a fortnight, a student volunteered to bring "better" music from a private collection. You can imagine how well that would have turned out.

The famous mummified Gorham lizard of song and legend did not survive the move to McCook. He or she disintegrated into lizardy powder a few miles south of the Kansas-Nebraska border. Consequently, lizard-inspired pep rallies did not survive. As a poor substitute for the lizard, the classroom began adding novelties, processed food items the kids could examine every day, check on their health or lack thereof.

A Twinkie on a small paper plate proved to have a shelf life of nearly 20 years. Intense summer heat during year four melted the marshmallow filling, which pooled under the Twinkie, where it grew green mold, eventually hardening into a jade-colored, concrete-like substance. A plate of McDonald's French Fries, when it reached year 15, appeared as fresh and tasty as the day it went on the shelf. A slice of Pizza Hut hamburger/cheese pizza showed not a hint of deterioration after spending 12 years on public exhibit. The humble Oscar Mayer hot dog, after 10 years of unrefrigerated existence, as pristine as the day it was born. Pretty much nobody speculated that the mysterious, effective embalming mechanism in these items might be a rich mixture of wholesome vitamins and essential minerals. The justification for the exhibits? Primarily, the entertainment value and convincing junior high students their instructor had a screw loose. If they gained a degree of cynicism regarding processed food, so much the better.

To further encourage students to believe their reading instructor had a loose screw, I added a couple of regular memes to the mix. Any news of an outbreak of poultry-related food poisoning went up on the bulletin board. And if you, like most conscientious reading teachers, have kept track of poultry poisoning events, you know there has seldom been a shortage, due in part to the hard sciency fact that all members of the poultry family pee through their feathers. During a rare poultry poisoning news outage, a possibly fictionalized news item might be posted. Typical news story:

"Four Dead, 27 Critical After Local Chicken Barbecue"

HUNTSVILLE, TX (AP)—Texas authorities questioned victims and witnesses Friday after an oil company employee chicken barbecue resulted in projectile diarrhea and dehydration for 200 attendees.

As a result of the most severe salmonella outbreak in nearly a month, four were known dead and 27, some of them 7th-graders, remained in intensive care.

Dr. Wyatt Service, head of internal medicine at Huntsville Methodist Hospital, warned citizens to be on high alert. "Until we discover the source of the chicken and determine how it was prepared, residents would be well-advised to avoid all contact with poultry."

Clare Mooberry, head of public relations for The National Poultry Council, said there is no scientific evidence poultry poses a health threat. "Doctors frequently jump to conclusions and make up stuff when fatalities are involved," Mooberry said.

Mooberry declined comment when asked if recent poultry-linked salmonella outbreaks would result in Congressional inquiries into the poultry processing industry.

I have always found the sight of otherwise sentient humans masticating chewing gum like rabid Holsteins personally offensive. If you want to appear a brain-deprived MO-ron, throw some chewing gum in the hatch and chomp. To discourage the disgusting, rude, mentally debilitating gum-chewing habit (strictly illegal in the reading classroom), news items went up on the bulletin board describing the latest scientific research from Yale University or UCLA Medical School, revealing the dangers of addiction and systemic poisoning from habitual gum chewing. Typical headline:

"Yale Med School Researchers Connect Swallowed Chewing Gum to Fatal Appendicitis"

Backed up by hard news:

"Chewing Gum Blamed in Latest Appendicitis Attack"

Baltimore, MD (AP)—A 13-year-old Baltimore girl died Monday after undergoing an unsuccessful emergency appendectomy. Holly Azula, former 7th-grade student at St. Matthew's Junior High School, was reported by her parents to be a three-pack-a-day gum chewer.

Dr. Adam Wheatly, head resident at Charity Hospital, said Azula's appendix, before it exploded, was enlarged to 20 times normal size. "We're talking about a large cantaloupe," said Wheatly.

Azula's fatal condition is the latest in a recent spate of gum-impared appendix found in preadolescent girls. Last month, identical twin Phoenix sisters suffered exploded appendix within 24 hours of each other. The distraught mother described years of gum dependency.

Speaking of loose screws, I'm remembering Amberette, a mosquito-sized, fart-in-a-skillet member of my first-period class. After school, Amberette and her brother donned bicycle helmets and played outside in a violent hailstorm. She said they had a blast. Connecting with junior high students often goes more smoothly if they believe their instructor capable of just about anything.

Precise-In gymnastics, the cowardnations must be precise.

The heavily promoted Friday spelling tests, the 20 words from the week's reading assignments, the same 20 words used in sentences which demonstrated mastery of meaning and usage, always included

216

five bonus words. Bonus words might be chosen from the frequently misspelled, like definitely or Albuquerque or Punxsutawney Phil or kaffeeklatsch. Or it could be random names in the news, like Arnold Schwarzenegger, John "The Wienie" Elway, Picabo Street, Wile E. Coyote, Duke basketball coach Mike Krzyzewski or Theodor Seuss Geisel. Chappaquiddick and Mary Jo Kopechne also made frequent appearances. The upcoming high school athletic opponent often made the list. With a twist. Instead of the Sidney High School Red Raiders, students might be asked to spell the Sidney High School Doofuses. Instead of the Lexington High School Minutemen or Minute Maids, they might be asked to take a crack at the Lexington High School Quivering Sycophants. Just another way of boosting school spirit by throwing sand in an opponent's face prior to the contest. And, be honest, who among us wouldn't be delighted if challenged to spell Lexington High School Quivering Sycophants?

Heinous-*Jerome got something shoved up his* _heinous_.

Then there was the money. Cold hard cash. Coin of the realm. Dough re me. Spelling the 20 assigned words perfectly earned the student a shiny new quarter, paid on the spot, slapped on the kid's desk with considerable force. The lucky devil who spelled both the assigned twenty and the five mystery bonus words earned one dollar and twenty-five cents, also paid out with emphasis. Might not seem like much, but despite the generous McCook wages, I had to watch my pennies. I well remember one unlucky Friday when too many 7th-graders intuited and studied up on the week's bonus words. I had to run to the bank over the noon hour to refresh the cash supply. You better believe the next week's bonus words were boogers.

Mid-semester during my first year in McCook, I added the Mattie E. Jones 7th-grade Spelling Award to the incentives. The student who missed the fewest spelling words during the year had their name affixed to a handsome walnut plaque and earned a $50 savings bond. My smart mother won the 1927 Franklin County spelling bee as a 12-year-old, earning a trip to the state contest, where she finished in 16th place. The woman could flat spell. Naming the award in her honor meant kids were curious about the identity of Mattie E. Jones. A good excuse to talk about my remarkable mother, who rode a horse to attend school and later rode a horse to teach school. A woman born on a windswept Wyoming homestead south of Devil's Tower, who later worked her magic with struggling readers in several schools. When Mom found out I was fronting a savings bond, she insisted on supplying the cash portion of the award. She wrote the check every year until she died, when I resumed funding the award. Winners typically missed two or three spellings during the year. Some years the winning student missed none. 720 spelling words, each one spelled correctly. One year, two students tied with perfect results. Two $50 bonds instead of one. The growing list of names on the prominently displayed plaque stimulated competition and diligent study habits. The contest sometimes came down to the last spelling test, as I often reminded my students.

Obtuse-*The angel is _obtuse_.*

In the late 1980s, McCook was and had been an athletic powerhouse, particularly in football and track. The community supported the athletic teams with a degree of enthusiasm familiar to those who follow Texas schoolboy football. Although Mr. Bennett saw to it the music and speech and drama departments were fed and watered, the athletic department had first call on resources, the newest buses, liberal budgets for assistant coaches and their salaries. No effort or expense spared when hiring a high school football coach. The newest one a refugee from coaching Texas schoolboy football. Girl's sports not so much. The new volleyball coach hired because, according to rumor, the athletic director thought she was hot.

At the five week mark of the first semester, when an unexpected flood of down slips arrived, multiple voices suggested students might not be focusing on academics. The building administrators called a meeting of the Junior-Senior High faculty to brainstorm solutions. Mr. Recent Hire 7th-grade Reading Teacher listened to a dozen half-baked suggestions. I knew how to fix this. Gorham mandated after-school study halls for everyone on the down list until they weren't. Resolved the problem in days. No students, including athletes exempt. Coaches not only supported Beeman's after-school study hall, but encouraged their athletes to get their grades up—now, if not sooner. Running lines and extra push-ups can be great motivators. Simple, effective. I should keep my mouth shut. I had no standing, no credibility. Worse, I would be recommending a solution from a foreign school district nobody had heard of. Let's just say McCook could be at least as parochial as the second most parochial community on the planet. Knowing better, I stood up and made my pitch to the teachers, most of whom did not know me or care to become better acquainted.

I barely finished expounding to the assembled blank faces, when the district athletic director jumped up.

"Am I to understand this would this apply to athletes?"

"Of course."

His face went purple. "It's always the athletes. Everyone picks on the athletes. You gotta problem, it's the athletes' fault. How can teams practice if half the athletes are sitting in study hall? Answer me that!"

He had me there, didn't he? The Hotshot New 7th-grade Reading Teacher's suggestion— DOA. Lesson learned. The first and last time I made a suggestion in a building meeting. Chat privately with an administrator? Many times. Casually float an idea with a colleague? You bet. But the first meeting was the canary in the lithium mine for subsequent teacher meetings. The loudest brayers almost always dominated. I learned to mute myself in meetings, conduct any serious business privately. None of my colleagues subsequently inquired as to why I never spoke at faculty meetings. Perhaps their interest in my well-informed opinions had been exhausted.

It must have cost him a fortune, but the AD later apologized, allowed he'd been a little rough on me. No shit. I would characterize our relationship over the next 15 years as civil. A competent athletic director and well-regarded track coach, I came to respect his talents and dedication. I should mention he did not wear golf shirts with little animals on the pockets. Snappy dresser. When he wasn't wearing high-dollar dress shirts with high-dollar ties and high-dollar slacks and high-dollar shoes, he wore high dollar red polo shirts with custom embroidered McCook Bison logos on the pockets.

Poignant-*After all, Max is a very sentinsive guy. It was no wonder he balled for the whole day when I read the <u>poignant</u> part of the story.*

Each succeeding year teaching in McCook became more rewarding, until it didn't. The next three 7th-grade English instructors came from the "write gobs and submit your writing to classmates for comment and revision" school of teaching writing. They worked miracles. Not only did basic student writing skills improve, but creativity bloomed as well. High reading scores on achievement tests joined by high scores on English usage tests. With science and social studies scores average or above, the 7th-grade faculty had a bit of chest-thumping *esprit de corps* going on.

Math. Always the math. 7th-grade math achievement test scores stagnated. Didn't matter who did the teaching. What the 7th-grade math teachers had in common was youth. I don't pretend to understand anything beyond basic arithmetic and therefore am not the best witness. Monitoring the 7th-grade math classes far above my pay grade and none of my business. According to student and parent complaints, 7th-grade math teachers weren't as interested in correct answers as in how well students could describe the process by which they arrived at the answer. This required a degree of abstract thinking which fit uneasily in the partially developed 7th-grade brain. The teachers also struggled to articulate what it was they were teaching. Long gone the memorization of multiplication tables I grew up with or anything which smacked of rote learning. The math fact flash cards I practiced with in elementary school not in evidence. Everything became fluid, an ongoing process which stretched far into forever—plus infinity.

I will stipulate it's always dangerous to assume. I assume the math teachers were only teaching what they were taught. Probably teaching out of a spiffy new model textbook chock a block with the latest edu math fad. It wasn't that some 7th-grade math teachers didn't take the job seriously and kept kids after school for extra help, worried their students "just weren't getting it." However, one rookie teacher actively discouraged questions and refused to help, happy to shut off her lights and flee the building when the clock struck four. Instead of changing gears or questioning their training, the young math teachers stayed the course, no matter how much frustration they created for students and parents, no matter how dismal the achievement test scores. Mrs. Hoehner, who could teach a doorknob passable math skills, and Mr. Berry tried and failed to right the ship. Parent-teacher conferences saw lines to the 7th-grade math teacher *du jour's* table stretched to the wall, then doubled and redoubled. Many parents abandoned the line and left for home in a mood. Parents unlucky enough to reach the head of the line went away scratching their heads, often after a 20-minute conversation. Following multiple years of frustration, after the standard of futility had been set in concrete, fewer parents waited in line. What would be the point? Of course, maybe discouraging disgruntled parents was the whole idea.

The math test scores would have shown disappointing progress even had the teachers been more flexible. The 6th-grade math teacher, whose students' scores the 7th-grade test scores were measured against, the best math teacher in the system. No student escaped her classroom without "getting it," whatever the hell it was they were supposed to get. She possessed matchless awareness of her classroom, sensing the instant a student's attention went off the rails. If a student's understanding hit an obstacle, she noticed and bookmarked the event. If a student's brow remained furrowed for any length of time, she moved in to ease the student over the hump. By the end of each class period, every student had mastered today's task and was ready for the next. Unless they weren't, in which case, they came in after school. Learning math, as you know, is like acquiring a foreign language. If you miss a step along the way, you're screwed. No wonder her students' achievement test scores sparkled. Those scores would have made almost any 7th-grade math teacher's efforts appear disappointing by comparison. She was that good. The young 7th-grade teacher disciples of the newest edufad in math instruction and their unlucky students never had a chance.

Fortunately, the 8th and 9th-grade math instructors usually rectified the damage done in 7th-grade. Not an easy task catching students up to where they were supposed to be after they returned in the fall, then securing adequate progress in acquiring the current year's math skills. The 8th and 9th-grade math teachers couldn't have been more different. One was a guy, the other wasn't. One had a well-developed, dry sense of humor. The other chewed on pickles. But they had important strengths in common: a clear idea of what their students should learn and the willpower to make damn sure they learned it.

It's a wonder any adolescent girls make it to adulthood. Changing bodies, self-loathing, self-doubt, too often create a depressed kid who would just as soon be someplace else.

Surprise and shock when Ginnie killed herself with a shotgun. No one claimed enough knowledge to have staged an intervention, even though she checked some boxes. Parental split. Family history of mental illness. Recent parting from a boyfriend. Always a top student, her grades slipped. A previous attempt only a few friends knew about. From her time in my classroom, I remembered a self-effacing but ambitious student. A member in good standing of the Class from Hell, she occupied a position on the fringes of a power group of girls. Kept her head down. Avoided being singled out for either admiration or disdain. In high school, she grew into a graceful but unathletic kid with good grades and average looks. If you're an unathletic McCook girl with good grades, average looks and family issues, you just might be a candidate to join the 20% of adolescent girls who've made a suicide plan.

McCook no stranger to suicide. Four teenagers, two boys, two girls, took their lives during my teaching tenure. This before the toxic influence of social media, prior to the introduction of the deadly iPhone, decades before the recent plague years, which bumped up teen suicides by 50%. In the wake of Ginnie's death, the community underwent intense self-examination. The impact on the school staff heightened by knowledge of Ginnie's gentle nature and the brutal method she chose. Not that we wouldn't have second-guessed ourselves absent those two factors. It's what you do. Why didn't we see the signs? Why didn't we get her help? Surely she'd hinted about her plans to someone.

Not hinted exactly, but a few close friends knew she was in trouble. After the fact, they blamed themselves, one or two decided they should join her as an act of contrition and solidarity. The school psychologist and school counselors went to work, heroic work—round-the-clock work. No lecturing. Intensive listening. They refused to give up until they'd convinced the last holdout her life could go on without betraying Ginnie's memory.

McCook Junior High lacked the Christmas traditions of the smaller schools where I'd taught. The last day before Christmas vacation, Bladen High School and Gorham Junior-Senior High Institute hosted all-school celebrations lasting most of the afternoon—board games, desultory carol singing, teacher-supplied treats, the ever-popular joke gift exchange. At Gorham, festivities included a grilled hamburger feast with Coach Tubby serving as head chef. Most McCook teachers celebrated during individual classes with candy and cookies, maybe a carol or two. But all school gatherings the day before vacation in the school library didn't exist. Had a McCook version of Lyle Kyle wished to incarcerate school children until one of them confessed to a felony, the logistics of locking every classroom door and interrogating the prisoners would have proved daunting.

Lacking a McCook rendition of Lyle Kyle, it was up to the rookie reading teacher to establish a distinctive holiday tradition. Following their last reading class before Christmas vacation, as each student scurried out of my classroom, they received, in lieu of cookies or candy, an official form to be filled out by a parent or guardian. Students were required to return in January with signed forms if they wished to collect the reward of an unimaginable number of bonus points. Many students forgot. Those who remembered to submit the forms the first week in January received a promissory note for an unimaginable number of bonus points.

AFFIDAVIT OF CLAIM

State of Nebraska

County of Red Willow

I _____, the undersigned parent or legal guardian and affiant within and for the County and State aforesaid, deposes and says that

(1)   _____ _____ is the (son, daughter, legal ward) of
_____ _____.

(2) (he, she, legal ward) is the student of Mr. Jones' ___ period reading class.

(3) (he, she, legal ward) spent the entire holiday vacation goofing off, sleeping in, staying up late, laughing too hard, and engaging in too many examples of lethargy to count.

(4) (he, she, legal ward) has not cleaned the house, scrubbed toilets, washed dishes or (his, her, legal ward's) own dirty clothes.

This affiant is familiar with the rules and regulations of 7th-grade Reading class, that according the said rules and regulations said Student is required to goof off during the entire two-week holiday vacation. Said affiant attests said Student, _____, goofed off during the entire holiday vacation and is entitled to a yet to be determined amount of extra credit, extra credit now due and owing and unpaid to said Student after the allowance of all just credits, deductions, and set-offs.

_____
Signature

Subscribed and sworn to this ____ day of January, AD 19__.

The purpose of the affidavits, which remained a mystery to a few parents, was to officially recognize the hard work most of my students produced during the school year. Lofty class expectations meant most students devoted considerable after-school time to their reading studies. They didn't require my encouragement to goof off during Christmas vacation, although implying they did served as recognition of the work they'd done that fall. The affidavits also paid homage to the average 7th-grader's keen appreciation of silliness. According the Harvard University School of Education, it's near impossible to foster too much silliness in a 7th-grade classroom.

The golden era of Harold Bennett and his talented brain trust too good to last. A series of unfortunate events prematurely extinguished the natural progression which should have morphed seamlessly from Mr. Bennett's successful tenure into Mr. Hoehner's.

If school boards take their responsibilities seriously, the #1 priority should be hiring the best available superintendent. The next priority should be making sure the superintendent is performing adequately. Akin to the old adage, it's better to put all your eggs in one basket, because you only have to watch one basket. But for goodness sake, don't take your eyes off that basket.

Even the most dedicated and responsible basket-watching school boards can be subverted by a determined crank or two. Maybe the crank's kid didn't make the starting five. Maybe the crank flunked geometry in high school. Maybe the crank is perpetually angry. If they're persistent and loud enough, they can sometimes sway the entire board into making unwise decisions. Given sufficient stubborn irresponsibility on the part of the crank and a willingness of other board members to placate the crank, the destruction of a well-functioning school system can be accomplished in months, not years.

For much of Mr. Bennett's superintendency he worked with above average school boards. Not only did they watch the basket, but if called upon, contributed in ways both measured and knowledgeable. Patrons of the McCook school district and most teachers did not realize how lucky they were. When two of the most competent board members retired, less talent and mean-spirited personal agendas filled the vacancies. One new member's primary agenda item was speeding up Mr. Bennett's retirement date. Nobody claimed to know the source of his grudge, although Mr. Bennett had a backbone made of titanium. An upstart school board member making ignorant suggestions for immediate changes wouldn't necessarily persuade Mr. Bennett to drop everything and jump on board. Bennett, nearing his planned retirement date, decided the new aggravation wasn't worth the bother and pulled the plug. The crank decided McCook should hire a search firm, make sure the best possible candidates weren't overlooked. The crank insisted the school board conduct an open and far-ranging superintendent search. The other board members, bowing to the loudest brayer, hired one of the two busiest superintendent search firms in the state.

Things proceeded down a predictable path. The search firm cashed the school district's check for several thousands of dollars. Administrators seeking new positions submitted resumes and, in some cases, substantial cash payments to the search firm. The search firm made multiple visits to McCook. First, they queried school board members on what qualities they sought in a candidate. White marker boards much in evidence to record brainstorming results. Additional visits to poll teachers and parents on their druthers. Not satisfied if the school board, teachers, and parents offered extemporaneous opinions, the search firm's polling process injected prefabricated, nothing-burger questions to shape the results.

Should the new McCook superintendent have strong communication skills?

Who exactly would disagree?

Should the new McCook superintendent be a whiz-bang in developing and implementing new curriculum?

Who exactly would say, "No way, Chester?"

Should the new McCook superintendent have a strong background in preparing budgets and financial reports?

226

Nah, we want a sup who doesn't know a spreadsheet from a cantaloupe.

I remain bitter my questions did not show up in the poll results:

"Should the new McCook superintendent be a thief?"

"Should the new McCook superintendent have his lips attached to the rear bumper of the Nebraska State Department of Meaningless Jargon?"

"Should the search firm make damn sure the new McCook superintendent does not have three dozen skeletons rattling around in his closet? For instance, should the new superintendent be in the habit of paying his bills on time with checks that don't bounce? Should the new superintendent have a clean criminal record?"

Guess which key qualifications, according to the search firm's vote tabulations, the school board, teachers and parents chose? Bingo, you win a Shetland pony.

The search firm's next order of business? Narrow the field of candidates to a manageable number, like three. Back at search firm headquarters, they compared candidates with the qualities listed by the McCook patrons. This process did not, of course, narrow the field. Any candidate with an administrative certificate and a pulse could boast of having the desired pre-determined qualities. Since the search firm didn't bother with serious background checks, any two-bit grifter/child molester/great uncle molester could make the cut. Inevitably, the search firm turned to the money question. Which candidate paid the firm the most money? As a general rule, the less attractive the candidate, the more money the candidate paid the search firm. Sometimes truly awful candidates paid thousands over multiple years. If they didn't land a job this year, they were encouraged to try again next year. If a failed candidate became discouraged and threatened to try his or her luck elsewhere, he or she might move into the coveted top three category for some lucky school district's search, guaranteeing, at the very least, an interview with a school board.

More accomplished candidates who could pick and choose between quality schools represented a more limited reward for the search firm.

For those candidates, one job application and done. Placing a compelling candidate an easy, inexpensive task compared to finding a job for some has-been with a nothing resume and too much baggage. The baggage carriers cost more to service, so it made perfect sense to charge them a higher rate.

The McCook School board chose to replace competent Harold Bennett with a simple protozoan. Why deliberately choose a candidate destined to flounder? Because the resident school board crank with the loudest bray wanted a superintendent he could dominate. No more Mr. Bennetts with brains and a backbone. The board granted Mr. Hoehner, Bennett's longtime heir apparent, a courtesy interview, but only for the appearance of a fair and open hiring process. The crank had his heart set on a compliant invertebrate for a superintendent, and he badgered the other board members until he got what he wanted.

The Mr. Klaus who welcomed us to fall teacher's meetings had no discernible administrative skills beyond a vacant smile. Soft, squishy-looking guy, speaking from a podium in the lunch room directly under a huge gob of calcified pink bubble gum. Said gum attached to that very spot on the same ceiling tile for as many years as I'd witnessed McCook superintendents welcoming us to school each fall. The tenacious gum outlasted every superintendent during my 20-year tenure at McCook Junior High. For all I know, it's still welcoming faculty members every fall.

Did I mention the English language did not come easily to Mr. Klaus? A harsh contrast to Mr. Bennett, who spoke in clear, concise sentences, the meaning of which could not be mistaken. Whatever random, nonsensical remarks Klaus intended to share during his welcoming speech did not emerge in translatable form. Whenever he stopped to think, which was always, he stared down at the lectern until a new batch of babble erupted. To his credit, the babble had a non-threatening, slightly musical quality. Although it wasn't possible to know for certain, the sounds he made indicated he liked all of us very much and wasn't going to fire all of us like certain infamous Bladen superintendents. (See Brommer, Richard).

During succeeding weeks, word circulated Klaus might be less of a cipher than we assumed from his first attempt at public speaking. The guy could delegate. Anything he didn't understand or know how to do, which covered most of his assigned tasks, he shoved on someone else's plate. Mr. and Mrs. Hoehner and other staff members were soon burdened with most of the superintendent's usual chores in addition to their regular duties. The district's business continued to be minded. Unfortunately, Mr. Klaus failed to remove himself completely from decision-making. Had he done so, the district's aimless drift and one fateful administrative hire might have been averted.

Klaus's tenure ended only when the board eased him out the door. Had they not done so, he might have delegated his ass off until he reached retirement age. School boards should be able to fire superintendents at will. No tenure law, at least not yet, protects Nebraska administrators. In practice, a school board with a reputation for firing superintendents, especially after a brief time on the job, can earn the reputation of being a rogue school board. Once the board earns the dreaded rogue rating, future hirings of administrators or even teachers can become difficult. Shedding the rogue label often takes years, long after the current board goes on to its reward, a key reason school boards tend to be cautious in dismissing superintendents, no matter how dismal. Not infrequently, a healthy severance package and a pile of positive recommendations will accomplish the task without repercussions. However, the process can involve delicate diplomacy, which may not be in every school board's skill set.

Klaus left behind no multitudes weeping copiously at the loss of his services. Although he hadn't earned anyone's intense dislike. He was too vacuous, too harmless, a genial, roundish blob of incompetence. The board's new superintendent search strove for less doofus and more competency. After the now familiar search process, with money changing hands, complete with white marker boards, brainstorming sessions galore and suspect polling numbers, the board made a sound choice. The hiring of Mr. Higgins, a well-qualified candidate, much admired in the smaller neighboring town where he'd served as school superintendent for several years, promised to return the McCook schools if not their former glory, at least a facsimile. The only barrier to Higgins' success? The high school principal, a particularly nasty form of bowel cancer, Klaus hired on his way out the door. Not Higgins, nor the next superintendent ever managed to control him or get rid of him.

Ignoramus-*Wade is an* *ignoramus*, *but without the inteligents.*

229

Ormly Gumfudgin, at the time the world's only living bazooka player and world-class chili judge, eventually challenged desiccated lizards, moldering Twinkies, and pristine McDonald's artifacts for classroom ascendancy. Ormly became a component of many a spelling sentence and made regular appearances on the list of bonus spelling words. (Close your eyes right this second. Try to spell Ormly Gumfudgin. Not as easy as you thought, is it?) Ormly proved both elusive and wise. Kids sometimes blamed Ormly for stealing their homework. Ormly often took credit for Krispy Kreme doughnut surprises. Ormly might be invoked to solve a complicated problem. "How the heck would Ormly deal with this?" If his name hadn't come up in a while, a kid might wonder what Ormly was doing these days.

If Ormly were still alive he'd be over 100 years old. Wherever he is, I hope he's still playing the bazooka and gifting nutritious Krispy Kreme doughnuts to 7th-graders.

Effluent- *Ormly Gumfudgin is <u>effluent</u> and has a fancy house.*

As much as I admired Mr. Bennett and his administrative team, it was difficult to suppress annoyance when they saluted a few too many times when the short-on-thought educrats in Lincoln ran a "new and improved" stupid idea up the pole. Mr. Berry shared my cynicism. He'd also seen these lame movies before. I suspect he did his persistent best during administrative team meetings to deflate enthusiasm. If he was ever once successful in dissuading the group, I never knew. Why would otherwise sensible, intelligent people give the time of day to any fad the brain-dead educrats in Lincoln promoted? Years later, I've come to believe the Bennett team, absent Mr. Berry, desired to be viewed by the State Department of Meaningless Jargon as team-playing progressives. You never knew when the school might find itself in need of educrat forbearance. If one of your teachers failed to obtain the proper credentials over the summer, you might need a waiver so the course she taught wasn't held against you. The State Department of Meaningless Jargon determined the spending of huge sums. Not an insignificant consideration when an administrator was deciding whether or not to sacrifice the school on the altar of a stupid idea. If the educrats thought your school could be relied upon to support this week's edufad, appointments to various statewide advisory committees and study groups would follow. You and your school would have a seat at the top table, presumably nudging state education policies in a good direction.

Given an invitation to attend two days of Six Traits Writing Assessment training in the Junior High cafeteria, I declined. No appetite for two days immersing in the latest edu-cure-all from the State Department of Meaningless Jargon. Our most recent state educrat-sponsored in-service, conducted by a "High-Performance Learning" nincompoop from Kansas City, still grated. Six hours of leaden lecture on the consummate evils of lecture-style teaching.

Six Traits. The title alone raised suspicion, reminiscent of check-out line tabloid cover nostrums. Six Ways to Lose Six Pounds in Six Days. Six Sure-Fire Ways to Keep Your Lover's Attention. Six Low-Cal Lunch Tips. Six Clues Your Lover's Attention Is Not Only Wandering, but Presently Traveling to Las Vegas with Your Best Friend. And what writing genius concluded the English language could be divided into six easily discerned subspecies? Why not ten? Fifty? Why any finite number?

The Six Traits creators advised writing instructors to assign the same value to Content (Trait #1) as to Conventions (Trait #6) or Word Choice (Trait #3). Creativity, a hard rascal to define, let alone measure on a rubric, did not make the cut, not even at #7. Once I absorbed the introductory Six Traits materials, I ran a Flannery O'Connor short story through the rubric. Didn't bother with William Faulkner or James Joyce. I chose a representative O'Connor short story, "A Good Man Is Hard to Find," which you'll be surprised to know didn't score high marks. O'Connor earned points for word choice, but didn't grade worth a darn in either organization or sentence fluency/structure. A pity O'Connor's teachers didn't have a handy teaching tool like Six Traits to help her improve her writing proficiency.

Foul doesn't quite do justice to my mood. For the two days of Six Traits in-service, my frisky students would be treating the poor substitute teacher like so much raw meat. Never mind the stacks of ungraded papers waiting my return. Never mind it always took the modified students, who weren't fond of change, several days to recover from one of my rare absences. Never mind being removed from duties some of us regarded as important. Never mind any writing teacher worth the title would regard the entire Six Traits recipe as what one colleague titled "How to Grade Papers for MO-rons."

I begged off on the excellent grounds of having better things to do than wasting two days being exposed to nothing of value. The unusual submission made its way up the food chain. Teachers didn't often choose their regular classroom drudgery over an in-service day when they might eat lunch with their buddies. Mr. Berry favored my polite request. Others disagreed. The verdict when it came was disappointing. "If it's good enough for most of 'em, it's good enough for Jones."

I'll admit to a chippy shoulder when I strolled into the cafeteria at precisely 8 a.m.— the only pigeon present. Our clinician, Ms. Luge, she of uncertain age, posed for dramatic effect, one elbow resting on the podium, helmet-haired, power scarved, heavily draped in a florid print number, adorned with ponderous Avon jewelry to a larger degree than in strictly good taste.

"You'll want to sit here," a nod to the condemned prisoner chair front and center. Hard to snooze in the front row. Hard to doodle and appear rapturous. I spotted a chair in the back, far to one side, and plopped.

"You don't want to sit there. You won't be able to see me." She batted her eyes. I'm not making that up.

"This chair is good." Heedless of the ominous flush traveling up her neck into her platinum helmet hair.

"You can't sit there. Take this chair instead." Pointing this time. Ms. Luge had firm ideas about seating. Fortunately, the doughnut and coffee crowd streamed in. Forty upbeat teachers, eager to trade irksome students for two days of anything. Lots of chatter. Lots of sorting. Junior High teachers back there, Middle School teachers in front, draftees from the smaller schools in our service unit district lumped here and there in groups of two or three. My junior high colleagues settled in my neighborhood. I was happy for the cover.

232

Our leader, red-faced and out of sorts, called for order. More chatter. She tried again with similar results. She reached under the podium for a tiny brass bell and tinkled—instant quiet.

"You remind me of some of my first students. (Dramatic pause) Second graders."

If you could pinpoint the exact moment when she lost her audience, it would be when she made that particular observation.

She switched on a tight smile, said she'd taught just about every grade possible, second grade, fifth grade, junior high, high school, a little college. It was junior high boys who did her in. No surprise that.

"One day I was walking down the hall and students were snickering and pointing. I reached back to find a big glob or purple chewing gum in my hair. One of those awful boys must have thrown it when my back was turned. I marched down to the office and resigned. I've never had the slightest interest in junior high teaching since."

Mr. Smock, the sumo-sized 7th-grade science teacher, known to his admirers as the U. S. S. Smock, slipped a note under my right elbow.

"Let's buy some grape bubble gum when we go for lunch." The note circulated, much suppressed laughter. Ms. Luge noticed. Blood pressure rising, she forged ahead, hoping, I suppose, things would get better.

"Every school in California has adopted Six Traits as the answer to their writing problems.

Note to Smock. "No foolin'? The state with some of the worst language arts scores in the country? Next thing she'll be telling us Texas is on board."

"Every school in the state of Texas has adopted Six Traits and is experiencing remarkable results."

Since Texas wasn't regarded as a state worthy of emulation, the audience held its applause. She scowled, then soldiered on.

"Of course, with so many coaches teaching English, it's no wonder achievement test scores are so low."

"Whaaaat?" The wrestling coach seated on my left took considerable pride in his teaching, conscientious to a fault. He'd wrangled hundreds of boys through 8th-grade English without getting gummed. Improved most of their writing in the process. He fixed Ms. Luge with his most ferocious death stare.

"What do you suppose is the most important constituent of good descriptive writing?" Nobody hazarded a guess. I wasn't about to volunteer. The proceedings had the feel of Mrs. Ebke's 7th-grade classroom in Chappell, where an incorrect answer could earn you a set of boxed ears. Our leader's neck reddened yet again. One pilgrim from the small school contingent took pity and raised his hand.

"Using fresh language?"

"Good job! You are almost one-sixth correct. Actually, we in Six Traits prefer the term word choice. But you came awfully close. To reward you for being awfully close, I'm going to give you something sweet. Isn't that what we should do when a student answers correctly?" She grabbed a handful of mixed candy from under the podium and dropped it in the guy's lap. After unwrapping and making short work of a Tootsie Roll, he decided to share. Candy flew everywhere. Some was caught, some was not, skittering along the floor, bouncing off an occasional forehead.

After some little time, the chaos subsided, followed by the faint tinkling of the bell. Our leader ordered a forced march out to the cafeteria's vast open spaces for "very special entertainment."

Bad luck no video of what followed exists. If it did, generations from now, when our descendants live on other planets, brain scholars could scan the visual evidence from the ensuing Macarena fest for evidence of rudimentary human intelligence.

Ms. Luge hadn't wasted all her brief time in Junior High. She cleverly organized the Six Traits attendees in rows by birth date, putting distance between the worst miscreants. Once she'd placed us in parallel lines, she announced she was going to teach us the Macarena, the current dance craze imported from South America. It soon became apparent Luge was more interested in showing off her mastery of the subject than in instructing the unwashed mob. Our leader flounced and wiggled. I'd never seen a more active set of drapes. She occasionally hit the wrong hip at the wrong time, but no matter. The infectious Latin beat soon had people old enough to know better working their saggy rear ends half to death. It was an awful thing to witness.

The wrestling coach stepped out of line to perform an energetic funky chicken, which morphed into the Bird and then the Jerk. Grizzled veteran teachers broke out lame versions of the Twist. The Hustle, a blow back to the 70s, proved readily adaptable to the Latin beat. Luge, deep in Macarena mode, deigned not to notice the bulk of her constituents dancing awkward renditions of every obsolete dance style imaginable.

By the time the tape ran out, Luge's mood had improved. Almost cheerful. After class resumed, she began guiding us through the mysteries of grading for content, organization, conventions, something she called voice/style/tone, sentence fluency/structure and the ever-popular word choice.

The wrestling coach gave her his undivided attention. Leaned back in his chair, hands folded over his steel-reinforced stomach, eyelids at half-mast, filing away every stray morsel, missing nothing. Even while he wrote notes to his friends. After he shared a Top Ten List—Top Ten Reasons You Know Your Macarena Instructor is Insane, the tittering became unseemly.

Luge opened every window in the joint. Fifteen degrees outside with a twenty-mile-an-hour wind. She apologized for the inconvenience, which she blamed on personal thermostat irregularities. The wrestling coach went to work on a new Top Ten list.

Day one dragged until lunchtime. Luge ignored the earnest provincial who shared a favorite instructional technique to teach one of the desired traits under discussion. A request for clarification drew a sneering, "I covered that five minutes ago. Check your notes." When the tinkling bell tinkled lunch, the rush for the exits could have hurt someone.

The wrestling coach and I were pulling out of the parking lot when the bossy 9th-grade English teacher waved us down. "You guys go back in there and apologize. She's really mad. She's going to report us and we'll all be in trouble. Maybe if you invited her for lunch?" Nope. Maybe the bossy 9th-grade English teacher should invite her to lunch. After all, she could apologize with the best of 'em.

Although no authorities appeared when the post-lunch Six Traits session got underway, a miasma of remorse settled over the assembled. No humorous notes circulated. No tittering. Ms. Luge lectured in the measured tones of a kindergarten teacher addressing a deaf flock, controlled, but highly pissed.

After the dismissal bell tinkled, a chastened crowd left the building. The 9th-grade English teacher shook the wrestling coach awake. "She's really mad. We're all in trouble and it's your fault."

"Tough. I'm mad too. This is worse than Vietnam."

"You never served in Vietnam. You've never even been in the Army."

"This is my personal Vietnam. It feels like I've just spent two years in a slit trench under Commie mortar fire."

Alcohol may have been involved, although we'll never know. Sometime around eleven o'clock that evening, Ms. Luge got on the motel phone, informing the upper reaches of our school's food chain of the day's events. That done, she moved on to the airy heights of the State Department of Meaningless Jargon. Not every phone call recipient was fully awake. The muddled messaging, translated days later by a friendly school secretary, cited inattention, note passing, improper Macarena dancing and that favorite incompetent teacher catch-all—disrespect. She wanted heads to roll—tonight if not sooner.

Day two. Unaware of last night's phone call binge, I arrived wary, but confident. Maybe we'd get chewed a bit. Maybe we'd act remorseful. It was worth a try. Maybe we'd put a little more effort into the Macarena thing if it meant so much to her. It was the least we could do.

I ran into the U.S.S. Smock at the doughnut table. And the bossy 9th-grade English teacher, who never ate doughnuts. She had news. "I told them she was awful, and I think they believed me, but for goodness' sake, behave today. No matter what she says, just sit there with your mouths shut. If you manage that, maybe we'll have jobs tomorrow."

"Sure," said the U.S.S. Smock, topping his doughnut collection with a couple of flashy chocolate sprinkle numbers.

Tight smile, but no creeping redness. At least not yet. Around four this morning, she said, she'd hit upon the terrific idea for a seating chart. And there it sat, mounted on a tripod, a seating chart to end all seating charts. Drawn in exquisite detail and shaded tastefully in four primary colors. So official-looking, even the wrestling coach settled into his front and center dunce seat without argument. I found myself in the back, as far away from the wrestling coach as was geographically possible. The bossy 9th-grade English teacher beamed a warning smile from her assigned seat among the provincials.

The chewing, when it arrived, proved as nasty and small-minded as you'd expect. But aside from unwarranted questioning of the motives of certain people, people who had abundant reasons to be provoked, it was a fair assessment of the first day's festivities. Nobody, I repeat, nobody attended the workshop with a premeditated plot to disrupt the seminar. We showed up, true, but innocent as newborn chinchillas. It was she, her, Ms. Luge, who provided the gasoline and the matches. If she wanted to share her pain and shun all responsibility, we'd take our public flogging like the mature adults we were. We'd had our fun. Done and done. I noticed the U.S.S. Smock waiting politely until she finished talking to take a dainty bite of his first sprinkle doughnut.

Thirty minutes into the mysteries of trait #5, sentence fluency, the baby sitters arrived—a stern-faced contingent of building principals, the service unit curriculum director, a couple of well-coiffed educrats from Lincoln. None of them appeared comfortable with the day's policing assignment. A few glared dares at us to misbehave. A few teachers glared back, daring them to do something if we did. But with nothing to see, the presentation beyond boring, the alleged unruly mob on its best behavior, the babysitters soon lost interest and fled to more pressing duties in a nearby saloon.

Once the enforcers left, Ms. Luge gave up any molecule of pretended affability. No tinkling bells, no Tootsie Rolls, no Macarena. She pounded Six Traits for the next seven, mind-numbing hours, less two bathroom breaks and a half hour lunch break. We were grateful the almost level lunchroom floor allowed us to drool out of both sides of our mouths. The bossy 9th-grade English teacher did not suggest we invite Ms. Luge to lunch.

Ms. Luge closed with an impassioned plea for the adoption of Six Traits throughout the entire world of education. If there were those in attendance who took the message to heart and found Six Traits useful in their teaching, far be it from me to criticize. I rejected the Six Traits model as intellectually repugnant, "How to Grade Papers for MO-rons" a well-earned appellation. But if this new-fangled educrutch inspired a few teachers to assign more writing projects than usual, I suppose it served some purpose. How much damage Six Traits in doltish hands was inflicted on students is a separate question no educrat ever asked.

We kept our jobs. Nobody chided us for bad behavior. According to stray whispers, the top of the heap Lincoln educrats were unhappy, especially after Ms. Luge briefed them in person about her ordeal. But after assurances from the McCook administrators their teachers were wildly enthused about adopting Six Traits, the educrats became less unhappy. Life at McCook Junior High went on as traitless as it had ever been.

The decks had been cleared for the next stupid edufad. And not just any stupid edufad. This would be the mother of all stupid edufads, the Mount Vesuvius of stupid edufads, the Krakatoa of stupid edufads. No obscure cranny of American public education would escape permanent damage from No Child Left Behind.

Schizophrenia-*Welcome to the mental illness hotline. If you have multiple personalities press numbers 1, 2 and 3. If you are paranoid press 4 and hang up. We know who you are and will get back to you. If you have* schizophrenia *press 5 and tell the 7 foot tall monster standing at your side you are his friend.*

April. Spring track season in full flower. I never lived in a community more enthused than McCook about the school's track teams. The perennial powerhouse football team, known for small size and superior speed, contributed elite runners to the boys' track team. McCook's 4 X 100 relay team often a heavy favorite at the state meet. The girls' track squad boasted traditional prowess in distance races and jumping competitions. McCook fielded competitive track teams every year, featuring enough winners of district events to make an annual splash at the state meet in Omaha.

McCook High School's track (now home to the annual LeRoy Hoehner Track-Field Invitational) located in a deep, sunny bowl behind the Junior High. The bowl sheltered participants and fans from frigid winds during early spring meets. By far the best track facility in the area, McCook regularly hosted fellow conference members and area smaller school conferences. Once school buses began arriving, hard-core McCook track fans, bag chairs and blankets in hand, filed out of their houses to watch whichever track meet was on the day's schedule.

Track meet this very afternoon. During a quick walk around during my planning period, I spotted yellow school buses from a six-county area lining the street next to the track. The assembled tracksters, small in stature, appeared to be junior high age. Likely a smaller school conference junior high meet. Fans, squinting against the blaring sun, sprinkled around the bowl on blankets and in bag chairs, the atmosphere almost festive.

I am no longer at the track meet. I am in the school library attending an emergency teachers' meeting. Mr. Berry, not his usual bantering self, sketching what little he knows. There's been a school shooting in Colorado. Horrific. Many might be dead. Cops have the shooters confined to the school. Columbine. Big school. No telling how long the standoff will last. School counselors will be here at the junior high all afternoon and evening. If a student scuffles during class tomorrow, the counselors and the school nurse will be available in the lunchroom.

"Be careful out there."

"Be careful out there," a line from the popular 1980s *Hill Street Blues* TV show, would become Mr. Berry's standard sign-off at the end of every faculty meeting.

Previous school massacres, usually by single attackers, many of them psychotic, had scant impact on the national consciousness. Hardly anyone remembered the Bath School massacre in 1927, when a farmer and former school board treasurer, disgruntled over property taxes, dynamited the Michigan school, killing 38 students and a half dozen adults. The massacre remains the deadliest school attack in US history. In 1999, hardly anyone remembered the 16 previous school massacres, going back to the Enoch Brown massacre of 1764.

The chilling, calm prepossession of Dylan Klebold and Eric Harris as they moved through Columbine High School shooting classmates and teachers provided the shock factor. The coordinated attack by two shooters rather than one marked Columbine as a frightening escalation in school violence. Klebold and Harris, exhibiting the classic symptoms of marijuana-induced psychosis (Harris died with his favorite weed pipe, "The Berserker," in his pocket), planned and executed their mission with meticulous precision. What kind of kids would do this? Do we have like-minded students in our midst?

In the moment, nobody realized how swiftly the dark tragedy at Columbine would change our world. School security studied and tightened. Cameras mounted at entrances, monitored in the principal's office. Clear glass framing classroom doors covered with construction paper. In the event of a real lockdown, a shooter would not be able to see or shoot at anybody in the classroom. Mr. Berry studied security protocols at other schools, led efforts to coordinate with local law enforcement agencies. Shooter drills. SWAT teams on the Junior High roof. Parents warned not to attempt retrieving students during a real shooter situation, which would expose both students and parents to danger. During the first shooter drill, law enforcement, city, county and state patrol, discovered the respective departmental radios could not communicate. Grants written. Changes made. Subsequent shooter drills went more smoothly.

The McCook Junior High School transformed overnight from lackadaisical peaceful to besieged. A rumor surfaced of an angry divorced dad on his way from Georgia to McCook to remove his kids. Armed, according to the tale, and willing to shoot anyone who stood in his way. A lockdown situation loomed. Extra police in the area. Teachers with outside windows searching the grounds for anyone resembling a pissed-off Georgian. A few clabber-brained teachers shared the rumor with their students, some of whom had cell phones. Terrified parents began arriving, demanding custody of their terrified children. And just before the situation spun completely out of control, word arrived the rumor was, in fact, a rumor, started by an angry ex-wife to make trouble for her ex-husband. An objective observer might stipulate the guy should have probably paid the child support he owed. Been easier on everyone.

How much long-term damage the rumor turned rumor inflicted on all concerned is hard to know. Kids tend to revert to normal-appearing behavior fairly quickly. However, the junior high students were more pensive than usual for a day or two. It's possible thoughts of homicidal, heavily armed Georgia fathers coming through the school doors weighed. Some teachers, on the other hand, couldn't get enough nervous conversation about the rumor turned rumor. One teacher announced she was bringing a gun to school. This the same teacher who accidentally shot companions during a recent friendly skeet shooting competition. (Although it should be noted none required long-term hospitalization) Nonetheless, if any teacher were to pack hardware, we hoped it wouldn't be her.

More than a few McCook teachers could handle a firearm responsibly. I counted myself as one of them. However, the idea of being part of an armed teaching staff did not appeal. Even a teacher competent to handle a firearm could become careless. What if a deranged student managed to grab a gun from a distracted teacher? Not likely, but McCook Junior High had been home to a representative sample of deeply troubled kids. One weed-addled student eventually advanced through a series of petty crimes to beating a former buddy to death with a fence post. Guards at the penal facilities he later inhabited regarded him as permanently dangerous. Not difficult to visualize him as a dope-fried 7th-grader grabbing a gun and using it.

While I didn't relish facing some gun-toting whack job with only a clipboard for a weapon, packing heat at school reinforced the impression I was fearful of an attack at any time. Of course, we were subject to attack at any time, but to serve up daily reminders to the students?

Students growing more anxious with each passing year? Whether teachers with guns would create anxious students was actually a moot point. There was the small matter of teachers packing heat in Nebraska public schools not being entirely legal. Like most other states at the time, Nebraska public schools, with the exception for trained security officers, were designated gun-free zones.

My concerns about guns in schools creating anxious students also ignored the trusting relationships between the students and security officer Calvin, who packed heat in a prominent location on his hip every damned day. Impossible to verify, but if Officer Calvin, with his unflappable, cheerful presence, didn't reduce student anxiety levels, it would be a shock. Since our building took security seriously and had competent people in charge, our students and teachers remained relatively safe. Had I taught in a different setting, say at McCook High School, where security was nonexistent, I might have wished for other choices.

Officer Calvin, our good-humored, levelheaded, well-trained school security officer, represented, in my view, the best bet to deal with a potential shooter. Not a particle of doubt he would put himself between students and teachers and a shooter. The school district's armed security officers appeared frequently in positive feature stories in McCook's newspaper, publicizing their presence. Potential shooters had to calculate their chances of success knowing a well-trained, armed peace officer protected a school building. Mr. Berry, for his part, put additional effort into dissuading parents from trying to pick up their kids during an active shooter incident and into coordinating training exercises. In doing so, he was adhering to the current wisdom, following the protocols established by many other districts. Current wisdom changed frequently and is still fluid. And, of course, every situation might require a different response.

Israel routinely offers rigorous gun training to teachers, some of whom choose to pack heat in school. Israeli schools, which face far more serious threats than deranged, preppy, dope-smoking weasels, have experienced only a handful of incidents in the last half-century. The general knowledge of armed teachers in Israeli schools may be partially responsible.

242

Israeli school security protocols remain the gold standard, have been the gold standard for the past 50 years. Any American school wishing to maximize protection of teachers and students has a proven blueprint as handy as the nearest internet connection. Israelis post armed guards in plain view outside the school, install high fencing, limit access to one bulletproof vestibule and meticulously guard the single entrance. First responders have copies of every local school's floor plan. One important Israeli school security tool remains unavailable in the United States. Israel's intelligence forces, unlike those of the United States, routinely share intelligence of potential threats with schools, intelligence gleaned from sophisticated electronic snooping, snooping beyond the capacity of a US school district, and not strictly legal if it were applied to United States citizens. (Although the FBI has no hesitation snooping on the parental rights activists they identify as insurrectionists). As almost every school shooting postmortem reveals, shooters often declare their intentions on social media. Identifying potential shooters before the fact is well within law enforcement's capabilities. Terrorist plots have been routinely uncovered and quashed ever since 9/11. It's those tricky constitutional questions and interpretation of same standing in the way.

After Columbine, schools pursued security with varying degrees of seriousness. Functional schools, like McCook Junior High, installed and trained in security measures deemed best practice at the time. For dysfunctional schools, schools incapable of teaching students to read or do math or tell time, securing a school building was and is a bridge too far. The school-wide discipline required to monitor surveillance cameras, lock and check exterior doors, stop and identify outside visitors, not achievable. Hiring skilled auditors to make unannounced probes of school security, not feasible. Even districts that take security seriously find it challenging to stay serious. Time passes. Columbine and the next dozen incidents pass into distant memory. Relaxation of protocols and enforcement follow. The next shooting incident might revive seriousness for a time, but a brief time. Concerns more immediate than random, unknown shooters regain ascendancy.

McCook Junior High remained vigilant for the balance of my tenure. Mr. Berry helped teachers prioritize security. The office staff laser-focused on monitoring surveillance cameras. Officer Calvin, our school security officer, quickly developed easy relationships with students, eventually assuming an approachable, big brother role. It was Officer Calvin who learned through his student contacts of a weed-addled student headed for the Junior High with bad intentions and a gun. It was Officer Calvin who handled the situation so skillfully it never made the news. Security at McCook Senior High? Not so much. The easily bored principal found new and superior interests. Maintaining school security fell off his radar. Tales soon circulated of unlocked outside doors outnumbering the locked, providing students and potential bad guys entering and exiting the building a wide range of options. The Gerbil's flagging interest in security replicated at many schools across the country.

Post-Columbine security protocols dictated repetitive active shooter drills for students, teachers and staff. Wise psychologists eventually questioned subjecting students to frequent active shooter drills. Students can easily learn the protocols they're supposed to follow. After all, most are easily frightened and wish to stay alive. If the faculty and staff are well-trained and receive continuous training, psychologists believe involving kids in every drill does little to boost security, but tends to frighten the bejesus out of impressionable students. Just as drug education programs often boost drug use among curious students, just as sex education programs often boost sexual experimentation among curious students, wise psychologists point out the role of continual, fear-inducing drills in creating a new generation of dope-smoking, trench coat-wearing school shooters. Aspiring school shooters can't get enough of the mythologized Klebold-Harris saga.

The role of heavy marijuana use by mass shooters has received limited publicity. Although the corrosive effects of marijuana use on adolescent brains have been documented for decades, a gullible public, heavily influenced by the Big Tobacco and Big Marijuana industries intent on legalizing dope sales, remains incurious. Marijuana is widely perceived as more harmless than alcohol and way more fun. The attitude of former Vice President Kamala Harris is typical. "Pot gives a lot of people joy, and we need more joy in the world."

Pot apologists ignore the geometric increase of THC content in marijuana sold in legal dispensaries compared to the hippie pot of the 1960s and 70s.

Certain legal concentrates may contain nearly 20 times the THC of earlier times, stronger than the potent hashish that has fueled so many Islamic terrorists and suicide bombers. Researchers have established chronic use of high-octane weed and THC concentrates leads to psychosis in adolescents at a rate five times greater than among those who do not smoke pot—not to mention a reported link between marijuana use and schizophrenia, paranoia, and other mental disorders.

The list of mass shootings linked to heavy marijuana use continues to lengthen. In addition to Columbine, April 20, 1999, (4/20, a date of significance to dope-smoking weasels everywhere), the shooter at the Uvalde school in the spring of 2022 complained the grandmother he shot in the face before heading to school wouldn't let him smoke dope in her house. Dope-smoking weasels were responsible for the shootings at Rep. Gabby Giffords constituent meeting in Tucson, Arizona, (2011), a movie theater in Aurora, Colorado, (2012), the Pulse nightclub in Orlando, Florida, (2016), Virginia Tech University (2007), the Marjory Stoneman Douglas High School in Parkland, Florida, (2018), the 2017 church shooting which who killed 27 people and injured 20 in Sutherland Springs, Texas, and the 2015 church shooting in Charleston, South Carolina, which killed 9. Acquaintances described the shooter responsible for the July 4, 2022, parade shootings in Highland Park, Illinois, as a "loner stoner." Robin Westman, the transgender woman who murdered children attending Mass at Minneapolis Catholic school on August 27, 2025, clerked in a retail marijuana store and, according to peers, vaped dope like it was his job. In addition to mass shooters, the Boston Marathon bombers (2013) sold hashish to regular customers and were heavy users of their own goods.

Speaking of unfounded rumors, we soon learned Klebold and Harris did what they did, not because they were dope-smoking weasels, but because they were misfits bullied by snooty Columbine athletes. This ignored both shooters working part-time jobs, belonging to a bowling league and having many friends, some of them snooty athletes. According to the mythical narrative, the shootings were not the dynamic duo's fault. Nor the fault of their parents, who'd ignored or downplayed the heavy marijuana usage. This single, fabricated out of thin air bullying rumor set off a mad scramble by the edu industrial complex to meet the heretofore limited demand for anti-bullying expertise. Herds of freshly self-minted experts dispatched to instruct teachers on how to persuade their students bullying was not only hurtful to the bullied, but might cause people to get themselves shot. Just look at what happened at Columbine. Schools bought it. Teacher's colleges went all in. Teachers, who might or might not be able to identify a single student bully in their care, bought it. An entire edu anti-bullying industrial complex created from a single rumor turned fact turned rumor. Within months, the hallways and classrooms of the nation's schools plastered with anti-bullying posters.

STAND UP FOR YOUR FRIENDS AND THEY'LL STAND UP FOR YOU

PUTTING OTHERS DOWN WON'T BRING YOU UP

GOOD GUYS DON'T BULLY

BULLY FREE ZONE

IF YOU SEE SOMETHING, SAY SOMETHING

Schools employed expensive anti-bullying experts to address student assemblies. The edu industrial complex churned out anti-bullying materials for classroom teachers. Teacher factories invented anti-bullying courses overnight.

The effectiveness of anti-bullying efforts remains largely unknown. It's possible districts capable of teaching math and reading lowered the incidence of bullying. Possible, but solid research is lacking. Schools with unmotivated administrators and lax academic standards failed miserably, continue to fail miserably. I failed miserably, as did most of my colleagues. Shutting down bullies is hard.

Think about it. Let's say a bullying incident were reported to the school authorities by the alleged victim. If the building disciplinarian calls the accused bully in for questioning, who do you suppose will be subjected to even worse bullying at the first opportunity? If a bullying incident is reported by a good citizen bystander, perhaps the disciplinarian assigns some form of punishment, although punishing students has gone the way of the dodo bird in many schools. Let's say the punishment is one day of in-school suspension with the threat of much worse should

246

the bullying be repeated. How exactly is the disciplinarian supposed to monitor the bully's future behavior? Follow him or her into school bathrooms, where a good chunk of bullying takes place? Shadow him or her while the bullies meander through hallways, lunchrooms, school locker rooms and playgrounds? Lower elementary teachers who typically teach the same students in the same room for most of the school day are in the best position to monitor and discourage bullying. But only if they are allowed to do so. The window on bullying for middle school and high school teachers is often limited to what they observe in the hallways. Even the most vigilant are at a severe disadvantage when it comes to monitoring bullying. Say Bluto stuffs the Prof in a locker. A teacher comes along, hears the Prof's cries for help, releases him, asks who did this. Would you predict the Prof would risk Bluto's revenge and spill the beans? Not if he's thought it through.

There is more than a little evidence active bullies learn more effective bullying techniques through exposure to anti-bullying programs, learn how to hide their crimes and avoid whatever weak disciplinary actions might be threatened. Bullies might not be the smartest specimens, but they're often cunning.

Bullies plied their trade at McCook Junior High. Most often with no teacher in sight. I was at least as oblivious as the majority of my colleagues, who used between class time to fetch bad coffee from the office or use the faculty restroom. The victims who suffered most were those incapable of fighting back or those who became upset at the slightest provocation. The later specimens might as well have worn "Kick Me" signs. Leonardo, a recent immigrant with limited English skills and a withered right arm, couldn't fight if he tried and flew mad under even mild teasing. It's usually best to allow kids space to work things out, but I made an exception for Leonardo. After visiting casually with his tormentors, I learned they were taking their cues from a teacher who disliked Mexicans. I appealed to their better natures, noted Leonardo was new, not only to McCook, but to the country. Not familiar with stuff they took for granted. I also noted his withered arm and inability to fight. Picking on him was not the studliest thing they'd ever done. Would it kill you guys to lay off for a few weeks, give him room to find his bearings in a new school and a new country? Put it that way, they mostly left him alone.

The offending teacher was hopeless. Too hardcore. No amount of sensitivity training or life experiences would ever penetrate. I sat Leonardo down and laid it out. Tap down your pride enough to let the small stuff slide. Somebody makes a crack you don't like, grin and bear it or at least bear it. If you don't fire up, they've lost any reason to provoke you. Can you make yourself ignore the bullies? I know it's not easy. You have so much pride, Leonardo. And reason to be proud. You come to school ready to work. You do good work. Your family is contributing to this community, making it a better place to live. I'll talk to the boys (not telling him I had already done so). Maybe they'll back off. If they don't, I'll talk to them until they do.

Hard to know how much of our conversation Leonardo understood, but he appeared to get the drift. We shook hands to seal a mutual agreement on something or other.

Against all odds, the bullies eased their bullying and Leonardo controlled his quick temper—most of the time. Even better, a half dozen excellent homemade tamales wrapped in corn husks appeared on my desk every Friday morning for the rest of the school year. I'm not holding up the Leonardo matter as a solution to school bullying. Leonardo's problems could just as easily have become worse. But any teacher connected to students can make a difference on the margins. If they are allowed to. More serious and persistent bullying requires a sure-handed administrator with appropriate penalties, including expulsion and sometimes criminal referrals. Penalties currently shunned by many public schools.

If the subject of bullying came up in class, I sometimes used Paul as an example of how a bullied kid might handle the situation. Paul, a diminutive, puny, near genius handled abuse with ease. Paul, who squinted at the world through smudged spectacles resting halfway down his nose, spectacles always askew. Paul, who dragged his bulging, filthy book bag around like a ball and chain. Paul, who beat the pants off anyone foolish enough to challenge him to a game of chess. Paul, who had the hide of an armadillo, fielded insults from the much larger muscle guys with a loopy grin and "Good one, Stewie, did you spend all night thinking that one up?" Didn't take long for the bullies to not only leave Paul alone, but to seek his friendship. Not many kids as clever as Paul, but his example was worth emulating.

248

This was prior to the 2007 introduction of the iPhone and the epidemic of cyberbullying, a far more insidious problem schools have struggled to address ever since. Teen suicides, especially among adolescent girls, have become a national crisis. The problem hasn't lacked for expensive solutions. The response of edu industrial complex including high-dollar cyberbullying consultants and canned teaching materials invaded the nation's schools. Predictable anti-cyberbullying platitudes appeared in school computer labs and hallways.

CYBERBULLYING IS A CRIME. DON'T BE A CRIMINAL

POST, DON'T ROAST

DON'T BE MEAN BEHIND THE SCREEN

Most school districts lack the technical tools to solve cyber crimes. Only by involving law enforcement, a step too far for many administrators, is there much hope of discovering the guilty.

The most effective method for addressing cyberbullying according the wise psychologists and the smart tech oligarch parents of Silicon Valley? Parents removing social media access from the bullied and non-bullied alike. Kids might be the target of bullying, but without social media remain ignorant of the attacks. According to wise psychologists and the smart Silicon Valley parents who design addictive social media algorithms for a living, without cutting access to social media, any massively funded edufad aimed at stopping cyberbullying will be an uphill battle, even with parents and teachers on high alert. Silicon Valley parents frequently take the next step and deny their children smartphones altogether.

Fear-inducing edufads spawned by the Columbine massacre were reminiscent of my introduction to the species while attending Chappell Junior High in the 1950s. Attendance meant nuclear attack drills. If we ignored the dire instructions from our *Weekly Readers* to avoid the most intense radiation clouds by heading directly for eastern Montana, the act of crawling under our desks during once-a-week duck-and-cover drills and placing our heads between our knees served as a grim second choice. Someone more sciency than I can explain the usefulness of hiding under a desk with your head between your knees when a Ruskie radiation-spewing nuclear device crashes through the roof of your school. No 24/7 news or internet in 1958 to spread the fear, but threats of nuclear winter circulated on television and in the print media. Most of us watched physically repulsive, murderous Russian dictator Nikita Khrushchev promise to bury us, pounding his shoe on a United Nations table for emphasis.

A few well-heeled Chappellites constructed secret bomb shelters in their backyards. The moral question of the day? Should you grant access to short-sighted members of the community, those who hadn't built shelters of their own, those who hadn't stocked a shelter with guns and ammunition and a two-week supply of water and dried food? Mr. Hall, our gargantuan science teacher, taught the no-mercy rule. Anybody too lazy and too stupid to prepare for nuclear winter needed to die (horrifying details of death by radiation poisoning attached). Mr. Hall, infamous for slapping Ricky Sneith so hard he lifted Ricky clean out of his desk, propelling him against the mopboard, where he lay in a sniveling heap until the bell rang. The hard-hearted students who agreed with Mr. Hall became eager, merciless guardians of their imaginary bomb shelters. Hall's preaching divided his students between paranoid nuclear war preppers and the insouciant prodigals. Former friends, none of whom was currently in possession of a working bomb shelter, soon eyeing each other with either fear or resentment. And fear, someone once observed, will turn anyone into a blithering idiot.

Demise-*Hey, Roy, the cows excaped and one just got the <u>demise</u> of its life.*

Late summer. A brilliant, blue sky Tuesday, the day students habitually handed in their weekly spelling sentences, the day they took a short quiz over the pages they'd been assigned the previous Thursday. Tuesday, the day they made a head start on Wednesday's reading assignment, hoping, no doubt, to encounter many examples of graphic sex and violence. First-period class filing out, second-period class filing in.

I am distracted. My smart mother dying in an Eastern Nebraska nursing home, IV fluids removed yesterday. Middle sis keeping vigil while I prepare for a substitute. Eldest sis should be airborne this fine morning, flying from Hartford to Omaha to join the vigil. I should be vigiling as well. Not for the first time, a deep distrust of substitute teachers outweighs what should be higher priorities.

Missy strolls in with news. In the classroom she'd just left, a TV tuned to events in New York City. A plane hit a building. "Mr. Jones, you should turn on the TV so we can watch."

Fat chance. We had work to do. Although distracted by my mother's situation, I was remembering a grainy newsreel from the 1940s when a B-25, lost in heavy fog, hit the Empire State Building. Fiery aviation fuel flowed into the gaping hole, incinerating most everyone working on the 79th floor. If Missy is correct and a plane hit a skyscraper in New York, it was probably because of fog. New York has lots of fog, right? Tragic, but nothing worth diverting my charges from their regular tasks.

Third-period students, having watched breaking news for almost two hours, proved more insistent. "It's terrorists, Mr. Jones. A plane hit another building. We should watch TV." Two skyscrapers on the same day? Not likely an accident. The TV replaced work until we were sent home early. To watch TV.

I was unaware of my eldest sis making an unscheduled stop in Chicago, where her plane was grounded until further notice. She borrowed a car and drove across Illinois, Iowa and eastern Nebraska to the nursing home. Even if I didn't, my two sisters had their priorities in order.

The Islamic terrorists responsible for the events of 9/11 had ambitious intentions, although if they could review the entire results of their handiwork from the back step of their current residency, they might be disappointed. Or not. Hard to impute rational thought to a religious fanatic or any other species of fanatic. One unintended result of that shocking late summer Tuesday was a brief reprieve from the usual political bickering in Washington, D. C. George W. Bush's diplomatic and military responses to the attacks received broad bipartisan support. During the short honeymoon, No Child Left Behind, Dubya's pet education initiative, blessed by both John Boehner and finally Teddy Kennedy, passed Congress despite containing irritants to all interested parties. Grafted to the renewal of Lyndon

Johnson's expiring Elementary and Secondary Education Act, the most corrosive, most destructive Krakatoa of stupid edufads to date was birthed.

What first saw life during the Reagan administration as part of the standards and testing movement, refurbished and trotted out during the Bush I and Clinton administrations, was transformed by the "compassionate conservative" candidate (which implied mainstream conservatives were heartless bastards) during the 2000 presidential campaign into the solution for what ailed the entire U. S. public school system. Minority student achievement lagging? Failing schools unaccountable to parents? Or anyone? Too many incompetent teachers? Urban school districts dysfunctional? Poor rural school districts underperforming? We're gonna fix all of it by installing a system of accountability. That means standards and testing, Chester.

The key to measuring is to test. And by the way, I've heard every excuse in the book why we should not test — oh, there's too many tests; you teach the test; testing is intrusive; testing is not the role of government. How can you possibly determine whether a child can read at grade level if you don't test? And for those who claim we're teaching the test, uh-uh. We're teaching a child to read so he or she can pass the test.

—George W. Bush

No acknowledgment, you'll note, of the existing, nationally normed achievement tests, including the Iowa Test of Basic Skills and the California Achievement Test, which provided accurate windows on student progress in major subject areas, including reading. Most school districts outside heavily unionized urban core areas had been using the tests and reporting the results to parents for decades. Any of the popular achievement tests could tell parents, if they didn't already know, whether their child could read or do math at grade level. In the rush to institute new, politically popular solutions to the most recent crisis in education and also, not incidentally, flood the Washington hog trough with billions in new spending, the old testing tools, tried and true, abandoned for mountains of pork and more intrusive federal control of local education.

Bush's résumé included a brief fling with imposing state-generated standards and testing on Texas public schools. Standards and tests initiated during his Texas governorship proved, at least to Bush, that if you wanted improved school performance, standards and testing worked. The new enthusiasm for accountability in education might have a political motive, but Dubya became a true believer in testing. Never mind if the stakes were high enough, for instance, if a lack of student progress meant the school lost funding or had to close, teachers and administrators might cheat. Most certainly would cheat. Never mind the validity of the newly minted tests, produced by 50 different state education departments, might not hold up to scrutiny. Never mind the inevitability of teachers dropping whatever else they were teaching to teach the test, narrowing a child's education to whatever a low IQ educrat thought the child should be learning. Details schmeetails.

Until the 2000 presidential campaign, Democrats more or less owned the education issue. Dubya and his political advisors saw "accountability" as the pathway to swaying urban and suburban voters, who might otherwise find a GOP presidential candidate objectionable, especially one to whom spoken English was a foreign language. On the campaign trail, Bush frequently voiced sympathy for students trapped by "the soft bigotry of low expectations," showcasing compassionate, big-hearted Republicanism to the voters. In promising major changes in the country's education system, the Bushies were taking a huge risk. Traditional conservatives (heartless bastards), Bush's base, wanted less federal meddling in local education matters, not more. Wealthy suburban and poor urban voters, the voters Bush hoped to attract, had leaned heavily Democrat for 40 years. The risky strategy aimed at changing entrenched voting patterns might not have been effective in any other election year, but in 2000 it worked.

Once elected, Bush lost no time sending the bare bones outline of No Child Left Behind legislation to Congress. After hundreds of amendments, hundreds of hours of committee testimony, hundreds of hours of House/Senate reconciliation meetings, the thing stalled. Among the intractable factions—conservatives, who wanted money for vouchers, and mainstream Democrats, who wanted to spend gobs of money (except on vouchers), but didn't want the penalties some parties proposed for schools and states failing to meet standards. Some Republicans wanted the bill to include the abolition of the Department of Education. Some Democrats demanded smaller class sizes and more money for teachers. At that point, the latest scheme to nationalize public education appeared as dead as every previous attempt.

Then the stone age came calling in the form of Islamic terrorists armed with low-tech box cutters, creating a fleeting Kumbaya moment in Washington D. C. Ted Kennedy, who'd been stand-offish to the Bush's signature legislation, jumped on board, although there's an outside chance his support did not come cheaply. For instance, Bush dropped inclusion of money for vouchers from his list of priorities. Ted Kennedy on the Senate floor, "No piece of legislation will have a greater impact or influence." He could not have known how prescient he was or how regretful he would become.

The bill which eventually passed both houses left most of the rule-making and implementation to career educrats serving in the Department of Education, each faction confident it could successfully lobby the department to its point of view. Not until ed department rules finally emerged and began to be implemented did the unanticipated consequences become visible.

Lactose-*I'm lactose and tolerant.*

While Congress manufactured bad sausage which federal and state educrats were about to churn into something much worse, I had more immediate concerns. My teaching certificate needed renewing, a process heretofore automatic, automatic unless you'd been tried and convicted of something unspeakable. No longer. Thanks to a new Department of Meaningless Jargon rule, successful renewal applications had to include evidence the teacher had completed a course in human relations. You would be excused for thinking human relations had something to do with being civil to one another. Maybe several hours of forced practice saying please and thank you? I'd taken several education courses with less utility. But no. Human relations meant being empathetic with minority and disadvantaged populations. Lincoln educrats assumed the state's teachers were even more ignorant of minority and disadvantaged populations than they were. By requiring recently acquired empathy for license renewal, Nebraska's teachers would presumably be transformed from redneck, racist bumpkins into sophisticated, empathetic advocates for the oppressed, similar to the smug educrats currently employed in Lincoln, Nebraska. Stop me if this sounds familiar.

According to the publicity blurbs, those taking the class would be tasked with acquiring six human relations skills. Why six? Why not four? Twenty-six? Maybe the edu guru who came up with the Six Traits writing assessment brain fart graduated to human relations? Most of the six (count 'em) assigned skills were pure oatmeal, of course. Exquisite examples of what the educrats at the Nebraska Department of Meaningless Jargon could crank out if they concentrated all their faculties plus infinity.

"An awareness and understanding of the values, lifestyles, contributions, and history of a pluralistic society."

"The ability to relate effectively to other individuals and to groups in a pluralistic society other than the teacher's own."

Out of respect for your safe space and to avoid marginalizing you, I'll spare you the rest. Except for, except for:

"The ability to recognize the ways in which dehumanizing biases may be reflected in instructional materials."

Uh oh. Mark Twain's days were numbered. Ditto almost any brand of satire or insightful exposition on the human condition. Once the book burners started combing library and classroom bookshelves for dehumanizing biases, no telling how far the crazed bastards would go. At least Dr. Seuss was safe. Seuss was an icon in as many communities as there were communities. Surely nobody would dare mess with Dr. Seuss. Or *Little House on the Prairie*. Or Harry Potter. Surely.

Doc Rider received the same license renewal notice. He wandered into my room in a complete tizzy, letter in trembling hands. "What does this mean? Are they going to take my license away?"

Once I explained, he had no objection to a class in human relations, whatever the hell that was, but was terrified he would fail. He had no understanding of a pud class. I don't believe he'd taken a pud class in his life. "This is fluff, Doc. Confetti. Window dressing for your résumé. A hoop for you to jump through. Nobody will be looking to flunk anyone. We could show up, sleep through class and still pass."

A trusting fellow, especially when it came to the advice found in gold bug newsletters, Doc had grown suspicious of my chronic optimism—a definite flaw in my ointment. Doc calmed down but remained trepidatious. I found a four-day summer class offered by Chadron State College in North Platte (an hour away), filled out the paperwork for both of us and promised to do the driving. After considerable backing and filling, he agreed.

By most yardsticks, Doc was already rich. His parents passed away leaving Doc their expansive country estate, a lake home, the stash of gold mining stocks, gold bullion in the basement and an impressive collection of more conventional financial assets. Doc's personal investments in gold mining stocks provided next to nothing in appreciation or dividend income, but he continued to believe his ship was about to dock. He salivated at signs of rampant inflation, became almost giddy at war news or rumors of war. Any spare dimes from teaching, paper routes, road construction flagging, helping senior citizens clear their leaf-infested gutters and occasional Keno winnings went into gold mining stocks. If he chose to cash out, Doc could kick back, smoke 25-cent seegars and fantasize about blondes for the rest of his days. By most yardsticks, Doc was already old. Well into his 70s, Doc could have retired with a full teacher's pension years before. The decision to renew his license, even at the risk of flunking a pud human relations course, a strong indicator he intended to teach forever. Doc removed any doubt on the drive to North Platte for our first day of class. "If I pass this course and they renew my license for ten more years, I hope I don't have to take another class to renew it the next time."

By my calculation, Doc would be well on his way to 90 by then. Not many 90-year-olds scuffling around the nation's Junior Highs. But no chance I would bet against him. Doc wrote the definitive, multi-volume treatise on bull-headed stubborn.

Our tag team of human relations instructors was as pleasant and vacant as you'd expect. They wasted no time making us comfortable, emphasizing the location of the handy bathrooms, making doubly sure we knew about the multiple scheduled class breaks, including the hour-and-a-half lunch. If you added up all the breaks and divided by infinity, we were looking at 2 hours of actual class time every day. Even if the 2 hours turned out to be painful, we should be able to handle it.

First, the usual touchy-feely self-introductions:

"I have taught for 15 years in the same school, have a lovely wife and two lovely children. I am a big Husker fan."

"After 12 years in the classroom, I'm looking forward to learning so much in this class. I love the Husker volleyball team." An oath of fealty that temporarily discomfited the Husker football fan majority.

"My family vacationed in Mexico two years ago, and we gained an appreciation of the wonderful Mexican people. And we root for the Husker *football* team." (A claim supported by the Husker fashion top with the ubiquitous Scarlet Letter N on the left breast)." Order restored.

I confess to a healthy interest in the Husker football program, including news about future recruiting classes. However, choosing Husker fandom as an important self-identifier would have never occurred. Didn't these people have lives outside Husker football?

Doc introduced himself as Dr. Eugene Rider and sat down.

Tomfoolery didn't wait to be introduced. When the class was asked to describe their experiences with minorities, Trail of Tears Boy stood up. He had a vague connection to a vague ancestor who had been death-marched on the Trail of Tears to Oklahoma from a vague location back east. Who was this ancestor and how was he related? Which tribe? Cherokee? Creek? Choctaw? Chickasaw? Seminole? Sycamore? We never found out. Just thinking about the thousands of needless deaths and the tragic suffering during that infamous march tortured his waking hours. He also had trouble sleeping at night. All of his impassioned maunderings complete with copious tears. As you can imagine, we were pleased and thankful he proved willing to share his emotional trash fire at every opportunity over the next few days.

Our tag team of instructors used any class time not taken up by bathroom breaks or Trail of Tears Boy to sharpen our sensitivities to minorities. Which if you chose to think about it, insinuated 1.) Our sensitivities needed sharpening 2.) These earnest white bread instructors were the most qualified people on the planet to do the job.

Films. Several hours of film. I would have traded the wasted class time for the mostly fictional *Roots* TV miniseries, but not an option. *Sounder and Lilies of the Field* were harmless enough and much preferable to listening to Trail of Tears Boy blubber. Doc started snoring as soon as the lights dimmed.

On the third day, as special entertainment, we were introduced to a visibly uncomfortable Hispanic employee of the local educational service unit. "Tell them about your experiences as a member of a minority living in a white majority community."

Which, after a few fits and starts, she did. Her experiences in North Platte so far had been very good. Her family treated very well. Her kids liked the North Platte schools very much. She thought they were learning very good things. She was surprised when she landed the job at the service unit because she didn't have much work experience. But she loved working there and everyone had been great.

Then she was done.

Nobody had any questions. Nobody said anything for an awkward spell. Even Trail of Tears Boy held his water. Our instructors jumped up to thank our representative minority person and scoot her off stage. They promised another rare treat on the morrow.

On the morrow, they scoured up a former resident of the Pine Ridge Reservation. According to our teaching team, an enrolled member of the Oglala Sioux tribe. They never explained where they found him or how they persuaded him to appear at their dog and human relations show. An older fellow, probably in his 60s, although he looked like a guy with quite a few extra miles. Tallish, cadaverous, long gray braids, eyes wrinkled into slits. He wasn't as uncomfortable serving as a public example of an oppressed minority as the previous marginalized witness. Consequently, his bitter words flowed easily and for some time. His topic? Reservation boarding schools. He'd been incarcerated in one as a small child and his tribulations at the hands of the ignorant and brutal school staff left lasting scars.

"I was only five years old when they took me from my home without any warning. The government cars drove in and took me away. My grandmother was crying when they put me in the car. At the school, they cut our hair short, made us wear uniforms, marched us everywhere military style. If they caught us speaking Lakota, they used a buggy whip. If we didn't shine our shoes they might use the whip or make us kneel on pencils for hours. If you ran away, they beat you even worse."

A depressing tale of man's inhumanity to man, or, in this case, man's inhumanity to little kids. A story all too familiar to those of us who subscribed to Tim Giago's *Lakota Times* newspaper or heard him speak at teacher inservices over the years. Giago, like this guy, never forgot his Pine Ridge boarding school ordeal or tried to forget. They both intended to tell their stories as long as they had angry breath.

Not that our speaker didn't have a riveting story, but I wished he talked a bit about how to avoid mistakes when teaching Native American kids. He might have explained students raised in a traditional home might not look a teacher square in the face. Not an act of defiance, but an act of respect. Why teachers should use gentle inside voices when speaking to the air above their students' heads. A teacher might be in the habit of asking a student to confirm what he's just been told. Not so with traditional Native American kids. They require space and more space. Why creating casual relationships with parents, grandparents and extended family members is vital. But I'm quibbling. The guy's story both captivated and horrified the class. It might not have altered anyone's teaching methods, but probably altered some attitudes. As an added bonus, Trail of Tears Boy had the good sense not to interrupt, although we could hear him snuffling and hiccuping just fine.

I asked Doc on the way home what he thought of the week's entertainment. He didn't know what to think. It's possible he tuned out the whole deal. I began to wonder if Doc's quest to renew his teaching certificate and continue to teach would end badly. How long could a guy 70-something years old who could no longer focus expect to survive teaching rambunctious 7th-graders?

Snow fence-*Dr. Rider is the opposite of a* <u>*snow fence*</u>; *everything flows over him.*

Parent-teacher conferences provided most of my contacts with parents. Unlike the smaller communities where I'd taught, McCook was large enough to accommodate a school teacher who wished to maintain a separate and mostly private existence. Had I been a joiner—church, service clubs, political organizations—I would have been familiar with more parents. On this teaching stop, I chose distance and detachment over community involvement. Writing projects requiring solitude and concentration consumed spare time. However, I always looked forward to the conferences, which provided opportunities to visit with a student's parent or sometimes both parents. I saw my primary task as informing parents about their student's progress beyond what was on the report card. Parents of an underperforming kid were often receptive to suggestions about how they could help. It does no good to talk about a kid's unsatisfactory performance if you don't present concrete measures a parent can take. For instance, telling a parent their kid needs to study harder supplies no actionable information. Suggesting a parent drill their kid on spelling words a couple of times prior to Friday's test could make a big difference, provides a road map anyone could follow. Or not. The parent might decide to use the time for more important activities, and often did. But they knew if the kid's grades didn't improve, part of the responsibility was theirs. Conferences also meant the opportunity to beat the drum for a private, quiet, kid friendly reading retreat in the home, as far as possible from a working television. This before the personal electronic device pandemic. Sending a kid to a private quiet place in the current environment would mean he or she would have to choose between spending time with a book or time on a laptop, Apple Watch, iPhone, Apple Ring or iPad.

With the exception of my first McCook Class from Hell parent-teacher conferences, subsequent meet-and-greets proved relatively conflict-free. Teacher and parents working towards mutual goals. Chatting casually with parents improved my understanding of my students. I might learn of a current family crisis or an undisclosed medical issue. I also gained an inside view of family dynamics. A pending divorce? A recent divorce? Did mom or dad have a healthy relationship with the student? Hinkiness going on? What sort of parental expectations, if any? Were the successes of older siblings creating unrealistic achievement targets? Then there was the old plant yellow corn, you get yellow corn dictum. The chance to size up parents often resolved remaining questions about what made a kid tick.

Contacts with parents outside formal parent conferences were not always as fruitful. The mother who came to my room after school to complain about *Tom Sawyer*. "Abby had trouble understanding those people. I tried reading a few pages. Those people don't talk normal. I can't make sense out of it. Neither can Abby. Why did you assign such a stupid book?"

The corrosive power couple who attended the annual fall open house when parents in assigned groups visited each classroom. My opportunity to lay out the goals of the course: expanded vocabularies, increased reading speeds, improved comprehension.

"This is not a literature class, but a skills class. Students read literature, some of it classic, some of it not. They will also spend a fair amount of their time and hopefully yours, preparing for Friday spelling tests. Spelling tests may not improve your student's spelling ability, but in conjunction with the vocabulary work they do on Mondays and the daily reading assignments, will improve vocabularies. See that plaque on the wall over there? Every year, 7th-grade reading students compete for the Mattie E. Jones Spelling Award. Mattie E. Jones is my smart mother who contributes the $50 savings bond to the winner, the student who misses the fewest spelling words during the year, and has his name engraved on that plaque. On your way out, you might want to check the names on the plaque. Names of some special students over the years.

"If your student shows up at home on Thursday, waving a list of spelling words, asking for someone to drill them, please oblige. A few times through the list will identify the problem words on which you and the student can then concentrate your attention. I know of no substitute for a student being drilled on their spelling words. If a student is going to compete for this annual award, someone at home needs to step up."

Ominous throat clearing and hand waving in the front row. A corrosive teacher from the middle school with her corrosive, stone-faced other half seated beside her in the next desk. Trouble. I remembered the teacher from a textbook adoption committee meeting where she'd ripped the pro-phonics building principal who dared disagree with her. This the power couple who'd made a local church toxic to its few gay members. Last year, her son had gone through a life-threatening health crisis. He'd survived, but showed up for 7th-grade still scuffling with serious fatigue. Sometimes the kid had trouble staying awake. Otherwise dutiful and compliant, but when his energy expired, it expired. He did his best, but not quite enough to avoid the first down list of the semester. Not flunking, but close. The back story? An older sister who excelled at everything, particularly athletics. The lad's parents attended every contest, no matter how far from McCook. And insisted, even on school nights, on dragging the kid brother along to wave the family flag. He could have been snug at home resting and studying, but he wasn't. Poor kid was exhausted, and not just from the long-term effects of his illness. As much as I sympathized, he'd earned the down slip. A down slip earned is a down slip delivered. Maybe, against all odds, the parents would realize the physical toll they were inflicting on the boy had something to do with his low grades. Not just the grade in my class, but the low grades in three other classes.

Infamous for the short temper and a mean mouth, which had mostly depopulated a previously functional area church. Infamous for bullying her teaching colleagues. More responsible than anyone for changing the middle school from the crown jewel of the McCook school system into a viper's nest of backbiting negativity.

"Why aren't you following the reading curriculum? We've seen nothing from you about voice or point of view or sense of place. Nothing about the author's background. Nothing related to common literary devices. All we're seeing in your class is spelling words and long reading assignments, which take up too much time. You should be following the curriculum. That's what it's for."

She meant to punish, make me look bad in front of the other parents. A secondary goal might have been forcing me to grade her son more generously. After all, no child of hers had ever received a down slip. But she wanted to inflict a bit of revenge, something at which she'd had more than a little practice.

I took my time.

"I was going to add the importance of your student having a quiet place at home away from distractions like the television. We increase daily reading assignments as students become more proficient during the year. Although your student may be able to complete an assignment at school, most kids will need time after school in a quiet, safe space. It's also important to have adequate light so your student can see the pages. The inside of a dark car traveling down the highway is not ideal.

"Since I wrote the 7th-grade reading curriculum, I can assure everyone we follow it religiously. As I may have mentioned, this is a skills class, not a literature class. Reading assignments are designed to improve reading speed, comprehension, and build vocabularies. Period. Spelling and vocabulary assignments also help build vocabularies. At the end of the year achievement tests measure student progress. During the years I've been teaching, 7th-grade reading, test scores have been encouraging."

"Any other questions?"

Then the encounter with the mother who didn't come to my room, but received special permission from Mr. Berry to use his office for a more private chat. She posed, bony hip resting on the side of Berry's desk, skirt slit clear up to beyond infinity. She was concerned about her mopey son's grades. College acceptance and all that. I didn't tell her Junior High grades didn't count towards a graduating senior's GPA, something she probably knew. The kid, currently experiencing his parents distinctly unfriendly divorce, (as opposed to all those friendly divorces we see every day), had been PSTDed by the ongoing nastiness. What little work he produced, sporadic and mostly crap. He might have a book in front of him but the pages never turned and his eyes seldom focused.

What to suggest? Maybe the kid could work through some issues with a competent counselor? Not the ghoulish North Platte psychiatrist who never saw a McCook kid who didn't require massive doses of Ritalin. I was thinking primarily of Jack Dodge, our gifted school psychologist and Mr. Irwin, our junior high counselor and Marge Malleck, the intuitive school nurse. Nurse Malleck had the magic touch. No telling how many potential suicides she prevented.

"Eric has been in therapy with a *real* professional since long before the divorce. She's just excellent."

Had to imagine what dire straits Eric would be in if he hadn't had all those years of *real* professional counseling.

Did Eric have activities he preferred to schoolwork?

"He's not a jock, if that's what you mean. He stays home when he's not in school. Sometimes he watches TV, but he spends most of his time reading. He's quite the little bookworm, you know."

No, I didn't. Eric and bookworm didn't belong in the same sentence. Which meant she was lying her slit-skirted, bony ass off. Which also meant persuading her to try something new and different with her kid was likely hopeless.

"Eric's already doing the best he can, even with all the stress he's under. You would not believe the awful lies his father tells him. Wouldn't it be the Christian thing to do if you gave him a little more latitude when you grade his work? He has his heart set on taking civil engineering at the university. He's a huge Husker fan. We wouldn't want this little grade hiccup in your class to destroy his dreams, would we?" With that, she fixed me with her best come hither look, slid off the desk and attempted an awkward slide onto my lap.

I have never been a quick thinker, but I moved my chair in time. A bony posterior glanced off the arm of the chair, her glide path continuing into the office wall. I remember the distinct thunk of a skeletal object hitting immovable plaster.

Mr. Berry waited in the outer office. He was smirking. "How did it go?"

Inertia- *If you hit a brick wall, your _inertia_ works.*

You'd never know Janeen *had a shy bone in her body the way she smiled her brilliant, horse-toothed smile every time I looked at her. She sat front and center, beaming away. She'd exchange harmless patter with anyone, but if asked a question not involving something innocuous like the weather, she'd duck her head forward, peer out from under crude brown bangs, mumble something unintelligible. Pen and paper proved a safer medium. Asked to write on any subject, Janeen's whimsical thoughts flowed. Her spelling sentences reliably entertaining, answers to essay questions often deserved framing. She directed her most ferocious smiles in my direction when she saw the grades on her corrected assignments.*

Janeen's parents didn't attend fall conferences that year. Just as well, since they had a reputation for showing up drunker than 1400 dollars. Instead, Janeen, an older sister well into her second trimester, a disgruntled infant needing a diaper change and a 20 something male of indeterminate relevance showed up at my table.

While Janeen ducked her head, I bragged up her work ethic and special achievements. Meanwhile, Big Sis tapped an impatient foot, wishing I would run out of gas. She had a burning question.

"Does she give you any trouble?"

The idea of Janeen causing trouble didn't come easily.

"Of course not."

Except for the baby, everyone accepted the news with solemn nods. The assemblage moved 15 feet down the line to ask the same question of the U. S. S. Smock. Surely, I thought, Janeen represented her family's best chance for an escape from the dysfunctional family recycle bin. The odds were against her, but I chose hope.

A few months later, a man came to Janeen's house to shoot her father. Love triangle turned violent. Janeen's dad sat alone in the darkened living room, expecting the man he knew was coming to kill him. He waited, unarmed, until the man kicked in the front door and shot him. With Janeen's father dead, the man returned to his car and shot himself. Community wags said it was a double suicide.

Janeen didn't come to school for a few days. The next Monday after school, one of her friends came to my room, led me downstairs to the main entrance. And there, just outside, was Janeen. She didn't pause, tucked her chin and ran, buried her head in my fat stomach, arms wrapping around my waist, holding on like everything.

"How you doin'?"

"Doin' okay, Mr. Jones. How you doin'?"

When she looked up, she was beaming.

Somebody once said that in looking for people to hire, you look for three qualities: integrity, intelligence and energy. And if you don't have the first, the other two will kill you. You think about it; it's true. If you hire somebody without integrity, do you really want them to be smart and energetic?

— Warren Buffett

Core members of the talented Bennett administrative team gradually departed, replaced by lesser mortals. Speaking of lesser mortals, during the last days of Klaus's forgettable tenure he hired a gerbil as high school principal. The first thing everyone noticed about the new principal was how little space existed between his beady eyeballs. The second thing everyone noticed was his sparse, wispy mustache, which paired with his narrow, beady eyes and his tendency to fidget when he talked, earned him the affectionate nickname Gerbil. No more enthusiastic advocate of the latest edufad ever walked the earth. Light on other redeeming qualities, Gerbil's whack-a-mole persistence proved unmatched. If his newest borrowed edufad were shot down by higher-ups, he tried again the next day, then the next. He came to see his job description as the district's Big Picture guy. Big Picture guys can't be bothered with the mundane stuff. Student discipline? Evaluating teachers? Being helpful to teachers and students with problems? Gerbil couldn't be bothered. The only exception? McCook High School boys' athletics. His sense of where the real power lay proved unerring. He granted any request from the coaches with an ingratiating smile and a hearty "we're all members of the guy club" chuckle. Talented football player on the down list and ineligible for the big game? Gerbil fiddled with the grades. Need another assistant coach? I can find the money. Not content to watch football games from the stands, Gerbil roamed the sidelines shouting encouragement. Nobody bested the Gerbil when it came to fawning worship of the Bison cause. Coincidentally, the Bison cause provided much of the motivation for many McCook residents to get out of bed every fall morning.

To supplicants without coaching credentials, he locked his office door and engaged in more important stuff. Long before texting, he emailed. Emails to administrators in other districts. Emails to Lincoln educrats. Emails to his much younger wife (his high school student when they met), now teaching in McCook, a wife requiring continuous care and feeding so she didn't email herself off the planet. When he wasn't emailing, he thought thoughts. Sometimes he concentrated on how he could improve the school. More often he meditated on how he could persuade certain attractive female teachers to embrace the big idea he kept (mostly) in his pants.

As with most of his ideas, his attempts to persuade certain attractive female teachers to his way of thinking showed remarkable persistence, especially since success always eluded him. When smarmy sweet talk didn't work, he'd cut their budgets, make sure his surprise classroom visits resulted in unflattering evaluations. The implied carrot suggested any unpleasantness could magically disappear under the right circumstances. Typically, his lack of success did nothing to discourage the Energizer Gerbil. His relentless, clumsy pursuits kept going and going until they finally yielded unintended results when young female teachers began resigning. All more talented than their replacements. A couple of them, who had built extraordinary programs, irreplaceable.

Teachers not currently identifying as female or identifying females older and/or less than attractive merited little attention. His failure to do the necessary spade work for firing a couple of grossly incompetents finally attracted public criticism. A teacher who spent class time on nothing beyond chatting with students, napping, showing up fifteen minutes late—every day, delegating students to fetch her McDonald's food during class escaped Gerbil's censure. A host of her former students might be bitching they were unprepared for the next class in the progression. Gerbil didn't care. Parents complained to the school board and the superintendent. As years passed and nothing changed, complaints grew harder to ignore. Gerbil gave lip service to official suggestions he take action. Not opposed in principle to firing a loser, tenured teacher, he simply didn't want to go to the trouble. He knew terminating a tenured teacher would take more time than he was willing to give. The first step required multiple, well-documented classroom visits. He would then be obliged to compose an improvement plan, giving the teacher adequate time to correct any official deficiencies. More class visits to document whether the corrections had been made. Assuming the teacher did not make the required corrections, Gerbil would have to compose an extensive official list of specific areas of underperformance and also document failures to address same. All of this had to be completed well in advance of the annual spring awarding of teaching contracts for the next school year. Way too much time taken from his Big Picture formulations.

Gerbil also knew a tenured teacher not offered a contract could ask for a hearing before the school board and, if a union member, could be represented free of charge by an attorney from the NSEA's strong legal department. Representation which would bear little resemblance to the rudimentary legal help the NSEA refused to the newly terminated Holbrook teachers so many years in the past. The NSEA, flush with new members and dues money, hired intelligent, experienced attorneys who could turn a hearing for a failed teacher into a trial of the entire school district. Few administrators who'd been subject to an NSEA attorney's questioning at a termination hearing, which often lasted into the wee hours, had any desire to repeat the experience.

Gerbil was just savvy enough not to flatly refuse the assignment. Obvious insubordination can get most anyone fired. But he dallied, promised, never quite got around to doing the necessary paperwork until it was too late, at least until the next fall. Frustrated parents became more vocal, their complaints focused not only on loser teachers, but on Gerbil. Additional school patrons were exposed to his chronic unavailability and lack of responsiveness. Gerbil and "lazy little prick" mentioned more frequently in the same sentence. The buzzards circled.

First-rate people hire first-rate people; second-rate people hire third-rate people.

— Humorist Leo Rosten

The Junior High managed to function almost as well as it ever had. However, the senior high principal managed to effect a general degradation, not only of the senior high school, but of the entire school system. His new hires often brought no exceptional qualifications to the job beyond showing little interest in rocking the boat. He continued to weed out experienced teachers with the temerity to complain about the lack of enforcement of rules covering attendance and behavior, his failure to secure the building. The senior English teacher who complained the loudest when he altered the grades of football players proved hard to move. His suggestions she retire rebuffed. He then spread rumors she had gone bat shit senile and lost control of her students. After the rumor pot bubbled for a spell, he began bringing her in for conferences where she had to defend herself against the false rumors. He dangled the substantial early retirement bonus she'd receive, suggested the extra time she'd have for family and grandchildren was too precious to postpone. "I understand you got into another altercation with a student yesterday."

The "altercation" might have been the teacher denying a student a second or third trip to the restroom. It might have been the teacher politely asking a student to remove a baseball cap (as per school rules). The students sensed a wounded animal. They'd heard the rumors. A teacher famous for her short fuse for the last 30 years an easy poke. That she, short fuse and all, was an excellent teacher, an irreplaceable teacher, didn't enter into a student's thinking any more than it entered into Gerbil's. Blood in the water meant more pokes, more "altercations," more Gerbil browbeating. The threat to transfer her to the junior high put her over the moon. Tough-minded though she was, the prospect of teaching junior high boys terrified her beyond all reason. The spring she quit saw other top teachers hit the exits, none replaced by anyone remotely their equals.

Notes from a Curriculum Coordinating Committee meeting: *Mr. Gerbil announced in no uncertain terms, the direction the senior high is taking is to focus on academic achievement and not on student compliance in handing in assignments or meeting teacher's behavioral expectations.*

The talent erosion took place throughout the district. Elementary teachers whose students regularly shone on reading and math achievement tests took buyout money and early retirement The buyouts, adopted by the school board to pare teachers high on the salary schedule, saving significant sums over the next ten years, had unintended consequences. Replacing the retirees with equal talent and dedication would have been difficult at any time or place. However, McCook's hiring practices hadn't changed since Harold Bennett was a pup. No longer could McCook post a job opening and expect a flood of worthy applicants. Colleges produced fewer top education graduates every year. Since women composed an increasing majority of licensed teachers, any decline in the number of women pursuing teaching degrees adversely affected the talent pool. Other, more lucrative opportunities in business, medicine, and law now open to women. Women graduates in marketing and accounting could earn two or three times a beginning teacher's salary the first year.

Larger school districts in Omaha and Lincoln, which previously favored experienced teachers with Master's Degrees, began hiring the cream of the new graduate crop. McCook, which for most of its history had been able to attract top graduates, found itself competing with smaller outstate schools for less attractive candidates. McCook, bleeding population and located 4 hours from Denver and 4 and a half from Omaha, lacked curb appeal for a new college graduate. Single teachers could secure jobs much closer to bright lights and higher populations of eligible mates. If potential candidates bothered to research, they found young adults in short supply in McCook because they'd left for college or better opportunities and hadn't returned. The only remedy, smart and active recruitment, was never seriously pursued.

A superintendent who'd attracted a slew of top education graduates to the tiny Nebraska panhandle town of Gurley (pop. 171) wrote the book on recruiting teachers to a small rural school. If his school anticipated a vacancy for a math teacher. He'd visit the math departments at Chadron,

Wayne, Peru, Kearney, and quiz the professors about their top three students. He did the same with other subject areas and elementary education majors. Once identified, he recruited the students. It didn't hurt that in an era with an abundance of teacher candidates, he'd talked his board into offering above-average starting wages. More importantly, he kept in constant contact with the top students through their senior years. The message? Gurley wants *you*. Gurley wants *you* because we think *you'll* be an exceptional teacher. Gurley places a high value on exceptional teachers. If you come to Gurley, you'll be surrounded by teachers as exceptional as you are. What can we do to make that happen? Housing? We have several rental houses in the community reserved for teachers. You can inspect them when you come for your formal interview. Or even before. Give us a call, we'll arrange everything.

Few other school districts in the state followed this strategy, although with the current paucity of teaching candidates, things may have changed. Who doesn't enjoy flattery, especially an about-to-be freshly minted college graduate? Gurley wants *me*. No other school is calling periodically. No other school promises a high starting salary or promises to help find housing. All the different places I've applied tell me they'll keep in contact, but don't update my application status. I could be at top of their list or the bottom. How would I know? Gurley wants *me*—no need to continue with the stressful application process anywhere else.

My friends may snicker when they find out. Gurley? Seriously? You're going to teach in a hick town with a hick name like Gurley? Are you going to milk cows before school? Do they even know about electricity? Where is Gurley anyway? Never heard of it. Despite Gurley's less-than-sophisticated name, the unusual practice of identifying top college senior teaching candidates early in the year and gangbusters recruiting frequently carried the day. The new recruits rarely taught for long in Gurley. Most had personal goals of graduate school, and many hoped for careers in college or university teaching. They left, to be replaced by new graduates of equal quality.

I suggested on multiple occasions McCook follow Gurley's road map. No interest. Too locked into the tried and true hiring practice of "we'll post the job and great applicants will show up by the busload," a policy which hadn't worked for years. Although, to be fair, an occasional diamond slipped through the process. Sometimes, a talented McCook alum returned to familiar territory. If, for whatever reason, a new teacher with brains and an idea of what they were about showed up at the Junior High, it was loud hosanna time.

Meanwhile, Gerbil preached to fellow administrators the value of mediocrity. "A teacher who thinks they're all that is usually a pain in the balls. Give me a teacher who does their job and keeps their mouth shut. They're grateful to have a job and they don't cause trouble. Maybe they aren't top-notch, but you know what? Nobody cares. Nobody. Cares."

And, at least in McCook, he had a point. Unlike wealthy suburban school districts, where parents expect high-performing teachers, most McCookians expected teachers to provide a smooth, stress-free educational experience and teach useful things. They also wanted their kids to have lots of friends, maybe play on a sports team. The community valued good grades and high ACT scores, but if the average kid muddled through high school with enough credits to attend Kearney or Chadron or a tech school or the University in Lincoln, the academic bar had been cleared. Parents prodding their children to set their sights on admission to an elite college or university were scarce to nonexistent. The football coach better make the playoffs, but the biology teacher could be a complete waste of skin without causing an uprising. There were exceptions, of course. Parents sometimes raised questions, demanded this principal or that biology teacher be given the boot. But they always found themselves pushing rocks uphill and any pressure for foundational academic excellence soon dissipated. Except for large, calcified urban school districts, a community's public schools usually reflect the goals and aspirations of its citizens. McCook's schools were no exception.

How much Gerbil's gospel of deliberate mediocrity affected hiring practices by his fellow district administrators is hard to determine. His preaching came at a time when talented teachers had already become difficult to recruit to McCook. On the off chance attractive new graduates accepted a contract, they sometimes backed out after giving the town and school closer scrutiny. Even during the Bennett regime, certain hiring decisions might be made based more on coaching skills than on promises of superior classroom performance. This was particularly true when it came to volleyball coaches. Although McCook's volleyball teams were competitive on occasion, the record over the past twenty years was nothing anyone would brag on. Smaller area schools regularly trounced McCook. Smaller schools in the area, unlike McCook, regularly qualified for the state tournament. The preferred solution, often tried and never rewarded, was to hire an inexperienced teacher who played volleyball in one of the more successful area small school programs. Maybe the magic pixie dust would rub off on McCook volleyball.

She'd played varsity volleyball for the small rural school a few miles east of McCook, famous for its volleyball success. She managed to start a few games as a high school senior but had never been confused with a star player. A few rough edges. Lots of alcohol and feral sex. She had enough ambition to earn a science degree with a minor in physical education, collecting a vaguely there husband and a small child along the way. McCook's Junior High science/high school volleyball coach opening coincided with her college graduation. Lucky us.

She showed up ten minutes late every morning looking and smelling like she'd dressed directly from the dirty clothes basket. If her students learned anything science-related that year, it was accidental. She spent class time either flirting with the boys or spinning salacious tales about her hobby. The hobby involved leaving her child in the care of someone all weekend while catching rides with her truck driver buddies to wherever they were going. Volleyball season, with its numerous weekend tournaments, cramped her style. Weekends lost to inevitable losing and long bus rides with cranky, sullen players. Her successful high school coach had been hard-nosed, freely handing out draconian punishments for everything from missed practices to general lollygagging. His methods tolerated because his teams won. McCook's rookie science teacher, emulating her mentor, handed out plenty of punishments, always accompanied by sneering references to how the lazy, no-talent players she'd inherited at McCook compared unfavorably to the awesome players of her alma mater. No wins resulted. Although she was allowed to finish the school year, she wasn't offered a contract for the next. Her classes lost an entire year of science instruction while the volleyball program suffered yet another debilitating blow. A familiar movie, versions of which played and replayed during my years in the district.

The only thing that you absolutely have to know is the location of the library.

– Albert Einstein

Given the shrinking talent pool, the McCook faculty retirements created too many vacancies to be easily filled by quality replacements. Case in point, the retirement of the long-tenured junior high librarian, who conducted library orientation seminars each fall for the new 7th-grade reading classes. Students practiced researching different topics using all of the library's considerable resources. Which meant they were required to consult thick volumes of the *Dictionary of American Biography* and fully fleshed encyclopedias like the *Encyclopedia Britannica* (not the cartoon online versions now widely in use). The act of merely opening serious reference works exposed 7th-grade minds to new, intellectually challenging vistas, the precise use of expansive vocabularies. Underneath her no-nonsense persona, the librarian nursed an abiding love for learning and books. Any kid with a book report due found her both willing and patient to find not just any book, but a book the kid would find engaging and challenging.

Her retirement represented loss on several levels. The Junior High lost its historian, the self-appointed curator of the joint's institutional memory. If someone wanted to know how we arrived at the fix we were in, she could draw the map. We also lost a voice of reason, who did not speak out often, but when she did, she chose her words carefully and teachers listened. You wouldn't think finding a replacement for a librarian who loved books and took pride in the collection she'd assembled should be that difficult. After all, wouldn't a book-loving, collection builder describe most librarians?

Although her replacement, bright and personable, was well-qualified for the position, she did not love books in the same way. Much of her recent graduate training focused on online resources and educating students to use them. I'm the last person to object to online resources. Online search engines and open-access materials have made research ridiculously easy. I wouldn't return to pre-internet days, even if it were possible. However, what's missing from easy online research is what we learn when the search takes time and becomes more complicated.

Look up Abraham Lincoln online. You'll probably hit a *Wikipedia* biography. Aside from the politically slanted editing we find so often in *Wikipedia* entries, the information will have some utility. On the other hand, look up Abraham Lincoln in the hard copy of the *Dictionary of American Biography* and you'll find an erudite entry written by a preeminent Lincoln scholar probably immersed in an all-things Lincoln-related career. As a bonus, during your search for Abraham Lincoln, you might take the time to read the biographies of several other Lincolns of note, some new to you.

The replacement librarian wasted no time cleansing the library of most anything published prior to the 21st century. Expansive gaps opened up on previously crowded shelves. Works as relevant today as they were thirty or fifty or a hundred years ago vaporized. She trashed literature and standard histories with equal enthusiasm. What she viewed as stodgy reference works, some out of print and nearly impossible to replace, never stood a chance. Most given away, the rest consigned to the school's incinerator. From her point of view, the carnage made sense. She would not be instructing students in the use of old fashioned, user unfriendly reference books. She directed student researchers to the computer lab and the growing plentitude of online resources. Only their education was diminished in the process. My personal library, on the other hand, gained classic literature and reference works worth thousands of dollars, worth even more years later. Try finding a pristine set of 1911 Encyclopedia Britannicas and, if you do, let me know the price. In a better world, I would return these jewels to the McCook Junior High library, but only with the pinky swear guarantee no Philistine would ever burn them.

The district's long time tech coordinator/advanced calculus instructor, who wisely convinced the district to purchase Apple computers, also took the early retirement buyout. At the time, competent techies were scarcer than librarians who didn't burn books. As his replacement, Gerbil hired a Canadian huckster with limited knowledge of PCs and zero knowledge of Apple products. Apple products, by the way, which were less subject to malware or system meltdowns than PCs. He and Gerbil, a fellow Apple hater, convinced the school board to replace the district's durable, well-functioning Apple computers with a semi load of dysfunctional PCs, manufactured by four Ontario tech whizzes in their rented garage. Because the computers turned out to be mostly useless, everyone assumed, with little proof, kickbacks were involved. Preparing students for the brave new computer driven world became more difficult. Entire computer labs on the blink for days. Teachers entered grades only to have them transported to super secret black holes nobody could even guess. Long abandoned physical grade books back in vogue as teachers returned to entering grades the old-fashioned way.

Staff members focused on Gerbil's dreadful tech hire after the garage-built computers failed and Huckster Boy couldn't fix them. But because he hired him, Gerbil protected him—for a while. Protection which did not extend to the altercations resulting after frustrated teachers caught Huckster Boy in the act of installing sociopathic software on their work computers, installations which invariably led to maximum frustration. Hard words and threats of bodily harm directed towards Huckster Boy. Although thick of skull, he eventually learned which computers he should never, ever touch. However, sparing a few district computers did not stop the district's tech education efforts from going so far backward not even Gerbil could save the Huckster Boy's job.

Holocaust-*Hitler did a very bad thing by showing no appreciation to the Jews and that would be called the* <u>Holocaust</u>.

An uncloudy February morning. *Unseasonably warm. I am sitting in the back pew of the McCook First Baptist Church. The pews ahead filled with unseasonably serious Junior High students. I wonder how many students would show up if I were in need of a public funeral. One? Two? But we're not here to speculate on low turnout funerals. We're here to honor Carl Smock, the beloved U.S.S. Smock, the former resident godfather of all things 7th-grade science.*

Underneath his gruff skin, a soft-hearted former state heavyweight wrestling champion. Mr. Smock did his practice teaching at Omaha Benson under the supervision of a crusty ex-Marine. At the time, Benson used a school gym to warehouse students not in class. Hundreds of them. Because students knocked out the lights as soon as they were replaced, the darkened gym hid a multitude of ongoing sins, both misdemeanors and felonies. If the violence became too pronounced, Mr. Smock's mentor opened the gym

276

door and waded inside, his baseball bat colliding with as many skulls as it took to restore order. He urged Mr. Smock to do the same. The bat was the only thing the animals understood. Former state heavyweight wrestling champ Carl Smock did not believe in violence. There had to be another way. And there was. Smock didn't hide outside the gym doors until a riot erupted. He circulated, got to know the troubleds and the untroubleds. Situations diffused before they spiraled. He became everyone's new dependable.

McCook students responded to his steady, predictable teaching style and the temperament of a sunbathing reptile. Nothing upset him. A scientist to his bones, his home-brewed experiments had students hauling everything from brackish Republican River water to coyote scat into his classroom. The greenhouse next door would have been the envy of a tenured professor of horticulture. Random cuttings from unfamiliar plants sprouted roots and prospered. Students assigned to make the appropriate identifications free to wander in and out, leading lives of discovery.

The old saw no one is irreplaceable is sometimes wrong. Carl Victor Smock proved it wrong. The rich traditions he left behind blown to teeny smithereens less than a week into his successor's first semester. Anyone, no matter how dedicated, would have fallen short trying to replace Smock. What wandered into his former classroom fifteen minutes late on the first day of the next term couldn't have replaced a light bulb—on her best day.

Now we got bad blood.

—Taylor Swift

The retirements and hirings at the elementary schools and the middle school took place mostly under my radar, although I mourned the retirements of the reading teachers at the middle school whose class placement recommendations over the years had proved prescient. However, the general loss of talent became apparent when achievement test scores began their steady decline. In the past, most students entering 7th-grade came equipped with a sound reading and writing foundation. The skill erosion didn't happen overnight, but the erosion became too consequential to ignore. This happened about the time the administration decided to move the 9th-graders and their teachers to the senior high and the 6th-graders and their teachers from middle school to the junior high.

Administrators spared nothing making sure the transition went smoothly. Next fall's 6th-grade students provided with multiple junior high orientations, 6th-grade teachers visited junior high classrooms, junior high teachers visited 6th-grade classrooms. The 6th-grade teachers weren't thrilled by the move from a much newer, fully air-conditioned facility, kept spotless by an OCD janitor, to the aging Nebuchadnezzar oven we called home. After junior high teachers visited 6th-grade classrooms, observed the obvious deficiencies of several teachers, we weren't thrilled with sending our talented 9th-grade colleagues to the high school in exchange for a set of mediocre 6th-grade teachers (with the notable exception of an extraordinary math instructor). The 8th-grade English teacher/wrestling coach spoke for many when he concluded, "The 6th-grade teachers are dumb and grumpy."

Boy, were they. Grumpy, not stupid. Constitutionally incapable of leaving anything alone that was working perfectly. The mutant spawn of medieval witch burners and the heathen Chinese Communist Red Guards. Some of them born in a disgruntled state. Others harboring long incubated resentments stemming from straying spouses, disappointing children, abandoned dreams, decaying, blubberous bodies. The invaders gave off the collective aura of curdled milk. Jovial chatter with colleagues in the hallways during class changes gave way to bitter carping and whispered finger-pointing. More concerned with colleagues backsliding in adapting the latest stupid edufad than with their own classes learning anything of value. It was as if the junior high had imported a handful of Maoist vipers, enforcing the party line by employing social ostracism and skillful backstabbing to enforce compliance. Within weeks, the vipers browbeat a few noodle-spined Junior High veterans, both men and women, into joining the cadre. As with most new converts, the Junior High veterans often became the most intolerant. I can only imagine the social pressure to adopt the latest edufad a rookie teacher with traditional teaching ideas would encounter in the current incarnation of public schools.

I would not describe the pre-invasion junior high faculty as one big happy family. I would describe it, nearly twenty years into Mr. Berry's benevolent tenure, as a smooth-running, semi-cohesive unit, cohesion destroyed in a few short months. It's what angry zealots do for fun.

If not for the loss of faculty collegiality, I might have been more welcoming. As a veteran teacher, I should have been more welcoming. After all, what the new transfers did in their classrooms or what unfortunate reality they adhered to was their business, not mine. However, I'd become so accustomed to the easy, supportive, nonjudgmental McCook Junior High School faculty, the new, cliquish, backbiting environment was hard to swallow. If I had it to do over, I would offer a few olive branches, been less standoffish. And been way less judgmental. A friendly, diplomatic welcome could have made a difference, at least on the margins. Coulda, shoulda.

The grumpy brigade did not limit their attentions to fellow teachers. They abused students, particularly of the modified variety, with the frequent sneer, the absence of expectations, an abundance of false, condescending praise. No wonder achievement test scores tanked. However, if a student belonged to just the right parents—parents deemed members of McCook's minuscule, self-appointed elite, the zealots spared no effort in sucking up. Favored students learned even minimal effort would be rewarded with towering grades and generous praise. Parents kept informed of their child's remarkable talents and accomplishments.

No wonder achievement test scores tanked.

Pity the parent of a struggling student summoned to school to meet with the student's unforgiving instructors. Prior to the grumpy invasion, parents, students and teachers met with teachers and the guidance counselor who served as moderator. The counselor supplied the student's record of test scores and grades. Without the history of test scores and grades, there was no way of determining if academic troubles were recent or long-standing. A sharp decline in grades and/or test scores could mean deeper problems requiring intervention from mental or medical health professionals. Meetings remained cordial. Sometimes good things resulted. Often, no change eventuated. But the Junior High had its best foot forward. Both student and parent made aware teachers cared. Areas needing improvement identified. Parent and student ideas for improvement solicited and heard. If the meetings accomplished nothing else, students and parents left knowing the school had their backs.

Once the grumpies became comfortable in their new surroundings, they began summoning parents for ad hoc meetings without the benign moderating services of the school counselor—and without notifying the principal's office. Leaving the counselor off the list of invitees not an oversight. The meetings were not about helping parents help their kids succeed. The meetings were about verbally abusing parents. I attended one such meeting—ignorant the school counselor was not involved and would not be providing wise and patient oversight, ignorant I would be attending not a constructive meeting, but a prearranged lynching.

I arrived in the classroom of the titular leader of the perpetual grumpies, a leader who by the way, taught 8th-grade classes. She'd never had the 7th-grade student under discussion as a pupil. The same could be said of two other 8th-grade teachers on the tribunal. The accused, a single mom with more troubles than a monkey on a rock, facing a panel of unsmiling teachers. I took a seat out of the line of fire. Mom represented the only household breadwinner, her nogoodnik ex supplying zero child support. She worked two jobs, keeping the roof over her family and food in the fridge. After her shift at the hose plant, standing at a table winding garden hose for eight hours, she drove to a local saloon to wait tables until closing. I never thought, and you shouldn't either, the tribunal didn't believe her bar duties automatically made her an unfit parent. Not only unfit, but so disreputable they did not have to be respectful.

Accusations flew.

"Don't you know your daughter is failing three classes?"

"Why haven't you done something about her grades? Don't you care what happens to your daughter?'"

"Do you have any idea how rude she is? I've never seen a student with a worse attitude. Don't you teach her proper manners at home?"

Let's see. On her feet 16 hours a day. Concerned about groceries and finances. Concerned what would happen if she were to miss work. Worried if her young children were surviving her long absences. Perhaps calculating the damage to her paycheck from taking time off to attend this kangaroo court. Just guessing, but perhaps her daughter's daily Miss Manners lessons didn't have a high priority. And even if they did, any red-blooded kid with an ounce of self-respect would react to these sneering, condescending bullyraggers with as much rudeness as he or she could muster. And Tonya wasn't just any kid.

Tonya came into my room the first day of school with a chippy attitude. Resting state? Pissed. Didn't take but a few minutes for her to run afoul of the no cell phone rule by checking the phone tucked in the front pocket of her hoodie. The phone went in the drawer to be relayed to Mr. Berry for disposition. Little activity from Tonya for the rest of the period, unless you count the steam coming out of her ears. The next day went better, although still cranky. By the next week, she'd settled into the modified class routine, working with a self-chosen partner, turning in perfect work. Her spelling test results not as good, but being drilled at home wasn't practical.

She chose to hold a permanent grudge over the phone deal. But as her work and grades improved, the grudge became a little less grudgy. She might let a smile slip every third while. When the fifth week grades came out, Tonya's reading grade was in the low 90s. An unexpected phenomenon noticed by the grumpy lynch mob. Especially after Tonya's mother, by now up to here with the Red Guards, pointed it out.

"If Tonya is such a bad student, why did she earn a 92% average in Mr. Jones' reading class?"

She had them by the short hairs, didn't she? Why indeed? Embarrassed, they fell back on their favorite theories. Theories about the relatively high grades the modified kids earned in my class compared to the abysmal grades earned in theirs. Theories hinting I made up the grades of whole cloth. They could not accept the passing grades as valid because they could not steer a modified kid to decent grades in their classes, not that they tried. They hinted at other, less flattering theories concerning my modified students' achievement test scores, scores which every year showed substantial progress in all phases of reading. These charges not plainly stated, but implied, a raised eyebrow here, a sarcastic inference there. All the adults in the room understood what was being said. Mr. Berry hadn't helped my popularity by pointing out at teachers' meetings the remarkable improvement in my modified class's achievement test scores. "Maybe some of you should visit with Mr. Jones, find out what he's doing right."

If you want to create internecine warfare, all you have to do is publicly compare a teacher unfavorably to another teacher. Thanks, Mr. Berry.

No grumpy inquired about my classroom practices—ever. No need. They knew beyond a shadow the high test scores were the result of cheating. Didn't know the mechanics of said cheating. Didn't need to know. They just knew. Because their modified students performed miserably, and they were, after all, the most talented, hard-working teachers they'd ever met. If the kids fell short, it was invariably the parents' fault. No objective person could expect a teacher to elevate a kid with a lousy upbringing. Couldn't be done.

Once the mob finished insinuating my reputation to holy shreds, they refocused the group glare on Tonya's mother.

"What are you going to do about Tonya's attitude? Just the other day in the hall, I asked her to spit out her gum and she called me a nasty name. It was under her breath, but I knew what she said. We can't tolerate that kind of disrespect."

Disrespect, the favorite crime of the incompetent teacher.

"Have you considered taking Tonya to a counselor? Several of our students have seen a therapist in North Platte who has amazing results. Sometimes a prescription for Ritalin can make a world of difference in attitudes and study habits."

Tonya's mother turned to me, diverting the hostile room's attention back to where I didn't want it. "How would you handle a situation like that, Mr. Jones? Do you consider Tonya disrespectful?"

I could have waffled, mumbled a vague response, chosen more diplomatic language, but I'd been poked. A hard-working mother abused, my honesty questioned, my students' accomplishments disparaged.

"Tonya does her work. As long as she does her work, whether she respects me or not is irrelevant. I don't plan on Tonya bringing me cookies. She doesn't bring any teacher cookies. She's cranky some days, but she may have reason to be. I'm not about to go all badge-heavy with

Tonya. If you want to make certain Tonya never turns a wheel in your class, just remind her how much power you think you have."

Sniffs and averted eyes from the tribunal. A brief pause before returning to their primary mission of browbeating today's designated pigeon. At no point did anyone offer a practical suggestion. Not—this is what you, the parent, can do to help Tonya do better in my class. Not—this is what I, the teacher, will do to help Tonya succeed. No soliciting Tonya's mother for suggestions. Nothing, in short, for Tonya's mother to implement, even if she weren't way beyond irritated and unwilling to cooperate—for the next 200 years—plus infinity.

Lacking the moral courage to call a halt, I bailed. Trotted down to Mr. Berry's office to rat out the lynch mob for parent abuse. Knowing the players as well as he did, he had no trouble grasping the scope of the evil being committed. As far as I know, that was the last ad hoc kangaroo court the grumpy brigade conducted. Their mischief days weren't over, of course, but they changed focus and adopted different tactics.

A few weeks following the mother lynching, McCook Junior High hosted a school assembly featuring a semi-famous motorcycle adventurer. Danny Liska rode his motorcycle - a BMW R60 - from Alaska to Argentina. Liska the first person to complete the overland route, riding over 95,000 miles between the Arctic Circle and Tierra del Fuego at the tip of South America. He followed that singular journey with a motorcycle adventure from Scandinavia to the beaches of South Africa. During those travels, he and wife Arlene rode through 60 different countries, learning languages and participating (most often Danny) in obscure and sometimes bizarre tribal rituals. And documented the journeys with a mind-numbing collection of photos. Liska sprinkled his presentations with personal Bigfoot stories and Ponca tribal legends. The Big Foot Ranch, his home base near Niobrara, Nebraska, the mother lode for Liska's offbeat inspirations. A bigger, hairier guy, a gruffier guy, a guy who talked with a heavy Czech accent. Kids couldn't get enough of Liska's folksy, slightly wacky charm and badass motorcycle persona. His photo-illustrated talks so popular with Nebraska school children, administrators hired him every couple of years for repeat performances.

A particular day in a particular late fall, leaves long gone, grass turned sere. McCook in late fall an ideal time to visit. The maddening sing-songy, dust-laden winds of July and August in abeyance. The threat of frost cleansing the air. The double gym doors standing wide open, welcoming a faint, football-scented breeze. Liska well-launched into an account of a meet and greet with the primitive, mostly naked denizens of an Amazon village. I am standing across the gym from the overflowing bleachers, taking my assigned crowd control duties seriously. Fat chance my services were needed. Liska's photos of mostly naked villagers could keep an entire geography of Junior High boys at attention. But when you're dealing with Junior High students, there are no guaranteed outcomes. Things happen. Like when violent coughing broke out in the audience. Eyes and noses streaming, students and teachers began exiting the bleachers and making their way outside through the open gym doors. Liska, coughing and sneezing, abandoned his program mid-remark and fled outside. A technicolor photograph of scantily clad Amazonians projected on the movie screen mute testimony to the interrupted proceedings.

My eyes began to water. I joined the crowd outside. Between mass coughing fits, general group speculation focused on what the hell was happening. A cherubic student teacher, currently assigned to one of the grumpies. Two weeks into her tenure, she'd already lost most of her curable optimism. Practice teaching under a perpetually negative senior teacher will do that. She stopped coughing long enough for a full confession. Accustomed to the crime-infested environment of the Omaha public high school where she graduated, she thought it prudent not to leave her purse in the unattended classroom. Not just any purse. This capacious specimen must have weighed ten pounds. She'd been digging through her crowded purse for a camera when she accidentally set off a can of Mace. Said can of Mace merrily spraying its disagreeable contents out and about for several crucial moments before she realized what had happened.

No harm done, except perhaps to the student teacher's fragile self-esteem. Liska resumed his engaging, well-illustrated presentation. Threw in a personal Bigfoot experience. Everyone except the student teacher and a couple of grumpies went home in a happier state than when the day began. McCook Junior High students gained new appreciation for mostly

284

naked villagers, Bigfoot and Mace exposure—all in all, a near-perfect Junior High educational experience.

Attention Deficit Hyperactivity Disorder—*Atenshun Defecate Hyperactivity Disorder is bad.*

Attention Deficit Hyperactivity Disorder did not become an official diagnosis until 1968. Ritalin, which had been around for nearly 20 years, did not become the preferred remedy until the manufacturer paid a captive group of public advocates to spread the gospel about the threat of ADHD and the magic cure. ADHD diagnosed children multiplied through the 1980s. By 1995, Ritalin and repurposed diet drug Adderall prescriptions were doubling every two years. Squirrelly McCook students were routinely referred to a North Platte psychiatrist who never saw a kid who didn't need heavy dosing with Ritalin or Adderall. I can't say with certainty the concentration of some students wasn't helped. Students didn't wear signs indicating they were amphetamine addicts. However, too often, a former fidgety kid calmed into a semi-vegetative state. Eyes glazed, movements robotic. And nobody talked about the drugs' serious side effects: cardiovascular reactions, including sudden death, stroke and heart attack, high blood pressure, increased heart rate, psychotic episodes, Parkinson's disease, poor circulation, stunted growth and weight loss, potential dependency, and too many more. Public knowledge of the considerable risks of the drugs took several more years to spread. Meanwhile, certain members of the grumpy brigade proselytized for Ritalin or Adderall or both at every opportunity.

For the most part, my drugged-up students came from middle-income homes. Modified class members, often representatives of the large squirrel component, not frequently trucked to the North Platte shrink by their parents, parents who may have viewed their kid's behavior as perfectly normal. Through trial and error, I began to allow freer movement in the classroom. Imagine you were confined to a cramped student desk for 7 hours a day with a half-hour respite for lunch. Try it and see how easy it is. And try to visualize a full-of-beans and hormones junior high kid trying to cope with minimal physical movement for an entire school day. It's a wonder they weren't all insane. Allowing students to move around the classroom helped. They were not chained to a desk in a particular spot for the entire class period. They chose their study partners, which meant the location of their work and the people they worked with were subject to change. If a kid was having a particularly hard time maintaining focus, I might ask him or her to take a note to the office or erase the chalkboard, anything to break the monotonous claustrophobia. Once they knew they were free to move around, the need to move around diminished. Sometimes in early fall or late spring, on a brutally hot day, I might take the students outside and find some shade. (Take that, Mrs. Roberts) Being set free from the desk and the classroom usually had a salutary effect on concentration.

Although the "more freedom is sometimes good" approach did not catch on at McCook Junior High, teachers at other times in other places have used similar means to help students struggling to concentrate. My smart mother, when she heard what I was doing, gave her stamp of approval, shared a story about a favorite squirrelly student in a one-room Nebraska Sand Hills school years ago who needed fewer boundaries to function.

Having a service dog is like having a guardian angel who never leaves your side.
                                                    – Anonymous

Not long after Mr. Smock left us, Max joined us. Max, a whip-smart, alert Welsh corgi (but I repeat myself), began patrolling the halls during class changes. Whenever Max appeared, frazzle and unpleasant vibes retreated: "Aw, it's Maaaaax," the most common student response. Max's cheerful demeanor restored the most troubled souls. Flunk a quiz last period? No longer a problem. Max is here. Stewie picking on me? So what? Max likes me. A student might not have developed a strong relationship with a dog before Max showed up. Not every kid is lucky enough to have a dog at home. A quick Max fix made the rest of everyone's day a little less dreadful.

Predictably, grumpy grumpiness proved immune to Max's charms. Private and public demands issued for his permanent removal from the Junior High. Max spread germs. Max might bite someone, and we'd get ourselves sued. Asthmatic kids would die. Max distracted students from their schoolwork. Worst of all, the teacher who brought Max to school every day occupied a prominent spot atop the grumpy brigade's shit list. Whether Max deserved expulsion or not irrelevant. His owner had irritated the perpetually irritated. Mr. Berry, solidly in Max's corner, did not bend, nor did he break. Max stayed on the job, helping kids through rough days for the duration of my teaching career. I only wish he'd shown up years earlier. I can imagine no quicker fix for a sour school building climate than a generous helping of calming emotional support dogs.

I am sitting in the guidance counselor's office waiting for a couple of 7th-grade instructors to show—five minutes past the designated meeting time. Jackie and her mother chatting with the counselor while they wait. The wayward teachers show up. They'd forgotten the meeting. Any kid who forgot an assignment would get his ass chewed. The teachers expect automatic forgiveness because they forgot.

After we went over Jackie's grades and test scores, it became evident she was outperforming her predicted outcomes by a generous margin, something I should have guessed from her relative success in reading class. No student outworked Jackie. According to her awful reading test scores, she should have been drowning instead of earning Cs and B minuses. How was she managing? Working ten times harder than anyone else.

Because reading represented her most difficult challenge, the counselor soon dismissed the tardy 7th-grade teachers to concentrate on the primary source of trouble. Jackie's mother reported Jackie had been diagnosed with dyslexia some years previously, but no one in the school system ever suggested a remedy. True dyslexia and variations thereof, as you know, aren't as common as is supposed. I am not a trained reading specialist, not qualified to judge such things, but perhaps two students out of the several thousand I'd taught over the years would have made the grade as true dyslexics. I'm sitting across from Jackie and her mother, thinking not so much about how painfully slowly she read, but about the garbled nature of the written work she produced in class, work she did not have a chance to labor over for hours and fix before she turned it in. My fault for not noticing sooner.

By happy coincidence, I'd recently visited with a real reading specialist who supervised a crew of reading specialists in an upscale suburban Omaha school district. She sang the praises of a Topeka reading clinic, which she said regularly performed miracles with perception issues. It was expensive, but well worth it. She wanted the reading specialists she supervised to adopt the clinic's best practices and was working to make that happen. Lacking the skills to help Jackie myself, I suggested the Topeka clinic, which employed several methodologies, including the Orton-Gillingham Approach, heavy on individual instruction, repetition and the use of multisensory pathways to rewire children's brains. The Topeka clinic might provide the answer to Jackie's reading issues, but tuition wasn't cheap. Wealthy only in bad luck with men, Jackie's mom was barely getting by. The chances of her financing Jackie's Topeka tuition weren't good, but at least the suggestion was on the table. Jackie's work ethic such she'd be worth betting on. If her mother couldn't come up with the money, maybe I'd uncle the deal. By then, I wasn't as broke as formerly, and a few thousand dollars wouldn't hole my bank account. However, my impulsive generosity died a merciful death when Jackie's grandmother, a practical woman who saved her money, wrote the check.

After attending a short summer session in Topeka and another at a sister facility in Oregon, Jackie returned to McCook Junior High an academic prodigy. Straight A student. Near the top of her 8th-grade class. Never an unhappy kid, she bloomed with confidence, trailed by a passel of brand new, suck up friends.

Jackie's mother initiated a conference the next spring in the counselor's office. The counselor, yours truly, Jackie, Jackie's mother, Jackie's grim-faced 8th-grade teachers—all members of the grumpy squad, doubtless puzzled at the purpose of the meeting but licking their chops at the chance to fit the mother, a former pole dancer, for a noose. Mom took over the meeting, announced she'd called the meeting to thank Mr. Jones for the gift of Jackie's miraculous triumph over her reading problems. None of Jackie's past teachers ever helped her. Mr. Jones the first one who cared enough to help. Blah, blah, blah. Ears burning, I tried to shift attention to Jackie's remarkable work ethic and willingness to take direction from the Topeka reading gurus. No luck. Jackie's mother kept returning to the importance of my role, which in truth was strictly minuscule. The question I hoped nobody would ask? Why in blazes didn't Jones suggest a solution much sooner?

288

Most sentient humans prefer praise to criticism. But the effusive thanks from Jackie's mother, while appreciated, did nothing to quiet boiling resentment in grumpy breasts. Slings and arrows hoarded for future use.

Lucky for Doc, he retired when he did, missing out entirely on the No Child Left Behind debacle. Lucky, but not by design. He might still be drifting around the junior high, checking his Keno computations, had not a slavering, unhinged mother invaded his room after school. Details sketchy. Snatches of yelling next door. Accusations Doc was the worst teacher who ever lived. Suggestions he drank at school. Bottle right there in the desk drawer (not true). Suggestions he should have been fired 30 years ago when it would have "saved the lives of thousands of innocent children." The attack came with no warning. The angry woman's daughter had been earning passing grades. Perhaps the woman's chronic, multiple unhappinesses boiled over for their own reasons and aging, eccentric Doc provided a handy scapegoat. And she wouldn't be the first parent to question whether Doc should still be teaching. None of the other parents, however, attacked him viciously and personally. Doc never talked much about the incident, except to say months later she was scary and he hoped he never saw her again. What he did after she left was wander down to Mr. Berry's office and resign, effective at the end of the semester.

In addition to harridan mothers, Doc had other reasons to take retirement seriously. A painful bout with gallstones that spring landed him in the hospital. Scared the crap out of him. The estate he'd inherited from his parents, high on a hill overlooking the town of Wauneta and the Frenchman River Valley, came equipped with a quarter mile of white board fence, requiring more or less constant scraping and painting. Every fall, starting after Halloween, Doc decorated the entire estate for Christmas, including the extensive board fence. Miles of twinkling lights. He littered the lawn with multiple versions of Santa Claus, Frosty the Snowman, the Holy Family, flocks and their tenders by night, and gift-laden Wise Persons. People came from a four-county area to view the spectacle—car lights laboring up the long, bumpy driveway. Doc added new and better every fall. Christmas decorating became a full-time job. Not incidentally, the current lofty price of gold made his financial outlook more secure. And it was time. Past time. The harridan's attack nudged him in the direction he was already headed.

He did not question the rightness of his decision to retire, at least to me. The self-imposed burden of working and earning until he died had been eased. Well, not entirely self-imposed. His dentist father set the family standard by maintaining his practice into his 90s, hands shaky, equipment far from sterile. Once Doc freed himself of his teaching obligation, he became a more cheerful guy. Spent long, sweaty summer days gardening and painting. Took his Labrador retriever Tess to the nursing home to entertain the residents with her deep repertoire of tricks. Played Keno at the Wauneta bar, but without his former obsessiveness.

I made regular stops at Doc's lofty estate when picking up freshly ground wheat flour at historic Wauneta Mills. I enjoyed his hilltop view, especially in October, when the ash and cottonwoods bronzed the Frenchman River Valley below. Doc always had projects—gardening, canning, scraping, painting, although Fox News took up several hours each day. Tess insisted the TV be tuned to Fox News. If it wasn't, she'd growl and paw the screen. With retirement came more exposure to TV politics and international affairs and with more exposure came firmer political opinions. Not necessarily a healthy development. He never once inquired about a previous student or indicated he missed the teaching grind. Whether he could have remembered the name of an individual student with a gun to his head is, of course, problematic. Every fall, Doc visited McCook in his beater Toyota pickup, handing out zucchinis, tomatoes and jalapeno dill pickles to his teacher friends—sporting a three-day, snow white homeless stubble, ivory hair disheveled, always in a hurry for the next stop on his distribution route. When he paused long enough, he'd talk about Tess, her latest tricks. Never mentioned his wife of umpteen years, nor his worrisome children. Nor did he mention the fabled blondes he used to date in his flashy red 1951 Ford convertible while stationed at Fort Benjamin Harrison during the Korean War. He was all about his garden, his pickles, his intelligent, loyal dog.

On rare occasions, in the dark hours, filled to the brim with Bible juice, Doc called.

"Is this my good friend Bryan? You've always been such a good friend. A good friend. Are you still my friend?"

"You bet, Doc. We'll always be friends."

"That's good, that's good. I'm worried, Bryan. Tess is worried. Have you seen the price of gold is down?"

"I saw that, Doc, but it went right back up."

'It did? Back up?"

"Yup. Closed ten bucks an ounce above last week's high. No worries, Doc. You can go to sleep now."

"Thank you, Bryan Jones. That's wonderful news. You're a good friend to me and Tess. A good friend.

Plague-*There was a* _plague_ *in Egypt during the Ten Commandments.*

Like I said, Doc was lucky to miss the No Child Left Behind clown show. Although he might have navigated the establishment of incoherent standards and infinite rounds of mindless testing better than most teachers. Wild hunch? Faced with an incomprehensible pile of edu crap, Doc would have ignored the whole deal, conducted his classes in the same eccentric manner he always had, including map-coloring and senses-numbing chariot races. If someone ordered him to take his students to the lab to be tested, he'd have done so. But would have been clueless as to why and been incurious about the results.

Not long after Doc retired to his Wauneta Shangri-La, the juggernaut of federally imposed No Child Left Behind implementation began rolling downhill. The legislation required states and districts to adopt achievement standards and develop new tests to measure how well students were meeting those standards. The initial NCLB legislation provided a little over $24 billion to encourage states to participate, enough to give every public school teacher in the country a $7000 raise. Those states that jumped on board incurred an annual increase in compliance paperwork requiring 6,680,334 employee hours to complete at a cost of $141 billion, enough to give every public school teacher in the country a $47,000 raise and a pet monkey. Money and time, critics alleged, that might have been spent on more fruitful endeavors. Or not. By the time NCLB had been euthanized and a stake driven through its moronic heart, public school teachers and students would have been much better off had taxpayers been allowed to keep their money.

States sued for relief, but lost in court because NCLB had been crafted not as a federal mandate, but as a voluntary program. Only those who took federal dollars had to comply. NCLB had gobs of dollars to hand out. Overnight, an entire edu industrial complex sprang up devoted to the creation of standards and the tests to measure progress towards those standards. Edu consultants sold expensive teacher training programs promising improved test results. College majors and graduate degrees in educational assessment, testing and measurement emerged full bloom in the teacher factories. Some states put together statewide standards and unified testing. Nebraska's commissioner of education, Doug Christensen, marching to his own muses, allowed schools to formulate their own standards and tests, a decision which eventually cost him his job. Christensen bridled at educrat-designed tests imposed on local districts, reasoning the people on the ground knew what needed to be tested and how to test it. I can't speak to what happened in every Nebraska school district. In our area, otherwise unemployable mopes with either teaching or administrative credentials volunteered their services at pay which often dwarfed anything they could have earned in the real economy.

Standard setters generally followed their whimsicals, sometimes creating grade-level standards with no applicability to the existing curriculum, curriculum traditionally developed after the expenditure of many staff hours and many thousands of dollars. McCook teachers complained of new standards stacked on new standards, with not enough class time allowed to teach them all. A standard might have little relevance to what was being taught or have little relevance to what, in a better world, should be taught, but the threat of lost school funding, public approbation when disappointing test results appeared in the local newspaper or time on the state's secret probation list kept teachers and administrators in the buggy. Meanwhile, incompetent test designers drawing enormous wages were creating discombobulated tests which might or might not match either the wacky new standards or the original curriculum. Conscientious teachers, too often the best veteran teachers, tore their hair in frustration, many quit. The loss of experienced teachers contributed to the general decline of public education in McCook and across Nebraska. Christensen might have been right to emphasize local standards and testing, but in Nebraska, the implementation of his theories resulted in needless chaos.

Not every state mimicked Nebraska. Instead of creating confusing standards and a testing mess, Michigan lowered its demanding state standards after over 1,500 schools landed on the NCLB's "needs improvement" list. Many states followed Michigan's example. The lower the standards, the easier the tests, the more states achieved proficiency goals and were allowed to exit NCLB scrutiny. Easy as falling off an Empire State Building.

Substandard teachers in substandard schools across the country didn't make the effort. To them, the goal of bringing 100% mastery of impossible standards was a fool's errand, dead on arrival. When threats of lost funding emerged, they screamed bloody murder to their union hierarchy, which in turn screamed bloody murder to their state educrats. State educrats, surprisingly, initially proved reluctant to adjust standards to reality. After all, the Federal money spigot was open and flowing. The Bushies at the Department of Education also held firm to the rule a student attending a school that failed to meet standards after two years was free to transfer to a better-performing district.

Eventually, public schools, in unison, argued that expecting special education students (who by definition had trouble succeeding in the classroom), reach 100% proficiency in math or reading was an unattainable goal. Averaging special ed student scores with regular student scores skewed overall results downward, making schools look bad. Never mind public schools in core urban settings rarely produced any flavor of student who performed within six hundred miles of grade level. Teachers union favorites, like Ted Kennedy, George Miller and Bernie Sanders, heard the whine and began lobbying more actively for relaxed standards and penalty-free testing. The push back coincided with teachers unions, flush with dues and new members, becoming the most powerful interest group in American politics, outspending the combined political contributions of all business groups. Not even conservative Republican politicians ignored teachers union concerns with impunity.

In the who could possibly have seen this coming department—school districts in at least 40 states and the District of Columbia responded by launching wholesale cheating initiatives. Administrators leaning on teachers to correct answers during testing or after tests were scored. Administrators helping with the tedious work of changing answers. The spectacle of educators tried and convicted of crimes and many others suffering lost jobs and teaching and administrative licenses only encouraged the defanging of No Child Left Behind. Although the pressure for teachers to cheat in our district was entirely self-imposed, teachers cheated. Not uncommon to see teachers circulating around the testing lab with cheat cards in their hands, encouraging students to change incorrect answers.

So many tests. State tests, local service unit tests, traditional achievement tests, STARS tests, ACT or SAT tests for high schoolers. Some school districts, with the incentive of wads of free money, developed their own. By the end of the second year of the NCLB testing mania, each of my students was taking reading standards tests and a Duke's mixture of other tests for eighty-two class periods annually, roughly half the available class time for an entire school year. Consequently, the year's reading curriculum had to be truncated, my students' progress stunted accordingly. Imagine, if you will, a school's entire student body threatened with an illness so severe, say a scary new virus originating in an Asian biological warfare lab, students were barred from attending half the year's classes. Imagine, if you will, how their educational progress would be negatively affected. Nothing I could do to stop the madness. But I refused to alter what was left of the regular 7th-grade reading curriculum to teach the test. I also chose to ignore any results not produced by tried and true, nationally normed achievement tests. The old "come and get me, coppers" attitude. Not surprisingly, no coppers ever showed up. I have no idea if my students did better or worse on the tests than other students. It's possible they managed decent scores. Or, more likely, the scores vanished into the local and state and national edu maw, where high-dollar educrats sorted and collated and filed into now long forgotten, dusty computer files.

From the minutes of a McCook School District's curriculum committee meeting of March 29, 2006:

The district testing coordinator made note that the RWSL and the Math STARS test data have been graphed as cohort data and program data. Secondary data includes AYP, ACT, PLAN and STARS data. All SIP graphs have been updated except for the NRT scores for this year, which have just arrived.

The last word of *The Bridge on the River Kwai?* "Madness."

Superintendent Higgins, successor to the regrettable Mr. Klaus, resigned earlier than he planned and earlier than most teachers hoped. A decent human being equipped with an overdeveloped conscience, Higgins cast an objective eye on the mounting damage Gerbil was inflicting on the entire school system. Despite the superintendent's earnest attempts to tighten control, Gerbil continued to ignore his actual duties in favor of percolating new and bigger big ideas, pausing only long enough to run off a capable teacher and hire a mediocre replacement. Parents, already critical of the high school principal, renewed calls for his removal. Higgins, had he been made of tougher material, might have engineered Gerbil's exit. Unfortunately, he was not composed of tougher material. Soft-hearted and empathetic to a fault. Admirable qualities, to be sure, but severe handicaps when dealing with a virulent, unprincipled colon cancer like Gerbil. When Higgins took stock of the current Gerbil situation, he concluded he had not only failed his constituents but was likely to fail them in the future. He chose the honorable retirement and more time with grandkids door. Like I said, he had a conscience. Which left Gerbil once again unscathed.

The surprise retirement launched a search for the new, new, new superintendent. Given the mixed results from the district's past superintendent searches and in the interest of self-protection, I decided to take a more active role. Maybe I could prevent the hiring of another single-celled amoeba like Mr. Klaus. Not the first time foolish optimism would get the better of me.

The McCook school board commissioned We Play Both Ends Against the Middle LLC, the Kearney-based headhunter firm that handled the district's two previous superintendent searches. With a substantial increase in fees. The firm's search team included the superintendent from an area school district, a personable guy with a reputation for running a shipshape school. It was he who conducted the marker board brainstorming sessions with the school board, faculty and parents. Smooth and effective. Took him no time to focus the various groups on the most important qualities desired in the new superintendent. The usual suspects: administrative experience, curriculum and staff development priorities, budgeting skills, proven expertise in public relations—if your school sucks, an expert in public relations might help keep the public copacetic. Personal honesty did not make the list, despite one sorehead on the faculty screening committee suggesting it several times. All I accomplished, besides irritating fellow committee members, was extracting a solemn promise from the marker board manager his firm, We Play Both Ends Against the Middle LLC, would subject the final candidates to "thorough and complete background checks." If any financial hocus-pocus were uncovered, the unworthy candidate would be dropped like the proverbial handful of molten lava. Ditto any candidate with a yen for underage humans. "We have a reputation to protect, which is why our background checks are the most thorough in the business." So thorough, at least one of us remembered a Both Ends Against the Middle LLC recommended candidate from the past, one superintendent Klaus, a unicellular amoeba with zero administrative skills.

Marker Board Manager, after he gathered the wants and wishes of the McCook school community, reported back to the home office in Kearney. Presumably, McCook's wants and wishes were compared to the credentials of the available candidates. Following a couple of weeks of fictional diligence, the headhunters presented the names of the three top candidates to the board. If accepted, the anointed three would sit for interviews with school board, parent, and teacher screening committees. Once the committees made their determinations, the board would offer a contract to the winner. Unless the board decided to back out, pay more thousands, and start over.

Before the first finalist arrived in town, I requested We Play Both Ends Against the Middle LLC supply the various screening committees with the promised background checks. No response. We were on our own. Which meant I was on my own. Although some teacher screening committee members said they'd help and wished me luck, I was the only one with enough curiosity to dig. By coincidence, a guy who'd been dabbling in investigative reporting for 20 years. Exposés on seed corn monopolies, radioactive waste disposal, corporate hog farms and the American Indian Mafia aka Movement. How hard could it be to check the oil of three school superintendent candidates?

Candidate A had been a principal in two small schools in the Nebraska Sand Hills. Although sturdy enough credentials and excellent references, he had no experience either as a teacher or an administrator in a larger school district. Not a deal breaker, but a consideration. Younger guy, late 30s, with a start-up family. Teachers who had taught with him or were currently teaching under him described him as "solid," not much of a talker, but merely conscientious and honest. No teacher working in his school would trade him off in the hope of replacing him with someone better. If I had the only vote, Candidate A would have been chosen by a landslide.

Candidate B, with superintendent experience at two schools the size of McCook and some smaller stops, had the backing of a former Kearney State classmate. The classmate a fellow member in good standing of the Dewey Adams fan club. English teacher/wrestling coach, we'd paired up on the same side in spirited class discussions in Dewey's reading methods class. Sometimes Dewey and the two of us against the world. I was impressed with his forthright nature. Prior to taking Dewey's class, he'd been using Dewey's preferred whole language teaching methods for two years, with, according to him, miraculous results. Under Candidate B, he'd been promoted to high school principal, earning a larger salary and the attendant headaches that came with the job. According to the former English teacher/wrestling coach, McCook would be hiring the best superintendent currently working in the galaxy. The guy was a genius administrator. Everyone loved and adored the ground he walked on. Teachers bottled the air in rooms he passed through, took it home to treasure forever—plus infinity. I believed every word.

A brief phone visit with a teacher from a smaller school where Candidate B currently served as superintendent. She refused to talk. She apologized, but said she needed the job. This a tenured, highly regarded teacher who'd worked under several superintendents. What could make the best teacher in the district (by reputation) so fearful? Spidey senses gone all red zone.

Two phone calls later, another teacher and a local school board member. The teacher as mute as the first. Terrified. No teachers at this school bottling up the air and stashing the bottles in a keepsake drawer. The board member chose her words. "All I'm willing to say is we didn't offer him a contract this spring." And hung up. No additional digging uncovered why the teachers were too frightened to talk. Usually, somebody talks.

A chattier school board member from an earlier Candidate B career stop. Small school, small community (380 people). Everyone knows everyone, plus all the relevant ancestors. There had been trouble with the high school boys. Draconian, arbitrary, all out of proportion discipline. Solid, hard-working farm kids, most of them. Unaccustomed to being treated like ax murderers for strictly minor violations of obscure school rules. They rebelled. Threw crap in Candidate B's yard. Beer cans. Flaming sacks of stinky cow manure. He'd come out of his house and cuss at them, though by then they were far down the block. More entertainment than the tiny burg had seen in a month of Tuesdays. Naturally, with 100% success came complacency. One early fall evening, a carload of mischief makers pulled up to deposit a large sack of foul-smelling something on the sup's lawn. A kid exited the car with a can of diesel, followed by a kid with a large sack. Candidate B jumped out from behind a tree, grabbed the kid with the sack and beat the crap out of him. Broke a cheekbone. The kid almost lost an eye.

Most in the community thought the kids bore the responsibility. They should have quit while they were ahead, left the man alone. On the other hand, you don't want your school superintendent beating the eyeballs out of students, even if the students have been over the top annoying. The incident occurred in a more relaxed era. No lawsuits filed, no assault charges, although the county attorney considered charges before the parents of the injured student asked him to drop the matter. Nothing good could come from making this regrettable incident a bigger deal. The school board did not renew the sup's contract, provided him with glowing references, wished him good luck, and see ya'. Which is how he ended up at a school where teachers were too scared to discuss him.

Which led me to reconsider the enthusiastic recommendation from my Kearney State College classmate. Where to start? A McCook teaching colleague had a former college roommate currently teaching in Candidate B's former school, the one with the former wrestling coach/English teacher serving as high school principal. The former roommate delighted to unload. Her pet theory? Her former superintendent hated women. Sure, he had a short fuse, but she wanted to talk about his treatment of women. Early on, women teachers began avoiding one-on-one conversations, not because he was handsy, although there was that too, but because he was so demeaning. After a few months, women teachers avoided talking to him altogether.

Long-serving school secretary. One of those invaluables who serve as reliable rudders, keeping a school district on a paying basis. This one had served for enough years to know where the bodies were buried, also knew the difference between right and wrong. In no way abrasive or power hungry, but if something were amiss and not being addressed, she spoke up. She shared a concern with Candidate B. Nature of the concern unknown. He fired her on the spot, told her to leave the building, do not to take anything with her. He requisitioned a cardboard box from the janitor, filled it with the woman's purse, her coat, family photos from her desk, anything he deemed as personal from her desk drawers, including a half bottle of aspirin. He toted the box to the slushy parking lot, where he gave it a mighty heave. Contents scattered. Picture frames broken. My source volunteered the names and phone numbers of two teaching colleagues. Both told similar versions of the same story. One added the rumor the secretary had uncovered fishy expenditures of Title I funds.

Had this happened during more litigious times, like now, the secretary could have owned the school district and anything of value Candidate B kept in his sock. However, her firing stood. Many school office workers, even the most talented and industrious, lack tenure or union representation. An outraged community could not overturn the decision, largely because the former secretary did not press her case. She wasn't interested in a rematch. Come spring, the board allowed Candidate B to depart with glowing recommendations. Nothing to see here. Nothing to alert a future school board he wasn't the top-notch candidate described in the recommendations. Business as usual in Nebraska administrative circles.

I assumed Candidate B was toast. Never assume.

Candidate C, better known as Dr. Hopps, had been there and done that.

Superintendencies in South Dakota, Nebraska and Kansas. Approximately ten years at each stop. Except at the last Nebraska post, where he'd only spent seven years before departing for South Dakota. Maybe Dr. Hopps had a financial plan? Most state pension programs required ten years of gainful in-state employment before participants became fully vested. Maybe with luck and dexterity Hopps could eventually draw full pensions from three different states? Nothing wrong with prudent financial planning, but might Dr. Hopps be more interested in money than was strictly healthy?

No luck finding witnesses to the Kansas or Nebraska superintendencies. Too much time had passed. My sole South Dakota contact led to a teacher in the district where Dr. Hopps was currently employed. Although short on specifics, she gushed. Great guy. All the teachers loved him. The best sup ever. She provided the name and phone number of the athletic director, who also gushed. Again, short on specifics. Ran out of superlatives and had to recycle. He professed to be deeply saddened to learn Dr. Hopps might be leaving for another job.

The teacher superintendent screening committee interviewed the three finalists in the cozy vastness of the junior high cafeteria, the ghost of well Macarenaed Six Traits wisping under the bubble-gummed stained ceiling tiles.

The Sand Hills guy, JC Penny sport coat and cowboy boots, string tie, reserved and stiff. Teachers asked him questions and he answered the questions. Short and to the point. No elaboration. No glib chit chat. He did not take the opportunity to expand an answer to extol his outstanding accomplishments or general wonderfulness.

Have you been in charge of your district's budgeting process?

Yes, Sir.

Have you instituted evaluations of your school district's curriculum?

Yes, Ma'am.

Have you made changes in your school's curriculum?

Yes, Ma'am.

Are you currently working on a higher degree?

Yes, Sir.

Short interview. The interrogators, relying heavily on the pre-packaged queries supplied by the search firm, soon ran out of questions.

Candidate B, a wider guy in his early 60s, dripping Grecian formula. Showed up in a killer suit and power tie, accompanied by a wife some 20 years younger. Not that there's anything wrong with younger wives. This particular younger wife, all sharp angles and heavy makeup, appeared to be boss of the cattle drive. Laser focused on the proceedings and the interrogators, she missed nothing.

Candidate B was not focused, but appeared in the grip of a comfortable, semi-comatose state. His wife moved her plastic lunchroom chair snug against his, facing the questioners, her hand high up on the inside of his meaty thigh, almost to infinity. As the interrogation proceeded, she whispered answers when he drew a blank, which was usually. If the prompt didn't work, a thorough kneading retrieved his attention from wherever it wandered. Even so, his answers infrequently addressed the questions. I'm certainly no eminent neurologist nor even an uneminent neurologist, but if the guy weren't suffering the introductory or even the handshaking stage of dementia I'd be shocked.

I again assumed Candidate B was toast. Never assume.

Dr. Hopps wouldn't win any sartorial awards. Cheap suit. Cheap shoes. Goodwill Industry tie with some added miles. Just guessing the savings he accumulated by not enhancing his wardrobe went into his retirement kitty. He made up for initial appearances by being relaxed and funny. Self-deprecating humor. If you want people to like you, just make fun of yourself. Unlike the first two candidates, he answered the canned questions in some detail. Not interesting detail. The same edu jargony crappola educators habitually to use for communication purposes. Which would have set the gathering to slumbering if he hadn't dropped a funny every time the interrogators were nodding off. After the interview ended, the job was Dr. Hopps and his low key, self-deprecating demeanor to lose.

I harbored no optimism the board would choose Sand Hills Candidate A. Honesty and a sturdy work ethic would not trump the lack of larger school experience. His plain-spoken manner and cowboy boots would not impress the easily impressed. That left comatose Candidate B and his long baggage train and Dr. Hopps, whose credentials and references appeared solid. Although his pension fixation bothered. Anyone so wrapped up in boosting his pension might not resist other, more shady temptations to add to his retirement nest egg. Still, I would have bet a nickel the board would choose Dr. Hopps. I was wrong.

Gerbil never slept. Especially if there were a chance to do mischief. Gerbil knew with community pitchforks being sharpened, any new sup would likely fire him. Not a stretch to imagine a conversation between Gerbil and Candidate B and/or Candidate B's wife. He might boast he could deliver the appointment to Candidate B, but needed to hear assuring noises about his own future. Candidate B, in his current unemployed state, could be expected to give the arrangement serious consideration. Gerbil promptly schmoozed the coaches, selling them on Candidate B. What promises, what side deals unknown. But he convinced the school's most powerful constituency Candidate B was their guy. Then went to work on some of the more influential members of the business community, enthusiastic Bison athletic boosters all. Not twenty-four hours after the screening interviews concluded, word filtered out Candidate B had the job locked.

Bypassing official channels not good form. And not something I did without trepidation. However, knowing what I knew and not sharing with the decision makers didn't sit easy. My personal job situation might not be threatened, but the school district's future was at risk. Two seasoned board members. I'd taught their children. Although I didn't know them well, both appeared to be in possession of good sense. They agreed to an emergency sit-down at the local bakery. They sat. I sat. Surrounded by inquisitive afternoon kaffeeklatchers. My show. I laid out everything I'd dug up on all three candidates. Neither school board member spoke during the briefing. I could have been talking to Egyptian mummies. Not a grimace, nor a thin smile, nor a slight inclination of a head. When I finally ran out of gas, they stood up, said they'd see me around. I might as well have filled them in on the most recent weather in Zimbabwe.

Nothing changed by morning. Candidate B and his troubling past in the driver's seat, about to be awarded a fat contract at any moment. Gerbil chortling over the strings he'd pulled.

A stern admonition from outgoing superintendent Higgins in the morning bulletin advising staff members not to conduct "unprofessional" amateur background investigations.

Done and done.

Then a small miracle. A Junior High colleague with friends at the elementary school fit to bust with news. During the administration/school board social hour following Candidate B's interview with the board, he'd been introduced to an elementary administrator wearing a name tag on her left breast. Claiming he was nearsighted, Candidate B clamped a hairy hand on the name tag and the underlying breast and pulled both much closer, giving both serious study before releasing his grip. "Nice," was all he said.

The school board president's wife, directing her staff in the school cafeteria, gave full attention to the story. She did not react in stoic, mummified fashion, but with the alacrity you'd hope for.

The next day, Dr. Hopps was in the driver's seat and Candidate B was back where he started, purchasing interviews with school boards where his wife would whisper and knead.

The contract offered to Dr. Hopps, in addition to a whopping raise over his current salary, came with the tacit understanding Dr. Hopps would rid the district of Gerbil. Hopps was agreeable to both.

I was not the sole person in McCook puzzled Gerbil had not only survived, but given generous pay raises every year. One theory held he was better suited to seducing his immediate superiors than any of the attractive, talented women teachers he pursued. He certainly had an uncanny nose for weakness—in men. If the target doted on little kids, Gerbil brought his own young children around, made sure they made a good impression. He never forgot the birthday of someone who could protect him from his critics. If a superior had a weakness for saloons, Gerbil became his most reliable drinking buddy.

Imminent trouble for the high school principal emerged with the fresh, high circulation rumors Dr. Hopps was bound by the informal condition of his employment to get rid of Gerbil. Said stipulation insisted upon by board members who had run for office on the promise of finally ridding McCook of the lazy little prick of a high school principal. The countdown began to the projected date in January when Gerbil was expected to receive his walking papers. No potential saviors, not the high school athletic department nor the powerful Bison booster business people, intervened. He was doomed.

Yet he survived. And thrived.

Dr. Hopps, in addition to the suspicious focus on boosting his retirement income, had another blot on his copybook, a blot neither the crack Kearney search firm nor his South Dakota cheerleaders saw fit to disclose. A shortcoming Gerbil soon uncovered and exploited. Dr. Hopps was a common drunk, a drunk willing to sell his soul for a couple of Bud Lights. Seldom appearing at the office before ten, he stuck around until 3 or sometimes 2:30, before easing out the door for the liquor store and home. He favored beer. Cases.

Gerbil, a resourceful little suck-up, found a seminar in Denver for administrators, invited Dr. Hopps to accompany him. They'd take the train, sit in the club car, drink all the way to Denver and back. Dr. Hopps, always looking for ways to spend time away from his unhappy wife, especially if it involved alcohol, took the bait. We can only speculate on what friskiness took place in Denver. Whatever happened in Denver stayed in Denver. But after the new best pals returned from the seminar, talk of Gerbil's imminent demise petered out. An attentive Gerbil showed up at Dr. Hopps' house one evening each week, always bearing a case of the good doctor's favorite brew. Joined at the beery hip, they were. The board found it difficult to proceed. No tenure law protected Gerbil. But absent a negative evaluation from the superintendent, the case for dismissal, according to the board's attorneys, might be weak enough to encourage expensive and embarrassing litigation. They couldn't fire the brand new superintendent without triggering the rogue board designation from the state's edu hierarchy. Until Dr. Hopps rode off into his three-pension sunset, Gerbil would keep Gerbiling.

Notes from the McCook Public Schools Curriculum Coordinating Council—*Dr. Hopps led the Curriculum Coordinating Council in a process to recommend methods of communication.*

And it was my fault. I should have visited the Kansas and Nebraska communities where Hopps held superintendencies, dug more deeply in South Dakota, not settled for the first enthusiastic reports. Also at fault were the Kearney headhunters, who promised thorough background checks. How thorough when you can't identify misogynistic, short-fused losers or hopeless alcoholic superintendent candidates? After all, few state secrets existed in the close-knit state school administrative circles the headhunters professed to monitor. I could kick my own ass at my leisure, but thought it important to share my pain. I rang up the head headhunter, suggested since the firm hadn't conducted the promised background checks, they should refund the school board's payment. Huffy bastard. Told me in no uncertain terms to never call him again.

Inebriated-*Skippy, if I've told you once, I've told you a thousand times, your inebriated is getting on my last nerve.*

Our regional educational service unit, headquartered in Trenton a few miles west of McCook, provided a range of services to the McCook schools and smaller area schools. A troubled kid in need of a school psychologist? We have three of those at your service. You don't have the money to hire a full-time speech therapist? Need the expertise of an Early Childhood Specialist? Interested in setting up an alternative education program? Give us a call. New family of freshly arrived migrant students and no English Language Learner specialist handy? Not only do we have the specialists, but a proven ELL program. In addition, the local ESU conducted technology trainings and planned in-service programs for area schools. In-service days, like the infamous Six Traits workshop, were always sited in McCook and proved popular with McCook merchants, whose sales surged from attending regional teachers hunting bargains.

The autumn Dr. Hopps assumed the McCook superintendency, the local ESU offered an in-service to beat all in-services. Any witless, well-jargoned educrat viewing the day's bountiful menu would have been gangrened with envy.

A partial list of the seminars offered:

(Fair warning—may contain toxic levels of edu jargon)

Fun in Learning: The Pedagogical Role of Fun in Adventure Education

Effectiveness of Cognitive Apprenticeship Instructional Methods in the Automotive Technology Classroom

Motivating, Enhancing and Accelerating Organizational Learning Performance Through User-Engaging Systems

The Virtual Company: Toward a Self-Directed Competence-Based Learning Environment in Distance Education

Make Financial Plan$ with Horace Mann

For those of you wagering at home, anyone who bet I chose the Horace Mann presentation over the other splendid offerings wins a lifetime, high commission, high service fee, low-performing annuity. Any of you who bet the smarmy Horace Mann salespersons fielded enough embarrassing questions about fat commissions, exorbitant surrender fees, and consumer-unfriendly fine print to wipe the smarm from their smarmy faces wins two lifetime, high commission, high service fee, low-performing annuities.

9/11 and the subsequent nation building wars in Iraq and Afghanistan provided background noise for the winding down of my teaching career. Buff, uniformed former students showed up unannounced in my classroom. Fresh from basic training, which changed indifferent Pillsburies into fit as fiddles men and women, imbued with confidence and purpose. The transformation so stunning I wouldn't have recognized half of them on the street without a formal introduction. One doughy 7th-grader morphed into a strapping Marine tasked with duties at Arlington Cemetery and the heavy lifting at state funerals. He said Gerald Ford's casket weighed a ton. The directionless freckle not enamored with 7th-grade reading, who later showed up in my classroom, could have been the model for a recruitment poster. Broad-shouldered, slim-hipped, muscled neck. His hopes for a long career in the Army keeping him warm at night. And the Matheny kid, who tolerated my 7th-grade classroom with quiet good humor, who made a slightly bashful appearance in my room after basic training, later killed near Baghdad by a roadside bomb.

Apocalypse-*Sarah always talks about the <u>apocalypse</u> and wobal glarming.*

During my final years in the classroom, NCLB and constant, time-wasting, mindless testing provided chronic irritation. As veteran colleagues became disgusted and pulled the plug, I began to question how much of my job remained worthwhile. The Society of Permanent Grumpiness maintained the dominant Junior High vibe. No longer the easy-going collegial workplace to which I'd grown accustomed.

To be fair, a smattering of the grumpies, when minding their own business, could be considered competent teachers. To be fair, a smattering of grumpies, if they momentarily strayed from the most recent grumpy warpath, could be warm, agreeable human beings. The desire to control others, in the absence of control over their own lives, and the desire to be included in what they perceived to be an exclusive club of movers and shakers led them astray. Once they joined up, one grumpy's anger became every grumpy's anger. Groupthink set pots to boiling and festering. A more chronically unhappy group of humans would be hard to find outside an Ivy League English department.

Unknown to both the happy and unhappy members of the junior high staff, hidden in the fine print in Section 1202 (C) (7)(A) (p. 114) of the No Child Left Behind legislation—a spiffy new reading program. In order to feed at the Federal edu trough (6 billion over six years) "an eligible local education agency…shall use the funds provided under the subgrant…to select and implement a learning system or program of reading instruction based on scientifically based reading research that includes the essential components of reading instruction."

"Scientifically based reading research" promised to replace presumably unsciency reading instruction and catapult student reading progress to Bush's goal of 100% proficiency and beyond. Masquerading as science-based, the Bushie educrats determined the new methodology would include five key components. 1. phonemic awareness 2. phonics 3. vocabulary development 4. reading fluency, including reading skills, and 5. reading comprehension strategies. They ran out of gas before they could think up a sixth component. After the Bushies characterized their proposal as "science-based," they quickly branded opponents as anti-science, even those who, unlike the Bushies, had some expertise in the teaching of reading. Stop me if this sounds familiar.

Successful reading teachers typically move students beyond phonics-heavy instruction as their abilities develop. If a student can read, the door to the entire universe of books opens. The sooner reading students have access to real books with meaty stories and strong characters, the sooner they become even better readers. In their desire to vaporize whole language instruction from the nation's schools, Reading First proponents ignored one of the key foundations of successful reading programs—giving students access to compelling reading materials which engage their attention and imaginations.

Struggling readers, due to either eye/brain processing issues or lack of prior familiarity, require intensive reading instruction incorporating repetitive phonics and word recognition exposure. The idea a disabled reader can learn how to read by reading is as silly as it sounds. However, by sentencing the vast majority of learning readers to three years of phonics drills, Reading First programs severely restricted their potential progress and did little if anything to inculcate a love of reading. As with most edufads, Reading First replaced the current reading materials with brand new, more expensive reading materials, teaching guides, audio visual aids, and teacher trainings. Reading materials composed of boring, simplistic stories guaranteed to induce sleep. Those receiving Reading First funding required to purchase the new, new stuff from approved vendors, a violation of Federal law prohibiting the Feds from mandating curriculum and materials for local school districts. In addition to providing a new stream of revenue to certain publishing members of the edu industrial complex, Reading First advocates hoped to kill the whole language movement dead, dead, dead.

For those of you spectating at home, whole language and phonics advocates have been warring for at least 200 years. Noah Webster incorporated phonics in his American Spelling Book in 1783. In 1844, Horace Mann's Seventh Report advocated whole language methods for teaching reading (long before he began selling annuity scams). In 1879, William Holmes McGuffey published a phonetic edition of his popular reading books. Dick and Jane appeared in 1930 using color illustrations coordinated with the whole language or look-say methods of word recognition. Although Dick and Jane led boring lives, occasionally interrupted by the barking of running dog Spot, the series proved wildly popular and helped certain authors very near here learn to read. We can speculate had the Dick and Jane series contained the red meat of interesting characters doing interesting things, I might have mastered the reading thing much quicker than I did. For example, what if Spot had brutally murdered an innocent squirrel, consumed the twitching carcass in one fell gulp and suffered a near-terminal case of projectile diarrhea? I'd have been in the Blue Bird reading group from the git go. Despite the thin gruel, Scott Foresman, Dick and Jane's publisher, dominated the reading series market for 30 years. Critics pointed to the lack of phonics emphasis and the boring, simplistic storylines, as well as the absence of racial diversity. Rudolf Flesch in *Why Johnny Can't Read* (1955) indicted the whole-language/look-say methodology for lacking phonics training. He also criticized Dick and Jane's simple-minded storylines and limited vocabulary for not preparing students to read more challenging books in upper grades.

Scott Foresman replaced Dick and Jane in the late 1960s with the Open Highways series with broader cultural content and more emphasis on phonics. By the 1970s, phonics fanatics were firmly in charge. Their reign was short. The 80s saw revamped whole language reading texts back in ascendancy. By 1993, Massachusetts linguistic professors were demanding the state commissioner of education halt the practice of whole language reading instruction. In spite of critics, whole language reading instruction, by 2002, had experienced two decades of dominance. The dominance coincided with a steep decline in reading proficiency in the nation's urban school districts, a decline due to many factors including dysfunctional school systems, but an embarrassing trend phonics enthusiasts never tired of publicizing. In the war over methodology, nobody examined school districts where students were learning to read at an acceptable rate. Nobody looked at the quality of the reading instructors or the relative academic strengths of the school districts or determined if districts had adequate school libraries and book-loving librarians. If kids weren't learning to read those factors didn't matter. The culprit? Faulty methodology. Out-of-date methodology as the main cause of educational failure remains a dependable excuse for failing public schools and teacher factories. If educrats could design a school where children were taught entirely by robotic androids programmed with the latest edu nostrum, they would have done so long ago.* If they deign to acknowledge teachers, it's to castigate the breed for failure to adapt to the latest new new edu thing with sufficient enthusiasm. The idea of creative teachers using brains, experience and ingenuity to educate students and caring about the results is as foreign to an edufadder as an actual, physical dictionary.

Each time the worm turns and either phonics or whole language regains dominance, the winners become increasingly intolerant of their adversaries. Open discussion and possible compromise never countenanced. It should be no surprise if one side, if not both, adopt stake-burning to advance their agendas.

The phonics/whole language battles flare every time a large district or powerful education departments in states like Texas and California adopt a new reading series and dictate its use. A state-mandated textbook or reading series in Texas or other large population state is assured of millions in sales. Dominant publishers like Centage Learning, Prentice Hall, McGraw-Hill, and Houghton Mifflin Harcourt ensure

*The reptilian Bill Gates, never one to ignore an opportunity to control human minds, promises AI platformed and programmed instruction delivered to students' personal electronic devices will replace human teachers within five years.

large profit margins by selling textbooks approved by large states to schools in smaller states. The more copies of a particular book and sets of study materials sold, the lower the unit cost to the publisher. No wonder textbook companies use every tactic, fair or foul, to gain the coveted stamp of state approval.

During the last half of the 20th Century, the nation's textbook selection process encouraged the choice of bland, heavily illustrated textbooks which irritated the fewest constituencies. As student reading skills declined, the percentage of textbooks and materials devoted to text also declined and the percentage devoted to snazzy color illustrations increased, as did the volume of pre-packaged teaching units, complete with lesson plans, downloadable materials and audio-visual aids. Consequently, I never met a state-approved history textbook worth the paper and ink. Now that textbooks and supplementary materials resemble cartoonish political propaganda, the textbook selection process has evolved into bitterly divisive conflict. In one corner, edufadders and their teachers union and left-wing nut foundation buddies. In the other, parents and teachers grown suspicious and critical of textbook content. With the dawn of the new century, edufadders and teachers unions acquired the smug certainty parents should never be allowed to question the wisdom of a textbook choice. If a parent had the temerity to do so, it was time to report them to the FBI.

The overweening arrogance embedded in the Reading First initiative implied all the teachers who'd been successfully teaching students how to read for the last umpteen years hadn't known squat about how to do it. I will stipulate I am no reading expert. Wouldn't know a phonic from a pheromone. But if I were the parent of a 3rd-grade child, I'd hope the teacher employed tools which produced the best results. Unless the student had resistant eye/brain processing problems, intensive phonics work might better be left to the first-grade teachers. Average 3rd-graders should prosper with spelling and vocabulary development coupled with reading material an objective person might care to read on a voluntary basis because it's interesting. As opposed to single sheets of canned, homogenized, sanitized SRA boredom. If a teacher chose to use *McGuffey Readers*, I'd be down. *McGuffey Readers*, first published in the mid-19th century and since refined, use phonetic instruction to introduce new vocabulary words in the context of actual literature, gradually acquainting students with new words and repeating the old. Each section increasing the level of reading difficulty. The basic drill reading classes followed during my time in Gorham and McCook. Homeschoolers use *McGuffey Readers* with outstanding results. Not that any self-deluding, thought-deprived educrat is paying attention to the enviable achievements of homeschooled students.

Once the Bushies at the Department of Education announced their approved phonics-centered material choices, significant Democrats and their favored edu industrial complex publishers protested. The education department's inspector general questioned the approval process, which favored publishers with financial ties to the decision-makers. One favored publisher, SRA/McGraw-Hill, by remarkable coincidence, happened to be habitual and generous with donations to George W. Bush's political campaigns. Other publishers vying for official approval imitated SRA's phonic-intensive products. Democrat George Miller, powerful chair of the House Education and Labor committee, subjected Christopher Doherty, DOE's Reading First director, to a thorough grilling. Smug as a sardine in a can, the Bushie educrat refused to admit wrongdoing. He had, after all, the firm backing of Education Secretary Margaret Spelling, former top aide in the Bush White House. And the Bushies were, after all, doing the Lord's work, stamping out anything casually related to whole language instruction, including actual books. Miller also interrogated the Education Department's Inspector General, who admitted he'd referred the case to the Bush Justice Department. You can read about the DOJ's investigation and indictments

Here

and

Here

The Reading First battles overshadowed the Neil Bush scandal, although the revelations rated a few back-page stories. In the 1980s, Neil Bush, Dubya's younger brother, set out to make his personal fortune in the oil bidness like his father. Instead, he assumed control of a sleepy Colorado savings and loan, began loaning outsized sums to his business partners. Attendant to the savings and loan debacle of the late 1980s, his failed bank cost taxpayers a cool one point two five billion dollars in bailout funds. Regulators criticized loans to entities in which the younger Bush had a financial interest and banned him from the banking industry for life. Never one to rest on his laurels, the younger Bush bounced back by assuming control of a struggling oil company, which promptly went broke.

Once George W. was elected and With No Child Left Behind lurking just over the horizon, Neil Bush began thinking outside the Bush family sandbox for the first time. He founded Ignite! Learning, an educational software/test prep company. Former President George H. W. and wife Barbara kicked in seed money as did a mixed bag of subterranean benefactors. Included were Middle Eastern oil sheiks, last seen cheering the 9/11 terror attacks, a couple of Russian oligarchs, convicted junk bond felon Michael Milken and Chinese chipmaker Grace Semiconductor Manufacturing, an outfit sporting close ties to elite members of the Chinese communist party and Chinese military intelligence. The younger Bush didn't know a computer chip from a raspberry, but Grace fronted him 2 million shares of stock and paid him $400,000 a year to lend his techie expertise to his fellow members of the board of directors. Not completely lacking experience in international commerce, Bush, according to his divorce testimony, had extensive dealings with the Asian prostitutes who showed up in his hotel room for reasons mysterious to him. Familiar territory for black sheep presidential relatives past, present and future.

Ignite! Learning developed "curriculum on wheels" or COWS, a cute $3800 purple plug-and-play computer/projector playing entertaining videos and cartoons illustrating various facts and concepts which might show up on a NCLB or state assessment test. The COWS machine also played catchy music, guaranteed to permanently cement random facts and concepts into impressionable student brains. Texas school districts, where the Bush name carried outsized weight, snapped up COWS machines, as did districts in 22 other states. Ignite! anticipated $5 million in revenue shortly after starting shipments. Districts typically employed a mixture of NCLB and local funds for the purchases. It was the use of NCLB money that sparked criticism. Why was the president's brother allowed to profit from the president's signature legislative program? Calls for an investigation by the Education Department's inspector general resulted in nothing much. Neil Bush emerged unscathed and soon expanded his business ventures with the Chinese communist elites. However, the scandal, when added to NCLB's and Reading First's well-publicized deficiencies, encouraged politically powerful critics to redouble efforts to dismantle NCLB.

Onomatopoeia—*Onomatopoeia is an example of <u>onomatopoeia</u>.*

What soon unfolded in the McCook Public Schools became the blueprint for how every national edufad during succeeding years overcame strong resistance from parents and experienced teachers to gain ascendancy. Abject failure of the new fads to demonstrate superior results didn't matter. If this last nostrum doesn't work, we have an even better one for you. Foreshadowing the jackbooted tactics employed to install the New Racism initiatives in Louden County, Virginia, and other school districts, effective teachers who knew their business found their views not only unwelcome, but experienced social ostracism and, in some cases, direct retaliation. Younger, less confident teachers often chose a path of least resistance and embraced the current fad. The gradual rejection of test results as unfair to disadvantaged students and unionized teachers led to the adoption of nostrums with zero academic value. In some cases, below zero academic value. Their one dependable virtue? Obfuscation of the lack of academic progress.

Reading First critics in the McCook elementary schools soon learned to keep their heads down and feign support for the new program. However, they remained convinced Reading First represented a terrible mistake, one which would inflict long-lasting damage on their pupils. They fought back, opening furtive lines of communication with sympathetic parents and school board members. Fat files of printed school emails and meeting notes exchanged on darkened porches between members of the rebel faction. Teachers provided proof the Reading First advocates, including administrators, were abusing teachers who showed insufficient enthusiasm. Friendly school board members requested and received current testing results from the district testing czar, which often contradicted the rosy statistics peddled by the administration. For instance, the year prior to the installation of the Direct Instruction reading program at the Junior High, not one elementary student, after multiple years of Reading First exposure, tested at mastery level. 70% of Junior High students, none of which had been subjected to Reading First instruction, tested at mastery or above. Concerned parents, armed with current testing scores, began attending school board meetings and asking hard questions. The board listened. Board support for Reading First weakened, then evaporated. Even after the Reading First advocates' favored school board candidate won a hotly contested election against an avowed anti-Reading First candidate, the program was doomed. Sort of.

Reading First proponents actively campaigned for a semi-deranged alcoholic board candidate, currently wearing an ankle bracelet so the cops would be alerted if he tried to patronize local liquor outlets. After multiple DUIs, a judge ordered an interlocking ignition device installed on the candidate's vehicle. If he breathed boozy breath into the device, it wouldn't start. At least that was the general idea. It might have worked as designed except his vehicle had a remote start feature, bypassing the interlocking device. He drove when and where he wanted, frequently to the local Walmart, where he purchased and consumed massive quantities of vanilla flavoring, littering the parking lot with discarded bottles and packaging. Local hobby bakers, inconvenienced by frequent vanilla extract shortages, may still be outraged.

The newly elected pro-Reading First board member/vanilla flavoring addict failed to save the program; an uphill battle had he been sober. The board pulled the plug on future funding, officially ending the unfortunate experiment. Officially. Teachers who had drunk deeply from the Reading First goblet continued surreptitiously using the program for several years. Not only continued but recruited new teaching hires to the cause. The board's action probably limited the damage to future elementary students but the civil war between teachers and teachers and teachers and parents continued, leaving lasting scars on the school and the community. Sorry, despicable business.

Meanwhile, ensconced in the McCook high school principal's closeted redoubt, Gerbil abandoned his usual preoccupation with avoiding his duties in exchange for active worrying. The future of Reading First in doubt. When McCook adopted the Reading First program, Mrs. Gerbil, her reading czar qualifications negligible, had been appointed elementary reading czar at a salary of $55,000 plus a generous $30,000 expense budget, a considerable raise from her classroom teacher wages. Three years later, the district's Reading First money trough was threatened by controversy and political squabbling. The school board's support vanishing. The school board unhappy, not only because the program's results sucked, but because they'd never approved the increase of an hour and a half of daily Reading First instruction to three hours. And why, they asked, should advanced second-grade reading students spend three hours a day pointing to their noses and ears relearning the parts of their bodies? The board also objected to the arbitrary ruling no student could be moved to a more appropriate ability grouping until eight testing periods had passed. Board outrage increased when it became known administrators had required elementary teachers to sign a loyalty oath to Reading First. (Years later, the Loudoun County, Virginia, school administrators not only insisted on teachers signing loyalty oaths to the New Racism curriculum but secrecy oaths as well). If the death knell for Reading First hadn't sounded previously, it rang after the Reading First rabids threatened to boycott the business of a concerned parent who hosted parents and school board members for a "listening" meeting at her house.

With Reading First's survival at risk, Gerbil's febrile brain went into overdrive. Reading First had been inflicted on grades 1-3. What if a canned reading program could be found to inflict on grades 4-8? Wouldn't the new program require administrative oversight? Like a czar? Or even two czars? Gerbil commenced digging. What he recommended to the compliant Dr. Hopps was Direct Instruction, a sister program to Reading First for older students offered by SRA, a division of politically connected textbook powerhouse McGraw-Hill.

What incentives, if any, the SRA reps offered McCook Public school administrators remain in the rumor bin. Maybe those hyperactive ferrets in the Bush DOJ could figure it out, but up to now, nobody knows nuttin'. In any case, the Direct Instruction bandwagon quickly gathered momentum. No significant opposition formed among teachers at Central Elementary, currently housing grades 4-5. The Junior High grumpies' embrace of Direct

316

Instruction could only be described as frenzied. These were irrationally confident teachers, mind you, who thought details and facts didn't matter and just saying something made it so. They preached and badgered their way to steamroller status. Focused on my students, I dismissed their enthusiasm as an annoying distraction. Why would anyone with a lick of experience teaching reading glom on to a canned program which on its phonics fanatical face was guaranteed to degrade the reading skills of most Junior High age pupils? Perhaps the grumpies genuinely believed the SRA salespeople's bogus claims of miraculous results. They certainly repeated the claims at every opportunity. It's difficult to completely rule out the desire to eliminate the 7th-grade reading program, long an example of actual accomplishment. I'm not saying that's what was really going on. But I'm not not saying that was what was really going on. There's also a possibility one or more of the grumpies hoped to gain appointment to the remunerative position of Junior High Reading czar. Freedom from dealing with actual students, many of whom remained stubbornly Ritalin/Adderall-free, and the opportunity to boss other people around an attractive prospect to many members of the brigade.

For its part, the administration promoted Direct Instruction as the cure for disappointing reading scores in grades 4-8. Leaving out, of course, any reference to the stubbornly high 7th and 8th-grade reading scores or the embarrassing test results showing lower elementary students currently enduring Reading First instruction falling below grade level.

The Gering school district, a Nebraska panhandle school roughly the same size as McCook, installed Direct Instruction the previous year. SRA encouraged a trip to McCook for Gering Middle School teachers to share their excitement. Excitement distinctly muted. Once the formal presentations ended and we visited candidly with individual instructors, doubts surfaced.

"DI might help your most disabled readers. Maybe. But it won't help your average to above-average readers. Most kids find the program boring. You'd probably find reading the same stupid sentence umpteen times, then repeating it umpteen times, then having your neighbor read the same sentence umpteen times a little boring."

"I hope we get rid of this program next year. It doesn't work and keeping even good students engaged takes way too much effort."

"Don't believe anyone who says this program worked miracles at this or that school. They told us the same thing and when we contacted teachers in those schools we found out it was mostly lies."

"We've heard SRA is paying administrators who adopt DI thousands of dollars. Could just be rumor. Don't know. But our administration has never pushed a new program as hard as they pushed this one."

The grumpy brigade's chronicle of the meeting with Gering teachers didn't exactly resemble what transpired. Their accounts awash with superlatives and nary a discouraging word. Some of us wondered if they'd attended a different conflab. Nonetheless, a collection of grumpies invaded the next school board meeting to spread the good news. They failed, of course, to discuss the miserable test results from the first three years of Reading First instruction in the McCook elementary schools.

One sorehead dissenter eventually wandered down to Mr. Berry's office. Mr. Berry always an attentive listener. When hearing the Gering teachers' unvarnished comments he nodded in the right places. He asked no questions. Mr. Berry always asked questions. When I repeated my objections to a canned reading program without books or interesting reading material, went a little overboard eviscerating the DeWitt reading program Direct Instruction closely resembled, he chuckled in the right places. Asked no questions. Mr. Berry always asked questions. He thanked me for checking in. Said we should find time for a drink sometime. Odd suggestion to a guy who didn't drink. Mr. Berry might have lost track of my weaknesses after I stopped attending his after-school soirées when he began inviting Gerbil. I left fearing the adoption of Direct Instruction was a done deal.

A few weeks later, Mr. Berry showed up in my room between classes with the bewildered 6th-grade reading instructor in tow. Mr. Berry not his usual relaxed self. Fidgety. Looking like he'd just swallowed a half pound of alum. "The district is adopting the Direct Instruction reading program next year. Your reading classes will not be offered. Sorry about this, but we'll need to find something else for both of you to teach. Any questions?"

Not from me. The 6th-grade reading teacher, too shell-shocked to raise her hand, left in a puddle. My path was clear. Resignation. I could no longer work for a district this ignorant and maybe, just maybe this corrupt. They'd flushed a proven reading program in exchange for predictable disaster. I won't say I went completely around the bend that day, but in the midst of the worst moment in my entire teaching career, I could have made some unfortunate choices. Instead, I went home, cracked an icy cold Coca-Cola, and reviewed the financial consequences of retirement. Not encouraging. I'd need to keep working. Starting over in a nearby smaller district at my advanced age didn't appetize. And no guarantee anyone would hire me. With my years of experience and accumulated graduate hours, I would be an expensive hire. Maybe the post office was hiring? Naw, grizzled McCook postal workers only retired when they aged out.

The next afternoon, a slightly buzzed Dr. Hopps granted me an audience. Yes, I qualified for an early district retirement buyout of this many thousands. Yes, I could qualify for a full state teacher pension if I purchased a few service years. Dr. Hopps knew a thing or two about state retirement requirements. Although the words Direct Instruction never passed my lips, he offered these soothing words:

"We owed it to the kids to do this."

It proved too late to line up all the unruly retirement ducks before the fall term. Purchasing added service years from the Nebraska pension system required tricky financial engineering and several months' lead time. Teaching elsewhere for a few more years offered the most practical path to pension nirvana. But where? Who would hire an expensive old guy so close to retirement? Many area schools were adopting Direct Instruction. Finding one that hadn't a tall order. I was already regretting cutting ties with McCook Junior High. Mostly warm memories, despite the current toxicity. McCook students were the same entertaining, hardworking students they'd always been. I'd miss the students if I quit.

Mr. Berry dropped by my room. More himself than the last time. He casually mentioned one of the leading lights of the grumpy brigade would be serving as Junior High reading czar. Perfect choice from my perspective. A teacher who lacked even nodding acquaintance with how children learn to read, nor with any genuine interest in her pupils. Infatuated with new, like the vehicles she traded for every six months, edufads held special fascination. In her lifelong search for gold stars and to be at the center of everything, nobody minded other people's business any better. Nobody gained more pure enjoyment from bossing people around. Like I said, perfect choice.

Mr. Berry stressed Direct Instruction's reputation as a proven program. Much success in other schools. I kept my mouth shut. Almost as an afterthought, he mentioned the 8th-grade American history position, now wide open. Didn't I have a history endorsement? No need to make a quick decision. Why didn't I sleep on it, talk it over with family, let him know. Next week too soon?

While I mulled the offer, the grumpy leadership marched into Mr. Berry's office demanding I be terminated. A sympathetic school secretary with large ears supplied the gory details. The Junior High, the grumpies claimed, was suffering from a sour attitude. Mr. Jones, they alleged, harbored a sour attitude. The success of the new Direct Instruction reading program required every teacher to buy in. Jones had never been a team player (almost entirely true). One bad apple could derail the whole deal. Curious charges since I'd been scrupulous in avoiding any conversation with anyone about the proposed new reading program, busy, as usual, minding my own business. How could my inner doubts about Direct Reading be public knowledge? Perhaps the grumpies consulted a local psychic? A Ouija board? There were other, more scurrilous charges, none of them based on anything but grumpy imagination. I had no idea the group possessed so much creativity.

Ouija board-*At my cousin's party, the _Ouija board_ pointed out there was danger! (Someone had farted)*

Never argue with an idiot. They'll drag you down to their level and beat you through experience."

—Mark Twain

You have to nip it. Nip it. Nip this kind of thing right in the bud.

—Barney Fife

And I should have let it ride, sticks and stones and all that. The smart choice? Walking away, not giving the grumpies any notion they'd touched a nerve. Let them stew in their own considerable juices. Mark Twain was right. Instead, I chose Barney Fife's solution and allowed myself a moment of delicious, self-righteous rage. After all, I'd been dutiful in following my smart mother's advice, keeping my head down and minding my own business. Maybe if I'd gone home, put up my feet, taken a nap. Not this genius. In a state of highly miffed, I placed a stiff letter in every grumpy's mailbox.

The following has been edited for length and word choice:

Dear Colleagues,

It has come to my attention a recent meeting in Mr. Berry's office was taken up by concerns about the sour climate at MJH. I understand I have been charged with contributing to the sour climate in these parts. In point of fact, I have been tending to my own knitting, something your group might well adopt as a mission statement.

A self-appointed community of ferrets spying upon and lying about other staff members shouldn't have to look far from the front porch to find the source of a sour building climate. The impressive list of lies and misrepresentations one or more of you volunteered at the meeting has become public knowledge. As much as I'm inclined to focus on my teaching and students, colleagues spreading vicious lies designed to damage my professional reputation rises to the level of gross provocation. Lies, as you know, develop a life of their own. Even if later refuted, the damage is usually irreversible. That is why the courts of this great country provide means of redress for victims of slander. I have yet to determine the names of the gutless cowards who spread their lies at the meeting. If you do a better job of policing your behavior and the behavior of your clique, I will not attempt to discover the identities of the scoundrels. I hope to never hear of another meeting devoted to assassinating my professional reputation or the professional reputation of any other teacher. However, if I become aware of the tiniest smidgen of speculative gossip emanating from your membership, you will be sued. You will be sued collectively. You will be sued individually. During discovery, my attorneys will depose Mr. Berry and each of you. When they are finished, we will know which of you are lying skunks. Then we will find out if those skunks have deep pockets.

In addition to taking legal action, I will file a formal complaint with the State Professional Practices Committee, which would guarantee the miscreants be subject to questioning and possible professional sanctions.

Respectfully yours,

Mr. Jones

The missive might have been impulsive and a tad intemperate, but had the desired effect, not that the mutterings or finger-pointings stopped entirely. I was grateful, lacking stomach for lawyers or legal wrangling. Life at McCook Junior High settled into an armed truce, neither side willing to let bygones go to wherever bygone bygones go.

If there's anything that upsets me, it's having people say I'm sensitive.

—Barney Fife

At the time, I believed I was the lone target, ignorant of the more vicious war on Reading First skeptics in the elementary school. McCook elementary teachers who voiced less than glowing opinions about Reading First subjected to the kind of intimidation the Junior High grumpies could only admire from afar. Threats of termination, unrelenting hostility from administrators, confrontations in the hallways, outlandish slanders repeated to colleagues and parents. As you might have guessed, the Reading First skeptics represented the most skilled reading instructors in the district, teachers who gave serious consideration to Reading First philosophy and materials and found both too focused on phorics and lacking quality children's books with compelling stories.

There have been hundreds of committee meetings in past years; hundreds, maybe thousands. There has never been any item of business conducted which was not subsequently changed or overridden.

—John Janovy, *Keith County Journal*

I was remembering, not so many years ago, before Reading First hit the fan, a meeting of the elementary textbook adoption committee I attended for no good reason. Reading textbooks being adopted, but not for my classroom, which had been and remained stubbornly textbookless. Mr. Berry suggested I attend the meeting, even if I wasn't buying. Wave the Junior High flag. Act interested. So I went. The current reading series having reached its expiration date, a new series needed to be chosen to keep the Lincoln educrats at bay. Why a reading series would outlive its usefulness never explained. Had the paper and ink suffered deterioration? Were the methodologies therein suddenly obsolete? The only disqualifying factor cited for the old reading series was the publication date—ten long years ago. An eternity in textbookland and a big no-no for the Lincoln educrats. Hardly a persuasive rationale to dump thousands of dollars of useful books and replace them with thousands of dollars worth of new books. As the meeting progressed, some elementary committee members voiced additional concerns with the old reading series. Too much emphasis on phonics. Whole language was all the rage. All the cool schools had adopted the whole language approach, similar to what Dick and Jane were selling decades ago. Salespeople peddling whole language reading series offered not only the latest in faddish reading materials but the cat's meow in teacher training, snazzy multi-media support materials and glowing reviews from districts using the new books.

The elementary building principal assigned to referee the meeting meekly opined he'd always believed phonics had a role to play in reading instruction, especially in first grade. The elementary teachers first drew him and then they quartered him. Scorn lay heavy on the arena. Phonics. They could hardly say the word without throwing up in their mouths. It was a

whole language reading series or nothing. No phonics. Phonics was old-fash-
ioned. Whole language was cutting-edge. The train leaving the station and
McCook better be on it. The only question? Which whole language series
to choose? The principal apologized, withdrew into his acquiescent shell.
My work done, I left for home. The committee selected a whole language
reading series and, at least initially, professed themselves pleased. Now, a
decade later, some of the same jackbooted whole language enthusiasts who
attended that particular meeting, the ones who berated the poor principal
for his positive view of phonics instruction in first grade, became the most
fanatical advocates of phonics heavy Reading First and the most intolerant
intimidators of those who disagreed with them.

Because I was self-isolating at the Junior High, tending to my classroom
and students, scant news from the elementary of the Reading First Civil
War reached my ears. Rumors, of course, but nothing directly affecting my
business. Unfortunately, adopting Direct Instruction at the Junior High
remained on the agenda for the next school year (Thank you, Gerbil). My
7th-grade reading classes toast. Although conflicted, I took Mr. Berry's offer of the 8th-grade history assignment. Accepting a new challenge while
sticking a sharp stick in the grumpies' rancid eyeballs. No third-rate bunch
of mirthless, mental midgets was going to bully me out of Dodge. Mr. Berry appeared genuinely pleased with my decision and promptly approved
my requests for new computers and history materials. As comfortable as
I'd become with 7th-graders and the reading program I'd put together, a
different subject assignment with a different age group might reenergize
this old fat man.

I set about transferring the reference books discarded by the new wave
Junior High librarian from my home to the 8th-grade history room—a
high-ceilinged former art classroom featuring a vast wall of west-facing
windows and one tiny window the size of a postage stamp, a window
which could theoretically be opened for ventilation. I also moved the
entire collection of Twinkies, McDonald's food items, and aging hot dogs,
which (mostly) survived the Gobi Desert-like summer temps in the new
classroom until the fall term.

Although the new teaching assignment occupied my full attention, a
nagging sadness accompanied me to my new room and new subject.

Mrs. Hoehner's $80,000 collection of splendid 7th-grade reading books did not survive the move. All but a handful found wanting by the inheritors from the grumpy brigade, the majority consigned to the school incinerator.

As an added bonus for switching teaching assignments, the longest-tenured teacher, that would be me, served as head of the 8th-grade "team," consisting of myself and a contingent of grumpies. I would determine meeting times and agendas and serve as moderator. As you might expect, this did not go over well with the grumpies, whose team meetings had produced so much sour milk. They marched to Mr. Berry's office intent on overturning the appointment. He said rules were rules. Longevity had its rewards. Sorry. He had a twinkle going when he told me about it.

A few days later, I received a call for assistance from the office. Mr. Berry out of town and a parent and an 8th-grade student wanting to visit with an 8th-grade teacher. The newly minted 8th-grade team leader arrived to find a blue collar dad and his 8th-grader daughter, a kid who was performing at a high level in my classes. A few minutes later, Mrs. Lund, co-leader of the grumpies and champeen NCLB test cheat, arrived. Lund had kept the daughter after school the previous Friday to make up missing homework. Dad, waiting in the parking lot and needing to report for work at 4 o'clock, had to leave before his daughter was released. The daughter ended up walking several miles home. He would be willing, he said, to deliver his daughter early before school to make up homework. But please don't keep her after school.

Lund claimed she had not kept the girl after 4 o'clock. Announced the girl could solve the whole problem by doing her homework in a timely fashion. Dad said he understood, but wondered, should the problem ever arise in the future, if teachers might call him so he could deliver the kid before school. I pronounced it a reasonable request and thanked him for explaining his circumstances. Lund reminded him this was all his daughter's fault and she could resolve the issue by doing her homework on time. I promised to inform the other 8th-grade team members the dad was willing to deliver his daughter early to school if necessary and thanked him for coming to school and for his patience. Lund, beyond pissed, reminded him his daughter could solve things by getting her work done on time. Stormed out of the room. I was reminded, not for the first time, of the elderly research paper which demonstrated students of likable teachers outperformed students of harsh disciplinarians by a considerable margin.

I was a short-timer at that point. And since the grumpies had lost interest in grade-level team meetings, I had no reason to interact with Lund or her cohorts for the rest of the school year. The warm camaraderie was not missed.

Looking back on nearly 30 years in the classroom, I cannot remember many examples of students not handing in homework on time. Two, to be precise. A smug, lazy, Bladen student who refused to correct his work and handed in the same crappy paper until he didn't and received his zero. A shy McCook girl being abused, along with her brothers, by an evil stepfather while mom held his coat. At the time, I had no understanding of the cause of the missing assignments, but knew her to be so conscientious it must have been something unavoidable. She invariably handed in the assignments, if a day or two late. Because she was usually reliable, I skipped penalizing her grade. Once news about the evil stepdad emerged (he earned a long prison sentence), I was relieved not to have docked her grade for tardiness. But why had I remained clueless about what she was enduring? Why didn't I ask more questions? How many months of abuse had she suffered because of my lack of curiosity? Sins of omission are the worst.

I might be forgetting a few examples of tardy homework, but my students tended to be punctual. Perhaps because they were required to finish an assignment before they moved on to the next. If the class were working as designed, most of the students competed for top grades. Getting a late start on the next assignment threatened their potential point earnings. The class culture fostered brisk competition and punctuality. Anything less considered bad form.

Late or missing homework, a favorite grumpy complaint, occupied many brigade hours of discussion and policy making. At times, the missing homework issue took more attention than their fellow teachers creating a sour attitude at McCook Junior High. Before I joined the 8th-grade team, they frequently published appeals to the entire Junior High faculty for solutions to the late homework crisis. Another instance where I lacked empathy. The issue seemed silly on its face. Let's see, you've been teaching for how many years and your students aren't handing in their homework? What does that say about you? However, the grumpies, with the cause embedded in their sharp incisors, wanted more than casual suggestions. As usual, they wanted rigid new laws, laws to be enforced by Mr. Berry. In-school suspensions or worse. Your math assignment goes missing, you'll be marched to Mr. Berry's office and punished—and punished some more.

Now, nearly 20 years later, the grumpies are long gone, retired to wherever grumpies retire. Had they stuck around another few years they would have been confronted by and perhaps discombobulated by the newest nitwitic edufad proclaiming homework to be a racist construct. Asian kids, in particular, spend so much time doing homework they shade every other group on the diversity paint sample. The result? Unequal grading. Average white students spend less time on homework than Asian students and receive lower grades. Hispanics and black students, who spend less time on homework than whites, receive even lower marks. As one of the most expensive, frequently hired grifter consulting firms (Crescendo Education Group) maintains, "The problem is that homework completion is more often a reflection of a student's income, language and family, and this grading approach places underprivileged students at a huge disadvantage." In the quest to rid public education of any objective measurements of student academic progress, the elimination of homework and the grading of same is but one initiative of many.

How would the grumpies have adapted to a world with no homework? A world where any teacher keeping kids after school to be individual-ly tutored was viewed as a racist, cultural suppressor? Hard to predict, although grumpy enthusiasm for a brand new nitwitic edufad wouldn't be out of character. Not difficult to imagine energetic sleuthing for evidence of fellow teachers assigning prohibited homework. Like I said, hard to pre-dict. By the time the grumpies had fully immersed themselves in blissful retirement, many American public schools had solved the problem of missing homework by eliminating homework altogether. No homework, no need to monitor or grade. No need to punish students or eviscerate parents.

That final semester before *I pulled the plug did not lack for school drama. The ace Junior High skeet shooter, the itchy-fingered teacher who following the Columbine massacre vowed to bring a gun to school, proved dependable at creating farcical situations. A lover of plants, she decorated her classroom with enough flowering, succulent herbs and spices to populate a small commercial greenhouse. Grow lights and an automatic watering system created a veritable jungle. The burgeoning number of plant stands sprouting abundant leaves and blossoms crowded her students into one corner of the room. Finding a clear path to and from their desks became difficult. Then the aphids arrived. And not just a few casual tourists—hordes of the voracious little buggers, consuming every edible in sight.*

When faced with a full frontal, in-your-face aphid attack, the skeet shooter did what any serious plant-based gardener would do. She hosed down the room with a potent combination of deadly pesticides. Mission accomplished. Dead and dying aphids everywhere. The downside? Once the fumes filtered into the creaky ventilation system and out to the hallways, formal inquiries resulted. Investigators determined the chemicals involved posed a grave danger not only to aphids, but to human beings. Mr. Berry took the only course available and dismissed school. A month later, he might have joked about skeet shooter's failed attempt at gassing every student and teacher in the building. In the moment, one of the rare instances when he failed to see the humor in a situation.

Not gonna lie, the year teaching 8th-grade history had its challenges. By creating the curriculum from scratch and adapting a range of materials (not including a useless textbook), each day required last-minute tweaking. Evenings spent making emergency lesson plans. Gone were the predictable 7th-grade reading classes on autopilot. Since the majority of my students had been 7th-grade reading students, most everyone knew the expectations and the drill. Because the library no longer offered bound reference works or much in the way of historical monographs, students conducted their research in the classroom using the actual, physical reference works formerly housed in the library. The room's four new computers offered limited access to additional source material. Class hours filled with diligent digging, historical questions being asked and answered. In a few weeks, the 8th-grade history classes resembled the Bladen worker bee classes from

30 years prior. Once again, I was being paid an unconscionable amount of money to enjoy myself.

That final year, the life after teaching financial plan came together. Debts paid. Assets moved. Service years purchased from the Nebraska pension system. Retirement now a feasible option. However, with the 8th-grade history program up and running, a few more years in the classroom beckoned—a choice which felt comfortable. But maybe, just maybe, the ideal time to retire is before they come for you, before a slavering, harridan mother storms into your classroom, as happened to poor Doc Rider. Maybe the ideal time to retire is before you've observed a grumpy brigade so long you've almost lost your faith in humanity. Gerbil and his protector Dr. Hopps gave no indication they were going anywhere. Watching Gerbil enjoying his metastasizing proclivities without fear of losing his job had grown dispiriting. Long-delayed writing projects beckoned. A book on the Nebraska Sand Hills in the hopper for over a decade, a project requiring numerous in-person interviews and thousands of driving miles. And who knows, someday I might find enough material for a teaching memoir?

I have to admit, however, it would be a kick to start over as a much younger, high-energy rookie, teaching in a school which values students and parents and books and learning, a school not preoccupied with political culture wars or passing edufads. Creating a classroom display of aging Twinkies and immortal McDonald's French Fries a simple task. Maybe I'd stumble over a desiccating male or female lizard during one of my pasture walks. Pretty sure the world would work the way it is supposed to.

Dinosaur-*The dinosaur is ex-stinked.*

EPILOGUE

One wonders how we ever survived as a species relying on the family unit to raise its children before the government came along to do it for us.

—David Spak

The sun-blessed May afternoon I walked out of McCook Junior High for the final time, no stirring martial music, no loud hosannas, no sneering jeers, no confetti infesting my not much there hair—as invisible an exit as I hoped for. My time, my choice.

The ancient (in Apple years) Macintosh computer in my home office welcomed me with open arms, as eager as I was to work on the much-delayed Nebraska Sand Hills book project, a project consuming my energies for the next 11 years. After hundreds of interviews and an unscheduled plane crash, *North of the Platte, South of the Niobrara: A Little Further into the Nebraska Sand Hills* emerged more or less intact from the tedious publication process. During the next two years, Kathy and I traveled the High Plains, meeting readers and conducting book talks. A handful of the book's primary subjects attended the talks and sometimes offered grudging approval of how they'd been portrayed.

Current developments in education did not appear on our radar.

Then COVID hysteria hit the fan. Our move to an isolated cabin in the high Rocky Mountains (so isolated the local Post Office from Hell refuses to deliver our mail) shielded us from the worst counter-COVID atrocities. Not that we were completely spared. During infrequent trips for supplies, we encountered mask-wearing, glove-wearing checkout clerks hiding behind plexiglass shields. Masked, fearful, sanctimonious shoppers scolded me for walking against the arrows directing traffic in grocery store aisles. Fortunately, local restaurants maintained relaxed, superficial obedience to the COVID police. High country cattle ranchers and hard-rock prospectors compose a significant chunk of our community—individualistic individuals not easily persuaded to join the sheep huddled behind masks and hand sanitizer. The unwarranted cancellation of two years' book appearances represented the most serious inconvenience. Some people around here suggest I should get over it.

Living a hermit's isolated existence at 10,000 feet in the Rocky Mountains—if you don't count the dope-smoking weasel who lives a half mile up the road— provides distance and perspective. Although we were subject to the same media/government-driven COVID panic as other Americans, most of our community took their cues from their sturdy, self-directed selves. Only a few gullible residents fell victim to the onslaught. They collected their mail at the Post Office from Hell so heavily garbed in masks and disposable paper booties and elbow-length rubber gloves any self-respecting COVID bug would have taken one look and fled the scene. Hell, I took one look and fled the scene.

Our local public schools, like schools in other parts of the country, locked out students and implemented poorly planned, poorly executed remote learning programs. Too many teachers chose not to participate, leaving students to study blank computer screens. Our county's charter schools reopened in May, as did schools in Europe and communist China. Unlike public schools in many other states, all our county public schools were back in business the next fall. Except for useless, psychologically damaging masking and distancing requirements, which sparked a geometric increase in speech impediments, depression and Adderall prescriptions, local schools returned to normal. For most of us, life as we'd known it resumed. Students, on the other hand, suffered from permanently stunted academic progress and regressed social maturity.

Despite our relative isolation, news from the COVID wars in other regions between parents and local schools filtered up the hill, news often difficult to credit as factual. Draconian school lockouts, some lasting two years, were imposed despite a lack of evidence children were at risk from the disease or were likely to spread it. Online lessons delivered by clunky technology to home computers alerted parents to what was being taught and what wasn't being taught. What was being taught and what wasn't being taught eroded faith in public schools. Parents who previously trusted public schools to educate their children, to produce students capable of reading a book, doing basic arithmetic, reading a map, telling time, counting their toes, or perhaps preparing for college, were disabused. While parents and the rest of us weren't paying attention, core academic subjects had been replaced in too many schools by anti-family, anti-country, anti-religious, self-hating racism and misogynist gender-bending propaganda. Parents began attending school board meetings and asking pointed questions. Parents soon discovered conscientious school board members in many districts had been replaced by resolute ideologues, elected with the generous assistance of the nonprofit bastard offspring of billion-dollar foundations. The humorless apparatchiks proved not only impervious but hostile to parental concerns. Too many school board members not only refused to answer legitimate questions but branded questioning parents as domestic terrorists and alerted the FBI. Too many school board members organized boycotts of businesses owned by concerned parents. Too many school board members mounted slanderous campaigns to persuade employers to fire engaged parents. Too many school board members and teachers reported concerned parents to social services for child abuse, putting parents' custody of their children in jeopardy.

Alarmed and a little bewildered. And sometimes scared. Undaunted parents researched the whos and whys of the decline in academic standards and the sources of the money, both public and private, financing the decline. Parent researchers, soon joined by professional journalists, determined the debasement of public education had been no accident. Teacher factories, state and federal education departments, teachers unions, a smorgasbord of nonprofits and billion-dollar foundations were intent on destroying two centuries of academic standards and teaching practices. The flight to public charter, private schools, and homeschooling alternatives became a mass exodus.

To summarize, well-financed bad guys have been up to no good. And if you paid attention to the preceding pages, you'll recognize many of the same bad guys were hard at work debasing public education long before I retired. I do not regret pulling the plug before their plans were fully implemented. Even from the distant sidelines in the high Rockies, bearing witness to the destruction of American public education is not for the weak of stomach. It is difficult to imagine the challenges of teaching in a school system devoid of discipline, devoid of academic standards, a system devoted not to meritocracy and student success but to rigid anti-child ideology. Students, of course, suffer the most serious consequences. But any conscientious teacher attempting to swim against the anti-intellectual riptide of the snot-encrusted, jargon-babbling, pestilence-spreading theology infecting the education-industrial complex has my devout sympathy. Bless you and good luck.

Like poor Doc Rider, hounded into retirement by a deranged mother, I was lucky to retire when I did.

ACKNOWLEDGEMENTS

Mattie Edith Tupper Jones, my smart mother, read to her children whether she had better things to do (always) or not. She read with a quiet, dramatic flair, transforming the books she chose into riveting entertainment. I blame my smart mother for her children's love of books and their appreciation for rich language. My mother enjoyed a lengthy teaching career, beginning in a one-room Sand Hills school when she was 17 years old. She became a reading specialist focused on addressing reading issues and helping students quick track back into their regular classrooms. During my teaching career, my smart mother shared her experiences, providing intuitive suggestions not found in tedious education classes or vacuous training workshops.

I will always be grateful for the sound education I received in the three small-town public schools I attended. Competent, dedicated elementary teachers taught me to read, add, subtract and do long division (fractional fractions and long multiplication remain elusive). My first-grade teacher, Mrs. Turner, spent many after-school hours helping a klutzy paster paste sticky strips of boring Dick and Jane prose into my reading workbook, easing the transition from the lowly Red Bird reading group to the smug Blue Birds. My sanctimonious temperance lectures to her bartender husband and his bemused customers while delivering the *Omaha World-Herald* newspaper to his saloon did not deter her from the task. "Mac" Martens, an impoverished widow teaching school for pitiful wages to help her two children through college. Her fourth-grade class was seldom dull, featuring snap Spanish instruction and spirited ad hoc spelling competitions. Mac Martens encouraged us to use recess time to hone our math skills by drilling each other with flash cards. Solving arithmetic problems in our heads became second nature. My high school instructors were not always top-notch.

But at least they didn't waste class time propagandizing their students. During my sojourn in higher education, I never felt ill-equipped for academic competition with students who had attended upscale urban high schools or when competing with Ivy League alums in graduate school.

Without the support and protection of extraordinary administrators, my teaching career would never have lasted three decades. Tom Kaufman, R. Keith Beeman, Dennis Berry and Pat and LeRoy Hoehner tolerated my iconoclastic teaching methods and shielded me from the worst consequences of my boneheaded mistakes.

Deep and abiding thanks to Laura Van Dusen and J. V. Brummels, who set aside more important writing projects to lend kind attention to the manuscript in progress. Any remaining deficiencies, including a few inadvertent bald-faced lies, are my responsibility.

Special thanks to photographer Laci Dinkler, who arranged with the bus driver for the cover photo shoot on Webster County's Dry Divide south of Bladen.

Our country owes a vast, non-dischargeable debt to the courageous parents who fought to reopen schools during the COVID hysteria and later questioned the substitution of destructive ideology for academic instruction. They risked not only public censure and presence on the FBI's domestic terrorist list but, in some cases, the loss of employment and custody of their children.

I have been crazy fortunate to have three fascinating children who take time from their creative endeavors to give the old fat man a timely "atta boy."

Daughter Erica accepted responsibility for formatting, book design and several hundred additional book production tasks, despite sharing oversight of an infant daughter deeply engaged in the teething process.

Without Kathy, who adds tech chops and unqualified support to my writing projects, no matter how many years they consume, we wouldn't be talking. But if you insist, I could elaborate for infinity plus 25 minutes on how lucky I am to have Kathy aboard.

Praise for Books by Bryan L. Jones

North of the Platte, South of the Niobrara: A Little Further into the Nebraska Sand Hills

Just a page or two of any of Bryan Jones' books reminds me why I'm a reader—I'm a sucker for great storytelling. At the heart of North of the Platte, South of the Niobrara: A Little Further into the Nebraska Sand HIlls are the stories of the region's residents—ranchers, school teachers, bull riders and war veterans—and of the historians, scientists and poets who've traveled and loved its rivers and dunes. This place, these voices, related by master storyteller Bryan Jones, compose a unique and unqualified treat.

—J. V. Brummels, frontpew@paradise and *Book of Grass*

Books about the vast Sand Hills region of Nebraska are scarce, and it follows that good books about the area are rare indeed. Bryan Jones has waded into this enigmatic landscape with tape recorder, wife, dog, and the tenacity of a much-admired 30-year teacher of junior high school students. He trains his persistence on Sand Hills folks until he unravels their affection for these hills and gets the story. While focusing on McMurtreys, Sandoz, Purdums, Kimes, Wards and other residents, Jones rounds up the whole neighborhood. He's found the people who love these Hills and lets them talk. Even Bryan's geologists and hydrologists reveal an enthusiasm for this region that is essential to helping us and them understand this very uncommon place. Bryan is a biographer of place and mostly keeps his prejudices corralled, but his love of our neighborhood is evident on each page. This is a great book about the Sand Hills of Nebraska and we will be forever grateful to Bryan Jones for the years he spent researching and writing North of the Platte, South of the Niobrara.

—Duane Gudgel, Plains Trading Company

The Farming Game

A former high school teacher turned Nebraska farmer himself, Jones has drawn on his experience to write a lively, practical guide to success or, more often, failure in small farming. What distinguishes The Farming Game from a mere how-to book is the author's sharp eye for the absurd detail in his portraits of people and his descriptions of the lending policies of banks, the government price controls and the production methods of agribusiness that make it difficult for the independent farmer to compete.
—New York Times Book Review

"Bryan Jones is that rare thing, a real farmer who also writes. The Farming Game is the one book I've seen that I would give to someone who was thinking of moving to the country and actually supporting himself or herself off the land. Anyone who picks it up won't be able to stop laughing. First, at the dozen portraits of different types of farmers. Then, at various barbed asides in the three long essays on how farmers can and do make money. Jones has a wicked wit. [And his] book is remarkably educative. Mixed with the humor is a mass of information and analysis. The reality of farming is here as other people very seldom see it."
—Noel Perrin, Smithsonian

"Characters like Crazy Billy the Fantasy Farmer make you think more of Damon Runyon than of a serious book on current problems with this country's agriculture. Make no mistake, Bryan Jones has written a serious book that probably offers the most cogent explanation of an extremely complex problem. For the avid city dweller, Jones explains why our food costs so much and why the farmers aren't making it."
—Philadelphia Inquirer

Mark Twain Made Me Do It & Other Plains Adventures

"I flat admire Bryan L. Jones's Mark Twain Made Me Do It—not only because it dramatizes a truckload of boyhood epiphanies, but also because it does the dramatizing with a flair and an attitude worthy of Twain himself."
—William Kloefkorn, Nebraska State Poet

"In recent years, the premature memoir of the young or floundering writer has established itself as a fledgling genre. While many of these hasty autobiographies seem of scant interest to anyone except the most dedicated literary groupie, Jones (The Farming Game) offers a collection of essays that recalls the youthful credulity of America in the '50s as much as it does his often hilarious, Huckleberry Finn-inspired misadventures. The son of a Methodist minister, Jones progresses from a four-year-old concocting gurgling chemical experiments in the parsonage's upstairs toilet ("Pot Roast Every Sunday") to a high-schooler recounting offbeat family legends at a typical '50s holiday get-together ("The Clan"). Over the course of these essays, Jones comes of age, which means he settles into living inside narratives he understands are larger than his own ("Polio," "Growing Up Methodist"). Though Mark Twain's two shortest essays--"Heading West" and "Back to the Basics"--prove transitional and a little sentimental, Jones's prose remains clear and energetic throughout. He's careful, as well, not to fall victim to cheap nostalgia. Leave it to a junior-high-school reading teacher to figure out how to get around that hazard."

—Library Journal

"These are the fond reminiscences of a boyhood in small-town Nebraska in the early 1950s. It is a rambunctious life, a la Tom and Huck, with Jones, the son of a Methodist minister, bolstering the stereotype of the preacher's kid as hell-raiser. Jones's charm lies in his ability to recount events from the perspective of a child with the droll humor of an adult ("The Reverend Bat C. Henry, he of the middle-aged shining head and ferocious windpipe, wrote the book on gasbags"). He also keeps his account relentlessly upbeat even in the presence of polio epidemics and teacher brutality."

—Jim G. Burns

For contact information, upcoming public appearances, and recent author news, follow Bryan L. Jones at bryanjoneswriter.com. The author's books, available with custom inscriptions, may be purchased on site. Books can also be obtained from independent bookstores and the usual online suspects.